The Post-Revolutionary Self

The Post-Revolutionary Self

Politics and Psyche in France, 1750–1850

Jan Goldstein

HARVARD UNIVERSITY PRESS

Cambridge, Massachusetts

London, England

First Harvard University Press paperback edition, 2008.

Library of Congress Cataloging-in-Publication Data

Goldstein, Jan.

     The post-revolutionary self : politics and psyche in France, 1750–1850 / Jan Goldstein.
     p. cm.
Includes bibliographical references and index.
ISBN 978-0-674-01680-4 (cloth : alk. paper)
ISBN 978-0-674-02769-5 (pbk.)
1. Self—Social aspects—France—History—18th century. 2. Self—Social aspects—France—History—19th century. 3. Cousin, Victor, 1792–1867. I. Title.

BF697.5.S65G65 2005
618.89 ′00944 ′09033—dc22   2005040206

To my family, old and new

Contents

Illustrations

Preface

This book grew out of my earlier work on French psychiatry. In studying the furor provoked in the first half of the nineteenth century by the diagnostic category monomania—one of the signal contributions of the new medical specialty during its formative phase—I encountered a distinctive and, from my perspective, decidedly odd mindset. I became aware of how intolerable to many Frenchmen of that era was the notion of a mental illness that might affect only a single idea or emotion or behavioral propensity, leaving the rest of the mind intact. Contemporaries offered a number of explicit rationales for their horror. Monomania, they said, destroyed moral responsibility by positing that a seemingly normal individual might lapse unintentionally into criminal conduct when a discrete, circumscribed pathology was activated; indeed defense lawyers were calling psychiatrists into court as expert witnesses to get their clients off the hook on just those grounds. Monomania, they additionally said, was an offense to religion because a mind divisible into healthy and sick portions had to be a brute material substance rather than a spiritual entity or soul. Behind these specific complaints, however, I detected a more general motif: a strong distaste for psychic fragmentation and a zealous insistence on the unity of the self. Indeed the fear of fragmentation and the fetishization of a unitary self, or *moi*—repeatedly named as such—were the opposite sides of the same coin. I had apparently stumbled on a historical moment in which the self, ordinarily an elusive and intensely personal concept, had come to the fore in no uncertain terms, announcing itself as an issue for public discussion.

I have been pursuing that nineteenth-century French self, and its eighteenth-century antecedents, for many years now, and it is hence with a mixture of pleasure and relief that I have reached the point of consigning the results of my quest to the pages of this book. Completing the book also enables me, happily, to record my gratitude for the abundant support, both material and moral, that I received along the way.

Financial support for leaves of absence from teaching to conduct the research for the book was generously provided by a National Endowment for the Humanities Fellowship for University Teachers, a National Science Foundation Scholars Award (Program in the History and Philosophy of Science), a grant from the Spencer Foundation, and a John Simon Guggenheim Foundation Fellowship. At a later stage in the project, a fellowship at the Center for Advanced Study in the Behavioral Sciences, funded by the Andrew W. Mellon Foundation, provided an ideal environment for writing. So did a stint as a visitor to the School of Social Science at the Institute for Advanced Study, which I enjoyed in the home stretch. The liberal leave policy of the Social Sciences Division of the University of Chicago made it possible for me to benefit from these other sources of largesse; it deserves special mention here as a force powerfully supportive of scholarship.

Earlier versions of many parts of this book were "tried out" on audiences in a variety of venues on my home campus, elsewhere in North America, and in Europe. I thank the participants at these assorted lectures, conferences, and seminars for having spurred me on through their lively engagement with the topic and having sharpened my arguments through the astute comments and criticisms that they offered. Let me list those venues here: the Workshop on Interdisciplinary Approaches to Modern France, University of Chicago; the Centre Alexandre Koyré, Paris; the Ecole des Hautes Etudes en Sciences Sociales, Paris; conferences on "The Modernist Impulse in the Human Sciences" at Bellagio, Italy, and the Center for Interdisciplinary Studies at the University of Bielefeld; the conference "Cultural History after Foucault" at the University of Amsterdam; the Max-Planck-Institut für Wissenschaftsgeschichte in Berlin; annual meetings of the American Historical Association and the Society for French Historical Studies; the Humanities Center at the University of California, Berkeley; history of science programs at Harvard University, the University of California at Berkeley, the University of California at Davis, and Cambridge University; Humanities and Social Studies in Medicine at McGill University; the University of Alberta; the Eighteenth-Century Studies Group, University of Calgary; the French History Colloquium, University of California at Irvine; the European History Colloquium at Cornell University; the Center for European Studies, Harvard University; Arizona State University; the New York Area French History Seminar; the conference "Enthusiasm and Modernity in Europe, 1650-1850" at the Center for

17th- and 18th-Century Studies at UCLA; the Institute for French Studies, New York University; the Department of History, Princeton University; the Triangle Intellectual History Seminar; the conference "Histories of Science, Histories of Art" at Harvard University and Boston University; and the conference "Generational Dynamics and Cultural Analysis," Internationales Forschungszentrum Kulturwissenschaften, Vienna.

In addition, parts of Chapters 3, 4, and 5 of the present work appeared in somewhat different form as "Mutations of the Self in Old Regime and Postrevolutionary France: From *Ame* to *Moi* to *Le Moi*" in *Biographies of Scientific Objects*, ed. Lorraine Daston (Chicago: University of Chicago Press, 2000), used here by permission of the publisher. © 2000 by the University of Chicago. All rights reserved. Parts of Chapters 4 and 5 of the present work appeared in somewhat altered form as "Saying 'I': Victor Cousin, Caroline Angebert, and the Politics of Selfhood in Nineteenth-Century France" in *Rediscovering History: Culture, Politics, and the Psyche*, ed. Michael S. Roth (Stanford, CA: Stanford University Press, 1994), used here by permission of the publisher. © 1994 by the Board of Trustees of the Leland Stanford Junior University.

The subtitle of this book deliberately echoes the title of the first essay in Carl Schorske's *Fin-de-Siècle Vienna* and is meant as a kind of homage to a scholar who, while never formally my teacher, influenced me by his writings long before I had the pleasure of knowing him personally. Indeed Carl Schorske's effort to think the history of politics simultaneously with the history of the psyche inspired the intellectual project that has occupied me for much of my career.

Aida Donald "signed me up" to do this book with Harvard University Press and, when she retired before I completed it, Joyce Seltzer graciously agreed to step in as my editor. I thank them both for their faith in the project and Joyce Seltzer for her expert guidance. Keith Baker and Sarah Maza, who read the manuscript for Harvard University Press, made characteristically shrewd observations that saved me from myself on multiple occasions. Jacques Guilhaumou, one of the editors of the Sieyès papers, supplemented my firsthand research in those manuscripts (housed at the Archives Nationales) with texts that he had transcribed; that he agreed to do so when he knew me only via e-mail is surely a testament to his scholarly generosity. The timely interventions of Luc Requier, of the Service de la reprographie of the Archives Nationales, Paris, ensured that a reproduction of a psychological diagram sketched by the young abbé Sieyès now appears in these pages.

Bill Sewell, who became my daily companion when the book was nearing completion, gave me some wonderful suggestions for pulling it all together. He also buoyed my spirits when the work did not. His analytic rigor and historical imagination have improved this book, just as his empathy and steady optimism have improved my life.

The Post-Revolutionary Self

Introduction: Psychological Interiority versus Self-Talk

Is the self a unitary whole, or is it fractured and fragmentary? That very general, open-ended question has been a recurrent one, assuming different forms and freighted with different meanings according to the historical context. In the aftermath of the Revolution of 1789, it took on an almost startling urgency in France; the highest social and political stakes seemed to ride on it. Spanning the period 1750 to 1850, this book explores a conjuncture between psychological discourse and sociopolitical change that, I argue, captures the French in the act of grappling with the newly imposed conditions of modernity. Hence this is a book at once about the self and about sociopolitical order.

As anyone who has embarked on research of this sort knows, basic definitional considerations make the self a treacherous object of investigation. Commonplace in present-day American English, the word "self" does not send us rushing to the dictionary; we have a firm if intuitive grasp of what it signifies and how to use it. At the same time, the word, which belongs both to everyday speech and to a variety of technical languages, steadfastly resists our efforts to pin it down. Surrounding it, moreover, are a cluster of similarly vague near-synonyms—individual, person, personality, subject, subjectivity, identity—with which it seems to overlap substantially and from which it can be distinguished only with difficulty, if at all. The historical dimension of selfhood adds another layer to this definitional complexity. Historians and anthropologists long ago denaturalized the self, asserting its status as a mutable object constituted historically and culturally. The resulting scholarly literature, dating back at least as far as Jacob Burckhardt's *The Civilization*

1

of the Renaissance in Italy (1860) and divided among several disciplines, has located so many putative births of the Western self—for example, with Socrates,[1] with the Stoics,[2] in twelfth-century religious devotion,[3] in the Italian Renaissance[4]—that, taken as a whole, it testifies to a widespread conceptual muddle about what, exactly, is the quarry being sought.

Rather than attempting to illuminate this muddle through a grand theoretical intervention, I have in this book adopted a minimalist position toward the self, though one, I think, that adequately serves my purposes as a historian. That position has three elements. First, I basically agree with the early twentieth-century anthropologist Marcel Mauss that "there has never existed a human being, who has not been aware not only of his body, but also at the same time of his individuality, both spiritual and physical."[5] Or as I would gloss and nuance Mauss's assertion, all human beings, with the exception of infants and some psychotics, recognize, to a greater or lesser degree, the fact of individuation; if pressed, they cannot help but side with Nietzsche's luminous Apollonians against his intoxicated Dionysians in their acceptance of the *principium individuationis*.[6] Hence all human beings regard both their bodies and their minds as discrete, self-subsistent entities. It is the individuated mental stuff, as well as the individual's own representation of it, that go under the name of self. Second, I would readily assent to the claims of Mauss, Michel Foucault, and others, that what passes for a self is not the same in all places and times. Or to return to my own vocabulary, there is no representation of the individuated mental stuff that universally obtains. Third, while I believe that the category of the self exists in some fashion in all cultures, I also believe that the cultural *salience* of that category—or the prevalence of what I will call self-talk—varies widely. Nor must we traverse vast temporal or geographical spaces to find noteworthy differences in salience. In fact, the story I tell in this book charts a dramatic shift in the salience of the self between the closely neighboring cultures of eighteenth- and nineteenth-century France.

Only in a culture in which self-talk is prevalent will people generally take the further step of worrying about whether the self is whole or fragmented. But that chronology may also be reversed: recognition of the pervasive existence of fragmentation coupled with a strong sense of its drawbacks may spur a rather abrupt introduction of self-talk. At least three different types of fragmentation have provided cause for worry. The type with which we are most familiar today was well evoked by Jean-Paul Sartre when he retrospectively described his first, youthful encounter with the work of Sigmund Freud, which took place in the early 1920s and resulted in a "deep repugnance": "When you have just taken the *bachot* at the age of seventeen with the 'I think, therefore I am' of Descartes as your text and you open *The Psychopathology of Everyday Life* and you read the famous episode of Signorelli with its substitutions, combinations and displacements, implying that Freud was simultaneously thinking of a patient who had committed suicide and of certain Turkish mores, and so on—when you read all that, your breath is simply taken away."[7]

Sartre is relating the shock that he felt when, thoroughly schooled at the lycée in the belief that his individuated mental stuff took the form of a self-evident, transparent, and seamlessly whole Cartesian ego, he confronted a powerful argument for the contrary proposition that it contained vast lodes of unconsciousness, could think multiple thoughts simultaneously, and might easily elude even its own possessor. His immediate reaction was to recoil in horror. Sartre's case is prototypical for the late nineteenth and early twentieth centuries, when a host of new psychological theories inspired by the empirical evidence of hypnosis—and most notable among them, Freudian psychoanalysis—argued for a fragmentation of the self along vertical, or depth-psychological, lines. According to this model, the self embraced significant expanses of deeply buried unconscious contents as well as a thin layer of readily accessible consciousness that floated atop them. I will call fragmentation of this type, premised on the existence of an unconscious mental substratum, *vertical fragmentation*. It figures briefly in the epilogue of this book but, as its point of historical origin alone indicates, it is not my principal concern here.

A second type of fragmentation, perhaps best labeled *segmentation*, refers to a disparity among the self's various roles. Unlike vertical fragmentation, which turns on the issue of the knowability of the self, segmentation turns on the issue of its sincerity and authenticity, its being all of a piece.

That role-playing is an integral component of the Western conception of selfhood was suggested by Mauss. He regarded the originary form of the self, found alike among indigenous Australian and Northwest American tribes, to be the persona, role, or mask, a concept referring to its possessor's social function. According to Mauss, an important evolution in this form occurred in early Roman society, which made extensive ritual use of ancestral masks. The name *persona* that designated the mask acquired an additional meaning; it became a technical legal term designating someone to whom the provisions of the law applied, the bearer of rights and obligations. Thus evolved, *persona* was for the Romans "synonymous with the true nature of the individual."[8] The legal persona did not give rise to concerns about fragmentation. In fact, as we will see later in this book, it seems to have functioned as the secure and stable template on which certain subsequent concepts of selfhood were drawn. But the intimate association of selfhood with something as superficial and inconstant as role-playing has at times provoked expressions of dissatisfaction and even moral outrage.

The court societies of the European monarchies of the sixteenth and seventeenth centuries were a locus classicus of inveterate role-playing. With brutal rivalry for the favors of the monarch as their central dynamic, they required participants to adopt public faces at odds with their private feelings. Widely circulated handbooks for courtiers even offered instruction in the art of prudential self-concealment and depicted achievement of an internal split within the person as a desirable goal. Such court-based codes of conduct, often transmitted as well to lower social strata, in turn produced a distinctive cultural backlash: criticism of the divided self and calls for the cultivation of sincere, holistic selves refusing to engage in flattery and other forms of calculated dissimulation.[9] The great spokesman for the unified, authentic self against the habits of segmentation ingrained and valorized by the court was, of course, Jean-Jacques Rousseau. While his railing against artifice and his endorsements of a "natural" authenticity were not carried out in an explicit language of selfhood, he nonetheless engaged in self-talk rather more than did his eighteenth-century contemporaries, famously reveling in the unmistakable self (*soi-même*) that he encountered as the simple "feeling of existence" while drifting aimlessly on a lake in a rowboat.[10]

The segmentation of the self through disingenuous role-playing continues to be an issue in our own day. For example, the historian George Chauncey has examined the imperative that dates from the 1970s for gay American men to "come out," or make their sexual orientation known in public. It derived, he argues, from a strong sense, not felt by members of this group in earlier eras, of the intolerability of donning different selves in different settings.[11] Similarly, concealment of ethnic background was once regarded as a prudential measure to facilitate getting ahead in America. But current mores placing a higher premium on authenticity now shun such segmentation of the self. Thus the celebrated architect Frank Gehry, born Frank Goldberg to Jewish working-class parents in Toronto, now bitterly regrets the new surname he adopted in Los Angeles in the 1950s. Musing about what a biography of him might someday contain, he said, "I haven't done anything bad, except for changing my name."[12]

Although I frequently mention Rousseau in this book, as is almost inevitable when discussing the culture of eighteenth-century France, the segmentation of the self that obsessed Jean-Jacques is not my topic here. My chief concern is rather a third type of fragmentation of the self, which I will call *horizontal fragmentation*. Unlike the much better-known vertical variety, it is not defined in terms of the depth, inaccessibility, and unconsciousness of mental contents. Instead, horizontal fragmentation refers to the status of the self in those psychological theories, rooted in biology, that build up mind from an accumulation of discrete pieces and have no obvious resources for joining them together under central, unitary command. All of the pieces are, epistemologically, on the same plane; there is no variance in our ability to know them; nothing is more hidden than anything else: hence the suitability of "horizontal" to describe the axis on which they are arrayed. Still, the composite whole is decentered, giving rise to concern about whether it qualifies as a true self.

As will be discussed at length in Chapters 3 and 7, two psychological theories that had currency in eighteenth- and nineteenth-century France routinely prompted charges of endangerment of the self through horizontal fragmentation: sensationalism and phrenology. A theory of seventeenth-century English vintage, sensationalism depicted the mind at birth as a blank slate subsequently inscribed by sensory bombardment, or by the stimuli picked up by the sense organs. Conscious awareness of those inscriptions was assumed. By contrast to the dark pockets of unconsciousness that give Freudian psychoanalysis its characteristic flavor, lucid consciousness was emphatically the medium of sensationalism; John Locke's version of the theory even helped introduce the noun "consciousness" into English.[13] But consciousness alone does not necessarily safeguard the integrity of the self. The starkly combinatorial logic on which the sensationalist model of mind rested riled its critics. They charged that such a mind contained no force or power that could overcome its fragmentary origins and subsume countless atomistic sensations into that active, holistic entity rightfully called a self.

Phrenology met with analogous criticism. A late eighteenth-century Viennese creation, it postulated an equivalence of mind and brain, further specifying that the brain was composed of some two or three dozen (the exact number varied according to the theorist) discrete organs, each responsible for governing an intellectual ability, an emotion, or a behavioral propensity. The relative size of the organs, which could be inferred from the contours of the skull, determined the particular psychological profile of the individual. All the organs were unproblematically knowable, just as all the sensations in sensationalism were conscious. Yet, critics alleged, the divided brain that phrenologists featured as the material basis of mind provided no support for the unifying agency called the self. An organ devoted to selfhood was conspicuously absent from the roster. Nor was there any logical place for it, given the lack of functional hierarchy among the organs.

The French critics who noted and bemoaned the fragmentation of the self entailed by sensationalism and phrenology were also the group who introduced self-talk into the culture of nineteenth-century France and who lent the category of the self its particular salience in that historical context. They were Victor Cousin, at once philosopher, philosophy professor, and academic administrator, and his large and well-organized cohort of disciples. They constructed their psychology around an immaterial self, or *moi,* that (they insisted) was given to its possessor whole and a priori. Such a construction avoided the insidious undermining of the self that, in their opinion, resulted from hitching psychology to biology: after all, spirit, unlike matter, was not susceptible of division. Cousin's stunning success in institutionalizing his doctrine in the national educational system vastly magnified the influence of his school. In fact, that institutionalization outlived by more than a half-century Cousin's roughly thirty-five years of personal power (1815–51) at the lectern and in the state educational bureaucracy. In more diluted form, it even continued well into the twentieth century.

While the proponents of sensationalism, phrenology, and Cousinianism all offered versions of "the post-Revolutionary self" (to cite the title of this book), the Cousinian *moi* emerged as the definitive version. It did so both because its institutional success swept the field and because, alone among the three, the Cousinians engaged extensively in self-talk. They persuaded people—ordinary people as well as the guardians of the French state—that the self, meaning the unitary self, was an urgent sociopolitical necessity; and that fragmented selves, which in their view were not selves at all, wrought sociopolitical havoc. A major purpose of this book is to show how they carried out their program and to examine the broad consequences that flowed from it.

A related purpose of the book is precisely to make and to operationalize an analytic distinction between psychological discourses in general and those psychological discourses, like Cousinianism, that feature the self. The wide diffusion of sensationalism in France, I argue, produced a heightened and systematic awareness of mental interiority without thereby encouraging people to dwell upon a single tight-knit unit comprising the sum total of mental states and processes. Less widely diffused, phrenology in France opened up a psychological realm while refusing to entertain a concept of the self. Psychological interiority can, in other words, assume a pointillist attitude; it is not necessarily tantamount to self-talk.[14] This book suggests that cultures reveal a lot about themselves by the kind of psychological discourses they adopt and, in particular, by whether or not those discourses generate self-talk.

The period 1750 to 1850, which forms the canvas of this study, has not, of course, been innocently or randomly chosen. It is the period, bridging the French Revolution, that marks the transition from the Old Regime to an ill-defined "modernity," or from early modern Europe to modern Europe properly so called. The period, and particularly its Revolutionary pivot, have been frequently, even obsessively narrated. Historians have methodically traced its major economic changes (from guild restrictions to laissez-faire), political changes (from monarchical absolutism to national sovereignty), and social changes (from corporate organization to the career open to talents). The self has figured incidentally in these narratives. Broad-gauged assertions about the transformations it presumably underwent when everything around it was in flux have become old saws: the individual as the subject of rights was born; the era of modern bourgeois individualism was decisively inaugurated.

Without challenging the fundamental validity of such gross character-izations, this book attempts to tell a more specific, finer-grained story of what happened to selfhood when it crossed the Revolutionary divide. In order to do so, it considers sources that have not been previously mar-shaled for this purpose: the prevailing psychological theories of the period and their conversion into pedagogy. Viewed through this lens, a basic plotline emerges. An ascendant sensationalism reached its apogee during the Revolutionary decade and then declined. With the establish-ment of the July Monarchy in 1830, it yielded its place more or less con-clusively to Cousinianism. Phrenology provided a contrapuntal movement. Presenting itself as an alternative to Cousinianism, it lost all the standard battles for preeminence and eventually turned its attention to the needs of socially marginal groups. For our purposes, its trajectory underscores the thoroughness of the Cousinian victory.

While I might have straightforwardly enlisted this plotline as the book's backbone, I have instead opted for a more unusual organization, one that warrants explanation here. The book begins obliquely, in medias res. Part I is devoted to the much-vocalized anxiety about the mental faculty of imagination in eighteenth-century France (Chapter 1) and the Revolutionary effort to render imagination non-threatening and to harness it for civic ends (Chapter 2). I thus plunge the reader directly into the sensationalist-psychological discourse of this period, showing its suppleness, liveliness, and many points of contact with discourses about society, economics, and politics. At the same time as these chap-ters tell their respective stories and familiarize the reader with the dis-tinctive psychological idiom of the era, they also demonstrate two points central to the argument of the book as a whole. First, far from being an arcane knowledge manipulated exclusively by philosophers, sensationalism served ordinary educated people in late eighteenth-century France as a general interpretive frame, capable of processing and decoding many kinds of information about the world. It thus set the pattern, later followed by Cousinianism and phrenology, for the broad cultural role that psychological theory played in this period.

Second, the occasion for and the incitement to the intensive develop-ment of psychological science in France in this period was provided by socioeconomic transformation. Anxiety about the workings of imagina-tion reflected a larger anxiety about the imminent breakdown of corpo-rate society and, after 1789, about its actual occurrence. As a careful examination of the discourse on imagination reveals, corporate structures were widely perceived in eighteenth-century France as integral to the regular and predictable functioning of persons. Thus the specter of a society without corporations effectively problematized the self for contemporaries: it posed the question of whether, in the absence of a corporate matrix, a person's own inherent resources were adequate to ensure that person's stability or whether, buffeted by an overactive imagination, the person would be thrown ominously off-kilter.

One logical response to this troubling question was to subject the mental workings of human beings to systematic scrutiny or, in other words, to develop a psychological science. Such a tack was very much in the spirit of the Enlightenment, which, taking Newton's science of the natural world as a model, had mandated a search for the lawful regularities governing the human world and had vested such human sciences with a high and reassuring degree of authority.[15] Of course, the eighteenth-century French already had such a psychological science in the form of sensationalism. Its initial articulation in seventeenth-century England may well have been prompted by the precocious appearance of a laissez-faire economy there, just as its gallicization by the abbé de Condillac in the 1740s was probably spurred on by intimations of corporate collapse. Hence, French attempts to tame the imagination and stabilize the freestanding individual, which occurred especially during the Revolution, took the form not of creating a psychological science from scratch but of more thoroughly and deliberately exploiting the one at hand, newly construing it as a resource in sociopolitical affairs. Whether or not the Revolutionaries' experiment in using psychology as an instrument of government succeeded (the question was made moot by the Napoleonic coup and the demise of the regime as a whole), its lesson was not lost on their early nineteenth-century successors. The post-Revolutionary generation faced sociopolitical problems of their own and had, moreover, in the form of Cousinianism and phrenology, brand-new psychological sciences to press into service.

Strictly speaking, the late eighteenth-century recognition of the perils of the imagination qualifies as a problematization of the self. For, to use the vocabulary I have introduced here, observers were expressing a concern about the capacities of the individuated mental stuff. Yet, significantly for our purposes, that problem was not cast as self-talk. It was not the "self" that seemed deficient or defective to pre-Revolutionary observers who apprehensively noted the high incidence of wayward imagination; to their way of thinking, the defect was narrowly lodged in the mental faculty of imagination per se and was then prone to exacerbation by certain social environments that dangerously overstimulated it. Likewise, in coping with the problem of wayward imagination, the Revolutionaries did not speak of stabilizing the self; they instead devised strategies targeting the single mental faculty in question. In fact, their ability to lavish so much exclusive attention on one element of the psyche confirms the characterization of sensationalism as producing psychic fragmentation. It also shows that a theory can foster psychological interiority while remaining aloof from self-talk. Hence, while Part I establishes many of the essential motifs of the book, especially the currency of psychological discourse in ordinary life, what is conspicuously absent from it is a culturally salient category of the self. Serious self-talk enters the book only in Part II.

That is why Chapter 3, which opens Part II, backtracks both chronologically and substantively. It treats from the angle of the self the sensationalist theory that, from other angles, already figured so prominently in Part I. It looks at what the key texts of sensationalism had to say about the self, starting with the seminal analysis in the second edition of John Locke's *Essay on Human Understanding* (1694). It shows that, in some quarters, expressions of concern and disapprobation about the flimsiness and fragmentation of the sensationalist self dated back as far as Locke's weighing in on the matter. But it also shows that a strong, unitary self was not a requirement for everyone: the chief French exponent of sensationalism, the abbé de Condillac, endorsed without apology the flimsy self that he derived from his own version of Locke's principles. The very minor place consequently occupied by the self in Condillac's psychological treatises coincides with and helps to explain the absence of self-talk even among psychologically attuned people in late eighteenth-century and Revolutionary France. Such people had, after all, basically learned their psychology from Condillac. Despite their marked tendency to understand the world in psychological terms, an entity called the self was absent from their preoccupations.

What vaulted self-talk into prominence early in the nineteenth century was, I argue, the rupture represented by the Revolution and the concerns unleashed first by the excesses of the Terror and then by the collapse of the moderate republican regime that attempted to undo those excesses. As observers sought to understand the agony of the French nation and to pin the blame for it on some plausible culprit, a group of thinkers, later to become influential, lighted upon the demoralizing effects of the long eighteenth-century reign of sensationalism and especially the pallid and passive self associated with it. Political stability, they contended, required a different psychology, which would in turn undergird—and create—a different kind of self.

The *moi* that the Cousinians made iconic was deliberately the antitype of its sensationalist counterpart: a robust, active, unshakably unitary self instead of a flimsy, fragmented one. The Cousinians not only taught this self as a doctrine. Their national educational program, which more or less persisted through the nineteenth century, routinized practices of introspection designed to ensure that students would directly perceive the activity of the self within them. The formidable cultural work performed by the Cousinian *moi* ranged even farther than this literal training in selfhood and inculcation of a newly lively belief in personal agency; it touched on the very organization of society. Because Cousin's philosophy specified that only certain people had the intellectual gifts necessary to actualize the *moi* that everyone possessed potentially, it established a hierarchy between the selved and the unselved. Based on class and gender, that hierarchy was then replicated and reinforced institutionally in the populations that were included in or, alternately, excluded from schooling in philosophical psychology. Through this combination of granting the self extraordinary cultural salience and providing a new criterion for ranking people, Cousinianism did nothing less than supply a structuring principle for the society—I will call it bourgeois society—that came into its own after the Revolution. The Cousinian *moi* effectively supplanted the structuring principle of Old Regime society: the corporate order that the Revolution had abolished.

I speak of "bourgeois society" advisedly. I am not using the term in a strict Marxian sense to refer to a society founded on industrial capitalism (which, economic historians have shown, had little purchase in France before 1850 in any case) or run by captains of industry. I use it more loosely to refer to that inherently fluid, individualistic social order that came into being in France once the corporations had been outlawed and laissez-faire economic principles gave free rein to individual professional ambition. This society was bourgeois in the sense that its characteristic elite was non-noble and readied for leadership by education rather than birth. The place of education is key. The post-Revolutionary French state demonstrated a marked zeal for the creation of central educational institutions—most famously, the lycées, founded in 1802—designed to train civil servants for the state administration. In all likelihood, its intense commitment to education grew out of its earlier destruction of the corporations. As Pierre Rosanvallon has argued, providing schools was one of several aspects of the singular function of "producing society" that the nineteenth-century French state took upon itself in order to compensate for its excision of the corporate bodies and for the brutally torn social fabric that resulted.[16]

I would be inclined to identify this state-educated elite as the most characteristic component of the nineteenth-century French bourgeoisie.[17] As befits the new structuring principle of French society that succeeded the corporations, then, the Cousinian *moi* was thoroughly embedded in the state education system, even using the lycées as its instrument of dissemination. In calling this self "bourgeois," I am not, it should be evident, conceptualizing Cousinian psychology as the ideological reflex of an already objectively existent bourgeois class. Rather I am suggesting that Cousinian psychology participated actively in the constitution of this social group, furnishing its members with a shared, highly articulated subjectivity or self-conception and providing them with a psychological justification for their social superiority.

In invoking the adjective "bourgeois" for the Cousinian self, I am not only utilizing the word's neutral, taxonomical sense—that is, its reference to the social elite that supplanted the nobility—but also exploiting some of the more colorful, barbed connotations that the word acquired during its long history in France. As Chapter 4 will show, specific attributes of the Cousinian *moi* make it a perfect epitome of colloquial bourgeois-ness: Cousinian psychology valorized in technical language both the positive self-image of this new French elite and its negative image in widespread antibourgeois satire. Thus the Cousinian *moi* was defined as a dynamic will capable of molding the world and as a foundational principle that endowed private property with metaphysical status. But at the same time that *moi* necessarily affirmed a set of values that, though lavishly praised by Cousin, destined it for all the unoriginality and conformism of Flaubert's Monsieur Homais.

Influences, Interlocutors

In trying to think about the self in terms simultaneously historical and theoretical, I turned to Michel Foucault as one of the few available guides. Hence it is fair to say that this book is in some ways Foucauldian in inspiration. One of Foucault's great theoretical contributions was to account for the new forms of individuality and subjectivity characteristic of the modern West by showing how they were, surprisingly, completely embedded in the new modalities of power that he called discipline and biopower.[18] As he extended the investigations begun in *Discipline and Punish* and the first volume of *The History of Sexuality* back into classical antiquity, Foucault built on this insight by formulating, with his usual keen sense of paradox, the category of a "technology of the self." It posits very concrete practices that a society recommends or prescribes to shape that intangible, even ethereal thing called a self.[19] My own study takes from Foucault the impulse to integrate historical variations in the self into a kind of *histoire totale* that includes social, political, and economic elements; and it shares Foucault's "technological" fascination by focusing on educational institutions and pedagogical methods as instruments of self-making. It moreover identifies the Cousinianism taught in the nineteenth-century French lycée as a superlatively influential technology of the self.

In another of its presuppositions, too, this study concurs with Foucault. While an investigation of the self in this period might have relied primarily on the looser and more intimate discursive forms of the novel, letter, and diary, this one, while not neglecting such sources, focuses on the psychological sciences—that is, the theories of the mind that claimed scientific status. It takes that approach out of a belief that in the modern period the psychological sciences have wielded a special authority and rhetorical power over the literate public. Ordinary educated people have readily, if informally, adopted their schemas as interpretive frames to make sense of their own mental experience and of the inner lives of others. I see sensationalism, Cousinianism, and phrenology as functioning in eighteenth- and nineteenth-century France much as Freudianism functioned in the twentieth-century United States. Freudian concepts became part of the mental furniture of the average educated American. One did not need to be a card-carrying adept of psychoanalysis to lend credence to such ideas as infantile sexuality,

Oedipal rivalry, and Freudian slips, and to use them in navigating the everyday world.

The central place of the human sciences and of the standard of scientific truth applied to human affairs was, of course, a leitmotif of Foucault's analysis of the modern West, one that figured in almost all his major works. In a metahistory of the self that he sketched out for an interviewer in the 1980s, too, Foucault identified the advent of scientific knowledge as the turning point. He distinguished between the "self," which had in his view existed at least since classical antiquity, and the "subject," a distinctly modern invention. The self, fundamentally ethical and aesthetic in nature, was capable of obtaining truth only if well cared for by its owner. The subject, introduced by Descartes, could obtain truth simply by seeing what was evident; it was thus the functional equivalent of all other subjects. With the mid-seventeenth-century arrival of the subject, in other words, evidence supplanted the vagaries of "care of the self" as the road to truth, and the enterprise of modern science was made possible.[20] Although I have not adopted Foucault's terminology of "self" versus "subject" in this book, I share his conviction that something fundamentally new and highly significant happened to the self historically when the language of science was applied to it.

But while Foucault's writings have been a frequent reference point in my thinking about this topic, I have never regarded his conclusions as dicta. I have used them heuristically, keeping them at the ready and drawing on them, where relevant, to interpret and organize the material that I turned up in libraries and archives. A strictly Foucauldian approach to selfhood would have ignored Cousin. After all, probably as a result of his desire to debunk the academic philosophy that had loomed so large over his own education, Foucault specifically excluded "philosophical theories of the mind, passions, or body" from the materials he regarded as pertinent to the constitution of the self.[21] It would, on those same grounds, have ignored sensationalism and probably phrenology as well. Foucault seems to have overlooked the fact that all three of these "philosophical theories of the mind" generated a widely deployed practical pedagogy and were thus, by his own criteria, entirely plausible participants in the project of constituting the self. Finally, a strictly Foucauldian approach to nineteenth-century selfhood would certainly not have countenanced the virtual silence about sexuality that the reader will find in these pages. In considering the construction of modern subjectivity, Foucault accorded a uniquely privileged status to the personal information about sexual desires, fantasies, and conduct extracted during asymmetrical, face-to-face encounters with scientific experts—a hypothesis that I have simply bracketed here.

In another important way, too, this study diverges from the conventions of Foucault's history writing. While his genealogies of the modern self concerned issues of power and were, in a very general sense, historically situated, they also lacked intentional actors and displayed structural dynamics of their own that set them apart from familiar historical narratives. The story of the post-Revolutionary self that I tell here is, by contrast, much more specifically grounded in a recognizable historical landscape. It includes consequential and willful actors, especially Victor Cousin and his chief ally, François Guizot. Its plotline features political calculations and strategies and is mindful of the bevy of distinct political regimes that characterize French history after 1789. In sum, while sympathetic to Foucault's perspectives, I have tended to see the blatantly public field of national politics, and not only the hidden recesses of insidious systems of micro-power, as the site of the constitution of the self. Mentioning "politics" (meaning national politics) in the subtitle of this book thus marks my distance from Foucault.[22]

Another recent commentator on the history of the self, the philosopher Charles Taylor, has had less impact on this study; indeed, it is my differences with Taylor, rather than my borrowings from him, that deserve mention here. Those differences focus on the way each of us has conceptualized the relationship between Descartes and Locke.

What I have called the horizontal fragmentation of the self occurred in early modern Europe when Descartes' picture of the human mind— an immaterial, indivisible, and ever-present thinking substance—gave way to the additive, biologically based Lockean picture. Hence, in its a priori holism, the Cousinian *moi* restored essential features of its Cartesian predecessor. Cousin acknowledged this debt to the founder of modern philosophy early in his career and then symbolically discharged it in the 1820s by preparing a new, eleven-volume edition of Descartes' collected works.[23] Similarly, the Cartesianism avowed by Sartre in the passage quoted earlier derived from his training in a lycée system still using, after almost a century, a version of the pro-Cartesian philosophy curriculum installed by Cousin in the 1830s. The story I tell here, in other words, turns on the *distinction* between Descartes and Locke and on the possibilities for the fragmentation of the self introduced by closely linking mind and matter.

In his *Sources of the Self,* whose canvas covers the more than two millennia from Plato through Derrida, Taylor makes no such distinction. He depicts the modern Western self as triply characterized by an inwardness, or sense of having inner depths, that began its career with Augustine; by an affirmation of the ordinary life of work and family as the arena for the realization of selfhood, a development that awaited the Protestant Reformation; and by a late eighteenth-century Romantic-inspired belief in the voice of nature as expressive of the authentic self. In this account, Descartes and Locke appear under the first rubric, inwardness. After Augustine accomplished the momentous feat of introducing radical reflexivity into the Western tradition by building an entire system of thought around the assertion that God was to be found inside our minds rather than outside in the world,[24] Descartes and Locke made the next significant contributions to Western inwardness. At more than a thousand years' remove from Augustine but a mere fifty years' remove from each other, they participated in a common project that Taylor calls disengagement. Following Augustine in finding more intrinsic interest in the mental processing apparatus than in the things "out there" that are processed, they inflected this Augustinian preference. They refused to inhabit Augustine's first-person standpoint or to immerse themselves in the "bewitchment" of experience. Instead, each chose to objectify the mental apparatus, thus acquiring a measure of control over it and depriving the experience it offered of normative force.[25] In Taylor's long view, Descartes and Locke appear more similar than dissimilar.

That Taylor has presented a striking narrative must be granted. But the very broad sweep of that narrative almost ensures the existence of valid subnarratives that fall within its chronological scope and go against its grain. One such subnarrative, completely effaced by Taylor but well documented in this book, is the concern about a specific quality of psychological inwardness: whether the inner space that is inhabited enjoys a structural unity that can ground a reliably coherent self or is so fragmented and diffuse as to preclude that outcome. While this concern, surfacing in the wake of Locke's *Essay* and marking the sharp divergence of sensationalism from Cartesianism, appears only as a wrinkle in the millennial trend that Taylor discerned, it was an event of no small magnitude at the level of a hundred-year *durée*. It obsessed many educated Frenchmen during the late eighteenth and the nineteenth centuries. It points, at least in France, to a massive change in the place of the self in the social imaginary. As such it will carry a driving force in this story.

The psychically fragmenting effects of sensationalism, as actually experienced by many educated post-Revolutionary Frenchmen, indicate a final intellectual context in which this book should be situated. Postmodern theorists of a Derridean stripe have typically portrayed the Western subject as monolithically logocentric—that is, as a unified "presence" serving a foundational function—all the way from Plato to Derrida.[26] According to their account, the possibility that this reassuringly stable entity might be illusory dawned on Western thinkers only in the late twentieth century. The account of the Cousinian project that I offer in this book casts doubt on this postmodern tenet. It shows that anxious awareness of the potential disintegration of the subject was a central fact of early nineteenth-century French intellectual life and describes deliberate political efforts to ward off that eventuality as early as the 1830s. It suggests that the conceptions of selfhood embedded in Western philosophy are considerably more variegated than the postmodernists allow. It furthermore suggests that postmodernism may have mistakenly assigned transhistorical status to a version of the self that is in fact quite historically specific. Its real nemesis may be the resolutely armored *moi* of Victor Cousin and his school, which—as this book will demonstrate at length—was summoned into existence in the name of post-Revolutionary bourgeois order and was destined for a surprisingly long reign.

I

THE PROBLEM FOR WHICH PSYCHOLOGY FURNISHED A SOLUTION

The Perils of Imagination
at the End of the Old Regime

Each artisan will regard himself as a solitary being, dependent on himself alone, and free to indulge all the flights of an often disordered imagination.

Remonstrance of the Parlement of Paris
against the edict abolishing the guilds, 1776

Among the many tensions that erupted in Paris in the critical year 1789, a relatively petty one can serve as a convenient frame for this chapter. At the beginning of January, and against the background of the elections for the Estates-General, a comedy by Philippe Fabre d'Eglantine entitled *Le Présomptueux, ou l'heureux imaginaire* opened at the Théâtre Français only to be hooted off the stage during the second scene. Disgruntled members of the audience alleged that the play "treated the same subject" as another play soon to be presented but written by a different dramatist.[1] In fact, the two works in question—the second was *Les Châteaux en Espagne* by Jean-François Collin d'Harleville—did, as their titles suggest, converge on a single theme: the impact on human affairs of an especially active imagination. (Building "castles in Spain" had the same colloquial and figurative meaning then as now. The abbé de Condillac wrote in his *Essai sur les origines des connaissances humaines* [1746] that all human beings tended in moments of idleness to spin daydreams in which they cast themselves as heroes and that these "castles in Spain" remained harmless products of the imagination as long as their creators faithfully distinguished them from external reality.)[2] The audience protest on the evening of January 7, 1789, crystallized a long-

21

standing literary rivalry. When Fabre d'Eglantine charged that the protesters who had rudely brought down his play with their allegations of
plagiarism were members of a "powerful cabal" devoted to Collin d'Harleville, he may have exaggerated the depths of the intrigue involved, but
he seems to have correctly grasped the gist of the story.[3]

How should we interpret this squabble? And how—if at all—should
we decipher its relation to the troubled political environment that
would, in less than half a year, issue in the collapse of the Old Regime?
One tack might be to highlight the mood of the theater-going public:
the certain low boiling point that prevented the audience from sitting
through the whole of Fabre's new play was perhaps symptomatic of a
more generalized spirit of agitation or even, as one nineteenth-century
commentator has suggested, of mutiny.[4] Another strategy might be to
emphasize the fact that Fabre would soon emerge as a revolutionary
politician. His pugnacious temperament (he affiliated with Marat and
Danton at the Cordeliers Club) was better suited for the new rough-
and-tumble world of popular participation than was Collin's gentility,
and hence it was no accident that the earlier maligned *Présomptueux*
was finally performed in its entirety—and to wide acclaim—in February 1790, when the Revolution was in full swing.[5]

But whatever merit these hypotheses might possess, they are not my
interest here. What interests me about the controversy is rather the similar content of the two plays involved—that is, their exploration of the
workings of imagination in ordinary life—and the relationship of that
content to the historical rupture brought about by the Revolution.
Briefly put, my thesis has two parts. First, the changes associated with
the Revolution and already adumbrated during the closing decades of
the Old Regime problematized for contemporaries the nature of the
human person, or self—or, more accurately, triggered one of those
reproblematizations of the self that punctuate the history of the West.
Second, according to the eighteenth-century understanding of psychology, the imagination was the most vulnerable component of the person, the one that would unfailingly wreak havoc (on its owner and on
others) if certain kinds of alterations in the social fabric were undertaken. However else the quarrel between Fabre and Collin might be
read as a presage of the Revolution, the fascination of two prominent
playwrights with the imagination at this particular historical juncture
and their conviction that the public would share that fascination was, I

contend, a discursive marker of sociocultural unease and of the seismic shifts that were soon to come.

Before explaining these assertions in detail, let me return to the Fabre-Collin *affaire*. A closer look at the documentation it generated as well as at the plays themselves will, while not proving my assertions, at least clarify them and render them more plausible.

Five days after the abortive premiere of *Le Présomptueux,* Fabre d'Eglantine published an open letter responding to the implicit accusation of plagiarism.[6] The text of this letter in effect doubles back on itself: it not only discusses imagination directly as a possible subject for a theatrical composition but also discusses it indirectly when offering an account of the creative process designed to exonerate Fabre from blame. This curious doubling back has the result—significant for us here—of underscoring Fabre's intense preoccupation with the category of imagination.

Fabre begins his letter by reconstructing the sequence of events by which he first learned that Collin was writing a play about imagination. He had encountered his rival at the theater when, at the conclusion of the evening's performance, both men paid a visit to a certain actress in her box. There the conversation turned to the difficulty of finding subjects suitable for comedy. After Fabre volunteered the four such subjects that seemed to him most obvious (natural man, ambition in the village, private life, and the hypocrisy of society), Collin ticked off his own list of three: the bachelor, the efforts of fathers to instruct their children, and, offered after a somewhat anxious pause, one that he found "especially droll" and about which he was currently writing—"castles in Spain." Upon hearing this third and final subject, Fabre's ears pricked up. He sensed that Collin was emitting important cues about the level of his artistic investment in this theme, and he describes his own mental response very explicitly, using the language of sensationalist psychology current in educated circles in France at that date. "The simultaneously impatient and circumspect demeanor of Monsieur Collin," he reports, "caught my attention"—attention was one of the key mental operations in Condillac's psychology—"and I confess that upon hearing that word [castles in Spain] I experienced the bedazzlement that an onrush of ideas produces."

In the midst of all this mental excitement, Fabre remained silent, keeping his counsel while his companions in the box continued to chat.

When the conversation concluded (all told, it had lasted less than a half-hour), he and Collin walked together as far as the Rue Dauphine, during which time his rival asked him to elaborate on one of Fabre's own preferred subjects for comedy: private life. "Not a word, not a word," Fabre insists, was said about castles in Spain during this stroll. Nonetheless, the earlier, chance mention of a play about imagination had stayed with Fabre, activating his own imagination: "My imagination was struck (*frappée*) by it, though without determinate plan." The next night he happened to choose for his bedtime reading Montaigne's "On Idleness," in which the essayist warns that a mind left unoccupied casts itself about in "disordered" fashion "in the vague field of imagination." Indeed, Montaigne confesses that he had believed when he retired to his estate that he would do himself a great favor by leaving his mind idle, only to find that his mind then chose its own work and, to his shame, "gave birth to an array of chimeras and fantastic monsters."[7] Thus, accidentally coming upon some of Montaigne's ruminations on imagination, Fabre "felt myself very keenly struck (*frappé*), for the second time, with the idea of castles in Spain." Ever alert to the nuances of his mental processes, he goes on to specify that this second *coup* was "absolutely different" from the one that had occurred in the theatre the night before. On that earlier occasion the ideas he generated had been—again the language of sensationalist psychology—"mechanically combined." This time, he "conceived of" a comedy on the theme in question "with such rapidity" and, apparently, with such holistic integrity that he "immediately got up" and wrote the entire first scene during the course of the night. A mere seventeen days sufficed for him to finish off the full five acts.

Fabre's pamphlet thus begins with an anatomization of the process of his own literary imagination: he describes the entirely automatic and thus implicitly blameless manner in which external stimuli had spurred it on to action, without the intervention of a malicious will to encroach on Collin's turf. In the mechanisms of psychology, he thus finds his first line of defense against the charge of plagiarism. Fabre then turns to imagination as a kind of topos, a subject matter for the genre of comedy. And here, too, analyzing imagination from a different psychological vantage point, he finds a second line of defense. He stole nothing from Collin because "this subject is inexhaustible; this disorder of mind is not [embodied in] a single character but is rather a modification belonging to all possible characters." To be convinced of the myriad forms that imagination can assume, the limitless number of plotlines that reverie can produce, "one need only look closely at oneself." Far from being unethical or narrowly self-serving, then, Fabre's variation on the theme of imagination that had first been chosen by Collin for representation on stage was, in fact, an artistic accomplishment from which all his colleagues could benefit, "a means," in Fabre's own words, "of expanding the resources of comedy."

Fabre thus offered up his reflections on the processes and nature of imagination in a bid to clear himself of charges of wrongdoing. But what, in particular, had attracted him and Collin to imagination as a subject for a theatrical composition at the end of the eighteenth century? To answer that question requires that we examine the plays themselves.

They are, in their basic contours, remarkably similar. In each, a young well-born man essentially defined by his overly active imagination believes that he can successfully woo the young well-born lady of the house; in the end, he fails. Yet, despite these fully comparable plotlines, Fabre argued in his open letter for the "inexhaustible" scope of the imagination theme by pointing out that he and his rival had given it fundamentally different comedic interpretations:

> His [Collin's] visionary daydreams for the sake of daydreaming. Mine daydreams because he is *presumptuous,* and if one studies nature carefully, one will see that *presumptuousness* is the most abundant— and the most dangerous—source of chimeras in the human mind.[8]

The contrast Fabre drew between the two main characters is apt, as is his intimation that, in terms of tone, his own play had the sharper edge. Set in an isolated chateau surrounded by forest, Collin's *Châteaux en Espagne* created a misty atmosphere of semi-reality that seems to encourage all the characters to give free rein to their imaginations.[9] The chief offender, d'Orlange, effortlessly wins the young lady's father, Monsieur d'Orfeuil, over to his cause. But the young lady, Henriette—who is chided by her maidservant at the opening of the play for her own dreamy tendency to imagine as her future husband a perfect man who could exist in a novel but not in reality[10]—dislikes d'Orlange because *his* head is in the clouds. (She judges him, she says, by his words, which are "empty, light, inconsequential, frivolous," indicating that he would make "an extremely pleasant lover, and a very bad spouse" [Act 2, Scene 5, p. 279].) Realizing that Henriette loves another man, however, d'Orlange cannot ultimately bring himself to capitalize on the paternal consent to his own match, and he goes in search of Henriette's beloved Florville, expeditiously returning him to the chateau. This good deed—and the almost palpable happiness and gratitude it generates in his entourage—apparently cures d'Orlange of his earlier need to take refuge in imagination:

> Me! I did my duty. Ah! let us draw a deep breath . . .
> We can feel how much a good deed refreshes the blood:
> And this kind of good is not imaginary;
> Henceforth I thoroughly renounce what are called "chimeras."
> It's done. I am forever corrected. (Act 5, Scene 10, p. 345)

The play thus ending with d'Orlange's "correction" ends on a gentle note of reconciliation and harmony. Having assimilated himself to the prevailing code of conduct, d'Orlange vows to buy a piece of land in the canton (M. d'Orfeuil volunteers his help in locating the real estate) and to settle down on it with a still-to-be-chosen wife. The "castles in Spain" have thus been officially banished (as his valet declares in the play's very last line),[11] but d'Orlange himself will be allowed to stay.

Fabre's play, by contrast, ends on a vindictive note. The d'Orlange equivalent, Valère, is rejected in his suit and, swearing that the young lady in question, Lucille, has "lost more than [she] knows," he departs the Franval estate "without pique but"—his imaginary world still intact—"not without hope." Unlike M. d'Orfeuil, who welcomes the transformed d'Orlange into the fold, M. de Franval bids the incorrigible Valère good riddance and ends the play by nearly cursing him and his particular mental state:

> Astonishing. . . . And, what's more, he believes what he says.
> Let us nonetheless conclude that the presumptuous person
> Is mad (fou) in his desires and is never happy. (Act 5, Scene 7, p. 133)[12]

What does "presumptuous" imagination and the fond attachment to castles in Spain connote in these two plays, and why is it so threatening in both—needing to be reformed and neutralized in Collin's version and altogether extirpated in Fabre's? For both playwrights (and despite the fact that neither of these plays concerns social climbing per se), the dominance of imagination in an individual psyche is explicitly associated with that individual's lack of fixed social position, with a kind of social floating that flaunts the requirements of order. D'Orlange's valet makes this association in the strongest possible terms by metaphorically likening his master to that most deracinated of Old Regime figures, the Jew. D'Orlange is, he declares, "a true wandering Jew, always roaming the world" (Act 2, Scene 1, p. 261). Soon after, d'Orlange confirms this description, acknowledging that he frequently, indeed purposely, goes astray, "know[ing] neither the roads nor the map" (Act 2, Scene 3, p. 265).

D'Orlange's propensity for geographical wandering has its mental analogue in his similarly unbounded and uncharted flights of imagination, one of which forms the centerpiece of the play (Act 3, Scenes 6–7). Optimistic about his pursuit of Henriette, he sees his presumed success in the marital arena as a sign of even bigger things to come: "I can make a name for myself and, in my Ministry, serve the King, the State, pacify the earth. . . ." He warms to his theme, "arriving by degrees"—as the stage directions specify—"at a kind of reverie and vision." A ship he has boarded in his official capacity is attacked by the Turks, whom he proceeds to fight almost single-handedly; and when he is finally forced to surrender, his assailants, "charmed by my valor, proclaim me their leader." His bold exploits continue, arousing the jealousy of neighboring princes, until the Sultan decides that it would be prudent to cement an alliance with d'Orlange by making him his son-in-law. The Sultan dies, leaving the Frenchman to reign over Turkey—at this point the stage directions call for d'Orlange to be "at the peak of delirium." He worries whether his religion is suitable for his new position but reassures himself that his dogma, "to adore the God of the universe," is also the dogma of the Turks and that everyone in the empire will, following his example, worship a single God. At this moment in the reverie, he is interrupted by his valet, who comes onstage prostrating himself and uttering the word "Sultan." Thus awakening the engrossed d'Orlange, the valet jokingly apologizes for having "dethroned" the Sultan. But d'Orlange refuses to allow his imaginative operations to be mocked, and he defends them at length and with a certain eloquence. His basic argument is that "everyone"—whether high or low in the social hierarchy— "builds castles in Spain." These "beautiful dreams" provide a necessary and "useful respite" from the "real cares" that would otherwise overwhelm us. It would be, he implies, foolish not to avail ourselves of this most powerful resource for the effective transformation of our emotional state: "When I dream, I am the happiest of men; and as soon as we believe ourselves happy, we are."

The ending of Collin's play thus derives logically from the link that formed its initial premise: the link between vagabondage as a lifestyle and giving oneself over to imagination as a psychological trait. Just as the valet's entrance awakens d'Orlange from the Turkish daydream, so—but more definitively—does the tangible happiness produced by his own altruistic act awaken him from his tendency to seek out the less real and hence inferior happiness afforded by imagination. Once cured of his mental wandering, he is cured of its physical counterpart, and he proposes to root himself in the soil for the first time through the purchase of a landed property. D'Orlange has never been a really bad man—his Turkish dream is not merely self-aggrandizing but also envisions the spread of a tolerant deism throughout the world—but he is, Collin would have us believe, a far better man for having renounced his self-generated chimeras in favor of a socially shared and validated reality.

Fabre's Valère is constructed on much the same model of a parallelism between lack of mental fixity and lack of social/physical fixity, but he is a far more negative creation. Utilizing a direct and extensive knowledge of sensationalist psychology and of its associationist corollary, whereby the ideas produced from sense impressions get linked and combined into propositional judgments, Fabre depicts Valère's imaginings not as an escapist's vague and misguided quest for happiness but rather as a mode of calculation. As Valère boasts to his valet:

> It is necessary, when one has plans,
> To be sure of success from the beginning:
> But to do so is the gift of a solid judgment,
> Of a mind that is vast, fervent, neither weak nor timid:
> I have that gift. There is a chain, you see,
> That links one object to another unexpected object. . . .
> At a glance, at first sight,
> I perceive in its full extent the chain of phenomena;
> I combine, weigh, and easily divine
> What will result from a given event.
> There, right beneath my eyes, I see a faithful image of the result.
> (Act 1, Scene 1, p. 7)

Imagination, then, is for Valère a means of projecting himself into the future coupled with a conviction that he has the mental acuity to forecast that future accurately, indeed to body it forth "there, right beneath my eyes." He is the visionary as young man on the make, hence his so-called presumptuousness. This variety of imaginative disorder—and the language of pathology is pejoratively invoked throughout the play to describe Valère[13]—has led him into a life of audacious risk-taking. It has also led to his refusal to commit himself to an *état,* where *état* is, in the eighteenth-century lexicon, both a line of work and a fixed place in the social universe. "He remains *sans état,*" his father complains in a letter to M. de Franval (Act 1, Scene 3, p. 23) and, much later in the play, Franval enters into a long dialogue with Valère that underscores just that failing. "Do you have an *état?*" the prospective father-in-law asks Valère pointedly, and the young man flippantly replies, "I have ten of them, if need be." The two then begin to catalogue Valère's *états,* which, it soon emerges, exist for the young man in an unalterably liminal realm between possibility and actuality. "Are you a military man?" Franval inquires. "No," Valère replies, but he easily could be, having the requisite noble birth and natural talents; he recounts in detail an (imaginary) interview in which he "enchants" the Minister of War with his grasp of strategy and tactics; he has, after all, "brought that great art to a state of ripeness in my head." He may, he adds a bit defensively, "give the impression of doing nothing, and yet I work":

> Would you believe it? There is already a battle
> So well imagined in the depths of my brain,
> By means so fresh, a plan so new,
> That to lose it would be, in a word, impossible.

A similar response is elicited by Franval's question as to whether he is a magistrate: "not yet or at least not *par état,*" admits Valère, "but possessing an in-depth knowledge of the legal code, the digest, the works of Domat and Beccaria," he would find nothing easier. Eventually Franval grows exasperated with Valère's imaginary careers and enunciates what Fabre probably intends as the theme or message of his play. "The most humble artisan in society," he declares, "is the proof of this verity: that a man *sans état* deserves ridicule, that the idle (*désoeuvrés*) are a burden to the world," and that Valère is "one of them." Continuing in the solemn voice of authority he has assumed, Franval intones: "To have an *état* . . . is the common duty, the order, the law prescribed by society." In his view, Valère's involvement in an imaginary life explains his blameworthy drifting: "Drunk on the future, . . . you are always hoping and never *are* anything" (Act 4, Scene 9, pp. 109–13).

In their different registers, then, these two plays of early 1789 concur about the dangers inherent in imagination, the threat that it poses not only to the particular individual in its thrall but, more globally, to social order and stability. Indeed the proper disciplining of imagination (be it through d'Orlange's happily spontaneous self-correction or through the ostracizing of Valère) is depicted as a necessary condition of social order. And Collin d'Harleville and Fabre d'Eglantine were hardly unique among their late eighteenth-century contemporaries in expressing this anxiety about the effects of overactive, disordered imagination.

Targeted Mental Operations

The standard eighteenth-century map of the human mental apparatus divided it into the three faculties of memory, reason, and imagination. So widely recognized was this tripartite division that it was used in the *Encyclopédie* to furnish an overarching scheme for organizing the branches of knowledge from a human rather than a divine point of view. As d'Alembert noted in his *Discours préliminaire* to the *Encyclopédie* (1751), all knowledge, as compiled within that ambitious multivolume compendium, was to be categorized by the mental operation primarily responsible for its production: thus history fell into the province of memory, philosophy was the fruit of reason, and the fine arts were born of imagination. The *Discours préliminaire* did not dwell on the connotations or affective charges carried by these three mental operations. But it is clear from d'Alembert's brief discussion that he regarded memory as the least problematic, a simple re-presentation by the mind to itself of objects that had earlier been firmly and directly apprehended by the senses. Imagination, on the other hand, inspired obvious indecision and a certain unease. Where, d'Alembert wondered, should it be placed in the encyclopedic scheme: before or after reason? In arguing for its placement after reason, d'Alembert hinted at some of the anxiety that typically attended any pondering of imagination in this period. Imagination must follow reason, he said, because reason in effect provided the standards and criteria necessary for containing it: "Imagination is a creative faculty, and the mind, before it considers creating, begins by reasoning upon what it sees and knows. . . . The more it departs from these objects, the more *bizarre and unpleasant* are the beings which it forms."[14]

One might speculate that at different historical moments, different mental operations—themselves constructed rather than given—are singled out as particularly anxiety-provoking and, hence, as the focus of cultural obsession. In the late twentieth- and early twenty-first-century West, that targeted operation seems to be memory. What to d'Alembert was the relatively uncomplicated retrieval from the mental storehouse of sensory data perceived at some prior moment—he used the phrase "purely passive and almost mechanical" to describe it[15]—has in our own day, and particularly in light of the mass exterminations of World War II, become fraught with epistemological, psychological, and moral difficulties. The number of recent historical works featuring the word "memory" in their titles bears witness to the strength of this preoccupation.[16] Memory was also highlighted in the United States in the 1980s and 1990s in the context of a rash of well-publicized lawsuits by adults for incidents of sexual abuse that they allegedly suffered, usually at the hands of their parents, in childhood. Such cases, in which distant but only recently retrieved memories were offered up as legal evidence, pointedly raised and even moved into a popular forum the issue of the nature and reliability of memory.[17]

The medieval and early modern Western world also lavished attention on the workings of memory, but the nature of its concern was less existential than straightforwardly practical. It took the form of a codified mnemotechnics that sought to train individuals in the art of remembering by instructing them to conceive of their memories spatially, as buildings into whose various rooms, antechambers, nooks, and crannies they carefully deposited their bits of data for safekeeping and swift recovery. Rooted in the texts of Latin antiquity, this mnemotechnics declined in importance during and especially after the Renaissance, a change connected in complex ways to the advent of printing.[18] At any rate, during the Enlightenment, the source of overt and generalized cultural worry was not memory—the various articles on memory in the *Encyclopédie*, largely drawn from Condillac's treatise on sensationalist psychology, devote only a line or two to dysfunctional excesses of forgetting (and remembering) and say not a word about the old discipline of mnemotechnics—but rather imagination. Allowed full and luxuriant freedom of expression during the Renaissance, imagination appears to have subsequently fallen under a ban.[19] Tellingly, the brunt of the main *Encyclopédie* article on memory is precisely the admonition to avoid the long-standing confusion between memory and imagination.[20]

That such an admonition strikes us as odd and superfluous is itself evidence of the continual reworking of cultural constructions and evaluations of the mental faculties. From the perspective of the early twenty-first century, we may wonder how memory and imagination could possibly have been routinely confounded, but, in fact, the traditionally close ties between the two went back to Aristotle's theory of knowledge. Aristotle had emphasized the necessary participation of imagination in human thought processes; he held that thought worked not on raw sensory impressions but only on those impressions already treated by the intermediary of imagination and consequently transformed into images. Aristotle bolstered his dictum that the "soul never thinks without a mental picture" by reference to the presumably self-evident experience of the necessarily imagistic operation of memory, and this rhetorical move led him to locate memory and imagination in the same part of the soul.

Once cemented by Aristotle, the affiliation of memory and imagination was destined for a long career in the canonical texts of the Western philosophical tradition. Indeed, it is not an exaggeration to say that one of the subthemes of Frances Yates's magisterial *The Art of Memory* (1966) is to trace the mutations of that persistent affiliation. Thus Yates notes that the scholastic theologian Thomas Aquinas, who regarded Aristotle as the Philosopher, echoed his mentor by insisting that "memory belongs to the same part of the soul as phantasy." For Aquinas, the linkage was in effect a concession to human frailty, a permission to make use of the corporeal similitudes of the lower power of imagination as an aid in remembering spiritual intentions. The formally anti-Aristotelian occult philosophy of such Renaissance thinkers as Marsilio Ficino and Giordano Bruno kept the affiliation very much alive, vaunting the power of a divinely or magically animated human imagination to grasp the intelligible shape of the cosmos and enlisting memory training to catalogue the features of a cosmos thus apprehended. Even Francis Bacon, dedicated to banishing "idols" and to approaching nature through observation and experiment, was, in

Yates's view, "profoundly imbued with the classical belief that the mnemonic image has power through stirring the imagination."[21]

Condillac would later complain, in his own voice and through anonymous excerpts in the *Encyclopédie*, that Bacon's empiricist successor and Condillac's own source of inspiration, John Locke, had been equally cavalier in his treatment of memory and imagination, failing to make an unambiguous distinction between them.[22] This complaint marks something like a historical rupture. Where a casual blurring of the two mental faculties had long prevailed, the French Enlightenment took pains to draw a sharp line between memory—now to be regarded as straightforward, objective, unproblematic—and an imagination flagged as harboring an intrinsic potential for danger. The drive to separate what had earlier been offhandedly lumped together signaled at once a neutralization of memory, its transformation into a dependable recording device, and a particular cultural obsession with imagination.

The Philosophical Discourse of Imagination

While the eighteenth-century French discourse on imagination spilled over into innumerable linguistic settings, its main lines were set in the quasi-technical domain of epistemology and philosophy of mind. Hence, before turning to its wider cultural existence, we need to grasp its basic characteristics in that formative domain, certain of whose marks it tended to bear indelibly. The two philosophical psychologies in question—Cartesianism and sensationalism—were both products of the Scientific Revolution, and both laid claim, implicitly or explicitly, to scientific status. This fact probably contributed to the authority granted them and, at the end of the Old Regime, to the popularity of the discourses of imagination that they undergirded.

The locus classicus of French Enlightenment discussion of imagination was Condillac's *Essai sur l'origine des connaissances humaines,* the mid-century treatise that naturalized on French soil a version of Locke's sensationalist epistemology. In Condillac's account of the origins of human knowledge, imagination was one of the earlier operations to be generated from the first, simple act of perception that inscribed the initially blank slate of the human mind. It was closely allied to memory, since both were powers of reviving past perceptions independently of the external objects that had initially given rise to them. But, in keeping with his critique of Locke, Condillac took pains to distinguish between the two operations, duly pointing out the benign nature of the one and the potential malignancy of the other. Memory, he noted, could revive only those past perceptions to which "conventional signs"—that is, language—had already been attached. More versatile than memory, imagination could either use these signs or make do without them. Hence, although beasts lacked memory, they possessed imagination; or to put this point differently, imagination was, in its capacity for nonverbal functioning, the more "bestial" of the two operations. The greater vividness and sensuous immediacy of its productions were attributable to the fact that imagination "revives the perceptions themselves," while memory "only recalls the signs."[23]

Imagination had, according to Condillac, a second power deriving directly from the first. Having once reawakened perceptions in the absence of objects, it could forge "new combinations of them at our pleasure." It thus presented itself as a potential danger to the sober workings of understanding, an obvious point of entry for error. It had the liberty to play, scramble, and embellish, to "transport the qualities of one thing to another"—in short, to dispose of our ideas in a manner "contrary to truth." Some of these new imaginative linkages were made voluntarily; others—like the sight of a sharp precipice evoking the idea of violent death—bypassed volition and were produced automatically under the influence of an external impression. Such automatic linkages were especially firmly cemented, leaving us powerless to undo them. We could, in effect, easily cease to be "masters" of imagination and instead become its "dupes," falling victim to "prejudices" that, while based on a chance experience of merely circumstantial juxtapositions, appeared to us as immutable principles.[24]

Imagination exposed us to another source of error as well: we might lose the capacity to distinguish the imaginary objects in our minds from real objects. In this connection Condillac considered daydreaming. Building "castles in Spain," or imagining ourselves as the protagonists of a pleasurable story of our own devising, was, he noted, ordinarily a safe and innocent pastime. But if Condillac thus far sounded like the visionary in Collin's *Châteaux en Espagne,* he soon adopted a critical stance much more like the playwright's. He observed that when chagrin and sadness led the daydreamer to withdraw from ordinary social contact, his or her mental productions could acquire a distinctly malignant cast; they could become more tenaciously rooted, and the power of judgment to categorize them as imaginary inventions could correspondingly weaken. "Little by little, we will take all our chimeras for realities." Hence, Condillac continued, the danger of reading novels—especially for young women, whose relative lack of education contributed to the native inability of their "tender brains" to discriminate between the fictive and the real.[25]

One did not need to subscribe to sensationalist psychology in order to view imagination as a potentially dangerous mental operation, for a catalog of its dangers had already been compiled during the previous century by philosophers of Cartesian persuasion. Even more than for Condillac, imagination was for the Cartesian Malebranche a profoundly, and suspiciously, corporeal component of the mind. The strict mind-body dualism that was the hallmark of his school led Malebranche to posit an active imagination dependent upon the soul (*âme*) and directed by the commands of the will, and a passive imagination exclusively bodily in nature, one composed of the "animal spirits that trace these images and [of] the brain fibers on which they are engraved." The power of imagination was thus never completely within our control because it necessarily resulted from the combination of two factors, only one of which was volitional and the other bodily and passive. As Malebranche described the latter by analogy: "Now, just as the width, depth, and sharpness of the strokes in an engraving depend on the pressure applied to the burin and on the tractability of the copper," so too the clarity and strength of a product of passive imagination depends on "the force of the animal spirits and the constitution of the brain fibers."[26] It followed that purely physical factors—the age and sex of the individual, the type and abundance of diet, the degree of nervous agitation—could render an imagination capable of overpowering reason and even, under certain circumstances, of permanently imprinting brute matter. Malebranche believed, for example, that the mother's imagination directly influenced the form of the fetus growing in her womb and was responsible for monstrous births—a belief that remained scientifically respectable in France until the early nineteenth century.[27] He also affirmed that an overheated imagination was contagious, spread from one person to another by propinquity.[28]

Imagination, then, was intimately linked by both Cartesians and sensationalists with error, defect, monstrosity, and disorder. But a difference in emphasis between these two strands of a single discourse should be underscored here. Because the external environment impinged less upon the Cartesian psyche than it did upon its sensationalist counterpart, the position of the individual in the social structure was in the Cartesian model far less implicated either in unleashing or in containing the perils of imagination than it was in the sensationalist model. Thus, as I will show at some length later in this chapter, the sensationalist construction of imagination had a more pronounced tendency to become involved in social, political, and economic discourse.

The article on imagination in the *Encyclopédie* was not, like that on memory, drawn from Condillac's treatise but was composed by Voltaire. While Voltaire adhered to a sensationalist epistemology, he organized his discussion of imagination around the traditional contrast between its passive and active varieties—an indication of the hardly surprising fact that, in the eighteenth-century discourse on imagination, Cartesian and sensationalist strands could be plaited together. Voltaire's active imagination (the "good" member of the pair) produced fertile new combinations of elements: it invented technologies and created works of art. Although "independent of us" in the sense of being a divinely implanted "gift" of "genius" (ask a hundred people to imagine a certain machine, said Voltaire, and despite all their efforts, ninety-nine will come up with nothing at all), still, in those who possessed it, active imagination was so thoroughly imbued with reflection and judgment that it could be trusted to stay on the course we chose for it. On the other hand, passive imagination (the "bad" member of the pair and the one that humans had in common with animals) escaped our control completely.

Voltaire's article is noteworthy for the degree to which it used politically inflected language, the language of power relations, to describe passive imagination and the evils to which it conduced.[29] According to Voltaire, passive imagination blithely and "in spite of us" re-plays what we have seen and heard and, under no obligation to reproduce those perceptions faithfully, adds or omits elements as it pleases. It acts so imperiously (*avec empire*) that "nothing is more common than the saying, 'One is not the master of one's imagination.'" Seducing us by the vividness of its images, this mental operation moreover subverts our will, "push[ing] us toward the objects it paints, or turn[ing] us away from them, according to its manner of representation." An imagination that thus bedazzles the will is the "ordinary lot of ignorant people." The ubiquity of this variety of passive imagination seems, in the Voltairean scheme of things, to furnish the psychological substratum of power relations in society since it provides the "instrument" that more clear-thinking men "exploit for purposes of domination." In other words, an imagination that utterly eludes volitional supervision marks someone out as a person who will be the dupe of others, ruled over rather than ruling.

Another frequent contributor to the *Encyclopédie*, the Berlin-based Huguenot J.-H.-S. Formey, who pressed sensationalist psychology into the service of moral and religious inquiry, likewise conceptualized the unruliness of imagination in political terms. His article on dreams asserts:

> The waking imagination is a policed republic, where the voice of the magistrate restores everything to order. The imagination during a dream is that same republic in a state of anarchy, with the passions making frequent forays against the legislator's authority even while his law is in force.[30]

In other writings, Formey was less sanguine about the degree to which the waking imagination was effectively "policed." He called the imagination a *coursier fougueux*[31]—that is, an impetuous or hot-headed steed, where the etymology of the noun *fougue* refers to sudden flight (*fugue*), to the propensity to lack or deviate from a fixed path.[32] The locution thus recalls Collin's characterization of the overly imaginative d'Orlange as a "wandering Jew."[33] In fact Formey's portrait of those who succumb to the *coursier fougueux* resident in our mental apparatus sounds remarkably like Henriette's disparaging assessment of d'Orlange. Said Formey:

> The imagination is a faculty prone to illusion. Those who begin by yielding to it, and who, so to speak, entrust it with the task of guiding their education, can become wits or clever persons, in the vulgar sense of those terms. They can excel in eloquence and poetry and acquire a brilliant reputation. But they will always lack solidity—a defect that will throw them into aberrant behavior (*écarts*)."[34]

Like Condillac, who singled out young women as a group especially vulnerable to the blandishments of imagination and novel-reading as the practice that maximized that vulnerability, so too Formey zeroed in on a high-risk population and practice—a kind of hygienic perspective that was, as we will see, a standard feature of the eighteenth-century discourse on imagination. Formey reserved his anxious concern for young children, who should not, he opined, "be too long left alone to their fantasy games." Such a nonchalant mode of child-rearing would, in his view, lead youngsters to "acquire the habit, very difficult to eradicate, of being unable to concentrate on anything and of having a distracted mind, an always wandering imagination, when one speaks to them of things that displease them."[35] (Formey's term for "wandering imagination" is *une imagination qui bat la campagne,* an idiomatic expression often found clustered with "castles in Spain," with which it not only shares a common theme but also rhymes in French.)[36] Note that Formey deplores both the cognitive ineptitude of a wandering mind and, perhaps even more vehemently, the fact that such a mind becomes so accustomed to the seductive pleasures promised by imagination that its possessor is inherently resistant to all discipline. A child raised in this fashion simply fails to attend to unpleasant verbal communications, including (we can assume) prohibitions, admonitions, and reprimands. Formey's warning is clear: overindulge a young child's penchant for imaginative play, and you will likely end up creating a social monster or, at the very least, a misfit.

Imagination in Socioeconomic Discourse (1): The Trade Corporation

So familiar a topos did dangerous imagination become in eighteenth-century France that it left its mark in unexpected places, places where it would seem not even to belong—most notably the discourse on the economy. A salient example of this discursive migration is the 1776 remonstrance of the Parlement of Paris against a royal edict of that year abolishing the trade corporations—that is, the guilds of artisans and merchants whose function was to regulate and monopolize the industrial and commercial life of the Old Regime. In part because of the protest of the Parlement, the edict, written by Louis XVI's "enlightened" chief minister Turgot, remained in force for only about six months; but it resurfaced during the French Revolution and, under the name of the d'Allarde and Le Chapelier laws, dealt its blow definitively in 1791. Hence the Turgot edict can be seen as a kind of dress rehearsal for the socioeconomic individualism that would be successfully inaugurated by the Revolution.

In opposing the abolition, the judges of the Parlement advanced an argument about the necessity of maintaining the integration of the individual within a corporate matrix. The corporate principle, they aptly noted, penetrated their society thoroughly, organizing it as a congeries of self-governing bodies, which included not only the craft and merchant guilds but also (to name just a few) the Church, universities, academies, and courts of law. The corporate structure, they continued, provided a means of mutual protection and of command and surveillance of inferiors by superiors; it thus produced a "general calm" which individual men echoed or responded to by an "inward calm." The tranquillizing effects of such an institutional arrangement were, they noted, all the more necessary for the "workers," who by contrast to the guild masters, joined to a "natural brute energy . . . passions less subdued by education."[37] Destroy the corporate structure, the judges warned, and "each artisan will regard himself as a solitary being, dependent upon himself alone and free to indulge all the flights of an often disordered imagination."[38]

While the socioeconomic reference and direct public policy implications of this psychological observation might strike us as curious, we are already quite familiar with the basic rhetorical structure: a group is identified as particularly vulnerable to the promptings of imagination (in this case, as for Voltaire, that group is the general mass of working people) and, in keeping with the main lines of sensationalist psychology, an external environment particularly liable to lead the imagination astray is also specified. That high-risk environment is (as for Condillac's disappointed young girls who withdraw from society and seek comfort in novels) solitude, isolation. The rhetoric thus tacitly assumes that a stable communal location exerts a restraining influence on a potentially unruly imagination, presumably by dint of continually reinforcing the "true"—that is, consensual—definition of reality and keeping before the mind a lively image of the boundaries that must not be crossed. Lack of such a fixed location will, conversely, tend to release the imagination from its requisite straitjacket. In this respect the artisan removed from his corporation, as envisioned by the judges of the Parlement, is another version of Collin's d'Orlange as wandering Jew or Fabre's Valère as a man *sans état*. But while d'Orlange and Valère are, to be sure, types rather than idiosyncratic individuals, the wholesale abolition of the corporations can be seen as threatening nothing less than the universalization of that type! In other words, given the prevailing discourse on imagination, and especially the sensationalist psychological strand of that discourse, certain kinds of large-scale socioeconomic change could be readily perceived in late eighteenth-century France as explicitly calling into question the psychological integrity and viability of the individual—as reproblematizing the self.

Jürgen Habermas made a related but by no means identical claim when he noted that "next to political economy, psychology arose as a specifically bourgeois science during the eighteenth century." Habermas's assertion capped his tracing of a particular line of historical development: as the scale of capitalist commerce and industry expanded, he maintained, the bourgeois household ceased to be a base of economic operations and, suddenly devoid of function, assumed the completely innovative task of cultivating intimate affective ties between family members and heightening the "audience-oriented subjectivity" of each.[39] In other words, political economy and psychology—the theorized forms of capitalist enterprise and personal emotional cultivation, respectively—became twin sciences as a result of an increasing division of labor and the consequent differentiation of social space. While I, too, am asserting that economic and psychological science unfolded in tandem during the eighteenth century, I have conceptualized the relationship between the two more locally. My claim is that contemporaries regarded the corporate structure of the Old Regime as the necessary underpinning of persons. Hence threats to the corporate structure (which were a routine feature of the new science of Physiocracy, the forerunner of political economy) produced anxieties about individual mental functioning, especially the possible swamping of reason by imagination. The basic premise of sensationalist psychology reinforced the link, already posited in such anxieties, between the (external) economy and the (internal) psyche. Thus responses to the Turgot decrees were often couched in a psychological idiom; and the actual collapse of corporatism during the Revolution served, to adopt a Foucauldian turn of phrase, as a powerful incitement to psychological discourse.

In their 1776 remonstrance against the Turgot edict, the aristocratic elite represented by the judges of the Parlement articulated a concern about psychological integrity with respect to their manifest inferiors, the people. But the aristocrats were not alone in attributing untoward psychological consequences to laissez-faire. The artisans (or more precisely, the masters among them) articulated much the same concern with respect to themselves. In their handwritten protest against Turgot's edict in 1776, the Paris glovemakers did not pinpoint the unruly imagination as the source of the trouble, but they sweepingly asserted that "each person (*particulier*) has an existence only through the corporate body (*corps*) to which he is attached."[40]

This psychological-*cum*-ontological comment, surprising to modern ears, was made in the context of the glovemakers' very first objection to Turgot's policy: merchants and artisans in a "city as highly populated [as Paris]" would, they said, fail to inspire confidence (*crédit*) if their "existence," that is to say their stable personal identity and their legal accountability, were not guaranteed in advance by the corporate structure.[41] Similarly ontological comments about the dependence of a stable personal identity on a stable corporate structure—and especially on the corporation's surveillance or "police" of its members—dot the protests of master artisans and merchants against the Turgot edict. The Paris tailors described the artisan removed from his corporation as a "faithless Proteus" undergoing a perpetual process of "metamorphosis."[42] Many protesters conveyed their ontological presuppositions by employing the polysemic term "subject," having both the active sense of a thinking and intending being and the passive sense of someone under the king's jurisdiction, to describe the artisan as that entity constituted and guaranteed by the corporation. Thus the bakers: "through granting admission, the community becomes in some fashion the guarantor of the subject with respect to the public." Or the buttonmakers: "the first [goal of apprenticeship] is to gain assurance of the capacity of the subject." Or the clockmakers: "A thrifty subject [i.e., one able to save the money necessary for corporate entrance fees], which is what the artisan in his corporate condition (*état*) is, is all the more esteemed."[43] In language anticipating that of the parlementary remonstrance, the ribbon and fringe makers of the capital stated that "by breaking the ties that bind [us] together, this new system [of limitless freedom] will turn each artisan (*fabricant*) into an isolated being." Such isolation was a dangerous condition because the artisan—or indeed anyone else in Old Regime society—was apparently assumed not to exist fully as a freestanding person, not to have internalized the basic moral norms required by his job but to need to have those norms imposed on him from the outside by his *corps*:

[Under the regimen of the Turgot edict], he will no longer have to dread the eyes of his colleagues; the corporation's opinion of him will no longer serve as a brake if he is inclined to embezzle, nor as a spur if he desires to distinguish himself in his art.[44]

By their own account, then, the incorporated artisans of the Old Regime seem to have lived in what present-day anthropologists call a shame culture, in which the gaze of the other was necessary for the moral and psychological completeness of the individual. In the master cobblers' formulation of essentially this same point, the public required *connaissance*—knowledge of or familiarity with—the artisan in order to avoid being "duped" by one who was acting in "bad faith." This indispensable *connaissance,* which got translated into reputation, derived from the fact that the incorporated artisan was "subject to the inquiries and examination of that police exercised in the interest of the corporation by its officers *(jurés)*." The gaze of the corporate regulators thus ensured the reliability and transparency of the incorporated artisan, while the unpoliced solitary artisan remained, from the vantage point of the public, an unknown and opaque quantity "hidden in the corners of the city."[45]

In their protests against the Turgot edicts, artisans occasionally sought to make their case through explicit reference to the mental operation of imagination. Predicting that the edicts would prompt "laborious [rural] colonists" *(colons)* to stream into the cities, the members of the affluent *six-corps* of Paris postulated as the mechanism for this demographic shift a change in the prevailing mode of imagining an urban future. According to this argument, agricultural day laborers had long been attracted to the reputed pleasures of town life, and only the burdensome obligation to enter a trade corporation in order to obtain work in an urban setting had prevented them from migrating. But, warned the protest of the *six-corps,* "once the barrier that instilled fear in their *imaginations* has been lifted," their movements would henceforth be governed by an unbridled imagination. The depopulation of the countryside would ensue, as well as the demise of the migrants themselves, whose pitiful lack of preparation for the rigors of survival in the city would be revealed. "Such will be the progress of the countryfolk, plucked by a *dazzling phantom* from their rustic and respectable occupations."[46] That a seductive fantasy of urban life would uproot rural laborers from the soil is another instance of the eighteenth-century association of imagination with deracination.

Also using the vocabulary of imagination, the master bakers predicted a different but equally ominous turn of events. The slackening of corporate ties would, in their view, increase the insubordination of apprentices and *compagnons*:

> The boys are bolder now that the King has made his intention manifest by sending to his parlement an edict suppressing the trade corporations. The master who needs 4, 5 or 6 boys can no longer find them because the boys, *imagining themselves* able to become masters without having any ability, fortune or means, no longer wish to work. They hold their seditious assemblies more regularly than before. . . .[47]

If the mere prospect of laissez-faire had so exalted the imaginations of the bakers' "boys" that they had lost touch with reality and ceased working, so, too, did eighteenth-century discourse make the reverse association—that regular and disciplined work habits enabled an individual to control the inherent waywardness of imagination. In 1753, some two decades before the promulgation of the Turgot edict, the academy of the city of Besançon held a contest for the best essay on the topic, "Which contributes more to society, assiduousness at work or superior talents?" Awarded the second prize was an anonymous composition which argued that an inextricable intertwining of the two, and a kind golden mean between them, was the real desideratum. "What sun is to plants," said this essayist, "work is to talent." Talent not only relied on outside sources of nourishment in order to flourish; in its primitive form it also carried within itself "great defects" that, to be rectified, required proportionally "great care and attention (*soins*)." Chief among those "defects" was imagination, which "operates without order," and chief among the remedial techniques for a disordered imagination was work. As the essayist put it, drawing upon the vocabulary of wandering so entrenched in the eighteenth-century discourse of imagination, "Assiduity at work is a counterweight which balances the *fougues* of the imagination."[48]

The Worker's Imagination Further Scrutinized

The fear of imagination—and of workers' imagination in particular—that animated the absolute monarchy and the upper orders of Old Regime society found its way into an extremely wide variety of texts. It even figures, for example, in the 1745 police interrogations of a chambermaid to the Versailles nobility. The young woman, Marie-Magdeleine Bonafon, had been arrested and detained at the Bastille for writing a clandestinely published *roman à clef* critical of Louis XV. Conducted by the highest official in the Paris police bureau, the Lieutenant-General, the interrogations touched several times on the issue of how this humble woman had acquired the knowledge necessary to carry out her nefarious project. Had a socially superior accomplice supplied her with information about recent goings-on in royal circles and with the obscure history books that enabled her to cloak her depiction of the French court in Persian garb, he asked, or had she "composed the work from her own imagination"?

The chambermaid repeatedly affirmed the latter alternative, stating that she had worked on the novel "all alone," that the details had come solely from her "imagination," that she had possessed a "head filled with everything that was being talked about at that time" and that it was upon this store of mental material that her "imagination [had] worked." While the Lieutenant-General eventually accepted her account as truthful, he was not reassured by it. After all, he mused, the novel contained "specific facts not naturally within the purview of [a chambermaid's] *état*." That feats of imagination might mentally propel a chambermaid beyond her *état* and transform her into a deft creator of seditious writings seemed to the police chief as much a threat to public order as that such a person might achieve the same end through conspiratorial intrigue with one of her betters. On the basis of the general discursive lines laid out in this chapter, we can hypothesize that the police chief regarded the inflamed imagination of an insufficiently supervised female member of the lower orders as a potential menace in its own right.[49]

Another example of the fear of the disorderly imaginations of working people can be found in the inaugural documents and institutional arrangements of the Ecole gratuite de dessin, the drawing school for young artisans established by private subscription and with royal letters patent in the late 1760s.[50] The prime mover in this enterprise was one J.-J. Bachelier, a member of the Royal Academy of Painting and Sculpture and a frequent recipient of commissions for murals in the king's chateaux. Having risen to this very comfortable status from modest, petit bourgeois origins (his mother sold porcelain in the Palais Royal), Bachelier seems, according to one modern commentator, "to have.

remembered his difficult beginnings as a penniless artist and to have wanted to provide a large number of children [in similarly disadvantaged circumstances] with the kind of formal instruction that he himself had acquired only by accident."[51] But whatever his personal motives in establishing the Ecole gratuite de dessin, Bachelier repeatedly stressed both in his public pronouncements and through his pedagogical regimen the need to subject young artisans, for the sake of their own cognitive development as well as for the good of society, to an appropriately strict discipline—one aimed at the imagination.

Education in drawing, Bachelier insisted in 1766, must begin with geometry, for geometry "alone can arrest deviant flights (*écarts*) of the imagination, contain imagination within the limits of reason, and make ideas circulate (if I may be permitted to express myself thus) within steady and legitimate (*réguliers*) channels."[52] Another proponent of the drawing school seconded this emphasis on geometry, citing the same rationale as Bachelier but couching it in the more perfervid rhetoric of "monstrous" imagination. Given the habits of "dangerous idleness" usually instilled "from the earliest years of childhood in every citizen destined to the occupation of artisan," the drawing school was obliged to inculcate an opposing set of mental habits. Hence, in its curriculum,

> *geometry must necessarily preside over the other sciences;* the certitude of its proofs, the self-evidence of its operations, the demonstration of its calculations, the order that it establishes in the train of ideas are just so many reasons to employ it in order to *put a brake on the boiling imagination of these youths,* who cannot be too much put on guard against the seductions of bad taste, the force of example, and the attractions of the frivolous and the outlandish. *Geometry is the womb of mental operations: it matures them, gives birth to them at term and in a condition when they can no longer be either abortions or monsters.*[53]

Bachelier in fact gave geometry pride of place in his curriculum,[54] but mathematical instruction hardly exhausted his disciplinary endeavors. He set up in the heart of the school a regimen of internal police that Michel Foucault could easily have cited as evidence in favor of his thesis in *Discipline and Punish*. Pupils received papers certifying their right to admission to the classes of the school, but those papers required formal renewal every three months; and renewal was in turn granted only on the basis of regular attendance, which was monitored by a system of tokens or *jetons*. The student received a *jeton* each day that he appeared at school, and his *jetons* were supposed to be submitted to daily inspection by both his schoolmasters and his parents. As the three-month admission certificate, signed by "Monsieur Bachelier, Director," admonished: "Parents, as well as Schoolmasters, are earnestly implored to watch over attentively the assiduity of those [pupils] for whom they have responsibility, making sure that on Monday they are presented with a *jeton* for Monday, and so on for the remaining days of the week. . . ."[55] Geometry instruction was thus only one feature of an environment deliberately designed to anchor the young, low-born artisan-in-training in real social demands and thus to substitute sober, instrumental reason for the seductive beckonings of imagination.

Imagination in Socioeconomic Discourse (2): Credit

The eighteenth-century discourse of imagination intersected in another way with that of the modernizing economy. Just as, for critics of laissez-faire, the artisan suddenly loosed from his corporate moorings became a hapless pawn of imagination, so, too, for critics of the so-called financial revolution, a whole series of sophisticated new institutions—banks, the national debt, the extension of credit—introduced into interactions among people an imaginary element subversive of social, political, and even epistemological stability. John Pocock's work on the civic republican tradition in early eighteenth-century England suggests the regularity with which this second rhetorical figure—the perverse permeation of the world of finance by imagination—was employed on the other side of the Channel. As Pocock tells the story, the seventeenth-century Harringtonian variety of English civic republicanism had linked the virtuous republican "personality"—the choice of word is Pocock's—to property ownership. But by the Augustan era, the financial revolution had called the very reality of property into question; property could now assume forms that were not merely mobile but also quite possibly imaginary! In the language of such commentators as Joseph Addison and Daniel Defoe, whom Pocock quotes at length, credit was a product of the imagination, a testament to the power of imagination, its fluctuations dependent upon imagination's caprices.[56] This new situation seriously undermined the integrity of the (property-based) political personality assumed to be the mainstay of a self-governing state.

Although France lagged behind England in creating modern institutions of banking and credit, a text that we have already considered indicates that by 1776 the concept of imagination had insinuated itself not only into the debate over the guilds but also into the financial branch of French socioeconomic discourse. That text is the parlementary remonstrance against the Turgot edict. Capacity for citizenship was clearly not at issue in the strictures against credit penned by these aristocratic judges serving an absolutist monarchy. But at the beginning of their remonstrance, they chastised the king for the ever-mounting loans taken out by the state, noting that this policy had "raised up, alongside of real assets *(fonds réels)*, a new sort of value which already constitutes the patrimony of many families." These "fictive assets *(fonds fictifs),*" they continued, had "with respect to real assets, a marked disadvantage" in that they did not "rest on an unalterable and certain foundation."[57] The king's penchant for borrowing had, in other words, indirectly undermined his subjects, eroding their ability to maintain an intergenerational stability and continuity.

The great historical moment for the flowering of a specifically financial discourse of imagination occurred not in 1776 but about a half-century earlier. It was the moment of John Law, of the feverish speculative ventures launched by that Scotsman in the several years before 1720 in his grandiose efforts to refinance the debts of the French and British states. In the English context, the South Sea Bubble was so widely depicted as an example of imagination run amok that the abundant pamphlet literature even ventured into psychopathology. (The regnant Lockean epistemology, which would later furnish Condillac with a model, defined madness as a disordered imagination.)[58] It included a tongue-in-cheek contribution by the pseudonymous Sir John Midriff, M.D., "Observations on the Spleen and Vapours: Containing Remarkable Cases of Persons of both Sexes, and all Ranks, from the aspiring Director to the humble Bubbler, who have been miserably afflicted with those melancholy Disorders since the Fall of South-Sea and other publick Stocks."[59] Dr. Midriff had a good deal to say about imagination as he recounted his case histories. One patient, complaining of giddiness, faintness, and a pain in the left side, traced his ailment to a day spent in "Exchange-Alley" waiting to sell stock; he believed his symptoms "occasion'd by a Jew who came to beat down the Price of Stocks, carrying a large Bag of Money, which, by reason of the Crowd, happen'd to be press'd several times against his Side." Learning that the afflicted gentleman "had been an Adventurer in the South-Sea [Company]," Dr. Midriff hastens to tell him that giddiness of the type he described "always denoted Trouble of Mind, either from some external Cause, which is able to make too violent Impressions on our Imaginations, or from our own distemper'd Imaginations alone." He opines that the pain in the side and the faintness stem not from the transient pressure exerted by the Jew's money bag but from that "same Universal Cause" of disordered imagination. As the narrative progresses and the physician is consulted by a long succession of ailing investors, his own imagination goes momentarily awry:

> The vast many miserable Objects I had seen dwelt so on my own Imagination, that I began to think the Distemper infectious; and for that Reason, I kept at Home one whole Day. . . . And just as I imagin'd, many of the Symptoms soon took hold of me, and no one can conceive the great Disorders I labour'd under for the Space of fourteen Hours. . . . But after I had slept upon it, I summon'd all my Reason, and found my Body was perfectly well, and that my Disturbances were only imaginary; I put on a Resolution not to give way to any such Prepossession. . . .[60]

The French version of the John Law moment entailed the establishment of a central bank, the issue of paper currency, and the floating of stock in the Compagnie de l'Occident (usually referred to by the name "Mississippi" because it monopolized the Louisiana trade). It amounted, in fact, to nothing less than the privatization of the French treasury, lately bankrupted by the wars of Louis XIV. Law's "System," as it was routinely called, was based on the Scotsman's monetary theory: that in an environment of unemployed resources, the issue of paper currency would permanently expand real commerce, thereby increasing the demand for paper currency to such a degree as to preclude inflation. In other words, to finance a great economic project, an entrepreneur manipulated the imaginary; he needed only the power to create claims that served as a mode of payment, and those claims would eventually materialize as real monetary value.[61]

Just as the aristocratic Parlement of Paris bristled at Turgot's abolition of the guilds, so, too, some six decades earlier they resisted the Crown's willingness to entrust the treasury into Law's hands. Most important for our purposes was the rhetoric of their resistance: in both cases, the radical changes involved in economic modernization seemed to the parlementaires a dangerous substitution of reality by fantasy—be that fantasy the solitary artisan's untrammeled imagination, the "fictive assets" of property in stocks and bonds, or the blatant manipulation of monetary value on the theory that a well-played confidence game would in time conjure up substance from illusion. If anything, the mechanics of Law's System—especially the repeated insistence on public *confiance* in a future, as-yet-unrealized economic vitality[62]—led more naturally and inevitably to a discourse of imagination than did Turgot's freeing of the market in labor.

Figure 1: *"Fancy, the Ruler of the Guild of Smoke-Sellers, Paints her Mississippi which Wastes the Treasures of France."* The satirical title of this Dutch broadside, published in 1720 in response to the John Law affair in France, reveals the pan-European scope of the discourse linking dangerously overstimulated imagination to the eighteenth-century financial revolution and its vast externsion of credit. (The British Museum, Department of Prints and Drawings, © Copyright The British Museum)

While initially cooperative about registering the edicts that put the System in place, the Parlement balked in 1718 when the Crown, reneging on its earlier promise to issue all paper currency in *écus* redeemable by specie at strict face value, decreed a devaluation and reminting.[63] What was, in part, intolerable to the judges about this new policy was that it injected the imaginative dimension into public affairs. Although the king had, they readily acknowledged, exclusive right to coin the money of the realm, "it is not his stamp that confers value"; rather, value was an inherent attribute, residing in the "quantity and purity of the precious metal" composing the coin.[64] By departing from the doctrine of bullionism, with its strict table of equivalences between signs and things, the Crown was, the parlementaires declared, tampering with the legibility of reality—creating "a chaos so great and so obscure that nothing about it can be known."[65]

The parlementaires did not in this instance actually use the word "imagination" (they summoned up a cluster of concepts associated with it). But the word itself was featured in other contemporaneous commentaries on the Law affair. In an anonymous pamphlet of 1721 taking the form of an exchange of letters between a French and a British nobleman, the French duke comes out against not only Law's scheme but any system of public credit. He believes that the credit extended between private individuals is both safer than the public variety and also "sufficient to enable the circulation of all the productions of Art and Nature in France." If the goal is to stimulate agriculture, manufacture, and commerce, then, says the duke, the correct course of action is to decrease the taxes that "weigh down the people and strip them of the strength and courage to work." Nothing is to be gained by Law's alternate route, defined here as "the multiplication of money by an *imaginary credit* that deters honest industry and augments luxury." The English lord, who thinks that his own countrymen have been more deeply scarred by Law's experiments than have the French, nonetheless believes in the necessity of a system of public credit. ("There is neither sufficient gold nor silver in Europe to enable the circulation of all the productions of Art and Nature.") But he echoes his French colleague in expressing a horror of "imaginary" credit:

> Public credit must be both supported by and proportional to real assets (*fonds réels*). In that way, it will always be convertible into specie by private persons and hence will remain free. . . . A credit founded on

the hope of distant gain becomes *imaginary*. If it exceeds the real assets that correspond to it, it loses its value; and if it is forced, it loses its nature as credit.[66]

Like the parlementaires of Paris and the anonymous author of the pamphlet, Montesquieu approached Law's System from an aristocratic standpoint, and his *Persian Letters* (1721) bitterly satirized it as an abuse of imagination. The "Fragment of an Ancient Mythologist" in Letter 142, a thinly disguised rendition of the Law affair, tells the story of the son of Aeolus. Although as a child he could distinguish so accurately between metals that he petulantly refused the gift of a brass ring, he attempts in adulthood to make his living by selling bags of wind. He travels to the land of Baetica and, displaying his airy merchandise, addresses the people: "You think you are rich because you have gold and silver. Your error arouses my pity. Believe me and leave the country of base metals. Come to the Empire of the Imagination and I promise you riches that will surprise even you." The next day he expatiates on the combined economic-psychological exercise that he is recommending: "Do you want to be rich? . . . Each morning put it into your head that your fortune has doubled during the night. Then arise, and if you have creditors, go pay them with what you have imagined and tell them to do some imagining of their own." In a subsequent pronouncement, the traveling salesman, sensing that his scheme is on the verge of failure, locates the source of the economic malaise in the insufficient liveliness of the people's imaginations.[67]

So regularly was Law's System attacked in France for its allegedly imaginary nature that Law himself—who, in the face of mounting opposition, directed considerable propaganda to the general public—replied to that charge. How, he asked rhetorically, could his System be "chimerical"? Didn't the successful examples of the Dutch, English, and Portuguese "furnish certain proof of its solidity and reality"? As for stock certificates, it was necessary to disabuse oneself of the "vulgar prejudice" that they were "imaginary property" just because their number exceeded the amount of gold and silver in the realm; not bullion but rather "the immense profits of domestic and foreign trade constitute the value of this paper."[68] An anonymous pamphlet of 1720, written in defense of the System, echoed Law's own rhetoric. Opponents of the System were said to dismiss stock certificates as "false and chimerical property" on the grounds that their cumulative face value exceeded that of the precious metals in the realm. But, rejoined the pamphleteer, the value of the capital inherent in the houses of Paris or the soil of France also surpassed that of the specie circulating within French borders or, for that matter, of "all the gold still contained in the mines of Peru"; yet no one would contend that such houses and land therefore sold for a "chimerical price." To those "rentiers" who saw dividend-yielding stock as "only imaginary property" and hence refused to invest their profits in it, the pamphleteer retorted: "They will soon see [in the development of sea and river transportation, the repair of roads, etc.] the fruits that *this imaginary property* is alone capable of producing and that *real properties* would have left in eternal nullity."[69]

The eighteenth-century discussion of credit was not, of course, confined to the period of intense debate over Law's System. As the 1776 parlementary remonstrance suggests, a nearly continual public conversation took place on the subject of the borrowing practices of a financially precarious monarchy. At the level of everyday practice, furthermore, credit impinged upon the consciousness of the humblest shopkeeper. By the eighteenth century, hard-minted coin constituted only a small fraction of the medium of exchange actually circulating in France; most sales of merchandise were made on credit, giving rise to written pledges of future payment—promissory notes and bills of exchange—that in turn circulated in lieu of specie, changing hands a multitude of times. Thus founded on a makeshift medium of exchange, the commercial life of eighteenth-century France was punctuated every few years by an occurrence that contemporaries called a "money famine" (*disette d'argent*). The perceived shortage of specie, usually of several months' duration, was in fact a fluctuation in the credit market. A widespread, panicky conviction that hard times were imminent, rooted perhaps in a few bankruptcies or the rumor of war, led customers to refuse to relinquish their cash or to buy on credit; it led the authors of promissory notes to refuse to pay them when they fell due. The initial fears thus proved self-fulfilling: debts were called in, purchases came to a halt, interest rates soared, and prices plummeted. For those contemporaries who realized that the so-called money famine was nothing of the sort but was rather a prevailing conviction of misery in the midst of plenty, this periodic phenomenon was another instance of the disruption caused by credit, which injected its pernicious dosages of unreality into the conduct of ordinary life.[70]

Self-Contained Persons: The Odd Trio

The belief that a laissez-faire economy would dangerously overstimulate the imagination placed the isolated *homo economicus,* whether in the form of an unincorporated artisan or an individual buyer of stock certificates, in the company of two other eighteenth-century figures whose solitary practices were also widely decried and attributed to overactive imagination—namely, the masturbator and the (usually female) reader of novels. Like the participant in the laissez-faire economy, the other individuals making up this distinctly odd trio were time-bound, historical products, the creatures of their era.

Masturbation was, to be sure, hardly a discovery of the eighteenth century, but not until that time was it singled out for serious scientific discussion and intense pedagogical condemnation. A much-cited anonymous English book of 1710 followed in 1760 by the French-language treatise of the Swiss Protestant physician Samuel-Auguste Tissot are generally cited as the origins of what Michel Foucault called, in a felicitous phrase, "the war against onanism, which in the West lasted nearly two hundred years."[71] The author of the *Onania* and Dr. Tissot defined masturbation as a disease, one threatening enough that its sequelae might include insanity and even death. But as the recent work of Thomas Laqueur has underscored, the brunt of their attack was not so much that masturbation depleted vital spermatic fluid or that it sexualized the young precociously but rather that, predicated upon the titillating charms of a fantasied partner, it was a transaction occurring entirely in the realm of imagination. Masturbation was for these eighteenth-century crusaders not primarily a sinful pleasure but a deceitful one, not an inappropriate satisfaction of a real desire but a succumbing to a made-up, artificial appetite. Its fundamental danger as a practice—its true scandal—lay in the fact that, by dint of its largely imaginary nature, it eluded all natural, interpersonal, and social limitation. Just as the imagination was susceptible to no external sanctions and could never be prevented from working, so masturbation opened the possibility of endlessly renewed desire endlessly gratified. In its ceding of ultimate authority to the imagination, masturbation effectively established an order of disorder.[72]

The Rousseau of the *Confessions* (a text composed during the 1760s) fits these specifications almost with the perfection of an ideal type, for he presents his eroticism as having been from early childhood bound up with the workings of his imagination. Describing the spankings he received at the age of eight from Mademoiselle Lambercier and the sexual feelings they perversely elicited, Jean-Jacques notes that he long failed to yield to those urgent sensations and "kept myself pure and unsullied up to an age when even the coldest and most backward natures have developed." Yet critically, what he denied himself in reality, he indulged in imagination—and indulged not merely eagerly but, in keeping with the peculiar unrestricted nature of the imaginative realm, limitlessly. "Tormented for a long while by I knew not what, I feasted feverish eyes on lovely women, *recalling them ceaselessly to my imagination,* but only to make use of them in my own fashion as so many Mademoiselle Lamberciers."[73] A decade or so later, already an adept of fantasied sexual experience, he expands his repertory by taking up masturbation (or, as he puts it, he loses his "moral" though not his "physical virginity"), fully cognizant of the gravely pathological nature of the habit ("various kinds of excesses that eventually imperil [young men's] health, their strength, and sometimes their lives"). In self-punitive tones, he notes the almost ontological deceitfulness of his newly adopted practice, calling it "that dangerous means of cheating Nature." And, even more strongly than in his discussion of Mademoiselle Lambercier, he underscores the peculiar omnipotence—the freedom from all natural and social constraints—with which its imaginary component endows him:

> This vice, which shame and timidity find so convenient, has a particular attraction for lively imaginations. It allows them to dispose, so to speak, of the whole female sex at their will, and to make any beauty who tempts them serve their pleasure without the need of first obtaining her consent.[74]

In terms of the widespread, nearly ubiquitous nature of the discourse on imagination that I have been arguing for and tracing in this chapter, it is worth noting that Rousseau's earliest indictments of masturbation, which linked that practice to imagination, were made in ignorance of Tissot's soon-to-be classic text. Only after Jean-Jacques' opinions had appeared in print did the Swiss physician write to him, exclaiming over the uncanny similarity of their views and the convergence of their independently pursued lines of reasoning.[75]

The debate about that new literary form, the novel, was likewise part of the discourse on imagination. When Condillac chose the example of novel-reading to spell out the sensationalist-psychological mechanism by which a combination of solitude and an overstimulated imagination might loosen a person's grip on reality, he was treading a familiar discursive path. Since the inception of the novel, contemporaries had been unable to separate the issue of its aesthetic validity from the hygienic issue of whether arousing the imagination on a routine basis would have salutary or pernicious effects. Imagination inhered, after all, in the very definition of the novel: "a fictive story of diverse human adventures, marvelous or plausible," according to the *Encyclopédie*.[76] Defenders of the genre were thus, ipso facto, defenders of the imagination.

The founding father of that school, the late seventeenth-century anti-Cartesian philosopher Pierre-Daniel Huet, even sought to make his case for the novel by radically redefining the imagination, endowing it with loftier attributes that it was usually said to possess. Humans did not, he protested, share the capacity for imagination with animals. Imagination was rather the answer to a uniquely and poignantly human sense of lack—a lack that could never be filled by objects present to the senses.[77] Seeking to account for the "vivacity" with which certain of his compatriots had "unleashed their fury against novels," Huet's supporter Nicolas Lenglet-Dufresnoy observed in 1734 that it was a "treat for bigots to proscribe everything capable of satisfying the mind and the imagination."[78] Conversely, Armand-Pierre Jacquin's 1755 polemic against the novel maintained that the "turbulent faculty" of the imagination served no useful purpose in the "career" of a mind that moved (in accordance with sensationalist psychology) from simple ideas to combinations of ideas and then to judgments and other forms of reasoning.[79] Imagination and gender were closely linked in this debate. The critics who took their stand on the side of imagination also articulated a version of French literary history—the version destined to be forgotten by posterity—which portrayed the female novelists of the late seventeenth century as playing a decisive role in the legitimation of the new narrative form. Those hostile to the imagination put forth the canonical version of that same history, in which any positive female influence was repressed: the early period of the novel's pariah status was said to correspond to the domination of the field by women authors, and the novel's subsequent acceptance into the literary mainstream to the better product turned out by the men who eventually assumed firm and sober control over the business of novel-writing.[80]

The debate about the novel was even more irrevocably a debate about the hygiene of the imagination because, during the eighteenth century, reading had become increasingly coded as a solitary practice. Whether or not a statistically significant shift occurred around the year 1750 from the intensive, often oral and group reading of a few venerated books to the extensive, purely personal, silent and one-time reading of many assorted titles—a shift that the historian Rolf Engelsing discerned in the German-speaking lands and labeled a "reading revolution"[81]—it seems clear that eighteenth-century French iconography abounded in images of solitary readers. When the chambermaid Marie-Magdeleine Bonafon, accused of seditious writing in 1745, told her police interrogator that she had never sought instruction in the art of composition but had rather "acquired a taste for writing by reading a great deal" and had worked on both those skills "all alone,"[82] her self-description jibed well with the paintings and drawings produced during that era.[83]

In terms of stock eighteenth-century anxieties, the Rousseau of the *Confessions* presents himself as the ideal-typical reader of novels much as he embodied the ideal-typical masturbator. He confides that his "restless imagination," acting very much in the Condillacian mode of that faculty, "nourish[ed] itself on situations that had interested me in my reading, recalling them, varying them, combining them, and giving me so great a part in them, that I became one of the characters I imagined, and saw myself always in the pleasant situations of my own choosing." But as always in the eighteenth-century scenario of a gratifying escape into imagination, the pleasures thus accrued come at a high price. Like Condillac's female adolescent reader, the young Rousseau moves inexorably from a "love for imaginary objects" and an ease in giving himself over to them to a rejection of "my real condition, which so dissatisfied me," and ultimately to a deeply entrenched "love of solitude." Unlike his Condillacian counterpart, he does not thereby lose his reason. But he does acquire a "misanthropic" character which, almost a variant of madness, he ascribes to a fundamental alteration of his relationship to reality: finding no living creatures akin to his own "tender nature," he chose instead "to feed upon fictions."[84]

The repeated linkage between practices—whether economic, sexual, aesthetic, or entertaining—that could or were alleged to be suitably performed alone and the specter of an unreined imagination enables a fine-tuning and further specification of the thesis of this chapter. Especially in the context of a widely accepted sensationalist psychology, which postulated the direct impingement of the external environment—including the *social* environment—on the mind, the fretful eighteenth-century preoccupation with imagination was, it appears, fed by a perceived increase both in the possibilities for and in the cultural valida-tion of satisfying solitary endeavor. In a variety of domains, the ability of the individuals to attenuate their reliance on organized society was being insistently advertised, both by those who commended it (the political economists) and those who abhorred it (the antimasturbation crusaders).

Michael Fried's argument for the "primacy of absorption" in French painting from roughly the 1750s through the 1780s points to yet another domain in which parallel assertions about individual self-sufficiency were being made. According to Fried, painters gravitated to—and anti-Rococo critics lauded—the representation of human subjects absorbed in their own interior states and oblivious to their environment. Fried contends that a new visual aesthetic was being hammered out by means of the preference granted to this subject matter, an aesthetic centered on a particular relationship between painting and beholder. According to this theory, best articulated at the time by Diderot, the self-absorbed subject ignored and implicitly negated the existence of the beholder of the painting; the beholder was in turn—and paradoxically—kept all the more riveted before a scene that was *not* being staged for his benefit and in whose veracity he was therefore more inclined to believe.[85]

Although, in tracing this shift in aesthetic values, Fried has no spe-cific interest in the discourse on overactive imagination, his argument helps to strengthen my claim about a late eighteenth-century French cultural preoccupation with the self-contained individual. That individ-ual could announce an independence of and indifference to society and its members in a variety of their guises: he had no need of them as orga-nizers of the production and distribution of goods, as sexual objects, as sources of amusement and distraction—or even, according to Fried, as spectators who witnessed his existence. Indeed the same logic seems to be at play in the new economic claim that the artisan can labor effec-tively without the eyes of the corporation upon him and the new aes-thetic claim that the subject of painting most worth viewing is the one who performs for no viewer. The more that practical possibilities and opportunities for individual self-sufficiency were recognized, the more danger seemed to inhere in imagination; for an imagination stimulated in solitude, without the forces for containment that social institutions provided, was the imagination most prone to go awry.

To be sure, the dangers of imagination were not in eighteenth-century discourse associated only with practices that occurred in full or relative isolation. Take, for example, the 1784 report of the royal commission appointed by Louis XVI to examine animal magnetism. It decried the contemporary vogue of the mesmeric *baquet*—the large tub equipped with iron rods around which Parisians clustered in order to be sent into convulsion by the mesmerist and thus, allegedly, to be cured of whatever ailed them by means of a redistribution of their personal complements of magnetic fluid. The convulsions were, said the commissioners, authentic enough, but Mesmer's explanation of them lacked all scientific merit and glossed over their perilous implications. Instead of being caused by the mesmerist's arcane tinkering with some universal magnetic fluid, they derived quite simply from his hyperstimulation of the imaginations of the persons congregated around the tub. Now in such a setting hyperstimulated imagination was obviously a collective rather than a solitary phenomenon. In fact, the commissioners explicitly and repeatedly noted its collective aspects: the mutual reinforcement of different individuals' vibrating nerves which, acting much like violin strings, intensified the overall effect; the possibility that the imagination-induced convulsions might spread by contagion to persons absent from the original scene. In recommending that public mesmeric treatments be banned, the commissioners, apprehensively extrapolating from the fairly modest attendance at the *baquet,* stressed the special vulnerability of the imagination in crowd situations. Contrary to the linkage of imagination and solitude that I have been tracing in this chapter, they intoned, "Imagination governs the multitude"; when "men [are] gathered in large numbers, [they] are more enthralled by their senses and reason has less power over them."[86]

From the perspective of controlling the imagination, solitary individuals and those in a crowd were, however, not so much antithetical terms as opposite sides of the same coin: both the isolate and the member of an ad hoc crowd led fundamentally extra-institutional existences; both were prone to mental wandering and aberration precisely because they were exempt from the rules that governed conduct and the tasks that demanded attention in institutional settings—from, in a word, the local reality that such institutions defined and enforced. It is difficult to say which of the two, the isolate or the crowd member, inspired greater unease and more apocalyptic musings in the later eighteenth century; very likely the two often went together, as in the example mentioned earlier of the "bakers' boys" who, having heard of the imminent promulgation of the Turgot edict, cease working because they imagine themselves able to get ahead without honing their skills and *then* find themselves drawn into "seditious assemblies." But I suspect that, before the mob violence of the Revolutionary decade gave a special affective charge to the crowd, the dominant specter was of a world of self-enclosed, atomistic individuals, so nourished on their own imaginations that they lost contact with a shared, consensual reality and were propelled away from the social center in innumerable directions as if by centrifugal force.

2

The Revolutionary Schooling of Imagination

What happened to the anxiety about the freestanding individual—an anxiety for which the discourse on imagination typically served as proxy—during the Revolution itself? Or, put differently, how could the Revolutionaries have confidently embarked upon such policies as the abolition of the craft guilds in 1791 and the abolition of a host of other corporate bodies on the night of August 4, 1789, if they believed that only a fully elaborated social matrix could contain the potentially unruly imaginations of the populace? Within a smaller compass, the oeuvre of Condillac poses much the same question. How could the master of sensationalist psychology, whose *Essai sur les origines des connaissances humaines* (1746) trenchantly analyzed the dangers presented to imagination by solitude, have unequivocally championed the laissez-faire market in his *Le commerce et le gouvernement considérés relativement l'un à l'autre* (1776)?

A basic, skeletal answer to these parallel questions—to be fleshed out later in this chapter—can be found in a short text from the republican phase of the Revolution: an anonymous journalistic account of the Festival of Reason held in the capital in the Year II (1793). Designed as a politically acceptable alternative to Catholic or, indeed, any sectarian religious worship, the Festival of Reason was celebrated in a specially constructed temple whose portal bore the inscription "To Philosophy." It culminated in the emergence from the temple of the figure of Liberty, "represented by a beautiful woman . . . a living woman and not a statue."[1] The overt aim of the article in *Révolutions de Paris* was to paint this particular festival, and the Revolutionary cult of the Supreme Being generally, in the most laudatory colors; the author was not explicitly concerned with the issue of imagination. Yet he employed the word "imagination" with notable frequency, unwittingly informing us about the new Revolutionary dispensation with respect to that mental faculty.

The article begins with a condemnation of all clerical institutions and casts a wistful eye at the United States, which has never known an established church or a powerful, entrenched priesthood. Going on to blame the Catholic Church for all the setbacks that the Revolution has endured, especially the counterrevolutionary insurgency in the Midi and the Vendée, it carefully specifies the manner in which the priests carried out their sabotage. Theirs was a psychological technique. In those regions that eventually turned against the Revolution, the priests had "directed as they pleased the *vagabond imagination* of the people."[2] Noteworthy for its familiar ring, the phrase "vagabond imagination" offers yet another variant on the metaphor that we encountered in Old Regime discourse: imagination as unstable drifter, or "wandering Jew," or *coursier fougueux.* If wily priests in the South and West had gained control over their parishioners' labile imaginations in order to inculcate a counterrevolutionary politics, it follows logically that in the name of survival the Revolution must exert its own set of controls over that pivotal mental faculty.

The author initially credits the French people with having in 1789 "shaken off the yoke of superstition spontaneously, by the sole impetus of wisdom and reason." But he recognizes that the Revolution cannot rely indefinitely on this glorious and unplanned moment of lucidity that was its point of origin. Instead, the Revolutionaries must hasten to develop a technique that will durably imprint the imaginations of the citizenry in a rationalist direction. The choice of a "living woman and not a statue" to represent the principle of Liberty in the Festival of Reason turns out to be a salient example of such a technique. According to the author, the festival organizers "wanted from the very first moment to break the people's minds of all habit of idolatry." Ever vigilant, they recognized that a stone emblem of Liberty would permit the maintenance of the fundamental belief structure of Catholicism, encouraging the simple replacement of "an inanimate simulacrum of liberty" for "the holy sacrament." A living woman would, on the other hand, help the people to resist that ingrained mental habit; as flesh and blood, she could not be so readily "deified by the ignorant." Rejecting the use of a statue, then, constituted the deliberate adoption for political ends of a kind of psychological pedagogy or collective mental hygiene. As the author puts it, care had been taken by the Revolutionary leadership to refrain from presenting to the people "objects that could lead their imagination astray."[3]

The *Révolutions de Paris* article can thus be read as a capsule history of sensationalist psychology with respect to the eighteenth-century understanding of imagination. Initially, as Chapter 1 of this book has shown, sensationalist psychology gave a particularly sharp edge to concern about the imagination. By identifying the environmental circumstances likely to conduce to disorders of the imagination, it heightened the psychological threat posed by certain social, economic, and cultural changes. But as this text from the Year II suggests, sensationalist psychology also provided contemporaries with a solution to the very problem whose contours it had earlier revealed. If, after all, learned men knew enough about the workings of imagination to pinpoint the situations likely to arouse that faculty and overstimulate it to a dangerous degree, then they could also figure out how to enlist countervailing forces to keep imagination in check. Once properly construed, scientific knowledge of the mind transformed an inchoate and somewhat mysterious problem of imagination into a concrete problem of psychological engineering.

The relative accent on science is critical here. The scientific credentials of sensationalist psychology remained more or less in the background when, under the Old Regime, commentators relied on that theory to flag the social circumstances that unduly excited imagination. But once, under the pressure of the Revolutionary moment, the same theory was put to use to stabilize imagination and, by extension, the individual psyche in the new noncorporate order, its scientific status tended to be emphasized. In the absence of traditional sources of social and political authority, the authority attributable to science increased. Psychological science became a precious sociopolitical resource.

After 1789, in other words, the changes associated with the emergence of modern economic forms could be safely carried out as long as scientifically inflected reason could find, or invent, *substitutes* for the restraints on imagination formerly exercised by the corporate bodies. Indeed, as this chapter will argue, much of what goes under the name of Revolutionary political culture was predicated on the tenets of sensationalist psychology and entailed the creation of just such substitutive restraints.

In order to understand how the discourse on imagination arrived at this happy point of locating the solution to a thorny problem within the problem itself, we need to return to an area broached in Chapter 1: the assignment (and reassignment) of words to things, and its perceived relationship to the putative sway of imagination over human affairs.

Renovated Sign Systems, or the Epistemology of Imagination

As suggested in Chapter 1, eighteenth-century critics of economic reorganization tended to point accusingly at the innovative vocabulary employed by their opponents. They regarded such vocabulary as codifying and tacitly granting legitimacy to the imaginative distortions introduced into human affairs by such economic changes as the expansion of credit or the dismantling of market regulations. One such early allegation of misleading vocabulary has already been cited: the complaint made by the parlementaires during the John Law episode about the use of the term "value" to refer to paper currency not backed by its equivalent in precious metal. Some decades later, however, more powerful critiques of this sort were generated, critiques that took as their target not a discrete linguistic maneuver but rather the whole science of political economy viewed as a thoroughly renovated, interlocking sign system for the re-presentation of the economy. The mid-century debate over Quesnay's Physiocratic theory provides a good example of this concern about comprehensive neologism[4] and its effects.

Quesnay depicted both sides of that debate in his *Dialogues sur le commerce et sur les travaux des artisans* (1757). The controversy rehearsed in these *Dialogues* turned on Quesnay's basic categories—that is, his tripartite division of society into a so-called productive class, a class of proprietors, and a sterile class. Physiocracy ascribed "real" productivity only to the soil and to the practitioners of agricultural occupations. Hence merchants, entrepreneurs, and artisans all found themselves tagged as economically "sterile." Many of them expressed "surprise" and "anger" at this "insulting denomination."[5]

Quesnay's *Dialogues* thus took up for discussion the novel alteration in the relationship between words and things allegedly effected by Physiocratic science. Defending commerce against invidious Physiocratic labeling, Monsieur H. argued that, especially under conditions of laissez-faire, mercantile labor "procured" even if it did not exactly "produce" profit and hence did not qualify as "sterile." The Physiocratic Monsieur N. replied that his interlocutor confounded the mere "absence of loss" in commercial transactions with "real product." In any case, Quesnay's own position (expressed in the prefatory remarks) was that the word "sterile," as he employed it, should not be construed as an affront. It was instead a rigorous scientific term and, as such, was utterly irrelevant to issues of "dignity" or social esteem.[6]

In the next dialogue, Monsieur H. became the spokesman of the maligned artisan, complaining that Physiocratic terminology "made [artisanal] production disappear." The unflappable Monsieur N. argued against that charge in part by expatiating on the relation between abstract scientific languages and ordinary languages. Since, he contended, "everything is intermixed in Nature and travels in crisscrossing circular paths," we can properly distinguish natural objects "only by means of abstract ideas, which neither arrange nor disturb anything in the physical world." These abstractions characterize relationships between such objects solely in terms of their causes and effects, speculatively teasing out a particular relationship from the jumble of physical phenomena. Thus the abstract idea of productivity that formed the basis of the Physiocratic social taxonomy was, in Monsieur N.'s formulation, "so narrowed in its physical sense, so rigorously reduced to reality," that it no longer conformed to "the vague expressions used in ordinary language." And rightly so. For "it is not for the natural order to conform itself to ordinary language, which conveys only confused and equivocal ideas; it is rather for [scientific] expressions to conform themselves to an exact knowledge of the natural order" by making "distinctions rigorously subjected to reality." Whether Monsieur H., or Quesnay's readers, followed the subtle reasoning of this disquisition, which hinged on the putatively superior ontological status of what the Physiocrats called the natural order, is unclear. But Monsieur N. nonetheless concluded it by casting himself in the role of the magnanimous protector of Monsieur H., admonishing his vulnerable interlocutor "to be on guard against the dominant illusion into which vulgar modes of expression have thrown you."[7]

The issue of the relationships between words and things, of the renaming inherent in new scientific conceptualizations, transported the problem of imagination and imaginative distortion, which Chapter 1 examined in terms of *psychological* integrity, onto the level of epistemology. Was affixing the label "sterile" to the work of artisans a praiseworthy act of scientific clarification, as Monsieur N. contended? Or, as Monsieur H. insinuated, was it a kind of magician's trick, an attempt to dupe the public by playing on the imagination and causing the concrete products of manual labor simply to "disappear"? In a paradoxical conjuncture, the same renaming of artisanal production was regarded as the height of irrationality and distortion by one camp and the height of rationality and lucid thinking by the other.

The allegation that Physiocratic theory was a deceitful product of imagination formed the central trope of *Les mannequins*, a pamphlet in the style of Montesquieu's *Persian Letters* that circulated in manuscript in 1776, at the end of the brief period of the Turgot reforms. Nominally set in "Persia," a country whose political situation just happened to mirror exactly that of France at the death of Louis XV, the pamphlet used its thin veil of exoticism to suggest how the Physiocrat Turgot (here, Togur) obtained the office of Comptroller-General in the first place. The story was as follows: While in a quandary over the choice a new Comptroller-General, Louis XVI's elderly chief adviser Maurepas (here, Alibey) dozed off. An evil genius bent on weakening the Persian state then "wrap[ped] himself in the artifice of a dream" and, thus disguised, "*seize[d] the imagination* of the sleeper," presenting to it a strange mechanical contraption in the form of a man. This anthropomorphic machine was bedecked in ordinances and edicts. It had for a head an active volcano discharging "gold, wheat, commodities of all sorts"; released into the open air, these commodities hurled themselves from the center to the circumference and back again. In the place of ears were two large canals exuding a viscous fluid that, upon condensation, formed the words of the key texts of Physiocracy. At the rim of the canals stood a half-dozen workers occupied with the task of keeping the volcano "effervescent," and at the base of the contraption a multitude of voices repeated incessantly the words, "Equality, liberty, net product."[8]

Clearly, the reader of the pamphlet was meant to identify the machine as the Physiocratic program, put into effect by an absolute ruler (hence the outer layer of edicts and ordinances), liberating goods onto the open market and keeping them in perpetual circulation, fully equipped with its slogans and its fundamental texts. "Astonished" by the mannequin, Alibey initially dismisses it as utterly unsuitable for Persia. But upon awakening, he cannot rid his consciousness of the dream image, and eventually he calls upon Togur, installing him in the office of Comptroller-General expressly to implement the economic policy emblematized by the mannequin. Alibey's imagination has been imprinted by the sight of the anthropomorphic machine, "struck (*frappé*) by this spectacle," and he in turn mechanically carries out its bidding. The way in which he has been won over to Physiocracy—against his better judgment and through the insidious capture of his imagination—makes especially appropriate the generalizing comment of his wife: "Don't you know that everyone is, after a fashion, a mannequin?"[9] In other words, we all have psyches capable of operating on mechanical principles outside our voluntary control, and hence we are all prone to manipulation by means of the faculty of imagination. Insofar as Physiocracy makes a convincing appeal, the pamphleteer would have the reader believe, it addresses the passive and impressionable imagination, not the faculty of reason.

The Well-Made Language of Science

Against the background of these polemics, we are better able to understand the internal logic of Condillac's oeuvre: the reasoning by which the anatomist of the psyche who feared imagination's power over solitary, novel-reading women could nonetheless champion the abolition of the guilds and express no anxiety about the resulting solitude of the artisan. Condillac came to the study of political economy late in his career, decades after he had hammered out the principles of his sensationalist psychology. He published *Le commerce et le gouvernement* hurriedly in 1776, spurred on by (accurate) rumors of the imminent fall of Turgot, whose high position had protected advocacy of laissez-faire from censorship.[10] Solidly within the Physiocractic mainstream in most respects, Condillac's treatise depicted the corporations both as a detrimental tax on industry (due to the payments the corporations were required to make to the Crown to assure their legal existence and to the costs of litigation between corporations over their respective spheres of monopoly) and as an "iniquitous" privilege which made it difficult for the excluded to earn a comfortable living and even "reduc[ed some] to mendicity."[11]

In arguing that artisans be released from the corporate structure, Condillac thus made no explicit connection between his psychological theory and his political economy, at least at the level of the mental apparatus imputed to the economic actor. In fact, and oddly enough for a thinker once so intensely occupied with the problem of psychological functioning, he never even highlighted the mental apparatus of the individual as an important issue for economic science—in stark contrast to his contemporary Adam Smith, whose *Wealth of Nations,* published the same year, conspicuously posited the pursuit of self-interest as the motive driving *homo economicus.* Instead, Condillac forged the connection between the components of his oeuvre at the level of methodology. Both his psychology and his political economy rested on the principle that a science is a "well-made language," one that is begun afresh, weeding out vague locutions and (often by means of neologism) precisely matching signs to their signifieds.

Condillac gave canonical expression to this principle in his last works, the *Logique,* published posthumously in 1780, and the *Langue des calculs,* not published until 1798.[12] But it is, with hindsight, fair to say that the principle already existed in germ and, perhaps in everything but name, in his psychological treatises of the 1740s and 1750s. Undertaking in these early works to decompose the human mind into its various operations and to explain its generation of ideas, he had stipulated that thought could proceed only by means of language, or the affixing of signs to sensory impressions.[13] Condillac's psychology was thus both the first instance of a well-made language in his oeuvre and the very grounding of that concept and of all its subsequent instances. In *Le commerce et le gouvernement* he came closer than before to articulating the well-made language formula. A footnote added after 1776 told his readers that his purpose in writing the treatise was not so much to add discrete new insights to political economy as to supply that entire science, often regarded by the public as an "indecipherable code," with the "particular language" that it, like all particular sciences, required.[14]

These epistemological principles shed important light on Condillac's assessment of the status of imagination under laissez-faire, but they do so only after we have painstakingly traced out the twists and turns of Condillac's argument. For while *Le commerce et le gouvernement* frustrates our inquiry by its failure to ponder the psychodynamics of the artisan, incorporated or otherwise, the *Logique* does address the issue of imagination on a theoretical plane in the course of specifying just what the laconic formula of science-as-well-made-language entailed. Condillac writes:

> The art of reasoning reduces itself to a well-made language only because the order of our ideas is itself nothing more than the hierarchy established between the names given to genuses and to species; and since we have new ideas only because we form new classifications, it is evident that we determine those ideas only insofar as we determine the classifications themselves.[15]

Knowledge, then, is a system of classifying things. That system, Condillac continues, articulating with greater clarity the point made by Quesnay in his 1757 *Dialogues,* does not exist in nature itself. Rather the various genuses and species indispensable to our efforts to acquire knowledge reflect the "relations that [things] have to us and that they have between themselves." Such categories are artifacts of purposive human thought, and it is precisely the recognition of their human origins that induces in us what is for Condillac the appropriate stance of epistemological modesty:

> If we perceive that these classifications are necessary to us only because, in order to make our ideas distinct, we must decompose the objects that we wish to study, we will not only recognize the limitations of our mind but will recognize the boundaries that we would not contemplate crossing. We will not get lost in futile questions. Instead of seeking what we cannot find, we will find what is within our grasp. For that purpose we need only construct exact ideas—something we can always do when we know how to use words.[16]

It is at this juncture that Condillac inserts into his argument a disquisition on the topic of imagination, considering its relation to the sought-after well-made language and evincing once again the preoccupation of his era with that particular mental faculty. He contends that the act of analysis, of decomposing the things we have experienced into their component sensations in order to label them appropriately, endows human beings with the capacity "to create the arts and sciences." Or "better still," as he refines and strengthens this position, analysis "itself created them" directly and "we have had only to follow it." How misguided, then, is the standard attribution of such creative powers to imagination! "Imagination," Condillac asserts, "would be nothing without analysis." After delivering this harsh assessment, he decides to make it more demeaning still. Imagination without analysis would not be merely a neutral lack or void but an active detriment, "a source of opinions, prejudices, errors." In the absence of the regulation provided by analysis, imagination would lead us to produce nothing but "extravagant dreams"—as do, in fact, those "writers who rely solely on imagination."[17] Condillac has, in effect, rewritten Voltaire's distinction, discussed in Chapter 1, between (bad) passive imagination and (good) active imagination, identifying the positive features of the latter as the contribution of analysis.

Continuing to pursue this theme of the opposition between analysis and imagination, Condillac locates what is for him the crux of the matter: the provenance ascribed to so-called "abstract ideas," which presumably include the classifications used to organize things into genera and species. Because abstract ideas "elude the senses" and appear to have nothing in common with sensory data, people can easily surmise that they come from somewhere other than the senses—for example, that they have an independent existence in our soul as innate ideas, or that they exist only in the mind of God. Seriously entertaining such propositions, says Condillac, "will necessarily lead us away from the path to discovery," dooming us to wander endlessly "from error to error." For it is precisely the conviction that abstract ideas originate outside human sensation that consigns us irrevocably to the realm of imagination: "Such are the systems that *imagination* produces: once we have adopted them, it is no longer possible to have a well-made language; and we are condemned almost always to reason badly because we reason badly about our mental faculties."[18]

Condillac's insistence that a reasonable person hold fast to the ultimately sensory origins of abstract ideas is strikingly similar to the anthropocentric requirement of the organizers of the Festival of Reason in the Year II—that is, their insistence that abstract ideas not be deified but be seen in purely human terms, that any other conception of abstract ideas marks the person holding it as under the baneful sway of imagination. As the author of the *Révolutions de Paris* article put it: "There is one thing that we must never weary of telling the people: liberty, reason, truth are abstract entities. They are not gods, for properly speaking, they are parts of ourselves."[19] The marked similarity between

Condillac and the festival organizers is hardly accidental, for as this chapter will go on to show, Condillac in many ways presided posthumously over the Revolutionary festivals.

An extrapolation from the *Logique* to *Le commerce et le gouvernement* offers a plausible solution—though, to be sure, one never spelled out by Condillac himself—both to the problem of the artisan's imagination under laissez-faire and to its corollary, the problem of stabilizing the atomized individual. It is clear that for Condillac the overhauling of terminology is anything but a conjuring trick or an effort to seduce the public by confounding the real and the imaginary. It is rather the supremely rational gesture, the laying down of the foundations of science, the definitive banishment of the deceits and beguilements of imagination. In Condillac's lexicon, imagination and a well-made language are radically opposed entities, and important consequences would seem to flow from that relationship. The unincorporated artisan in the laissez-faire market will, we can surmise, work within a thoroughly rational economic structure, one that operationalizes the well-made language of political economy; and hence in that new environment, by definition inimical to imagination, the artisan's solitude will harbor no psychic dangers. (In the absence of such a considered scientific rationale, on the other hand, Condillac would probably not countenance the release of the artisan from the corporation. For let loose into a society at once socially unstructured and intellectually unenlightened, the imagination of the solitary artisan would encounter no countervailing force and would thus continue to pose genuine threats.) Even without the benefit of a dense customary routine regulating the artisan's daily activities, the pure rational transparency of a social situation created according to a scientific blueprint will effectively constrain imagination; in this regard, science-as-well-made language will replace the corporate structure.

The criteria for a well-made language were not, of course, as perspicuous as Condillac seemed to assume. Take the reception of *Le commerce et le gouvernement*. Members of the Physiocratic community, sympathetic to Condillac's basic position on the freedom of the market, nonetheless bristled at the terminological pretensions of this relative newcomer to their fold. Both Guillaume François Le Trosne and the self-identified Physiocrat, the abbé Nicolas Baudeau, for example, questioned Condillac's division of society into two classes (landed proprietors and wage earners), firmly convinced that the tripartite division initially laid down by Quesnay (landed proprietors, cultivators, and wage earners) accurately translated reality. As Le Trosne put it, Quesnay's categories corresponded, quite simply, to "what goes on right beneath our eyes." The founder of the discipline had, after all, "taken great pains to fix the meaning of words properly."[20]

Quarrels such as these underscore the vast, uncharted territory opened up by the eighteenth-century mandate to use neologism in the service of science. Was anything possible in the well-making of languages, or should specific guidelines be applied? What was the court of last resort when new terminologies conflicted? An astute observer of the scientific and philosophical scene like Condorcet quickly recognized the problem that issued from Condillac's formula. Brooding on it in writings of the 1770s and 1780s, he reached the conclusion that all classificatory systems interpreted nature rather than merely transcribing it; hence, none could ever be definitive. Even the ones that fostered scientific progress at a given moment introduced obstacles into the process of observation that would eventually erode their utility. Yet however imperfect, classificatory systems were all that we had in our effort to gain accurate knowledge of the world. Or, in Condorcet's phrase, "If there is little philosophy in mistaking these methodological arrangements for science itself, there is still less in despising them."[21]

Condorcet's sophistication on this issue was, however, rare in his era. Most people who regarded themselves as enlightened knew only that the specially constructed languages of science were a hallmark of enlightenment, that they were far more reliable than ordinary language, and that they could serve as levers for intellectual and perhaps social change. The basic lines of intellectual battle were drawn not over the status of rival classificatory schemes but between the supporters of the new well-made languages on the one hand and the supporters of the traditional terminology (and practices) of corporate society on the other.

These two camps represented alternate epistemologies, although only the advocates of science proffered an epistemology in the conventional sense—that is, a set of explicit claims about the nature and scope of knowledge rooted in an explicit model of the human mind. For the traditionalists, a particular *social* structure was, in effect if not in name, epistemologically foundational and, like a model of the mind, could be used as the basis for truth claims. Thus traditionalist discourse included the locution *faux ouvrier,* or false worker, by which was meant a person who attempted to make a living without membership in a guild, either living a clandestine existence in a furnished room or working openly in a juridically privileged enclave, such as the faubourg Saint-Antoine in Paris, where unincorporated labor was tolerated.[22] The falsity of such a worker was determined not by reference to any insufficiency of productivity (as was the "sterility" of a worker and the "reality" of a product in the Physiocratic scheme) but purely by social location—that is, the worker's refusal or failure to find a corporate niche. Presumably, the falsity of the *faux ouvrier* extended to the incorrectness of his judgments, clouded as they were by the flights of imagination that his unsupervised situation did nothing to restrain.

Other corporate locutions formed on this model bore witness to the same assumptions. Members of the textile guilds decried Turgot's 1776 edicts by pointing to the resultant arrival at the marketplace of what they called "false dyes," in this case blue dyes whose ingredients differed from those stipulated by corporate regulations of 1669. The falsity of the commodity was gauged not only by its departure from the legal standard but also by the effect of such a deviation on the attitude of the public: blue dyes not containing the expected indigo were a "deceptive practice" that would destroy public confidence in the products of French artisans and cause consumers to look abroad to satisfy their needs. Here again truth (or falsity) referred to social location—to the supervised (or free) artisan whose productions were a known (or unknown) quantity and who consequently generated either a stable nexus of trust between producer and consumer or an unstable environment of mistrust. Worse still, the "false dyes" produced colors that were "brighter" and "more seductive" than those of the true dyes. The language here, designed to emphasize the potential for fraud in an unmonitored market, recalls typical eighteenth-century descriptions of the duping power of appeals to imagination.[23]

Corporate discourse, in other words, did not directly address the question of how we know, but it did specify the social preconditions for an accurate apprehension of reality. Both sets of categories, the traditional corporate ones and the deliberately renovated ones of the well-made language, thus had in common a self-ascribed ability to obtain truth and, in the service of truth, to stand in a prophylactic relationship to imagination.

Revolutionaries Confront the Imagination

The fears that the parlementaires had expressed preemptively in 1776 about the psychological effects of laissez-faire were, not surprisingly, voiced again when the Revolution actually began to dismantle traditional legal and social structures and boldly inaugurated a policy of "liberty." Consider the long letter that Jean-Baptiste-Antoine Suard, a second-generation philosophe, addressed to Condorcet in 1789 arguing against the latter's blanket advocacy of liberty. Condorcet wanted to end censorship in the theater as well as in the domain of the printed word. In declaring himself a supporter of freedom of the press only, Suard pointed to the serious drawbacks of an unsupervised theater. What filled him with foreboding was the impact of such a theater on the imagination—not the imagination of the isolate but that of the crowd member:

> One ordinarily reads a book alone and in a cool manner, communicating only to a few persons the impressions that one has received.
>
> Theatrical representations, by contrast, speak to the *imagination* and the senses; they can set all the passions in motion, and the impressions they produce acquire an extraordinary energy by the fact that a multitude of assembled persons experiences them simultaneously. Everyone knows the story of the people of Abdera whose imaginations were exalted to the point of insanity by seeing a performance of a tragedy by Aeschylus.

To the problem of imaginations brought to a fever pitch in the milieu of the theater, Suard offered a fundamentally conservative solution: restrict liberty and maintain censorship. To be sure, he had no use for the censorship of the Old Regime, which he characterized as capricious, secretive, cowardly, and inquisitorial. Instead he proposed a new-style Revolutionary censorship employing mechanisms of public deliberation. The system he envisioned would be administered by "wise and educated men, who love the arts and liberty"—even, presumably, when they are engaged in curtailing them—"who could not refuse their approval to a play or even a single feature of play without articulating their reasons, who would allow the author to defend his work and would invoke a police tribunal to decide between the author and the censor."[24]

Also writing in the early years of the Revolution, the comte de Mirabeau expressed similar worries about imagination but took, in assuaging them, the opposite tack, the one that the First Republic would later cultivate intensively. Imagination should be controlled, Mirabeau apparently believed, not by placing external limitations on human liberty but by a form of pedagogy that would mold the imagination directly, thus fortifying the psyche at its point of maximum vulnerability and enabling the citizen body to enjoy liberty without sinking into psychological and, eventually, social disorder.

Even before the Revolution, Mirabeau was alert to what might be called the sensory pedagogy of everyday life, or the continual impingement of the environment upon the mental apparatus to produce, for good or ill, certain prevalent sociopolitical attitudes. Thus his "Considérations sur l'ordre de Cincinnatus" (1784) expressed dismay at a new institutional development in the United States, a country that he had regarded as politically regenerated by its recent revolution. The order of Cincinnatus was composed of the veterans of the revolutionary wars, including George Washington. Membership in it was to be hereditary, passed on from father to son. The group had its own "mark of distinction": a gold medal in the form of an eagle suspended from a dark blue ribbon edged in white. "Each member," noted Mirabeau, "is to wear this ribbon and medal, just as in Europe the cross and other marks of chivalry are worn." The order of Cincinnatus was, in other words, an incipient American nobility. Military in origin just like its European counterpart, it appeared to Mirabeau to be clearly en route to becoming an entrenched civil aristocracy.[25]

Especially odious in Mirabeau's view was the order's adoption of an insignia, and he dwelt at length on the perverse power of such badges. Seemingly frivolous, they in fact "tightened the chains" of oppressed people through their direct appeal to the imagination. By its particular color and configuration, a ribbon or medal "seems to render visible to the eye the artificial inequality that usurpation and insolence began"; as an "imposing sign," it "engraves the imagination of the weak" and thereby actually succeeds in producing an attitude of servility in those that gaze upon but do not wear it. In an extraordinary passage, Mirabeau then generalizes this theme.

> Man is a natural labeler; he associates or substitutes the sign for the thing. The sign so subjugates him that he places more importance on his conformity with an established formula than on true sentiments, honest motives, useful actions ... Every sign is redoubtable and produces a great effect on the weak imagination of men. It is by

striking their eyes that one endows them with whatever passions one chooses. . . . It is by the use of signs that several revolutions, either for the sake of liberty or of tyranny, have been prepared and carried out in certain states.

In other words, hereditary nobility can gain acceptance only when its proponents exercise sufficient control over the everyday visual environment to penetrate to the imaginations of ordinary people and to convince those people—wordlessly, repetitively, and without use of reason—of their baseness. A visual motif predominates in this sensationalist-psychological analysis of social relations: his eyes once struck by decorative signs of honor, the honest man "lowers his eyes" before them in implicit acknowledgment of his own inferiority. If the order of Cincinnatus threatens to corrupt American democracy, then the gold medal in the form of an eagle and the blue ribbon edged in white will be among the causes of that corruption, and the eyes and the imaginations of the American citizenry will be its chief instrument.[26]

A man so attuned to the connection among visual images, the faculty of imagination, and sociopolitical structures could hardly fail to apply these insights to his own country in the aftermath of the 1789 Revolution. Newly and suddenly liberated from the straitjacket of traditional economic, social, political, and religious authority, the French people must have struck Mirabeau as possessing an extreme psychological plasticity that, although filled with promise, might just as well issue in disaster. Thus it is not surprising that found among Mirabeau's papers at the time of his death in 1791 were drafts of three speeches on the subject of public education that he had planned to deliver before the Constituent Assembly. Two of the speeches concern the foundation of schools and school systems; the remaining one, of special interest to us here, proposes that classroom instruction be supplemented by another pedagogical medium: an annual cycle of "public festivals." Under this heading Mirabeau, in effect, continued the ruminations of his essay on the order of Cincinnatus, pondering the way that images, and the impressionable imaginations to which they are relayed, can determine the political propensities of a people.

"In his capacity as a sensitive being," Mirabeau asserts, "man is led much less by rigorous principles . . . than by majestic objects, striking images, great spectacles, deep emotions." Put more baldly, man "obeys his impressions rather than his reason." Merely showing him the truth is futile if you do not give him a passion for it—if you do not, in other words, "lay hold of his imagination." Decisive political negotiations take place at the site of this mental faculty because, when appropriately stimulated, imagination can readily win men over to a "social organization that is entirely absurd, unjust and even cruel."[27]

The radical indeterminacy of imagination in its native condition necessitates that a polity, especially the new French polity hoping to infuse its citizens with generous ideals, undertake a schooling of the imagination by means of the public festival. "Up to now, Gentlemen," Mirabeau warned his fellow legislators, "your institutions bear the imprint of a cold wisdom, of justice, of truth; but they still perhaps lack that which seizes man by all his senses, which fascinates him and sweeps him away." The architects of the new France needed to learn more about the "secret ties that bind free peoples to their political institutions" and the "ties of happy fraternity that unite [citizens] among themselves." In particular they needed to understand the use of public festivals, deployed to such great effect in ancient Greece and Rome, to create and reinforce such ties. Mirabeau recommended that nine festivals be held each year throughout France, four for civilians, four for soldiers, and one all-embracing national holiday. The festivals would bombard the citizenry with sense impressions—music, dance, paintings, sculpture—chosen for their ability to instill civic sentiments. Plays would be mounted at public expense with the same end in view: "to nourish both enthusiasm for liberty and respect for the public power that protects it."[28] The extraordinary energy of shared impressions, so feared by Suard within the context of an uncensored theater, would be deliberately channeled and exploited by the Revolution. The festival life of the new national community would join the rational science of political economy as a potent substitute for the restraints on imagination formerly exercised by corporate membership.

The Progenitor: Rousseau on the Training of Imagination

As the Idéologue physician P.-J.-G. Cabanis noted in 1791 in his introduction to Mirabeau's posthumously published speeches, the count "often made use of other people's ideas but almost always recast and improved upon them."[29] In the case of civic education through the imagination, the "other people" whom Mirabeau mined for inspiration were, it seems, Condillac and Rousseau: Condillac for the psychology that highlighted the volatility of imagination and its extreme sensitivity to its surroundings; Rousseau for the pedagogical strategies aimed at that mental faculty. To be sure, both Condillac and Rousseau wrote significant works of pedagogy. But while Condillac's *Cours d'études pour l'instruction du Prince de Parme* mentions the imagination only twice, Rousseau's *Emile* invokes it more than sixty times.[30] Although never explicitly cited by Mirabeau, the *Emile,* a text widely read in France in the second half of the eighteenth century, clearly forms the backdrop of his advocacy of public festivals. It also served other Revolutionary policymakers as a basic discursive resource. Hence its sustained meditation on imagination deserves consideration here. For just as Jean-Jacques' discussion of masturbation in his *Confessions* contributed, if belatedly, to the discourse on the dangers of imagination (see Chapter 1), so the *Emile* contributed both to that discourse and, more pointedly, to its antidote. It proposed practices that could actively harness the imagination for positive ends or neutralize its potential for harm.

Implicitly building on Condillac's sensationalist psychology, the *Emile* places the imagination close to the heart of its theory of education. It describes a double movement on the part of the tutor with respect to the pupil's imagination: at times an effort to keep that faculty dormant, to refrain from stimulating it; at other times, an equally deliberate effort to arouse it. Rousseau sets forth the problematic of the imagination early in Book I. Our desires and abilities are, he postulates, evenly matched in the state of nature. However, the awakening of imagination vastly extends our desires without a corresponding increase in our abilities, thus making us prey to unhappiness. This disequilibrium argues powerfully for curtailing the activity of imagination: "The real world has its limits, the imaginary world is infinite. Unable to enlarge the one, let us restrict the other."[31]

Imagination exposes us to unnecessary unhappiness not only through its kindling of insatiable, artificial desires but also by its propensity to excite fear:

> Do I hear absolutely nothing? I am not for that reason tranquil because, in the last analysis, even something without noise might surprise me. . . . Thus forced to set my imagination in motion, I am soon no longer its master, and everything I do to reassure myself only alarms me further. If I hear noise, I hear robbers; if I hear nothing, I see phantoms.

In this situation, too, imagination requires careful management. Rousseau proposes the basic technique: "In everything, habit kills imagination." The way, then, to rid ourselves of imaginary fears is by repetitive counterphobic behavior; if we thoroughly accustom ourselves to the objects of our fears, encounters with those objects will stir only the safe and sober faculty of memory and utterly fail to rouse the notoriously unreliable faculty of imagination. "Do not, then, reason with him whom you want to cure of loathing of the dark. Take him out in it often. . . ."[32] Rousseau's dictum on this subject became widely known and inspired other eighteenth-century French pedagogues to propose comparable techniques for subduing the fretful imagination. Thus, in Madame de Genlis's epistolary novel, *Adèle et Théodore, ou Lettres sur l'éducation* (1782), where Rousseau's "night games" are explicitly recommended "to preserve [children] forever from those gloomy ideas that have so much power over the imagination," the Baron also offers comparable pedagogical inventions of his own—for example, a glass-enclosed armoire displaying anatomical specimens that, placed in a corridor of the house regularly traversed by his offspring, allegedly neutralizes their superstitious, infantile fear of skeletons.[33]

But if Emile's tutor frequently takes pains to extinguish his pupil's nascent imagination in childhood, the boy's subsequent development—from a virtuous but self-enclosed to a fully social being—demands that his imagination be not globally dampened but selectively kindled. For according to Rousseau, we exit the narrow circle of ourselves and form attachments with others only by means of imagination. "The first act of [a meticulously raised young man's] burgeoning imagination is to instruct him that he has fellow-creatures (*semblables*)." Our ties to our *semblables* depend upon an imaginative identification with them and, more specifically, a capacity to commiserate with their pain. The phenomenology of such attachment is a taking up of temporary, imaginative residence in the other. "It is not inside ourselves but inside [the *semblable*] that we suffer [. . .]. Thus a person becomes sensitive only insofar as his imagination comes to life and begins to transport him outside himself." Though written in a lyrical, evocative prose, Rousseau's comments obey a strict, underlying systematicity. Thus he observes that the habituation techniques that the tutor recommended to keep a fearful imagination in check have the comparable effect of dulling an empathetic imagination and are, for that reason, to be studiously avoided when empathy rather than sangfroid is the desired result: "What one too often sees, one no longer imagines, and it is only through imagination that we feel another's sorrows. By dint of seeing death and suffering [on a routine basis], priests and physicians become pitiless."[34]

The tutor declines to assume the task of transforming Emile from a social being into a full-fledged political one, regarding the young man's exceptional virtue as incompatible with the corruption of contemporary politics. Yet if a complete education for citizenship is not on the agenda, he nonetheless draws on political examples in the final stage of his pupil's training. Before instructing Emile to seek a wife, the tutor launches on a long digression about constructing one's public persona: how to make one's verbal utterances count and to "engrave [them] on the memory" of one's audience. Once again the imagination is key:

> One of the errors of our era is to employ reason too nakedly, as if men were only mind. In neglecting *the language of signs that speaks to the imagination,* we have lost the most forceful of languages. Speech always makes a feeble impression, and one speaks much better to the heart through the eyes than though the ears.

In support of this proposition, he cites the practices of the Romans ("How great was the attention that the Romans paid to language of signs!"), who reserved different clothing for different ages and stations, who insisted that accused persons and candidates wear special costumes, whose warriors vaunted their bravery by displaying their wounds, who heeded the minutiae of ceremonies: where the people were assembled, whether they could see the Capitol from that spot, whether they were turned in the direction of the Senate.[35]

From the discussion of a pedagogy of imagination in the *Emile* to Mirabeau's proposal for public festivals in 1791 is only a short step. Clearly Mirabeau draws on Rousseau's suggestions for an active exploitation of imagination rather than on the tactics designed to prevent the premature awakening of that faculty. However, with respect to the creation of fraternal social ties, he sounds much like Emile's tutor. Man possesses in a higher degree than other animals, Mirabeau asserts, the capacity to "share in the affections of all beings, and especially those of his *semblables.*" Furthermore, this essentially imaginative identification with the other, or installation of oneself into the psyche of the other by imaginative means, is the "wellspring of all benevolent sentiments, of the enthusiasms of friendship," and of supreme importance in the new French polity born of the Revolution, "of devotion to the fatherland."[36]

Revolutionary Political Culture: The Refurbished Environment of Everyday Life

Speaking before one of the legislative houses of the Directory in the Year VII, an obscure deputy spelled out a basic principle of sensationalist psychology. Said Joubert (de l'Hérault), "[E]ducation does not consist solely of formal instruction. . . . [W]e are much less the pupils of our teachers than of the circumstances that have surrounded us, of the objects that have frequently attracted our glances and captured our attention."[37] Joubert complained that his colleagues had not yet fully grasped the import of this principle, that it cried out for intensive cultivation. But in fact, many Revolutionaries had already applied it quite assiduously, attempting to turn the French population into a nation of stable, civic-minded citizens by creating new practices and institutions that would alter the environment of everyday life for the express purpose of altering the mental furniture of everybody. Those new and presumably transformative practices and institutions included four that will be considered here: the regular cycle of festivals favored from the outset by Mirabeau; the wearing of special clothing by public officials; the renaming of city streets; and the adoption of a new Revolutionary calendar. In surveying the components of this Revolutionary culture, it is for our purposes most important to notice how closely its advocates hewed to the tenets of sensationalist psychology and, especially, how concerned they were in their tinkerings with the environment to harness the imagination for civic ends. The political pronouncements examined below reveal that the psychology of Condillac had become nothing less than a quasi-official component of the Revolutionary ideology.

Most supporters of the Revolution shared the belief contained in Mirabeau's posthumous papers: that the regenerated French nation required a series of national festivals to commemorate Revolutionary milestones and to renew the fraternal and patriotic bonds forged at those peak moments. Supplementary articles to the 1791 Constitution announced the desirability of such a festival cycle. But, only under the Jacobins in the Year II was a coherent system of festivals finally devised and enacted into law. It would last until the end of the Directory in 1799.[38]

The spectacular political festival was hardly a new idea. Historians have noted the continuity of the Revolutionaries' project with the practices of the Bourbon kings, even at the level of the decorative motifs employed and the bureaucratic agencies charged with responsibility. Nor was it outside Louis XVI's repertory to celebrate the French nation and its component regions as well as the French monarchy.[39] Specific to the Revolutionary era, however, was the self-conscious effort to turn the festival form into a civic pedagogy grounded in psychological theory. Even the location of the festival—the revolutionaries preferred an open space that provided an uninterrupted vista, making every movement of the participants immediately visible—testified to the guiding role of sensationalist principles.[40] A sampling of deputies' speeches and pamphlets from the periods of the Republic and Directory reveals the extent to which the festivals were construed as an exercise in applied sensationalist psychology.

Thus, in the course of advocating that civic festivals be staged at regular, closely spaced intervals, one deputy declared, "Speak to the senses and to the imagination of the people if you wish to exalt their enthusiasm for your institutions."[41] Other legislators added a historical dimension to this argument, indicating the precedents on which the Revolutionaries ought to draw. They depicted Catholic priests as intuitive sensationalist psychologists *avant la lettre,* clever manipulators who had long ago learned to use sensory stimulation to produce and sustain popular loyalty to clerical institutions. When Constantine converted to Christianity, one deputy remarked, the personnel of that religion refused to allow any other power within the Roman Empire to sponsor festivals and ceremonies or, what is the same thing, "to have a language for the senses and the imagination and to speak to men by means of images." It would ill behoove the French Revolutionaries, another deputy asserted, to let this priestly wisdom lapse. They must embrace the weapons of their enemies and bend them to their own purposes.[42]

Yet another deputy, Merlin de Thionville, argued for the national festivals in a more philosophically elaborate fashion by expressing the goal of the Revolution in terms of Condillac's celebrated definition of science as a system of pellucid signification. Citing Condillac by name, he noted that the "art of reasoning well can be reduced to the art of skillfully speaking a well-made language, and the art of making oneself understood by a great people can be reduced to pronouncing a sonorous language adeptly." What he called the "analytic part of the Revolution" was the transformation of France into a kind of communicative utopia where "no one can speak without knowing what he means and without making himself understood." In Merlin's scheme, the national festivals, although operating primarily at the prelinguistic level, fostered and indeed served as the prototype of this political-cum-epistemological goal of perfect transparency. Take, for example, Merlin's description of choral music at the festival. The "common organ" created by the "limitless association of thousands of human voices," all "united by fraternity and warmed by the same sentiment," would achieve "direct communication"— presumably communication by means of sentiment and sensory stimulation, largely dispensing with the mediation of words, and infallibly able to "make [its message] understood by all who wish to understand."[43]

This rhetoric eventually came around full circle. When, after the Napoleonic coup, the national festivals fell into official disfavor, those who denounced them likewise drew their arguments from sensationalist psychology. A comprehensive report on Parisian cultural institutions commissioned by the municipality in 1801 recommended the abolition of the annual cycle of festivals and its compression into a single national holiday on July 14. The report emphasized the anomaly of the Revolutionary practice ("the annals of all the world's peoples offer us no other example of a purely political festival") and the sheer wrongheadedness of attempting an exclusively political commemoration of founding principles. Insofar as such commemorations sought to perpetuate the political order, said the report, they required the sanction of religious institutions, which alone were lasting. Their singular durability derived not only from the intrinsic truth of their doctrines but also from their leaders' intuitive grasp of sensationalist psychology.

Thus the detractors of the Revolutionary festivals took over wholesale a discursive motif dear to their champions: the wisdom of emulating priestly techniques. The report criticized the Revolutionaries for having concocted festivals whose dry pedagogical component evinced a foolish disregard of the lessons of religious ritual, with its arsenal of "signs evoking respect and confidence." Any effective ceremony necessarily employed a semiotics that addressed the "senses by means of emblems that at once signify, express, and are analogous to ideas." The people were capable of learning this "language of allegory," though not overnight. In this area, too, the organizers of the Revolutionary festivals had blundered, frequently changing the signs and symbols they presented to the public. Since the political festival was originally "a borrowing from religion," the government could do no better than to continue its imitation of the Church by restoring the divinity to the festival and establishing a fixed ceremonial language of signs.[44] Penned at the very opening of the new century, this pronouncement exemplified a typically nineteenth-century tendency to embrace religion as much for its utility as for its truth. It also indicated the axiomatic status still enjoyed by sensationalist psychology at this historical juncture.

Supporting the mission of the national festivals during the period of the Republic were other cultural contrivances similarly reliant on the mechanisms of sensationalist psychology for their presumed effects. Two of these were proposed by the abbé Henri Grégoire, the Revolutionary legislator whose most celebrated project, that of "annihilating patois and universalizing the French language," had also sought legitimacy from an explicit invocation of Condillac. In Grégoire's view, French was a better-made language than the various patois spoken in the countryside, which preserved antiquated opinions in their very vocabularies. The "linguistic imperfection" of such crude idioms, said Grégoire paraphrasing Condillac, was "a major source of error." Universalizing French would, by contrast, help to spread enlightenment evenly throughout the population, enabling intellectual consensus and fostering social unity.[45]

The very next year Grégoire appeared before the Convention with another report and draft bill, soon to be enacted into law, on the "costumes of legislators and other public functionaries." He recommended, for example, that all legislators wear long robes, which would be white for the members of the Conseil des Cinq Cents, and blue violet for the members of the Conseil des Anciens.[46] His report was a kind of mirror image of Mirabeau's observations on the Order of Cincinnatus. Whereas Mirabeau had faulted the use of insignia that operated on the imaginations of the people to create and enforce an unwarranted distinction between noble and commoner, Grégoire proposed to use costume to operate on the imaginations of the people to produce an entirely justified awe for the guardians of the Republic. To make his case, he raided the arsenal of sensationalist psychology and came up with the usual discursive maneuvers. He observed that the "language of signs has an eloquence all its own" and that "costumes form a part of that idiom"; their sensuous properties revived pertinent ideas and emotions, "especially when they take hold of the imagination by their splendor." Nor did he think that "this [sartorial] apparatus ought to strike only vulgar eyes." The language of signs was a legitimate and suitable means of communicating with every sort of person and a necessary supplement to a theoretical discussion of politics:

> We all have senses, which are, so to speak, the doors of the soul. We are all susceptible of receiving, by their mediation, deep impressions. Hence those who would pretend to govern a people by philosophical theories can hardly be called philosophers. The man who is most detached from everything material responds to the glamour of decorations and to the magic of the imitative arts. The one who most prides himself on having only reason for a guide has perhaps followed its voice less often than he has yielded to the illusions of the imagination and the senses.[47]

So, too, Grégoire's proposal for a new "system of topographical denominations for the public places, streets, embankments, etc. of every commune in the Republic" derived in part from his belief in sensationalist psychology. Expecting his colleagues in the Convention to oppose such a project as "too finicky and painstaking to occupy the legislature," he countered preemptively, "When a government is completely overhauled, no abuse should escape the reforming scythe; everything must be republicanized." To refrain from renaming the elements of the urban landscape would be to miss an opportunity for quotidian civic instruction—in this case, by displaying at each corner "names and emblems capable of exercising the mind for useful ends, acting on the heart, and arousing patriotism." Each name, Grégoire specified, should be carefully chosen to function as the "vehicle of a thought, or better still of a sentiment which causes citizens to remember their rights and duties, which tightens the bonds of fraternity and strengthens the love of liberty." This omni-pedagogic urban environment would work primarily through the eyes that read the street signs. (Grégoire was, in this instance, proposing a quite *literal* language of signs!) The pedagogic city would also have a deliberately auditory component since Grégoire recommended that the topographic denominations be "short and sonorous," not only easy on the tongue but also attractive to the ear.[48] As singular as Grégoire's proposal might appear, it actually had roots in the mid-eighteenth century, when the abbé Etienne Teisserenc, similarly imbued with sensationalist psychology (as were so many architects and urban planners of the era), proposed renaming the streets of the capital. His goal was not, of course, revolutionary regeneration but the statist-cum-nationalist one of making provincials feel immediately at home in Paris and thus cementing ties between center and periphery.[49]

Grégoire's street name project never mentioned the imagination as the mental faculty to be targeted by euphonious and meaning-laden signs. But the chief spokesman for the Revolutionary calendar did have recourse that much-used topos, frankly depicting the part of the reform concerned with verbal renovation (as opposed to the arithmetic renovation that divided the year into units calculated according to the decimal system) as a technology of the imagination geared to nation-building.

That spokesman was none other than Fabre d'Eglantine, whom we already encountered in Chapter 1 as the playwright whose preoccupation with uncontrolled, overactive imagination had, five years before, found expression in his comedy *Le Présomptueux, ou l'heureux imaginaire*. There is evidence that Fabre had long been steeped in Enlightenment philosophy, including its psychological branch. A poem that he wrote early in the 1780s thanks Buffon for having converted Nature into "my supreme lesson" whose observable features "disclose precious secrets to humans." Fabre's new relationship to Nature has, he attests, changed him personally from a timid, rudderless creature into an astute and unflappable student, "a telescope at my eye, a sounding line in my hand," so persuaded of a fundamental order that he feels no alarm even if the earth shakes under his feet. Fabre-as-poet avows that he sometimes extends this mode of calm scientific observation to the psychological realm, "into the shadow and the silence of my own individual being." Here he "probes the movement" and comes to understand the channels by which he "senses, touches, and knows."[50]

The adept of sensationalist psychology comes through clearly when Fabre, as deputy to the Convention, reported to his colleagues on the reform of the calendar: his commission would believe itself to have carried out its mission if it "succeeded in striking the imagination" by means of the names that it affixed to the months of the year. "We conceive nothing except by means of images," he intoned in the didactic style favored in Jacobin political discourse. "In the most abstract analysis, in the most metaphysical speculation, our intellect registers only images." Long habitual use of the Gregorian calendar under the Old Regime had already stocked the minds of the people with a "considerable number of images." In their effort to subjugate the human race, the priestly inventors of that calendar had, after all, shown great skill at "seizing the imagination of men and governing it as they pleased." Fabre recommended the retaliatory strategy much touted by republicans: opportunistically imitating priestly techniques (which were, he implied, formal equivalents of the techniques suggested by sensationalist psychology) in order to instill reverence for secular objects of "public utility."

Hence Fabre proposed that the names of months summon up images of the soil and the sky. These real, natural objects would banish the "fantastic objects" of religion with which the priests had so cleverly cluttered their calendar—for example, saints' days presenting St. John as the distributor of the harvest or St. Mark as the protector of the vine. Honest, mundane gratitude for the bounty of nature would replace servile dependence on saintly or priestly intercession as the dominant calendrical motif. The new months of republican provenance would work on the imagination, in part, by auditory, onomatopoeic means: the autumnal months (for example, Brumaire) would have a serious sound and a medium tempo; those of winter (for example, Pluviôse) a heavy sound and a slow tempo; those of spring (for example, Floréal) a gay sound and a brisk tempo; and those of summer (for example, Fructidor) a resonant sound and a broad, relaxed tempo. Visual images would be at least equally powerful. For example, on the first day of the month of Germinal, the beginning of spring "will be effortlessly painted on the imagination" because the initial syllable carries the image of a shoot, a sprouting seed (germe).[51]

The world ushered in by the French Revolution was, as these four cultural innovations indicate, a world in which the viewpoint of sensationalist psychology was validated by official discourse and used as the basis of official policy. The embrace of sensationalism meant that the objects of the material environment were not regarded as dumb and inert but rather as "speaking to" human beings, who were in turn construed as organisms sensitive almost to the point of quivering, and not sealed off from but readily permeated by their surroundings. While this situation of human porosity harbored dangers, it could also be turned into an opportunity and a boon. The mental faculties—and, in particular, the notoriously plastic imagination—could be affected in ways inimical to social order. But, if the initiative were seized by right-thinking people, imagination could also be intentionally shaped and cultivated for social ends. Based on scientific principles, psychological engineering could thus make a virtue of the vulnerability inherent in imagination.

The Central Schools and the Teaching of Condillac

At the beginning of his famous "Report on the Principles of Political Morality" delivered to the Convention in the Year II in the name of the Committee on Public Safety to anticipate and justify the Terror, Robespierre disclaimed any tyrannical intentions or Machiavellian strategies on the part of the highly centralized Jacobin republic. Proof of this irreproachability would, he said, be found in the "Report" itself, which laid bare the goals of his government, the obstacles in its path, and the means proposed to surmount those obstacles and reach those goals. Providing such information was a tack that a "lax and corrupt government" would never dare to take. "A king, a haughty senate, a Caesar, a Cromwell are obliged above all to cover their plans. . . . For ourselves, we come to make the world privy to your political secrets."[52]

The same argument might have been adduced—though I do not think it ever was—to explain the establishment of the *écoles centrales*, or central schools, by the law of 3 ventôse Year III and the so-called Daunou Law of 3 brumaire Year IV. Although the Republic had been applying the tenets of sensationalist psychology to inculcate civic principles in the population, it had no desire to mold citizens behind their backs. Sensationalist psychology was not, in a republic, a secret tool with which to fashion a fundamentally passive and pliable citizen body; republican leaders were not like priests, using crucifixes and incense to overawe the imaginations of their gullible flocks. Instead, the citizens would be taught all they needed to know to understand their own genealogy as patriots; they would appreciate how their sensory organs had, at the national festivals and on renamed city streets, been deliberately bombarded to shape their intellects. In short, the Republic gave high priority to teaching sensationalist psychology to its citizens, thus making them conscious collaborators in their own political education. In the name of individual autonomy, it politicized a commitment to cognitive self-reflexivity already evident in Condillac's 1775 pedagogical treatise. "Why then," Condillac had mused in his capacity as tutor to the prince of Parma, "couldn't one make [the child] notice what is happening within him when he judges or reasons, when he desires or forms habits?"[53] The pupil should not merely be educated at the hands of the tutor but should actively understand the process of education transforming his mind.

The central schools were secondary schools, designed to replace the *collèges* of the Old Regime by providing instruction to adolescent males. They were established on a uniform plan, one per department throughout France. To some extent they embodied laissez-faire in the realm of education: they had virtually no admission requirements, no required courses, no graded classes or fixed term of enrollment, and they awarded no degrees or certificates.[54] On the other hand, their curriculum did not reflect a free play of divergent approaches but rather a single, coherent epistemological and pedagogical position, one organized around and thoroughly permeated with sensationalist psychology. For example, courses in drawing and natural history aimed, in part, to strengthen the students' visual acuity and powers of observation in order to improve the quality of the sensory input from which all mental processes were supposed to derive. In the case of natural history, a discipline centered on the taxonomy of the plant and animal kingdoms, the student would also learn rudimentary skills connected to the great epistemological principle: the correct assignment of words to things.[55] Furthermore, the drawing course, although primarily geared to training artisans and fostering the observational skills of ordinary citizens, was also conceived as serving the long-term needs of the republic in its role as producer and consumer of patriotic spectacle.[56] And just as Fabre d'Eglantine, the author of a pre-Revolutionary play about imagination, reappeared after 1789 as a legislator intent on striking the imaginations of the citizenry by means of a new calendar, so too J. J. Bachelier, who had under the Old Regime attempted to discipline artisans' imaginations at the Ecole gratuite de dessin, resurfaced during the Directory as professor of drawing at the central school of the Pantheon in Paris.[57]

Explicit instruction in the tenets of sensationalist psychology at the central schools, as well as in the theory of language derived from it, formed the task of a more advanced course, that in "general grammar."

The unusual name of the course[58] tended to raise false expectations and inspire a slightly comical confusion in the student body. Thus the professor of general grammar in the department of the Ardennes recounted ruefully that his course

> had initially had about thirty students, but this large number was the result of a misunderstanding caused by ignorance of the subject matter treated: the students generally believed that the purpose of the course was to teach the French language, and they appeared very surprised that they had been mistaken.

The students listened respectfully to the professor's explanation of general grammar and seemed to accept his reasoning. However, voting with their feet (the terms of the law gave them complete freedom to choose their courses from among the various offerings that the school was obliged to provide), they nonetheless deserted Citizen Magin, whose enrollment plummeted to ten within a month.[59] His colleague in the Creuse told a similar tale. In that department, the prevailing opinion that general grammar meant French grammar had a negative impact on the morale of the pupils who, upon entering the course, were shocked and "repelled to hear talk of the generation of ideas, the development of the intellectual faculties, and sensations as the rudiments of our ideas."[60]

But if the term "general grammar" perplexed some of the students— and if certain more remote regions of France were unable to find local men qualified to teach that newfangled subject matter[61]—the cadre of professors of general grammar recruited to the central schools displayed an impressive readiness for their job, unprecedented as that job was in the history of French education. Their descriptions of the course, written to satisfy an exigent minister of the interior or printed on posters for the information of prospective pupils, followed no standard model or rote formula. Though they had common themes, the words were those of the professors themselves.[62] Perhaps the most sophisticated rendition was the semiotic one offered by Citizen Thiébault, assigned to teach the course at one of the Paris central schools. The government had, he said, substituted a chair called "general grammar" for the more traditional one in speculative philosophy to make a critical point: that insofar as philosophers have access to ideas, judgments, and mental operations, insofar as they gain familiarity with them and are able to meditate on them, they do so only by means of language.[63]

References to Condillac abound in the copious ministerial archives that document the state's oversight of the new educational system. Citizen Gattel, who taught in the central school of the Isère in Grenoble, where he numbered among his pupils the young Henri Beyle later to become the novelist Stendhal, told his superiors that insofar as the course in general grammar derived from any single thinker, it followed most closely the lines laid out in the oeuvre of Condillac.[64] A table compiled by the state bureaucrats to summarize the results of a questionnaire sent to all the professors of general grammar in the Year VII reveals that well over half reported heavy reliance on Condillac's works in preparing their lessons.[65] One even grafted onto Condillac the nationalist gloss featured in Grégoire's language project, saying that he sought to teach his pupils "how the mind of an individual or a nation becomes true or false, deep or superficial, in accordance with whether the language spoken is well or badly made."[66] Another wanted the government to buy Condillac's complete works for the central school library, complaining that its collection currently reflected the intellectual "taste of monks" and that it was unfair to expect the professors to supply the necessary holdings at their own expense.[67]

Reviewing the lesson plans of the professors of general grammar, the Council on Public Instruction called the one they received from Chambéry "a small masterpiece," adding, "It is at bottom just the doctrine of Condillac but expounded by a man capable of one day evaluating that doctrine and improving upon it."[68] Among the many adepts of Condillac should also be mentioned Citizen Merlet-Laboulaye who, precariously perched in civil-war country "between the unfortunate Vendée and the Chouans," embodied the spirit of this pedagogy by teaching both the general grammar and the botany courses at the central school in the Maine-et-Loire. Working in a garden laid out according to Linnaean classifications, Merlet-Laboulaye recognized all of his pupils as "capable of observation" and admonished them to study the plants at leisure before or after the lesson; the test of pedagogical success was the pupils' ability to identify the new plants that they encountered "without committing prejudicial errors." Small wonder that this amateur botanist referred to the material covered in his general grammar course as the "natural history of speech."[69]

That the Republic was able to enlist a sizable corps of professors of general grammar at such short notice to staff the central schools certainly bespeaks an extensive and serious dissemination of Condillac in France by the end of the Old Regime. The main locus of that dissemination was not the universities, though even in those bastions of tradition, Cartesianism had waned and the philosophy professoriate could at least entertain the tenets of Lockean empiricism.[70] Rather, insofar as it was associated with any formal institution, Condillac's epistemology seems to have flourished in the *collèges,* especially after the expulsion of the Jesuits in 1762. After that date these schools fell into the hands of orders, principally the Oratorians and Pères de la Doctrine Chrétienne, which by the mid-eighteenth century were losing their character as religious communities and taking on a new identity as secularized organizations of teachers. Their members tended to postpone or avoid altogether their ordination as Catholic priests; they were loath to wear cassocks; they mingled in the world. Their intellectual tastes ran to Enlightenment philosophy. And they tended to greet the Revolution with sympathy, more than half of them playing an active role on its behalf between 1789 and 1792. Not surprisingly, then, the central schools of the Directory recruited their faculty very heavily from among former members of these orders.[71]

The professor of general grammar at the central school of the Var emblematizes this type. Citizen Ortolan had been a teacher with the Pères de la Doctrine Chrétienne for fourteen years before the outbreak of the Revolution and was recruited to the central school shortly after its foundation. In his response to the ministerial questionnaire, he mentioned Condillac as the primary source of the instruction in general grammar that he dispensed to the adolescent boys of Toulon. Recognizing his pupils' poor preparation and, as he put it on the official poster, wanting to render himself "more useful" to his fellow citizens, he secured municipal approval to open a private course in French and Italian. Since the course mingled ordinary language instruction with training in Condillac's epistemology, the pupils would, Ortolan promised, emerge from it with "their minds fortified by the analytic method and by the knowledge of true principles." They would then be ready to embark on the public course in general grammar—where they would receive an even stronger dose of Condillac![72]

The efficacy with which professors conveyed the fundamentals of general grammar to their central school pupils no doubt varied widely. At one extreme was the experience of Citizen Magin: he said of the faithful remnant who remained in his course after two-thirds of their classmates had abandoned it that they "encouraged me more by their goodwill . . . and their industry than by their progress."[73] At the other extreme was Citizen Gattel, who so indelibly imprinted his pupil Stendhal with general grammar that in his autobiographical *Life of Henry Brulard* written some four decades later, Stendhal hailed the "excellent law on the central schools" and fondly remembered the advice of his professors, "'My child, study the *Logic* of Condillac, it is the basis of everything.'"[74] But if degrees of actual success are extremely difficult to measure, pedagogical intention is easier to discern.

Despite the highly abstract nature of general grammar, the charge of the central schools at their inception was to disseminate that novel subject matter widely and democratically. It is true that two twentieth-century historians retrospectively called the general grammar class of the central schools a "factory of the elite"[75] and that A.-L.-C. Destutt de Tracy, who wrote the basic textbook for the central schools after the Napoleonic coup d'état, contemplated separate educational regimens for the working class (*classe ouvrière*) and the intelligentsia (*classe savante*).[76] Still, the republican policymakers never envisioned general grammar as a master foundational theory to be reserved to the leaders of society and used by them to keep the mass of the population appropriately tractable. After all, students at the central schools chose their courses freely, and those students came in roughly equal numbers from the bourgeoisie and the working classes.[77]

The democratic assumptions and impulses behind the teaching of general grammar in the central schools can be seen in the comments made by professors of that subject in the materials they submitted to the Ministry of the Interior. Citizen Descoles at the central school in Nîmes noted that "the [physiological] organization of men being everywhere the same, apart from certain minor differences of no importance here, we must conclude that men are everywhere endowed with the same faculties, . . . that they receive the same impressions at the sight of or by contact with the same objects, that they have the same simple ideas arrived at in the same manner, etc." To be sure, Descoles worried about the lack of preparation of his general grammar pupils ("it is not very easy to make oneself understood when speaking a more or less abstract language to young people deficient in complex ideas"), but his egalitarian credo boosted his courage. Lack of preparation had a distinctly positive side in that "prejudices have not yet given false directions" to "fresh minds." Furthermore, the appropriate pedagogy could make any subject matter accessible to anyone. "I am convinced," he asserted confidently, "that there is a simple metaphysics within the capacity of even the youngest children. . . ."[78] Similarly, a public poster for Citizen Ortolan's private course, envisioned as a prologomenon to his general grammar course at the central school in Toulon, attested, "I will try to put within the grasp of the most mediocre minds all the most metaphysical writings" of such theorists as Condillac, Court de Gébelin, Dumarsais, and Beauzée.[79] Citizen Laurent, an ex-Oratorian, assured his bureaucratic supervisors of the ease of teaching Condillac, the "ingenious author" whose simple and precise style was readily understandable by young people—apparently even those in Laurent's general grammar class in the Haute-Saône who spelled so poorly that they could not read what they had written and had thus caused their professor to forsake dictation as a pedagogical exercise.[80] And even the class-conscious pronouncements of Destutt de Tracy after the fall of the Republic did not diverge from the principle that the working classes would, in some fashion, learn general grammar rather than being unwittingly manipulated by it. If the education of the poor was to be "distinct from" that of the comfortable classes, the distinction would reside in the depth and intensity of instruction rather than in the subject matter expounded. The poor would, Tracy stipulated, learn a "summary" and "abridgment" (*abrégé*) of what had been taught to the well-off, future savants.[81]

Nor was instruction in sensationalist theory confined during the Revolution to the adolescent age-cohort recruited by the central schools. Under the Directory, at least one private evening course in the "art of reasoning" based on "physiological observations" sprang up in Paris. The instructor, a certain Pinglin, attested that he had boiled down that indispensable art "to a single principle," which he promised to place "within the grasp of people of all ages and all mental capacities" if they congregated near the Louvre at 5:30 PM for his lessons.[82] (See Figure 2.) Pinglin, we can assume, sought a predominantly adult clientele in this forum. Another venture of his, the periodical *L'Ami des campagnes*, transferred his project of dissemination to a print medium and targeted not Parisians but rural people. His goal as editor was to make "common knowledge accessible to the least cultivated minds," and to this end he supplied not only the political news that concerned the country dweller as a citizen, the medical

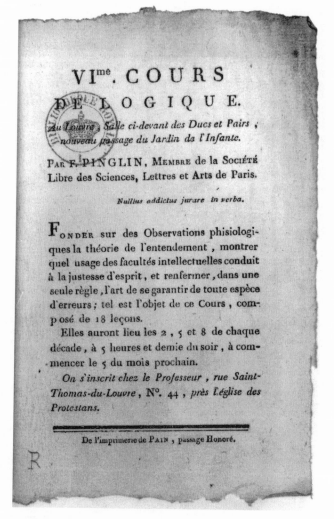

VIme. COURS DE LOGIQUE.

Au Louvre, Salle ci-devant des Ducs et Pairs , nouveau passage du Jardin de l'Infante.

PAR F. PINGLIN, MEMBRE de la SOCIÉTÉ Libre des Sciences, Lettres et Arts de Paris.

Nullius addictus jurare in verba.

FONDER sur des Observations phisiologiques la théorie de l'entendement , montrer quel usage des facultés intellectuelles conduit à la justesse d'esprit , et renfermer , dans une seule règle , l'art de se garantir de toute espèce d'erreurs ; tel est l'objet de ce Cours , composé de 18 leçons.

Elles auront lieu les 2 , 5 et 8 de chaque décade , à 5 heures et demie du soir , à commencer le 5 du mois prochain.

On s'inscrit chez le Professeur , rue Saint-Thomas-du-Louvre , N°. 44 , près l'église des Protestans.

De l'imprimerie de PAIN , passage Honoré.

Figure 2: The Popularization of Sensationalist Psychology. This handbill advertises the logic course of a freelance teacher, one F. Pinglin, held in Paris, probably under the revolutionary regime of the Directory in the closing years of the eighteenth century. Using the idiom of Condillac without mentioning him by name, Pinglin promises his prospective students that they will learn the theory and practice of correct thinking and the "art of ensuring against error" if they sign up for lessons three times a *décade* (the ten-day period that replaced the week in the revolutionary calendar). The total length of the course and Pinglin's fee are left unspecified. (Bibliothèque Nationale de France)

principles that would help him protect his health, and the literary news that would give him a patina of enlightenment, but first and foremost, in a treatise on "intellectual education" serialized over more than ten issues, the outlines of a sensationalist psychology that would "teach him to direct personally the first developments of [his children's] minds."[83] Like Destutt de Tracy, Pinglin put his faith in the *abrégé* as the means of disseminating difficult epistemological concepts among the *vulgaire*. "The more a science is perfected," he stated confidently, "the less space it takes up in a library."[84]

Pinglin was not the only self-appointed grass-roots propagator of sensationalism. In 1789 Laurent-Pierre Bérenger, a former professor of rhetoric at the *collège* of Orléans who several years before had run afoul of the royal censor because of his anticlerical writings, published a two-volume anthology of selected texts called *Esprit de Mably et de Condillac*. Featured in the Condillac volume was a condensation of the master's pedagogical classic, his plan of study for the prince of Parma.[85] Still further abbreviated, that condensation found its way into a handy forty-page pamphlet that appeared shortly after Thermidor, billed as the work of an anonymous "Citizen B***."[86] And in eerie fulfillment of Berenger's 1789 wish that powerful European nations might one day consider institutionalizing Condillac in state-sponsored schools, Berenger himself became a professor at a central school in Lyon under the Directory.[87]

Combating Imagination with Condillac's Philosophy

As was the case with Condillac himself, the administrators of the central schools believed that the subject matter that went under the name of general grammar was the best prophylactic against disorderly flights of imagination. Thus a flyer distributed in the Ariège railed against those who tried to undermine the local central school by alleging the irreligious nature of its curriculum and by touting to parents the superior virtues of the pre-Revolutionary *collèges* and of the private schools that were currently seeking to imitate them. Such backward-looking assertions were simply false:

> In the old *collèges,* young people lost a long series of years painfully learning a language that no People any longer speaks, learning words, words, nothing but words. And if they finally reached philosophy,

which is supposed to teach things, those things were most often false or uncertain notions, *imaginary systems, chimerical things devoid of reality.*[88]

Citizen Thiébault, an elderly professor of general grammar in Paris, concurred with this assessment of the "old" philosophy as recklessly exposing students to the perils of imagination. Except for a philosophy based on sensationalist psychology and the analysis of language, he declared, "Every other route threatens us with wandering in the void or in illusions." If philosophy as traditionally construed had so often led men astray, it was because "abstract conceptions" have "no purchase on man." Presumably because it revealed the man-made and ultimately sensory origins of abstract ideas, general grammar was "the sole instrument that they can use with certainty."[89] Several years later, in a published version of his curricular recommendations, Thiébault made the same anthropocentric, Condillac-inspired point with greater elegance and economy. He denounced all previous philosophical instruction as so much "hairsplitting," noting that the attempts, characteristic of speculative metaphysics, "to study the mind of man outside of man himself" doomed the philosopher to the "vast regions of the imagination," where he chased after chimeras and ended up with mad, irresoluble questions. Condillac's method of studying reason through language, by contrast, banished the imaginary from philosophy and gave the investigator "a tangible and real hold on himself."[90]

Citizen Magin, who had the demoralizing experience of watching most of his students desert his general grammar course in the Ardennes, lost none of his enthusiasm for that subject matter and later wrote of its particular suitability for the age group recruited by the central schools. Since the physiological changes associated with puberty overstimulated imagination, adolescents urgently needed general grammar for the "regulation of [their] reason." As Magin described the situation, imagination and general grammar were opposing forces:

> The topic of this course [general grammar] is the study of the intellectual faculties of man; its goal is to learn how to direct them toward the truth and to lead the human understanding to its full perfection. The professor receives his pupils during the precious time of adolescence, when nature completes its development of the organs of sensitivity, renders them susceptible to all impressions and foments an unavoidable revolution in the mind and heart of man. This revolution

must be guided with all the more attention because its consequences are dangerous and because, *with imagination seizing hold of every perception, the linkage of ideas is carried out in a bizarre manner, unlike anything that occurred in childhood.*[91]

Responsibility toward Possessors of a Wayward Imagination

Chapter 1 showed that eighteenth-century discourse identified certain groups as particularly vulnerable to disorders and flights of the imagination: workers, women, and children allegedly had a special propensity to flee the harsh demands of reality and to seek shelter in more congenial, imaginary worlds. Hence we should not be surprised to find that, once the Revolutionaries embarked upon the project of citizen-making through schooling the imagination, they not only addressed their efforts to the population at large but also acknowledged that certain groups, starting from a lower baseline of rationality, demanded special consideration and protection. Thus the Société des amis des noirs, lobbying during the early years of the Revolution for the abolition of the French slave trade and of slavery on French-owned Caribbean islands, leveled the accusation that the slave trade was nefarious in part because of its psychological dynamics. Its agents preyed on the African native, who was of weaker than average mental constitution and whose imagination was so susceptible to stimulation that he could be easily induced to act against his own best interests. Said the deputy Viefville des Essars in a speech to the Assembly in 1791:

> It is laughable to suggest that the slaves that we take from the coasts of Africa have all been condemned to torture or other such painful punishments. Let us be honest: *we excite the desires of these simple men by all sorts of ruses, by a host of objects that we present to their eyes to seduce their imaginations.* Thus we force these unfortunates, who otherwise have nothing to offer us, to make constant war on one another in order to procure persons to sell to us.

So crass, reprehensible, *and* effective was the psychological manipulation that undergirded the slave trade that African merchants frequently went so far as to sell their own children "when they have no other means of satisfying the passions that we have aroused in them and of which they would still be ignorant if they had not had the misfortune of knowing us."[92] Viefville spoke in the first person plural, taking "we" to mean not only white European slave traders but the societies that condoned them. He thus invited all his fellow deputies and fellow citizens to share in the blame for this unconscionable exploitation of psychological weakness.

The motif of the unevenly matched psychological contest can be found in much Revolutionary discourse, and the standard Revolutionary solution to the problem of hyperactive imaginations in flimsy mental constitutions is—as the central schools with their general grammar courses exemplify most perfectly—education. The nation had an obligation to fortify the mental faculties of all its citizens so that they would not be in the generic position of African natives yielding themselves up, with disastrous consequences, to clever people who appeal to their imaginations by means of their senses. A classic Revolutionary text setting forth this obligation is Condorcet's *Sketch for a Historical Picture of the Progress of the Human Mind* (1793). The discovery of the doctrine of natural rights, says Condorcet, means that men no longer "dare to divide humanity into two races, the one fated to rule, the other to obey, *the one to deceive, the other to be deceived.*" He later restates this point in a favorite Enlightenment idiom, that of dupes and charlatans. A republican government can reasonably hope to attain among its citizenry not a complete equality of education or mental acuity but that adequate degree of equality that will enable every citizen

> to be no longer the dupe of those popular errors which torment man with superstitious fears and chimerical hopes; to defend himself against prejudice by the strength of his reason alone; and, finally, to escape the deceits of charlatans who would lay snares for his fortune, his health, his freedom of thought and his conscience. . . .

The duality between "dupes and charlatans, . . . clever men and men readily deceived" is, Condorcet informs us, a universal one, arising everywhere as a consequence of the naturally unequal abilities of human beings. But a government committed to the rights of man can, for all practical purposes, eradicate that duality, converting the difference between charlatans and dupes to that between "men of learning and upright men who know the value of learning without being dazzled by it."[93]

So, too, did a less lofty thinker, the lecturer and journalist Pinglin, find in an education in Condillac-style logic a protection of weaker minds from dupery and its painful sequelae. In Pinglin's view, most people qualified as weaker minds. The average run of mankind was "naturally docile, trusting, credulous," impressed by appearance, deluded even by figurative speech. Theirs was a condition of great vulnerability. When such a person "allows himself to be duped, he becomes misanthropic, no longer sees an honest man anywhere but believes himself surrounded by rascals. He takes his bad humor for philosophy. . . ."[94] Hence the necessity of a course in logic with M. Pinglin, which would level the playing field between dupes and charlatans and create an effective, though imperfect, mental equality among members of the citizen body.

The same topos of the unevenly matched psychological contest between dupes and charlatans was part of the repertory of Louis-Marie La Reveillière-Lépaux, a minor Revolutionary politician who, after helping to draft the Constitution of 1795, was named to the five-man Directory that served as the executive branch of the new regime. At that juncture, he championed the survival of the republican festivals but wished to supplement them by an austere deistic religion, one utterly lacking the pomp and sensory appeal of Catholicism as well as its state support. The chief beneficiaries of this religion would be the popular classes, who would be saved by it from descent into dupery. Without it, "they will throw themselves into the crudest superstitions because *they will always find charlatans to alarm their imaginations and profit at their expense.*" The vulnerability of the people stood in stark contrast to the imperviousness of the "well-educated man accustomed to reflection." Such a man "drew from his studies and from all the circumstances of his life . . . a rational love of order" that preserved his psychological autonomy and enabled him to "exercise all the social virtues without religious belief or worship." But the multitude lacked this acquired psychological ballast; their minds were in chaotic flux. Unless provided by others with a fulcrum, "they will lose themselves in the surge of their ideas."[95]

Sensationalism Reconsidered

The two chapters comprising Part I of this book have told a seemingly self-contained success story. Through the lens of the theory of sensationalist psychology, the growing pains of modernity were perceived and interpreted in eighteenth-century France as environmental changes threatening to overstimulate the mental faculty of imagination. Once the Revolution endorsed and actualized those changes, that same psychological theory became a scientific resource, deliberately mined for the purposes of stabilizing the new laissez-faire, republican polity—at once prudently containing individual imagination, cementing the social bond and infusing it with patriotism, and committing the citizenry to the egalitarian ideal that everyone should have the capacity for autonomous reasoning, that the nation should not be divided into charlatans and dupes.

But given the brevity of the sensationalist experiment in political culture, its success must be regarded as more logical than actual. On its own terms, it should have worked. It was, however, so short-lived that no one could know whether it actually worked and would continue to work over the long haul. The demise of the Directory and the dismantling of central schools and Revolutionary festivals signaled its decisive end. What remained was a dual legacy: a widely shared horror of the political instability that the Revolution had unleashed; and a belief that psychological theory could be pressed into the service of sociopolitical engineering.

At the same time, certain observers turned against the type of reasoning so powerfully exemplified in the Revolutionary psychological experiment. Revolutionary politicians had, after all, targeted a single faculty, the imagination. That they had adopted such a strategy evidenced a conception of the psyche in which the parts overshadowed the whole and could be readily detached from it. The Revolutionaries had, in a word, ignored the totality called the self. If psychological theory was to figure in the post-Revolutionary solution, this argument ran, then the very absence of self-talk in *sensationalist* psychological theory had to be seen as contributing to the problem.

II

THE POLITICS OF SELFHOOD

3

Is There a Self in This Mental Apparatus?

The difficult thing is forming the *moi*.
                                        Sieyès, 1773

No one could have been more committed to the psychology of Condillac than the minor historical figure Dieudonné Thiébault, who made a cameo appearance in Chapter 2. A professor of general grammar at a Paris central school under the Directory, Thiébault had earlier done a stint in Berlin teaching the sensationalist epistemology at a new school personally founded by Frederick the Great to foster the spread of enlightenment in his domains. Hence it is of no little moment that, addressing the French fathers who had sent their sons to the central schools in the Year XI (1802), he listed among the goals of secondary education that the students become "accustomed to that inner life (*vie intérieure*) that assures us of so many resources in times of trouble and vexation," that they "learn to descend into their own thoughts and to search deeply (*fouiller*) in their heads, everyone's richest and most fecund book, the most important for all of us to study."[1] In other words, Thiébault, the veritable ideal type of the sensationalist psychologist, referred to the psychic apparatus by invoking the metaphors of depth, excavation, and interiority that we typically associate with that entity called the self, indeed with a highly elaborated, modern version of that entity.[2] Such a self was, we might infer, part and parcel of sensationalist psychology, a psychic space grounded and secured by its tenets.

But in fact the relationship between the self and sensationalist psychology was far more complicated than Thiébault's casual remarks intimated. Misgivings about that relationship clouded discussions of

sensationalism, prompting certain contemporaries to doubt the ade-
quacy of the sensationalist model of the mind for the purposes they
wished it to serve. This chapter will survey the early installments of
those debates, thus marking the transition to Part II of this book by
pushing the concept of the self into the foreground of the story. Spanning the long period from the 1690s to the 1820s, the chapter begins
with the dawning recognition that the newly minted theory of sensationalism might not be entirely hospitable to the entity that John Locke,
undertaking a bit of influential neologism, called a "self"; it ends with
Maine de Biran, who, in a series of highly original manuscripts, abandoned sensationalism for the express purpose of accommodating a
robust self. The chapter thus takes up the theme, highlighted in the
Introduction to this book, of the gap between psychological interiority
in general and self-talk as a particular subset of it.

Two analytically separate questions are in play in a consideration of
the relationship of sensationalism to the self. The first is whether belief
in the principles of sensationalist psychology gave adherents a particular optic through which to experience psychic inwardness—both their
own and, by extension, that of their fellows. Was there, in other words,
a distinctively sensationalist encounter with what I have called in the
Introduction the individuated mental stuff? Material cited in Chapter 2
has already suggested an affirmative answer to that question. In inventing a new republican culture replete with civic festivals, a revamped calendar, and renamed city streets, the Revolutionaries had conceptualized
the individual citizen along sensationalist lines. They postulated a being
whose convictions could be shaped by means of selective sensory bombardment, whose psyche, sensitive to the point of quivering, existed
(for good or ill) in a state of porous exchange with the environment.

A characteristically sensationalist confrontation with the individuated
mental stuff can also be found, to cite just two more examples, in the
writings of the Revolutionary politician La Reveillière-Lépaux and the
novelist Stendhal. La Reveillière was entirely typical of his confreres in
his employment of the rhetoric of sensationalist psychology to argue for
the efficacy of the national festivals[3] and, as discussed in Chapter 2, to
explain the difference between charlatans and dupes. Less typically, he
also left behind evidence of his application of that same psychology to
himself. His memoirs revealed that he had always "been inclined to a
deep melancholy which . . . has given my moral feelings a compelling

force" and that the faculty of imagination was likewise prominent in his mental life, having consistently "produced singular effects on me." Recalling an unshakable conviction, acquired during a childhood promenade around the chateau of Angers, that he could see the living bodies of St. John the Baptist and the lamb, he mentioned the episode as an instance of the way "our senses are abused by that remarkable faculty called imagination."[4] To such episodes he traced his anticlerical politics and his belief in psychological engineering. Firsthand experience of the potent combination of melancholy and overactive imagination that Condillac had flagged as undermining an individual's ability to distinguish fact from fantasy alerted him to the collective problem posed by religion:

> I have been very incorrectly labeled an enemy of all religion. Born, perhaps unfortunately, with an excessive sensibility, *endowed with an active imagination,* and prone to a deep and chronic melancholy, how could I not have been susceptible to religious ideas? Religious feeling was never foreign to me. But if I have a warm heart and a passionate expressiveness, I have a cool head, and that has perhaps protected me from the errors into which dispositions like mine are often led.[5]

The novelist Stendhal, who retrospectively praised the instruction in Condillac he had received at the central school of Grenoble, used sensationalism as a resource in creating his literary characters. The first time that the young, unpolished Julien Sorel attempts to speak from his heart to Madame de Rênal, the mistress of the house in which he serves as tutor, he effusively describes surgical operations whose gory details cause his beloved lady to cringe. Stendhal comments that Julien's outlandish conduct derived quite logically from the fact that the only person whom he had ever before addressed with complete sincerity was his mentor, a surgeon in the Napoleonic army, who often regaled him with stories of his wartime ministrations to wounded soldiers. Hence surgery automatically sprang to Julien's mind as an appropriate topic for a conversation in which no defensive masks or postures would intervene between him and his interlocutor. Julien becomes a figure of fun because the mechanical principles of association that invariably guide human thought processes effectively sabotage his romantic intentions.[6] And Julien was a representative instance of the Stendhalian species: *un mouvement machinal* always governed the lover's declarations to the beloved,

Stendhal announced in his "book of *idéologie*," the nonfictional *De l'amour* (1822).[7] Indeed the trope most characteristic of Stendhal's prose—irony—may be enmeshed in his sensationalist presuppositions, which routinely drew his attention to the disjuncture between the loftiness and delicacy of human aspiration and the coarsely mechanical and corporeal instrument of thought upon which all human beings necessarily rely.[8]

The ability of sensationalism to provide contemporaries with a distinctive psychological language, and hence a distinctively inflected experience of mental inwardness, thus seems clear. But a second, more stringent question can be posed—and, indeed, was posed at the time. What is the overall *structure* of the individuated mental stuff when it is described by means of the language of sensationalism? Does the mental apparatus postulated by sensationalism actually contain a self? And if so, is it a true self (sturdy, unitary) or a pallid simulacrum of a self (flimsy, fragmented)? This is a very different question from the first one. A theory can facilitate psychological inwardness and give it a characteristic stamp without forcefully conceptualizing the individuated mental stuff as a centered totality. Inwardness can be a pointillist attitude; it can focus on a specific mental trait or mental conflict, or a specific mental faculty like imagination, while ignoring or leaving blurry the contours of the mental entity as a whole. Individuals can be habitués of the inner life without seriously engaging in self-talk.

Certainly the cases of La Reveillière-Lépaux, Stendhal's Julien Sorel, and the citizens envisioned by the architects of republican political culture all suggest that a psychic apparatus conceived on sensationalist lines had conspicuous weaknesses and vulnerabilities, that it lacked protective armor and full control over its processes—that it was, in a word, disaggregated.[9] But the question of what kind of self was consonant with sensationalism did not initially arise from pondering concrete exemplars such as these. It arose rather as a highly abstract, philosophical investigation in the pages of Locke's *An Essay on Human Understanding,* the late seventeenth-century treatise that crystallized the sensationalist paradigm. In that form it occupied philosophers intermittently for a good two centuries, becoming nothing less than one of the classic questions of modern Western philosophy as well as a standard reference point for many of the psychological theorists who figure in this book. To be sure, the question generated a rarefied, technical disputation among philosophers that most often seemed irrelevant to mundane concerns. Thus one late twentieth-century analytic philosopher, crediting Locke with setting the terms of the modern debate on personal identity, could attribute Locke's pioneering role in this regard to "his vital insight that different sortal terms convey different criteria of identity."[10] But it is not such technical glosses on the debate that ultimately interest me here. Rather, as the eighteenth- and especially nineteenth-century developments traced in this book indicate, the appearance of Locke's question on the horizon of philosophy heralded a sea-change of some consequence for ordinary people: the increasing salience of the self as an everyday category. It is precisely one of the themes of this book that (at least in the historical context under discussion here) the propositions of philosophical psychology had, through a series of institutional mediations, definite repercussions on lived experience.

The Lockean Self and Its Critics

Locke's question was originally a question posed to him by his friend William Molyneux. In a letter of 1693 replying to Locke's request for "any new heads from logick or metaphysicks to be inserted" in the forthcoming edition of the *Essay*, Molyneux urged that a discussion of what he called the *principium individuationis*—the distinct, indivisible nature of our personal mental stuff—be included.[11] That small historical datum demonstrates on its own the gap that can exist between turning inward and engaging in self-talk. Apparently the consummately inward-turning thinker, who in the first edition of his *Essay* (1690) had painstakingly derived the numerous features of a human mind from sensationalist suppositions, had never thought to ask how he could account for a self in his model. Only as a result of his friend's intervention did the now celebrated chapter "Of Identity and Diversity" make its appearance in the second edition of 1694.

In that chapter Locke sizes up the implications for the status of the human person of his jettisoning of Cartesianism. If, he asks in effect, we discard the Cartesian contention that the indivisibility of the self or thinking substance is a self-evident, a priori truth and postulate instead that all our mental contents are derived from a combination of discrete sensory impressions and our mind's ability to reflect on its own operations, what is the ground of selfhood, of (in Locke's words) the "sameness of a rational Being" that persists through space and time?[12] Why should a human psychic apparatus constructed bit by bit from atomistic sensations ever constitute or house that stable, unitary entity entitled to the name of self?

In a long and rambling argument (Book 2, Chapter 27, is nothing if not a difficult text), Locke located the sought-after ground of selfhood in a combination of consciousness and memory. We cannot think, feel, sense, or will without being reflexively aware that we do so, he asserted, and the consciousness inevitably accompanying our mental processes "makes every one to be, what he calls *self;* and thereby distinguishes himself from all other thinking things, [and] in this alone consists *personal Identity.*" Still, in order to ensure this identity, memory must be added to consciousness because, as Locke readily conceded, consciousness is discontinuous, "being interrupted always by forgetfulness, there being no moment of our Lives wherein we have the whole train of our past Actions before our Eyes in one view." Sometimes sheer absorption in present thoughts momentarily obliterates our awareness of our past selves; once a day consciousness itself is suspended in sleep. Hence memory must be enlisted to fill in the gaps and restore that unbroken continuity of consciousness to which Locke gave the name of self.[13]

But Locke probed further, submitting as a more strenuous objection to the coherence of the concept of selfhood the possibility that certain portions of lived experience might be lost beyond retrieval—those, for example, that occur when an individual is drunk or in a state of somnambulism. Locke now salvaged his basic contention about the persistence of the self through recourse to what he termed a "forensick" conception. A court of law, he said, lacks any sure means of assessing the authenticity of a plea that an accused should be found not guilty for reason of drunkenness or sleepwalking. Hence convention deems that the court avoid the issue entirely, ignoring any alleged gap in consciousness and, hence, any lapse in moral responsibility attendant upon it, and punishing the person in question on the purely factual basis of the crime committed by his hand. But this pragmatic arrangement lasts only as long as our temporal existence, becoming irrelevant on the Day of Judgment, "wherein the Secrets of all Hearts shall be laid open . . . [and] no one shall be made to answer for what he knows nothing of; but shall receive his Doom, his Conscience accusing or excusing him." Presumably, then, the postulation of the unity of the self was for Locke a necessary expedient to sustain the concept of moral responsibility in daily life in face of the ultimate imperfection of our terrestrial knowledge about other people's states of consciousness.[14] Locke had thus accurately pinpointed morality as a major area of concern to himself and to consumers of his psychology more generally: it was to ensure moral behavior that he believed a unified self indispensable.

As tentative and full of loose ends as this winding argument might seem, Locke audaciously presented it in the *Essay* as definitive, laying all doubts to rest. Not surprisingly, however, his claim that a stable and coherent self could have its genesis solely in sensation and reflection soon met with a barrage of criticism. In Britain, Bishop Joseph Butler and Thomas Reid attacked Locke's argument as circular, presupposing what it allegedly proved by defining personal identity as consciousness of personal identity.[15] In his *Treatise of Human Nature* (1739–40) David Hume began by noting, with historical acuity, the brouhaha that had only recently surrounded personal identity: it had become, he wrote, a "great a question in philosophy, especially of late years in England, where all the abstruser sciences are study'd with a peculiar ardour and application." He went on to offer a more elaborate critique of Locke than had Butler and Reid—and one all the more devastating because, unlike those two earlier critics, he shared Locke's sensationalist epistemology.

Postulating that there "must be some one impression, that gives rise to every real idea," Hume argued that no such single impression could possibly be found to undergird the idea of a self. Ordinary reflection revealed that far from being unitary creatures who are "every moment intimately conscious of what we call our SELF," we are instead "nothing but a bundle or collection of different perceptions, which succeed each other with an inconceivable rapidity, and are in a perpetual flux and movement." Hume therefore concluded that the self was a "fiction" or "artifice." As such, it was a construction of that most unreliable of human mental faculties, the imagination, here aided by our characteristically sloppy perceptual processes, which tended to ignore slight differences between objects and to register sameness where none existed.[16] Hume's argument bears a family resemblance to that of the critics of Quesnay whom we encountered in Chapter 2. A new scientific system—be it political economy or sensationalist psychology—that is supposed, by dint of its remade and well-made language, to elude customary error and provide reliable knowledge is turned on its head and exposed as a product of error-prone imagination.

In France, some of Locke's earliest readers responded to his argument for personal identity in what is to modern ears a surprising register. Accepting the proof at face value, they lauded the chapter added to the second edition of the *Essay* because it showed sensationalism to be fundamentally consistent with the Christian doctrine of the resurrection of the flesh![17] More usual, however, was the diametrically opposite reaction: a critique of the Lockean self undertaken by Catholic Cartesians intent on exposing the immoral and atheistic implications of sensationalism.[18] Preaching to the converted, these critics tended to be more declamatory than analytic. Their main point was that a sensationalist epistemology could never satisfactorily ground a self recognizable as such to a Catholic. Hence recourse to a philosophy that postulated a self given all at once as a spiritual substance, instead of being assembled serially from material sensations, was necessary.

The Reverend Father Hayer readily admitted that the alleged unity of *physical* bodies was "only an abstraction of our minds." But, he continued, in the essentially *spiritual* creature that is a human being, "we find a really and substantially indivisible center, where everything that interests man is brought back to unity." And how, one might ask, do we find this center, which Hayer called the *moi?* Hayer's facile answer is that the situation simply could not be otherwise. "If for this unique self *(moi)* we substituted a multitude of selves, what strange confusion would result!" The hypothetical multiple individual would be like an "anarchical society" composed of isolated, self-absorbed parts functioning as wholes, each in perfect ignorance of the needs of the others.[19]

Hayer went on to invoke other so-called proofs of the unified and spiritual nature of the human *moi,* some of which relied—as was typical of this mode of Catholic-Cartesian apologetic—on the self-evidence of introspective experience. ("Having retreated into a pleasant solitude, solely occupied with the desire of knowing myself, I begin to consider with the eyes of my soul, my soul itself. That is to say, my *moi,* folding back upon itself, . . . contemplates itself. . . .")[20] Introspection and the psychic reality to which it irrefutably bears witness were also at the heart of the abbé de Lignac's multivolume attack on the "doctrine of Locke" and its theological implications. In his preface, in which he also states his intention to enlist contemporary philosophy to vindicate the

wisdom of the Church Fathers, Lignac explains and justifies his confident, declamatory tone. "Just as a witness ought to be firm when, before
the court, he makes a deposition concerning what he has seen, . . . so
ought I to refrain from weighing pros and cons or appearing to have the
slightest doubt about the verities I discover."[21] Lignac gave his book a
title consonant with that motif: he called it "Testimony of the *sens
intime.*"

Lignac's role as an apologist was more complicated than that of Hayer
because, as he confides to the reader much later in the book, he had
once seriously flirted with Locke's argument. He had believed that the
âme could be justly compared to a tabula rasa or a "canvas prepared by
the Painter for painting whatever it pleased him to imagine," that the
soul was in fact "a pure capacity suitable for receiving any sentiment or
thought." He had gone so far as to accept Locke's characterization of
sleep as an authentic interruption of the consciousness required to sustain personal identity. But the fatal flaws of the Lockean position eventually became clear to him as a Catholic. He realized that a group of
simple, indivisible parts, each sensing its own "numerical identity"—
Lignac is apparently referring here to the discrete sensory impingements
postulated by Locke—would cast doubt on personal identity because it
would contain "nothing that would sense the numerical identity of the
mass." Armed with this understanding, he then refuted Locke by affirming that the *sens intime,* the mental attribute roughly equivalent to what
Locke called reflection, did not operate (as Locke's reflection did) by
adding up discrete sensations; it did not construct personal identity by a
process of assemblage. Rather it apprehended all at once and as a self-
evident whole the invariable spiritual substance that was the soul and
that served as the stable foundation of all a person's multifarious
thoughts, sensations, and affections.

The key to Lignac's refutation was the distinction between Lockean
reflection and the *sens intime,* between the sensationalist's perception
and addition of atomistic parts and his own apprehension of the whole.
Lignac knew that the *sens intime* functioned in this holistic manner
through his introspective experience of it, which he supposed was representative of the experience of mankind in general. ("If this experience
is peculiar to me, I am wrong in proposing it to the public as the sole
means of knowing the essence of the soul; but if it is common to me and
all other men. . . .") Once he had nailed down the *sens intime* in this

way, Locke's objections about sleep as an interruption of consciousness vanished. He realized that, although he experienced deep sleep or even religious meditation as a void (*dénuement*) "similar to the state of death," he in fact conserved upon awakening a memory of that "inert" interval of time and hence knew himself to be the same person who had lived through it. As Lignac explains this basic difference between Locke's dubious power of reflection and his own *sens intime*, from which the principles of Catholic orthodoxy happily flow, "I sense myself perceiving while perceiving something, as Locke says. But what Locke does not say is that, when perceiving the letters that I am now tracing, I sense myself as the same being who received his first writing lessons so many years ago."[22]

Condillac and the Minimalist Self

While Locke, once alerted by Molyneux, recognized the magnitude of the problem of personal identity for the sensationalist epistemology and spun out a long and tortuous argument attempting to resolve it, his French successor, dependent on Locke in so many other ways, displayed an odd and surprising nonchalance about the unity of the self. In fact, Condillac's first psychological treatise, the *Essai sur l'origine des connaissances humaines* (1746), mentioned the self only in passing. In the course of describing the generation of the various mental operations from the primal capacity for sensation, Condillac paused to observe that the operation of reminiscence enables us to preserve the sequential linkage between perceptions that we have experienced at different moments in time. As such, he opined, reminiscence is a necessary condition for a persisting, unified self. "If this linkage were each night interrupted, I would so to speak begin life anew each day, and no one could convince me that today's *moi* was the *moi* of the day before." Condillac then went on to analyze two distinct aspects of reminiscence, one that "makes us recognize our own being," the other that "makes us recognize the perceptions that are there repeated." The first of those two phrases thus tersely and elliptically predicated selfhood on memory, apparently identifying memory as its sufficient condition. Yet Condillac failed to acknowledge the immensity of that claim, which went even farther than Locke's comparable one.[23] Invoking the dual principles of sensation and reflection to account for the contents of a fully developed mind, Locke based the self on both memory (construed as a direct development of sensation) and reflection. Condillac aimed at greater parsimony and, by attributing the invention of linguistic signs to the elementary mental faculties, sought to make do with sensation alone.[24] Hence Condillac's minimalist self relied solely on memory.

By the time of his second psychological treatise, the *Traité des sensations* (1754), Condillac was somewhat more deliberate in his treatment of the self, but he still disposed of that topic promptly and without obvious intellectual agony. Condillac's hypothetical case history of a statue gradually endowed with each of the five senses included, in Book I (in which the statue's exclusive sensory organ is his nose), a succinct chapter entitled "Of the *Moi,* or of the Personality of a Man Limited to the Sense of Smell." Here once again, selfhood and memory are tightly bound. The statue, we are told, could not say "I" at the moment when it first experienced an odor. "Insofar as a being does not change, it exists without any folding back on itself. But insofar as it changes, it judges that it is still in some manner the same as it previously was, and it says *moi.*" Condillac then recasts this point in a stunningly pared down definition of the self: the "*moi* is nothing but the collection of the sensations that [the statue or person] experiences and of those that memory recalls to it. In a word, it is the simultaneous consciousness of what [the statue or person] is and the memory of what it was."[25]

Condillac thus seemed oblivious to the controversy swirling around Locke's concept of personal identity, curiously detached from the concerns that so passionately exercised others in his intellectual community. He engaged neither the aggressive French Catholic critics of that concept nor Hume, whose *Treatise* was not translated into French during the eighteenth century.[26] With respect to the former, he seems to have shied away from polemics on religious matters. His reply to Lignac's 1756 critique of his *Traité des animaux,* for example, counsels the Catholic apologist simply to accept or reject a philosophical argument on its internal merits, bracketing its doctrinal consequences. A valid argument, Condillac promises, will never harbor danger for religion because "Truth cannot be contrary to truth."[27]

With respect to Hume, whose *Treatise* he probably never read, Condillac is in the odd, almost perverse position of appearing to side with Locke about the cogency of a self founded on sensations while sounding a great deal like Locke's Scottish detractor. The very same image of the mind as a "collection" of fleeting sensations and perceptions, which Hume deliberately employs to damn Locke's theory of personal identity, is employed by Condillac in a completely neutral register, simply to describe the *moi* as Condillac believes it is, without commentary on the cogency or absurdity of the concept. For Hume, the presumed fact that the self is nothing but an arbitrary collection of sensations and their by-products reveals the fictive nature and hence the scandalous bankruptcy of Locke's claims about personal identity. But for Condillac, the self as an empty space, as the theatrical stage (to use Hume's metaphor)[28] where a succession of sensory events are momentarily enacted, seems all the self that he could ever envision. Condillac evinces no discomfort, certainly no horror, with the flimsiness and lack of grandeur of such a self. He behaves much like the intrepid truth seeker, the unflinching philosopher committed to exploring the limits of human knowledge at any cost, that he would later depict in his reply to Lignac.

Somewhat comically, Condillac's only affirmation of the unity of the *moi* occurred not in his treatises on the human psychic apparatus, where it logically belonged, but in their bestial analogue, the *Traité des animaux* (1755). There he seems to have inadvertently backed into such an affirmation in the course of criticizing his sometime rival, the comte de Buffon. Known today as a taxonomist of the animal kingdom, Buffon had in his own era an additional reputation as a psychologist. In the *Discours sur la nature des animaux* (1753) that opens the fourth volume of his *Histoire naturelle,* he even offered a full-blown definition of the *moi*—an idiosyncratic definition blending Cartesian and sensationalist elements.[29] Careful to reserve possession of a *moi* to humans even though he granted animals consciousness of their own existence, Buffon followed the sensationalists in binding selfhood closely to memory. Beasts are conscious only of their present existence, he said, while the specifically human *moi* has a decisive temporal element, complementing the animals' perpetual present with "memory of our past existence." But Buffon also maintained a Cartesian allegiance, insisting that human beings, as instances of "homo duplex," were formed through two types of sensation, a purely material or corporeal one, which they shared with beasts, and a spiritual one, which was unique to them as a possessors of a soul (*âme*).[30]

Angrily, Condillac set out to refute Buffon's dual sensation theory. His crowning refutation concerned the implications of that theory for the unity of the self:

> [I]f one were to admit these two kinds of sensation, it seems to me that those of the body would never modify the soul and those of the soul would never modify the body. There would thus be in each man two selves (*moi*), two persons which, having nothing in common in their manner of feeling (*sentir*), could have no commerce with one another. Each would exist in absolute ignorance of what transpired in the other.

There is thus no doubt in Condillac's mind that the premises of sensationalist psychology, when not perverted by Buffon's odd brand of dualism, can undergird a unified self. "The unity of the person necessarily supposes the unity of the sensing entity," he says, implicitly denying that such unity might require the importation of some suprasensory principle.[31] His is an argument rich in irony for the philosophically sophisticated reader, for it turns on its head the argument that seventeenth-century Cartesians like Hayer mounted against Locke: remember the specter of the hypothetical multiply selved individual that Hayer raised as part of his denunciation of Locke's sensationalism. In Condillac's somewhat carnavalesque rendition of philosophical polemic, monism unproblematically produces a unified self, while Buffon's Cartesian-inflected dualism endows the individual with a grotesque double personality. Most important for our purposes, these passages are an aberration in Condillac's *oeuvre*. He seems to have gotten involved in the debate about the unity of the sensationalist self unintentionally, only because he felt compelled to rebut Buffon, not because he believed that the debate had much intrinsic worth.

New Terminology: From *Ame* to *Moi*

The increasing interest in the self evinced by Locke's famous chapter and by the eighteenth-century philosophers who parsed it was accompanied by a shift in French vocabulary. The traditional term *âme*, usually translated by the English "soul," but in fact combining the meanings of soul, mind, spirit, mental life, and consciousness, gradually gave way to the term *moi*, which was in turn eventually replaced by the nominal form, *le moi*.[32]

The *Encyclopédie* of Diderot and d'Alembert reflects the status quo ante. The long article "Ame" defines that time-honored term as "a principle endowed with consciousness and feeling" and goes on to ponder, with reference to Western philosophy from the ancient Egyptians and Greeks forward, whether soul is a pure quality or a substance, how it is related to the divinity, and in what sorts of beings it resides. Unlike the species-specific "self," always reserved for humans, *âme* was potentially more capacious in its reference: hence the old quarrel that could still rage during the Enlightenment over the existence of an animal soul, or *âme des bêtes*. By contrast to the article "Ame," the article "Moi" in the *Encyclopédie* concerns nothing so elevated as consciousness. Only a few paragraphs in length, it makes short work of a suspect term whose sole meaning is grammatical:

> MOI   It has been contended that this personal pronoun has the same meaning as the *je* or as the Latin *ego*. The *je* has been condemned by the word *egotism*, but that does not prevent it from being suitable on certain occasions. It follows still less that the *moi* cannot sometimes be sublime or admirably placed. Here are some examples. . . .[33]

In fact, this article was already out of date when it was first published in 1765. For as the eighteenth-century French texts just cited make plain, the term *moi* had, by mid-century, expanded its meaning beyond the workaday first-person pronoun; in philosophical discourse of both the Cartesian and sensationalist varieties, it was being used as a noun to denote the human being's individuated mental stuff. It was not, however, being so used in any consistent fashion. On the one hand, Condillac's 1746 *Essai* implicitly defined the *moi* as that aspect of the *âme* that has cognizance of its persisting sameness and is the locus of personal identity.[34] On the other hand, both Hayer and Lignac, as quoted earlier, used *moi* and *âme* as synonyms and seemed simply to equate the spiritual substance with the sense of personal identity. In addition, at least one eighteenth-century figure scrupulously avoided using the term *moi* altogether to refer to enduring personal identity: Locke's first French translator, the Huguenot emigré to England, Pierre Coste. In a fascinating footnote to his translation of the chapter "Of Identity and Diversity" of Locke's *Essay*, Coste explained why he had selected the terms *le soi* and *soi-même* to translate Locke's "self." One reason for his choice was the indelible coloration that Pascal had, in Coste's view at least, imparted to the term *le moi;* the other reason was Locke's own neologizing in English:

> The *moi* of Monsieur Pascal in some manner authorizes me to make use of the words *soy, soy-même,* to express the sentiment that each one has within himself that he is the same. Or, better put, I was obliged to do so by an indispensable necessity, for I would not know how otherwise to express the meaning of my author, who has taken a parallel liberty in his language. The roundabout terms I would have to employ on this occasion would clutter the prose and perhaps render it completely unintelligible.[35]

In some famous passages in his *Pensées,* Pascal used the noun *moi* to refer to the fallen self that had not yet found God. "The *moi* is hateful (*haïssable*)," he declared bluntly. Its hatefulness derived from its exclusive self-love ("it makes itself the center of everything") and from its desire to rule tyrannically over others. One version of the *Pensées* had Pascal pronouncing the rhetorical rule, similar to the one later disputed in the *Encyclopédie* article "Moi," that an "*honnête homme* ought to avoid . . . using the words 'je' and 'moi.'" In Pascal's theological scheme, conversion to the love of God would bring about not merely a forgetfulness of the *moi* but a total annihilation of it.[36] The noun *moi* was so thoroughly imbued with these Pascalian associations for Coste that he regarded it as inappropriate to signify the respectable entity, the bearer of moral responsibility, that was the Lockean self.

But while Coste is basically correct that Locke's "self" was a philosophical neologism in English,[37] the French *moi* as a philosophical equivalent, or near-equivalent, of *âme* antedated Locke and appears to have been the contribution of no less a thinker than Descartes.[38] In the paragraph of the *Discours de la méthode* (1637) immediately following the celebrated announcement, "I think, therefore I am," Descartes set forth his terminology: "This *Moy,* that is to say the *Ame* by which I am what I am, is entirely distinct from and easier to know than the body."[39] The successive paragraphs of this text are larded with uses of *moi* lacking an article: "thoughts that I had of several other things outside of *moy,* like the sky, earth, light, heat . . ."; questions about whether these things were "superior to *moy*" or perhaps "in *moy.*"[40]

Moi as a philosophical term was thus both relatively novel in the eighteenth century and shot through with a fundamental ambiguity: it referred both to the Cartesian self, that unextended and hence indivisible *res cogitans* given all at once to consciousness as a self-evident truth, and to the more flimsy and tentative Lockean self, that temporal accumulation of sensory impressions whose unity might be open to question. The increasingly widespread use of the term thus indicated a growing interest in the totality formed by individuated mental stuff without expressing a preference between its robust Cartesian variety and its precarious sensationalist one.

The Deaccentuated Self of Later Sensationalism

Although French sensationalists participated in the linguistic shift that replaced the premodern *âme* with the modern *moi,* and although, when backed into a corner, Condillac explicitly asserted the fundamental unity of a self assembled from discrete sensations, sensationalist psychology can hardly be said to have emphasized the concept of the self. In the final analysis, that concept seems to have occupied a decidedly peripheral place in Condillac's own vision of things. His posthumously published *Dictionnaire des synonymes* contained no entry at all for the term *moi.*[41] The theorists and pedagogues he inspired likewise relegated the self to the bottom of their conceptual toolboxes.

The national archives of the central schools suggest that very few of the cadre of general grammar professors bothered to include an exposition of the *moi* in their courses. Citizen Baradère, who sent the minister of education a particularly copious set of lesson plans from his benighted provincial outpost in the Basses-Pyrénées, may have been the exception that proves the rule. His account of how he taught his students "what constitutes the *Personality,* or the *Moi*" shows just how feasible, indeed how easy, such instruction was for a professor familiar with Condillac—and, as Chapter 2 showed, there were many such in this particular school system. Making implicit reference to the hypothetical statue in Condillac's *Traité des sensations* and dipping into the *Essai sur l'origine des connaissances humaines* as well, Baradère instructed his young charges that "the personality or the *moi* is thus the linkage between the sentiment of one's being on the one hand and the set of present and remembered sensations on the other. Without that linkage, no one could persuade me that today's *moi* was the same as yesterday's."[42] The raw material for this demonstration was all readily accessible in Condillac's texts. Yet few professors availed themselves of it, indicating a widely shared judgment that the demonstration was fundamental neither to Condillac's system nor to the worldview they wished to impart to their students.

As sensationalist psychology developed in France after the outbreak of the Revolution, assuming the newly coined name of *idéologie,* or the science of ideas, and gaining an institutional foothold in the Institut de France, founded in 1795, the deaccentuation of the *moi* persisted. In his master textbook of general grammar intended for use in the central schools, the *Elémens d'idéologie* (1st ed. 1801), Antoine-Louis-Claude Destutt de Tracy remained true to Condillac's strategy of treating the *moi* in passing rather than as a topic in its own right. If anything, he marginalized the *moi* even more than his teacher had, scattering his comments throughout the text, never presenting an unequivocal definition.

Dropping Condillac's device of tracing the successive operations of the *âme* that unfolded from an originary capacity for sensation, Tracy posited a so-called faculty of thought divided into the four elementary faculties of: (1) sensitivity; (2) memory; (3) judgment; and (4) will. It was an odd and rather misleading taxonomy because, while Tracy had apparently placed all four components on a par, the last three in fact derived logically from the first, as he was at pains to point out. Thus, memory was the "kind of sensitivity" that enabled one "to be affected by the recollection of an impression experienced [earlier]"; judgment the "kind of sensitivity" that was alert to the "relations between our perceptions"; and will the "kind of sensitivity" that afforded us a capacity "to feel desires."[43] In other words, all four faculties were "only a result of our [physiological] organization."[44]

Within this structure, Tracy first treated the *moi* not under the rubric of memory, as Condillac had done, but rather under the rubric of will. Observing that "the use of our mechanical and intellectual forces depends in large measure on [our desires], with the result that it is by means of our desires that we are a power in the world," Tracy then went on to link the will and the self. "That is why we tend to confuse our *moi* more with this faculty than with any other and that we say, as if they were equivalent, 'that depends on me' or 'that depends on my will.'"[45] Tracy's formulation here is decidedly ambiguous: the reader cannot tell whether he is talking about popular prejudices embedded in vulgar language or about his own scientific rendition of psychology. And that ambiguity persists, even when the reader assiduously gathers up the scattered passages in which Tracy discusses the *moi*. Sometimes the Idéologue asserts categorically, "I am my will" ("ma volonté c'est moi"), a phrase reminiscent of Louis XIV's famous identification of his royal person with the state. Sometimes he speaks more embracively of "our sensing and willing *moi*" or muddies the water still further with the dictum that "a pure and simple sensation teaches us the fact of our own existence."[46] The reader intent on pinning down Tracy's position on this matter is forced to become an exegete and, scouring the text for clues, comes to the following conclusion: that Tracy's is a highly nuanced position in which the capacity for sensation suffices to produce the *moi*, or the recognition of one's personal existence, but a manifestation of will, in the form of our own voluntary movement and the resistance that it encounters, is required for the recognition of other existences.[47] But if the position on the *moi* in Tracy's textbook is relatively coherent, the very difficulty of discerning it indicates that his interest in inculcating it in his students was virtually nil.

The *Rapports du physique et du morale de l'homme* (1802) of the physician P.-J.-G. Cabanis reveals once again that Idéologue discourse incorporated the concept of the *moi* while theorizing it rather haphazardly. Cabanis takes up the concept for the first (and only) time in this treatise in *Mémoire 10*, which covers a veritable grab bag of topics: its title lists "animal life, the first determinations of sensitivity, instinct, sympathy, sleep, and madness." His main point about the *moi* was so avant-garde that it would have little resonance or impact in France for nearly a hundred years. Cabanis wanted to do nothing less than decouple sensitivity and consciousness, to argue that sensitivity was alive in parts of the body "where the *moi* catches absolutely no sight of its presence" nor "receives any notification of its action."[48] In other words, Cabanis put forth a position that adumbrated the kind of vertical fragmentation of the individuated mental stuff that I discussed in the Introduction. His position thus shared certain structural features with the one Freud would much later advance. Far from accentuating the conscious self, he demoted it and diminished its sphere of efficacy.

Such a free and heterodox spirit was Cabanis that his emphasis on what he called "internal sensation" even had the effect of undermining the key sensationalist credo about the blank slate. While accepting that the newborn infant was a "tabula rasa with respect to the external universe," he insisted that at the moment of birth the infant's "cerebral center [had] already received and combined many [internal] impressions." Thus, while endorsing provisionally the sensationalist wisdom that the *moi* was the product of post-uterine experience, he added the important caveat that no one had yet undertaken "a detailed and complete analysis of the ideological condition of the infant" during the brief period before external objects began to make their impression on the sense organs. His ultimate inconclusiveness on the issue of the moment of origin of the *moi* underscored the relative indifference of the sensationalist tradition to the issue of selfhood.[49] So did Cabanis' obvious pleasure in entertaining the audacious hypothesis that, since the body's different organ systems were served by separate neural webs, there might even be "a kind of partial *moi*," one that existed in the plural in each individual. His taste for philosophical play had its limits, however, and in the end he supported the conventional view by stipulating that "the *moi*, as we conceive it, resides in the shared center" of our nervous system and was, hence, presumably unitary.[50]

With respect to its treatment of the *moi*, the work of Pierre Laromiguière, the main academic continuator of the sensationalist tradition during the Napoleonic Empire and the Restoration, diverged noticeably from the pattern set by Tracy and Cabanis. For one thing, it showed signs of linguistic archaism. Laromiguière was capable of using the term *moi* not only in a modern neutral register to mean the human subject but also in the antiquated, Pascalian, pejorative sense of vile selfishness and egotism.[51] In addition, much more attached to the literal texts of Condillac than were the other Idéologues, Laromiguière revived the term *âme*, going so far as to give his collected Sorbonne lectures the subtitle, "Essays on the Faculties of the Soul." His students called attention to this surprising word choice. Why, they asked, did "this word *âme* recur in each sentence of [his] lectures"? He had not, after all, "demonstrated that we have a soul." Laromiguière replied that he would, in due course, provide a proof of the existence of the soul, inserting it in its proper place once he had prepared the ground. Until then, and even afterward, they could regard the phrase "intellectual faculties" as synonymous with "faculties of the soul."[52]

Hence Laromiguière deemphasized the *moi* by diluting his use of that term with his use of the term *âme* and by implicitly assigning to each term the meanings that they had held for Condillac over a half-century earlier: the *âme* was the general spiritual stuff, and the *moi* the differentiated part of that stuff possessing self-awareness.[53] Linguistically archaic, Laromiguière also displayed a concern for the ontological status of the *âme* that was at once a throwback to the pre-Enlightenment era and a timely mark of early nineteenth-century preoccupations. He was bent on rescuing Condillac from the charge of materialism. It was true, he conceded, that the master had derived all the mental faculties from sensation. Still, Condillac did not regard sensation as a property of matter but rather as a "spiritual modification of a spiritual substance."[54] To be sure, Laromiguière could have extended this spiritualist argument to argue forcefully for mental unity. But he did not do so—and, besides, his spiritualist argument concerned the *âme* and not its modern, highly personalized subset, the *moi*.

Although the renditions of latter-day sensationalism offered by Tracy, Cabanis, and Laromiguière each have their own particular accents, all three theorists concurred in placing the *moi* at the periphery of their psychological systems. If none seemed to doubt that there was a self in this mental apparatus, none seemed exercised about demonstrating, elaborating upon, or hammering in that point.

Contrapuntal Rumblings

It would be wrong to give the impression that Condillac's enlightened audience universally shared his ease with a minimalist self. In the 1750s and 1770s at least two fundamentally sympathetic readers privately protested this aspect of his system. Thus Jean-Jacques Rousseau, annotating his copy of Helvétius's *De l'Esprit* (1758) not too long after its publication, objected to a principle articulated in that book that, he believed, Helvétius shared with Condillac: the essential passivity imputed to all the faculties of the human mind, including the capacity to make judgments through the comparison of ideas, once it was granted that mind originates solely in the reception of sensations. "[E]specially in the first part of the profession of the Savoyard vicar," Rousseau wrote testily in the margins of his Helvétius, "I have tried to combat [that principle] and to establish the activity of our judgments. . . ."[55] But public loyalty to sensationalist psychology seems to have been so integral a part of Rousseau's enlightened identity at this date, perhaps because its reverse connoted Catholicism and clericalism, that he took pains to keep his strictures secret during his lifetime.[56]

The abbé Emmanuel-Joseph Sieyès, who burst on the scene in 1789 as the author of the superlatively influential political pamphlet, *What Is the Third Estate?*, is not a figure routinely inserted into the history of psychology. Yet, on his own initiative, Sieyès studied Condillac intensively while a young seminarian at Saint-Sulpice during the 1760s and 1770s. Reluctantly obeying a paternal injunction to enter the priesthood, he described himself (in an autobiographical pamphlet written anonymously in the third person in 1794) as having "contracted a sort of savage melancholy" as soon as he found himself "sequestered" within the seminary's walls. In that despondent condition, an "involuntary penchant inclined him to meditation," with the result that "no books procured him a more lively satisfaction than those of Locke, Condillac, and Bonnet."[57] Sieyès left behind dense and copious reading notes on Condillac bound together in a "Large Metaphysical Notebook" (*Grand Cahier Métaphysique*), as well as individual note cards devoted to different operations of the understanding, such as "memory," "reminiscence," and "imagination."[58] He even left behind a drawing of the psychological apparatus. (See Figure 3.)

The young Sieyès became a thoroughgoing enthusiast of the French sensationalist, lauding his methodology against the deductive reasoning of the Physiocrats ("It will be absolutely necessary to follow Condillac if we wish accurate knowledge of what we know and how we know it").[59] He endorsed the posture of empathetic self-reflexivity that Condillac associated with the *spectateur philosophe*: that of putting oneself in the place of the statue whose sense-by-sense unfolding was hypothetically recounted in the *Traité des sensations*.[60] At times, he evinced total comfort with the minimalist Condillacian self. Thus we find him cheerfully, even a bit triumphantly, offering his own metaphorical rendition of the self (here called, simply, "man") as an empty, unstructured room awaiting the random arrival of sensory impingements and combinations and, as such, delightfully transparent:

> Man is, as they say, a mystery to man, [but] that is really his own fault. I regard man as a large ballroom. It has five doors [i.e., the five senses] by which a prodigious number of people enter, commence motion, part company, and finally arrange themselves in a thousand ways. He who would wish, without entering this room, to number each one, to

know it and its relations with the others, would never reach the end of his quest. But since it is certain that this place contains only people who entered by one of the five doors, nothing is easier than getting to know them. Let us place at each door observers who have the right of interrogation, and we will not only know the exact number of people who entered but will know the people sufficiently well not to lose track of them in the different relations to which chance gives rise among them.[61]

But even in this early phase of infatuation with sensationalist psychology, Sieyès gave voice to a certain area of disagreement: like Rousseau, he was concerned, at least sporadically, to rescue human mental processes from the passivity to which the sensationalist paradigm seemed to consign them. For example, reading Charles Bonnet's 1760 *Essai analytique*

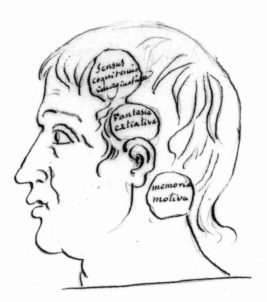

Figure 3: Diagram of the Psyche by the Young Sieyès. The archivist has dated this drawing, found among Sieyès' early papers and labeled in Latin, as 1773 or 1774. Although the psychological model depicted is very different from the sensationalism that the young seminarian embraced around the same time, the drawing provides visual evidence of Sieyès' long-standing fascination with the task of conceptualizing the mental apparatus. (Centre historique des Archives Nationales [CHAN], Paris, Sieyès papers 284 AP 2/1/155. Photo courtesy of the Atelier photographique of the CHAN.)

sur les facultés de l'âme, which made use of Condillac's statue model, he asked impatiently, "But when does the directing *moi* arise?" He then went on to supply the explanation that the author had, in his view, so annoyingly omitted:

> In any whole subjected to the action of beings around it and capable of reaction, it is impossible that a *center* not be formed from all the actions that it experiences. It is there that I establish the source of reaction. Out of this single point I constitute the soul of all. Beforehand there had been as many souls as parts; now there is a *moi* to which all responds, all is subordinated.[62]

Similarly, he dismissed with the terse phrase "very limited" Condillac's definition of will as "an absolute desire that occurs when we think that the desired thing is within our power." Such ex post facto tailoring of desire to capacity apparently struck him as a passive, defeatist attitude. "By will I mean action," he rejoined.[63]

Around 1798, when he was a thoroughly public man, deeply immersed in the politics and philosophical debates of the Directory, Sieyès read Condillac again; he even jotted down fresh thoughts in the "metaphysical notebook" of his seminary days.[64] It is unclear whether his view of Condillac had measurably evolved during the long, eventful period that intervened.[65] On the one hand, he still evidently regarded Condillac's texts as foundational and, on the other, he continued to express dissatisfaction with the unorganized, decentered *moi* Condillac had postulated. For example, now using the physiological language into which Idéologues like Cabanis translated Condillac's sensationalism in the 1790s, he again postulated the need for a "general center" in the brain, or alternatively, a "common node" of nervous fibers, which would bring together the "knowledge of all sorts acquired by interior and exterior observation," thus combating the aimless dispersion of mental contents that the sensationalist model of mind seemed to encourage and achieving the critical "separation of the *moi* from exterior objects [and] from my sensations."[66]

The political vicissitudes of the years following 1789 may well have provoked Sieyès' return to Condillac and his reexamination of the sensationalist doctrine of the *moi.* An engaged politician from the beginning of the monarchy's constitutional crisis in 1788 until he resigned the presidency of the Senate under the First Empire, he had obviously endured considerable personal upheaval as France careened from one political regime to the next. Optimistic and militant about the emancipatory possibilities of overthrowing absolutism in 1789, he initially had the gratifying experience of seeing French history unfold in accordance with the blueprint he offered in his pamphlet, *What Is the Third Estate?* But that political accomplishment had later been eradicated by the Terror, which Sieyès, then a deputy to the Convention, managed to weather by lying low. By 1798, the year when he resumed his reading of Condillac, the deliberately moderate republican regime called the Directory, in which he had once placed his hopes, was disintegrating; he would soon hasten its demise by helping to engineer the coup d'etat that brought Napoleon to power. Whether Sieyès saw any relationship between the political instability that had plagued France since the Revolution and the passivity and fragmentation of the *moi* postulated by the Revolution's quasi-official psychologist, Condillac, we can, for lack of direct evidence, only conjecture—although his use of the language of activity-passivity in both psychological and political contexts at the very beginning of the Revolution certainly suggests a propensity on his part to make that linkage.[67] Another event, intellectual in nature, seems, however, demonstrably connected to Sieyès' resumption of his psychological studies and of his critique of Condillac.

That event was the importation of German philosophy into France after Thermidor. Hoping to lower the political temperature of an overheated country, the Directory revived, in the form of the Institut, the officially sponsored academic culture to which France had long been accustomed and attempted to assert its predominance over the freewheeling literary culture that, since 1789, had been produced through the mechanism of the commercial marketplace. Introducing Kantian philosophy, with its appropriate tone of sober rationality, was part of this project. The government thus subsidized the publication of a French translation of Kant's *Perpetual Peace* in 1796.[68] This work of political philosophy was especially dear to Sieyès' heart, and its pacific universal republicanism seemed to the leaders of the Directory to furnish just the philosophical ideal that could end the seemingly interminable radicalization of the Revolution.[69]

More relevant to our concerns here, Kant's epistemology and that of his rebellious student Fichte also made their way to France during the same period. One of their earliest envoys was the young Prussian savant Wilhelm von Humboldt, who arrived in Paris in the fall of 1797 and quickly infiltrated the philosophical circles of the capital. In May 1798 Destutt de Tracy invited him to a day-long "metaphysical symposium" with Cabanis, Laromiguière, and Sieyès, among others, in attendance. The prospects for real dialogue were not bright, for Tracy had already expressed his suspicion of the new German transcendentalism by telling Humboldt frankly (and in typically sensationalist language), "I fear that your imagination works overtime and embroiders nature."[70] Nonetheless Humboldt's vivid accounts of the symposium in his private journal and in a long letter to Friedrich Schiller inadvertently reveal a good deal about the conceptualization of the *moi* among leading French intellectuals at the very end of the eighteenth century.

Humboldt put the *moi* and its assumed activity at the center of the discussion, informing his French colleagues that "our [German] metaphysics is nothing but a perfect development of the actions of what we call our *moi*." Or, as he rephrased the point toward the end of the same journal entry: "all philosophy rests on the pure intuition of the *moi*, outside all experience; either explicitly—that is, if one departs directly from that intuition, as Fichte does—or implicitly," if one traces the apprehension of phenomena to the categories in the manner of Kant. That basic proposition met with fierce resistance from most of his French interlocutors, resulting in a debate that Humboldt wryly characterized as "sterile but simple to conduct because everyone [on the other side] expressed easily refutable ideas." Laromiguière, whom he sized up as the most clear-thinking and confident of the French group but also the "most negative and dry," was obdurate in his wholesale rejection of the German approach: he "affirmed a total *passivity* (Humboldt's emphasis) of the mind in the production of representations." Not surprisingly, the one Frenchman present who showed any receptivity to the German mode of philosophizing was Sieyès; he stood out as the single exception to all of Humboldt's generalizations about the mindset of his colleagues across the Rhine.[71]

Of those colleagues Humboldt said damningly: "They have no idea, not even the slightest inkling, of anything other than appearance; pure volition, the true good, the *moi*, pure self-consciousness—all this is totally incomprehensible to them. Even when they use the same terms, they always impute a completely different meaning to them."[72] Only Sieyès departed from the accepted sensationalist wisdom, once even voicing the heterodox opinion that "the philosopher brushes aside sensory judgments; he closes his eyes."[73] Humboldt sometimes seemed filled with admiration for him: "He manifestly has a more profound mind than all the others," he reported to Schiller. "He says things that sound simply like they came from Kant or Fichte."[74] But while Sieyès may, at some point, have had a direct encounter with the German philosophers and their works—he briefly served the Directory as ambassador to Berlin—his affinity with their style of thought seems to have been thoroughly self-generated and homegrown, the fruit of his own native tendency.[75] A cluster of German Jacobins who made contact with him after 1795 regarded him as a Kantian who didn't know he was a Kantian.[76] And Humboldt found his insights so half-baked, unsystematic, and obviously untutored that he was almost driven to distraction by his efforts to communicate with Sieyès on a philosophical plane:

> [I]t is not pleasant to get into a debate with him. He obviously has new ideas, but he is not yet certain of them, he is too preoccupied with them to listen carefully to someone else, and his inadequate mastery of them prevents him from explaining them. That's why he so often argues, so to speak, in desperation . . . [77]

Writing to Schiller, Humboldt further detailed his frustration with Sieyès. The man who so splendidly "avow[ed] the inadequacy of all French philosophy" presented his own philosophical ideas in a totally disorderly fashion and was "too proud and impatient" to accept advice about reformulating them. "If he could decide to develop a [philosophical] system in the German manner . . . he would surely produce something great." But he was "too French for that," Humboldt opined, meaning that he was so caught up in "public life" and attuned to the response of the public that he would desist if his ideas failed to gained widespread acceptance. In another way, too, Sieyès seemed to Humboldt to lack the resolve and the perseverance necessary to produce a rigorous German-style philosophy. His thought had an irritable, mordant quality; it "penetrates deeply, but with lightning bolts that suddenly plunge into the interior of the thing, not with a slow penetration accompanied by steady effort." While Humboldt knew that Sieyès had been, as he put it with unwitting understatement, "very important during the Revolution," he suspected him of harboring a fundamental character flaw.

Sieyès, he opined, had the misfortune to be at once a philosopher manqué and a politician manqué:

> He is one of those rare men of whom it can be said almost truthfully
> that for all their strength of intellect and of character, they were made
> neither for thinking nor for acting. That is because their entire makeup
> is passionate—not that this or that particular passion really dominates,
> but because everything that surges within them bears the mark of
> passion.[78]

Moreover, for all the un-French philosophical tendencies Sieyès
sometimes expressed, at other times he appeared resolutely stick-in-the-
mud. Visiting him at home shortly after the metaphysical symposium,
Humboldt encountered a Sieyès (dressed in a night cap and complaining of a headache) disappointingly conventional in his views. Said
Humboldt: "Among all metaphysicians, today it is Condillac and Bonnet—surely the most superficial—on whom he lavishes his highest
praise." Faced with such retrograde opinions, Humboldt feared that
Sieyès' genuinely metaphysical spirit had been "corrupted by the
[French] national character or, at least, by national habits."[79]

In Sieyès, then, we see a man with his hand on the pulse of French
Revolutionary politics struggling to break loose from the sensationalist
paradigm. But, deeply loyal to Condillac and to the Frenchness he represented in an international context, Sieyès always struggled ambiv-
alently. As defective as he found the Condillacian *moi*, he lacked the
patience and determination to devote more than intermittent effort to
the task of repairing it.

A Columbus of the Self

His contemporary, Marie-François-Pierre Gonthier de Biran, called
Maine de Biran, took on that task and brought it to something akin to
completion during the opening two decades of the nineteenth century.
Starting out as an Idéologue—Destutt de Tracy and Cabanis selected his
Influence de l'habitude sur la faculté de penser for a prize awarded by the
Institut in 1802—he gradually chipped away at that psychological
model until he achieved an alternative that could properly be called
"Biranian."[80] Its main features were the postulation of a self, or *moi*,
existing before sensory experience and as the precondition for it; a

phenomenological elaboration of the nature of experience and the radical separation of the domain of external or sensory experience, labeled "objective," from a privileged domain of internal experience, or consciousness, labeled "subjective"; and the postulation of consciousness of the *moi* as a so-called *fait primitif,* or originary fact, that grounded the theory at a fixed and stable point. In addition, Maine de Biran's *moi* was active, appearing in the space between the psychological and the physiological in the form of the voluntary movement of otherwise inert muscles. Such willed movement conveyed the sense of one's own causality; being a cause in the world was tantamount to and an essential attribute of selfhood. Biranism did not constitute a full-fledged, self-enclosed system. Its author never completed the synoptic work he had long intended to produce, leading one commentator aptly to compare Biranism to a "Chinese painted scroll whose significance emerges as it is unwound."[81] But even if unsystematic, Biranism offered a thoroughly transformed version of the fragmented and passive sensationalist self.

The son of a physician in the Périgord whose ancestors had inhabited that southwestern province for centuries, Maine de Biran was in some ways the diametric opposite of Sieyès and in some ways his analogue. The two men's responses to 1789 could not have diverged more sharply: while Sieyès was busy radicalizing the constitutional crisis that had prompted Louis XVI to call the Estates General, Maine de Biran was serving in the *gardes du corps,* devoted to preserving His Majesty's physical safety. Wounded near Versailles in the chaotic October Days of 1789, his military unit soon disbanded by the king, he decided to retool as an engineer and began to study mathematics in Paris. But once the Terror began, he prudently withdrew to his family estate in Grateloup where, Montaigne-like, he turned his attention to philosophizing and almost constant self-observation.[82] A royalist all his life, he became reconciled to the more moderate face of the Revolution that surfaced after the fall of Robespierre; at that juncture, he added a public political role to his private philosophical one, thus replicating Sieyès' pattern of operating simultaneously on those two separate tracks. Possessing the local notable's sense of civic duty, he occupied a long succession of offices, including administrator of the department of the Dordogne in the Year III, deputy from that department to the Council of Five Hundred under the Directory, member of the Legislative Body under the Empire, and member of the Chamber of Deputies under the Restoration monarchy.[83]

Like Sieyès, if at a more modest level of participation, he had a day-to-day experience of the political vicissitudes of the Revolution and its aftermath and, as a result, a highly developed political consciousness.

Where Maine de Biran differed most dramatically from Sieyès was in his well-documented habit of minute self-observation. Much like Sieyès, he looked inward in his scientific quest after the general laws of the human mind: already in 1794 he called for a "psychology" modeled on "experimental physics," one that would oblige researchers "to do experiments on themselves similar to (though different in kind from) the one Spalanzani had courageously repeated at his own risk of swallowing various substances in order to confirm how digestion works."[84] But unlike Sieyès, he also, and perhaps mainly, looked inward to explore the particularity of his own interior landscape. Physically sickly since childhood and exquisitely sensitive by nature, he lived with a chronic malaise that solicited his concerted investigation and analysis. "It is only unhealthy people who [actually] feel themselves existing," he observed while in his twenties, at a time when he explicitly traced to his proclivity for self-examination to his pathologically "weak constitution."[85] By contrast to the *cahier métaphysique* that Sieyès filled with matter-of-fact reading notes and abstract philosophical speculations, Maine de Biran kept, in 1794–95 and again, intermittently, from 1814 until shortly before his death in 1824, a *journal intime* in which his own interior life was the central datum. Obviously many stories can be told on the basis of so rich a text, which put Maine de Biran self-consciously in the tradition of Montaigne and Rousseau.[86] The story I will tell here aligns Maine de Biran's need to narrate his interiority with two other factors: the political consciousness that he acquired in the course of traversing the Revolution, and his philosophical project to renovate the sensationalist self.[87] It was, I will suggest, his deep and anguished personal investment in that latter project that fueled his engagement with it, lending him the perseverance that Sieyès lacked.

Maine de Biran's triple cluster of preoccupations, and the odd juxtapositions to which they give rise, can be found repeatedly in the pages of his journal. Take, for example, the autumn of 1814, the period when the larger portion of the journal begins. Our protagonist is in Paris, a member of the Chamber of Deputies of the newly restored Bourbon monarchy. In the opening sentences of most entries, he reports the weather and assesses its impact on his mood. A cool, rainy week in early October is credited with turning him "melancholic" and thus "much less disposed to unfurl myself outside" than to "come back to myself; thus I incline toward psychological meditations as if by an instinct that is periodically renewed with marked force." (Throughout the journal, *méditations psychologiques* is his preferred term for his intervals of self-searching, and he is also fond of the verb-and-adverb form, *méditer psychologiquement*.) He devotes his mornings to such meditations but for the rest of the day is "swept up in the active life" despite himself. He attends legislative debates about granting French citizenship to the inhabitants of Napoleon's fallen empire (he began to express his opinion on the floor but was interrupted by a more talkative deputy) and debates about the restitution of the property of the returned emigrés (this time he utterly failed to speak, doubting his ability to intervene extemporaneously in such a weighty matter, and then berated himself for his shameful silence); he regularly dines at the home of the minister of the interior.[88] He is a man enmeshed in politics, who recognizes the seriousness of his historical moment and feels duty-bound to help puzzle out France's post-Revolutionary future, even while he strongly suspects that he is not up to the job. So he goes back and forth, somewhat jarringly, between the nuts and bolts of national legislation and a never-ending fascination with his delicate and hypersensitive psyche. The sheer, repeated contiguity of politics and psychological meditation suggests that some deeper thread of significance joins the two activities for him.

The third recurrent motif is plaited together with these other two: a small, newly founded philosophical society meets at his home on alternate weeks. Its members include the naturalist Georges Cuvier, Maine de Biran's close friend the physicist A.-M. Ampère, the Idéologue Joseph-Marie Degérando, philosophy professors of a newer stripe like Pierre-Paul Royer-Collard and his young colleague Victor Cousin, and the future politician François Guizot. Maine de Biran is not always completely efficacious in this setting either: at least once he failed to complete a paper he had promised to present, leaving the disappointed group to its own devices.[89] But in general he feels far more competent among his fellow philosophers than in the Chamber of Deputies. As he describes a dinner in the bosom of such companions in May 1816: "I felt like chatting; I speak the language of metaphysics with more facility than that of politics or business; several strings vibrate when I have the occasion to talk about a science that is familiar to me."[90] The common interest responsible for bringing together the members of the informal philosophical society has great significance in this vignette of Maine de Biran's daily life. Though it is never expressed in general terms, the cumulative effect of the topics addressed at the individual sessions is unmistakable: "psychological language"; "the sentiment of the *moi* and activity"; "the *moi* and the originary fact (*fait primitif*) of consciousness."[91] The assembled company is, in other words, participating in the overhaul of sensationalist psychology. They are marking their distance from their eighteenth-century forebears by engaging in serious self-talk.

Maine de Biran's personal need to supplant the sensationalist self with something more robust can be seen in the 1794–95 installment of his journal, begun at his estate at Grateloup while he hid from the Terror. He appears here, not surprisingly, as an adept of sensationalist psychology, accustomed to depicting himself to himself in its terms. That very depiction, which includes evocations of passivity, mobility, and precarious malleability, functions simultaneously as a complaint. In his opening paragraph, Maine de Biran writes:

[T]his unhappy existence is only a series of heterogeneous moments lacking all stability. They go floating, fleeing rapidly, without our ever having the power to fix them in place. Everything influences us, and we change ceaselessly in accordance with our surroundings. I often amuse myself by watching the flow of the different states of my mind. They are like the billows of a river, sometimes calm, sometimes agitated, but always succeeding one another without permanence.[92]

The same basic complaint reappears pages later. The sensationalist psyche lacks a master ("I am going to prove how little influence [*empire*] we exercise over our own ideas, how these light phantoms appear and disappear . . . sometimes in an orderly manner, sometimes in an intolerable hodgepodge, while the mind, a pure spectator, is incapable of rectifying the disorder . . ."). The psyche follows the mechanistic pattern of cause and effect that Stendhal, similarly reliant on sensationalist psychology, would later highlight in his portrayal of Julien Sorel ("[A] fiber accidentally rattled will produce a rattling in those with which it is linked, setting off a sequence of perceptions that I can neither arrest nor foresee").[93] Just as the organizers of the Revolutionary festivals described those patriotic displays, positively, as imprinting the soft wax of spectators' minds (see Chapter 2), so Maine de Biran twice uses the word *mollesse*—softness—to negatively describe his own character, formed as it is by chance environmental factors outside its control.[94] "I am merely passive," he laments, "I say what I would not wish to say, I do what I would not wish to do."[95] Even more than twenty years later, when Maine de Biran had long since transformed his understanding of human psychology, he retained an acute, almost painful awareness of the shaping force that his physical environment exercised over him. Here he is in Paris in November 1816, having just attended a meeting of the Conseil d'Etat:

> I returned to my new lodgings and began to settle in. There is in the *strangeness* of the impressions of all the environing objects something that distracts the mind by shaking up the senses and calling forth a sort of *sensitive* attention. We must mold ourselves to these objects, they must become very familiar in order that they cease making on us that distracting, tiring impression.[96]

Perennially assailed by melancholy and a humiliating sense of inefficacy, then, the Maine de Biran of 1794 keenly disliked his "softness" and lack of control, his being held hostage to the mental imprinting of his physical environment. His personal discomfort translated into a recognition of the disadvantages of a sensationalist model of mind and, in particular, of what I have called the horizontal fragmentation of self effected by that model. As early as 1794 he resolved—if so tentative a statement can be called a resolution—one day to repair the model: "I would like, if ever I could undertake something sustained, to investigate the degree to which the mind is active, the degree to which it can modify external impressions, augment or diminish their intensity by the attention it gives them; I would like to examine the extent to which it is master of that attention."[97]

His uncomfortable sense of horizontal fragmentation was exacerbated by a related sense of inauthenticity, or segmentation of self. He did not blame this condition entirely, à la Rousseau, on the inherent nature of society; he also faulted his own psychological weakness, his tendency to be imprinted by whatever or whomever was around him. The Terror over, Maine de Biran had emerged from hiding; he could freely leave the solitude of his estate and show his face in the town of Bergerac. It was not a pleasant experience:

I saw a lot of people and received courtesies and expressions of attachment and concern, but coercion and dissimulation broke through those affectionate transports. So many masks and not a single heart! Nonetheless I was obliged to respond as if these compliments were truthful—that is, to disguise myself, too, and put on a mask like everyone else, for it would be ridiculous to remain in a natural state (*à visage nu*) when everyone around you was in domino.

Maine de Biran finds this game of deception, of "lying to oneself," a "torment." He believes that he would be able to avoid it and, hence, to "live fruitfully in the social world (*le monde*)" and "derive some advantage from the commerce of men" if he had a "great firmness of character" enabling him to defy "opinion." Of course, his lot is just the reverse: softness rather than firmness. "[A]ll the fibers of my brain are so mobile that they yield to the impression of objects. . . ."[98] What Maine de Biran offers us in this passage from his journal of 1794–95, then, is a rendition of Rousseau's *Discourse on the Origins of Inequality* inflected by individual psychology. In his view, those people endowed with sufficient personal "firmness," or imperviousness to their environment, can escape from the amour-propre and corrupt artifice that otherwise infect society.

The first installment of the *journal intime* thus enables us to see the personal emotional logic behind Maine de Biran's philosophical project: if he could find, outside the framework of sensationalist psychology, a self that would function as a fixed and invariable yet active center, he might alleviate his own daily suffering. The political logic behind that same project is less clearly spelled out but can be roughly inferred from the portion of the journal covering 1815–16.

It was not, of course, for the sake of democratic participation that Maine de Biran wanted to strengthen the self. The notable from the Périgord had no interest in the political capabilities of the masses. He regarded popular sovereignty as an "anarchical and revolutionary principle, the source of all the evils that have befallen France in the past twenty-five years."[99] But he did believe that a nation got the government it deserved, with desert defined in moral terms. When the exiled Bonaparte returned to France in 1815 for what turned out to be another hundred days of rule, a desolate Maine de Biran observed, "The French people deserve only to be conquered. . . . Born amidst the storms of the Revolution, depraved and deeply immoral, the present generation is not susceptible of good government."[100] Furnishing France with "good government," we can assume, would require not only the return of the Bourbons but, to ensure their continued presence on the throne, also some sort of remedial moral education for the "depraved" Revolutionary generation.

Two weeks later, he recognized a link between the moral failings of that generation and the sensationalist philosophy imbibed during the previous century. Picking up a recently reprinted eighteenth-century edition of Pascal's *Pensées,* he was struck by the inadequacy of its scholarly apparatus, which was the work of two great Enlightenment philosophes: Voltaire had provided "extremely ridiculous notes, to which Condorcet had added ones still more ridiculous and inane." As a result of the psychology to which they subscribed, these two eminent thinkers appeared to lack any appreciation of human interiority. "[T]o cultivate, to exercise the internal sense, that means nothing to our sensualist philosophers"; since they held fast to the proposition that "we get ideas only from the outside," they dismissed self-contemplation as a useless, contemptible pastime.[101] (To be sure, Maine de Biran greatly admired the founders of sensationalism, Locke and Condillac, for their personal powers of self-reflexivity.[102] But he believed that adepts of their completed systems could readily bypass the inward-turning moment and focus on the external environment.) For Maine de Biran, by contrast, the domain of subjective, inner experience—or, in other words, the *moi*—was the key to our moral being. At the time of the first restoration in 1814 when he was appointed to the administrative and financial post of *questeur* in the Chamber of Deputies, he noted in his journal that, despite his high salary and new level of material comfort, he had "never been less happy." He attributed this mental state to the balance between his inward- and outward-turning activities: "Since I arrived at the *questure*, I have been constantly dragged outside and *enveloped* in all the impressions of the exterior life; it is only in the interior life and in the exercise of the active faculties, only in the depths of the soul, that one recovers one's moral being. ..."[103] Sensationalist psychology, with its marked orientation toward the "outside," would, then, sap the morality necessary for a sound political community.

Armed with this reconstruction of Maine de Biran's logic, we can make sense of the repeated alternation between political and philosophical-psychological preoccupations that marks his journal. It is by constituting the self on active, nonsensationalist lines that Maine de Biran seeks to make good government again possible in France. Thus one of his most complete statements of his political credo, culminating in the rousing sentence, "Without monarchical feeling, without respect and love for the legitimate king, there can be neither religion, nor morality nor fatherland in France," is followed the very next day by the entry, "I began to piece together the psychological materials I gathered during the past two months in notes on Kant, Lignac, etc."[104] Turning inward to find an active and unified self and then to theorize that self was thus partly a political strategy for Maine de Biran. It was a way to mend the broken moral compass of the Revolutionary generation and to revive royalism. In his quest for a robust self, moreover, Maine de Biran looked not only to the recently imported German transcendental philosophy but also to an indigenous, old-fashioned French source: the abbé de Lignac's early eighteenth-century Catholic apologetics, which, as we have seen, sought to refute Locke straightaway by invoking the self-evident testimony of the *sens intime*.

Interiority was thus a multiple resource, even a kind of panacea, for Maine de Biran. In a memorable passage in his journal, written in a calm moment about a year after Louis XVIII had been re-restored, he contemplated the limits of our ability to penetrate into the "intimate constitution of this *moi*" and wistfully mused, "Who knows [. . .] if there is not an *interior* New World one day to be discovered by some *metaphysical Columbus* . . . ?"[105] His conversation seems to have been so full of references to the *moi* that his old friend, the abbé Morellet, then ninety years old and still adhering to an Enlightenment intellectual style that failed to privilege self-talk, asked him "brusquely: 'What's the *moi*?'" Like anyone asked to define a term that is so basic to his thought that he cannot tease it out from all the things to which it is connected, Maine de Biran was nonplused. "I could not reply," he recorded in his journal. He went on to suggest that the *moi* could not be objectified for purposes of definition but could be known only performatively and from inside: "One must place oneself in the intimate viewpoint of consciousness and, thus having present that unity which judges all phenomena while remaining invariable, one perceives this *moi* and ceases asking what it is."[106]

By emphasizing "unity" and invariability," by criticizing as shallow and amoral the sensationalists' fixation on the external environment, by changing the assumptions and methods of a psychological science, making its data the internal ones of consciousness,[107] Maine de Biran had succeeded brilliantly in locating a self in the mental apparatus. However, he entrusted his findings to a bundle of manuscripts that, despite his friends' prodding, he refused to publish and that, by the time of his death, weighed some sixty pounds.[108] Only his immediate circle, including the metaphysical society that had regularly met at his home, knew of his endeavor and his accomplishment, and at his funeral Royer-Collard, speaking for that select group, rightly called him "the teacher (*maître*) of us all." But Maine de Biran's renovated model of the self was not entirely lost, even in the short term. To be sure, his manuscripts would not be published until the Second Empire was in full swing. But at the time of his death, one member of his circle was already adapting his doctrine of the self, albeit selectively, for consumption on a vast scale.

4

An A Priori Self for the Bourgeois Male: Victor Cousin's Project

Dinner at the Ecole polytechnique with Monsieur D . . . and the
young philosophy professor Cousin. We spoke a great deal about
metaphysics, and I was pleased with myself; I thought the others were,
too. I laid out my mode of conceptualization . . . , explain[ing it] to my
young professor, who grasped it wonderfully (à merveille).

Maine de Biran, Journal, 1816

Among the educated Frenchmen troubled by the defective, fragmented
sensationalist self, none was more dogged in his pursuit of it than Victor
Cousin. A junior participant in Maine de Biran's exclusive metaphysical
society during the early years of the Restoration, he had a glint in his
eye, a capacity to grasp ideas "à merveille," that made a strong impression on the philosopher from the Périgord. By 1821, Maine de Biran felt
sure that, despite his excessive fervor (une tête trop ardente)—apparently
a coded reference to fondness for German idealism—the "young professor Cousin" was the "hope of the true philosophy among us."[1] In fact,
even as the older man penned those lines, Cousin was busy rescuing
Biranian insights from oblivion. What he chose to leave out of his own
philosophical mix would prove almost as significant as what he selected
for inclusion.

A derivative philosopher, though one who enjoyed a vastly inflated
reputation in his own era, the mature Cousin possessed in the more
workaday occupation of academic entrepreneur a degree of talent that
bordered on genius. By producing and then successfully institutionalizing a new system of psychological knowledge designed to usurp the

place of sensationalism, he stamped on French culture a mark that lasted at least until the end of the nineteenth century. Scholarship on Cousin has long stressed his achievement in professionalizing philosophy as an academic discipline in France and implanting his own brand of it in the state system of higher education.[2] My argument in this chapter and the next builds on that foundation. At the same time, however, it shifts the focus to the specifically *psychological* component of Cousin's philosophy and the way it served, in the context of the classroom, deliberately to inculcate a certain kind of selfhood.

Though a sworn enemy of psychological fragmentation, Cousin proved addicted to fragments of another sort. He never produced a sustained, synthetic work of philosophy. The volumes that he named (ironically, for a man so devoted to holism) *Fragmens philosophiques* comprised a large portion of his philosophical output; and *faute de mieux*, the carefully worded prefaces to those volumes, which contained some of his most important statements of philosophical position, were treated by contemporaries as intellectual events of the highest magnitude. Published versions of his university courses made up the rest of his philosophical corpus. The master did not literally write this latter group of works, which were instead direct transcriptions of the notes he had used in class, sometimes supplemented by the notes taken by members of his student audience. No wonder that Cousin defended himself preemptively against charges of incompleteness and incoherence, observing early on that "a course should not be judged like a book"[3] "Entirely fragmentary, fine *aperçus* on a large number of philosophical topics but no developed system"—such was the verdict on Cousin's philosophy that the basically sympathetic philosopher Adolphe Garnier delivered privately to the young Ernest Renan in 1846.[4]

In the 1826 preface to one of his collections of fragments, Cousin rehearsed his complaint against sensationalism, the "sad philosophy" that had immediately preceded his own. "It is an incontestable fact," he asserted, "that in eighteenth-century England and France, Locke and Condillac supplanted the great antecedent schools and that they have remained supreme until today. Instead of being irritated (*s'irriter*) by that fact, we must try to understand it."[5] Even in this brief and apparently straightforward remark, Cousin displays his pugnacity and sharp wit. In the scientific idiom of the period, irritation was a manifestation of nervous sensibility, a virtual synonym for sensation. Cousin was saying, then, that sensation-irritation is only the first, primitive stage of mental response to a phenomenon; understanding is a higher stage and, *pace* Condillac, is not reducible to sensation. Far be it from Cousin, then, who predicated his entire philosophical career on transcending mere sensation, to cease his examination of Locke and Condillac at the elementary stage of irritation! His epistemology shielded him from such pettiness.

Before considering Cousin's larger agenda, we need to look once again at the predecessor who so famously got under his skin and ask in what the ascendancy of Condillac consisted in the several decades following the Revolution.

Vernacular Knowledge: The Status of Sensationalism circa 1830

Part of this story is well known and has already been alluded to in Chapter 3. A group of continuators of Condillac, wedded to *idéologie*, or the newly invented science of the generation of ideas from sensory impressions, and calling themselves *idéologistes*, were catapulted to positions of institutional power under the Directory and the Consulate. Most important among them were A.-L.-C. Destutt de Tracy and the physician P.-J.-G. Cabanis. From an informal organization centered on the salon of Madame Helvétius in Auteuil, the group rose to control of the Second Class (Moral and Political Sciences) of the Institut de France, founded in 1795 as a restoration of official academic culture; at the same time, they propagated their views through their journal, the *Décade philosophique*.

During this period sensationalism continued to be the intellectual fashion in many strata of society. In the early years of the nineteenth century, for example, the Duchesse de Courlande, a member of the transnational European aristocracy, chose as a tutor for her daughter a certain Florentine abbé, Scipion Piattoli, "who believed that Condillac . . . [was] a surer guide than the Gospel."[6] At about the same date, the bourgeois Stendhal larded his letters to his sister Pauline with admonitions to read Condillac. Sending her a pocket-sized edition of the *Logique*, which he described as the book "people are making such a fuss about"—the year was 1802—he proposed that they work together on a page a week and predicted that once they had completed two chapters at this pace she would be able to tackle the rest alone. The *Logique* was "the easiest thing in the world if you come to it with a mind free of prejudice." And once having mastered the book "your progress will no longer be impeded in any science," whether algebra or grammar, "for logic is nothing but the art of reasoning."[7]

The official ouster of the Idéologues was as swift their entry into official favor. A period of mutual infatuation between the group and Napoleon succumbed to misgivings on both sides as the authoritarian streak in Napoleon's politics intensified. As early as 1800 the government press referred to the self-identified *idéologistes* as "idéologues," a new coinage meant to smack of derision that became, ironically, the standard name for the group.[8] The Law of 11 floréal Year X (May 1, 1802) abolished the central schools and replaced them with lycées, a new institution that, purged of such characteristically Idéologue courses as drawing and general grammar, restored Latin to its pre-Revolutionary pedagogical prominence.[9] In 1803 Napoleon's Minister of the Interior Chaptal reorganized the Institut, purposely closing the Idéologues' base of operations, the Second Class. And in a famous tirade before the Conseil d'Etat in 1812, the emperor declared his former intellectual allies proponents of a "dark metaphysics" who, believing they could found laws on abstract philosophical principles, were responsible for "all the misfortunes that have befallen our beautiful France."[10]

The chief carrier of the philosophy of Condillac during the philosophically confused periods of the Consulate, Empire, and Restoration (1800–30) was the minor Idéologue, Pierre Laromiguière, whom we already encountered in Chapter 3. A representative instance of the species, Laromiguière had taken the cloth in 1773 as a member of the Pères de la Doctrine Chrétienne, one of the secular teaching orders that served as an important locus of the dissemination of Condillac under the Old Regime. True to type, Laromiguière had experienced an intellectual conversion when, sometime after 1780, he happened upon a copy of Condillac's *Logique* and, the scales duly falling from his eyes, he renounced the Aristotelianism and Cartesianism in which he had been educated. It was the philosophy of Condillac that he taught at the Collège d'Esquile in Toulouse, entering into a polemic on the subject with the Aristotelian rector of the institution who, true to the reputation for intellectual freedom enjoyed by the Pères de la Doctrine Chrétienne, never prevented the younger man from speaking his mind before his students. In 1790, when the Revolution abolished the religious orders, Laromiguière continued to teach at Esquile, though in the new status of an employee of the French state. He soon renounced his religious vocation, minimal to begin with, and wholeheartedly embraced the identity of philosophy professor.[11]

At the height of the Terror, Laromiguière published his class notes on Condillac in the form of a concise manual for students entitled *Projet d'élémens de métaphysique*. This little brochure attracted the attention of several of members of the Committee on Public Instruction (then charged with producing a curriculum for the new republic), including that avid reader of Condillac, the abbé Sieyès.[12]

Fortified by powerful patrons, Laromiguière continued to advance on the career ladder. Clearly ripe for the picking when the central schools were founded, he was named professor of logic, then of history, and finally and appropriately, of general grammar in the central schools of Paris.[13] In 1809 he received a post of uniquely strategic importance, the professorship of philosophy at the newly established Faculty of Letters of Paris. His lectures, praised for their clarity, elegance and vivacity, soon attracted a large audience that included not only students but a broad swath of intellectually cultivated Parisians.[14] Although Laromiguière's adherence to Condillac may have become subtly inflected by this date—some commentators would later see his emphasis on an active faculty of attention as a bridge to the Cousinian philosophy[15]—his first lesson proudly bore the hallmarks of Idéologie, announcing that the philosophical method was one of "decomposition, that is to say, *analysis*."[16] Indeed in his formal opening lecture, given belatedly in 1811, he read from the job description drawn up by the University Council (*Conseil de l'Université*), indicating the administration's assumption that he would construe his subject matter in a thoroughly sensationalist fashion: "He [the philosophy professor] will principally set out to show the origin and successive developments of our ideas."[17]

Despite the small size and somewhat "shadowy" existence of the Paris Faculty of Letters at this date,[18] its philosophy chair had a symbolic importance that enhanced the status—and the vulnerability—of the occupant. Any changes in the philosophical preferences of the political regime would be registered at this extremely visible point in the academic hierarchy. Thus in 1813, when Napoleon had become convinced that Idéologie was absolutely inimical to the Empire, he removed

Laromiguière de facto, allowing him to retreat into nonthreatening obscurity as a university librarian. Replacing him in the spotlight was Pierre-Paul Royer-Collard, the spokesman of a new and still inchoate French philosophical tendency that would subsequently be nurtured by conversations with Maine de Biran and, eventually, flourish luxuriantly at the hands of Royer-Collard's *suppléant,* or substitute lecturer, Victor Cousin.

But this conspicuous removal did not put an end to Laromiguière or his school. Laromiguière published his *Leçons* in the waning days of the Empire and continued to attract disciples, whom he trained informally through daily chats at the library. In 1820, shaken by the assassination of the Duc de Berry, the Restoration monarchy made an unexpected and perhaps erroneous calculation. It decided that the government of the reinstalled Bourbons was more philosophically jeopardized by the new school of Royer-Collard and Cousin, which had by that date declared for the liberal opposition, than by the old, Revolution-tainted school of Condillac. Accordingly it silenced Royer-Collard and his substitute, Cousin, and brought back Laromiguière to his podium at the Faculty, investing the old Idéologue with the power to determine the official philosophy of the now thoroughly royalist and pro-clerical regime.[19] This surprising reversal may well have stemmed from the conviction of the abbé de Frayssinous, as minister of public instruction, that the anti-metaphysical nature of sensationalism made it far less dangerous to Catholic orthodoxy than was the new school of Cousin, with its combination of resolute secularism and metaphysical pretension.[20] In any case, the reversal must have gladdened the heart of Stendhal, who had earlier envisioned a rapprochement between the Restoration monarchy and the intellectual currents of the Enlightenment. Almost immediately after the fall of Napoleon in 1814, he had prepared a proposal to Louis XVIII for the establishment of a Royal College of Peers that would give the sons of the nobility the sort of "liberal education" of which they had been robbed by "our civil dissensions." The projected curriculum included Bentham, Adam Smith, J. B. Say, Montesquieu and, one of the few texts mentioned by name, "the *Idéologie* of Tracy."[21]

In an intellectual climate in which sensationalism still enjoyed support in important circles, it is not surprising that a *Cours d'etude pour l'instruction des jeunes gens par Condillac*—a selection from the master's key texts along the lines of Bérenger's 1789 anthology—appeared in ten pocket-sized volumes in 1821, its front matter noting that the "success enjoyed" by the unspecified original had inspired this new edition.[22] Or that early in 1830, shortly before Charles X was dethroned, the University Council approved as a textbook the *Abeille encyclopédique,* a brief survey of the sum total of human knowledge that included a long entry on Idéologie.[23] A recent quantitative study of the editions and reeditions of Condillac's logical, psychological, and grammatical works from the mid-eighteenth century through the early decades of the nineteenth makes the point clearly. It found that the "dizzingly steep increase" after 1770 tapered off only around 1830, leading the author to conclude that, for the entire period in question, "Condillac's influence simply cannot be overestimated."[24]

Nor, then, is it unusual that Jean Saphary, a disciple of Laromiguière, used his position as professor of philosophy at the Royal College of Nancy to disseminate sensationalism in Lorraine in the 1820s.[25] Or that another disciple, A. J. H. Valette, whom Laromiguière chose as his substitute at the Faculty in 1829, delivered in that year a rousing defense of the school of Condillac scarcely qualified by his acknowledgment of the validity of certain typically nineteenth-century criticisms of the Enlightenment. Yes, Valette conceded, the eighteenth-century philosophes had relied excessively on the rhetorical device of ridicule; yes, they had lacked that historical sensibility that accords respect to the past and seeks to fathom it; and yes, their project was more successful in the domain of the physical and mathematical sciences than in that of the moral sciences. But, he continued, they had nonetheless "left a long streak of light." Through their devotion to disseminating their philosophy and its practical applications, they had changed the face of France:

> Had they done nothing more than to popularize *(rendre populaire),* by their many fine applications of method, the need to see each thing clearly and to make oneself understood, what gratitude would such a service merit! However "impoverished" or "meager" one finds the philosophy of Condillac, experience still proves that young minds that have . . . been early on habituated to the [mental] procedures that it reveals to us under so simple and naive a guise are soon filled with wonder at the rapidity of their progress in the quest for truth.[26]

For Valette, the heart of the school of Condillac was its pedagogy. He dwelt at length on Condillac's course of instruction for the prince of

Parma, the late text that the Revolution made canonical. "Called to the education of a prince, whose life can so powerfully influence the future of the people who must live under his laws," Condillac had stressed cognitive self-knowledge, familiarity with the operations of the human understanding, and the use of the method of genetic analysis to foster reliance on the individual's own intellectual powers. "In every case, only one thing is important, to figure out how we took the first step because, in order that there be progress, it suffices that we continue as we began." The method of analysis had, Valette attested, served him well as a young man assailed by competing intellectual currents in the opening decades of the nineteenth century. "The study of the [mental] faculties that was prescribed to us as the way to attain necessary truths enabled me to find a resting place [literally *oreiller*, or pillow] sweeter than the one afforded by doubt." Valette declared himself convinced of the continuing ascendancy of sensationalism in France: "The school of Locke and Condillac is still that of the great majority. . . . [T]he distinctive taste of our nation for perfect clarity will last a long time still."[27]

That the sensationalist camp had not given up the fight even after the July Revolution is evident in the attempt of the aging Idéologue P. C. F. Daunou to block the automatic inclusion of Cousin in the Academy of Moral and Political Sciences when that body was founded in 1832 as a self-conscious reincarnation of the Second Class of the Napoleonic Institut. Reportedly, and no doubt rightly, Daunou feared that Cousin's partisanship would dominate the election of new members, causing eclecticism, the so-called "German school," to wipe out Idéologie as an intellectual force within the new institution.[28]

But even if sensationalism eventually lost the battle for the Academy and other such institutional contests, it displayed impressive staying power. The sensationalist philosopher Valette was not alone in his early nineteenth-century testament to the perdurance of sensationalism in France. Several mainstays of the Cousinian camp echoed him. Perhaps the Cousinian philosopher Francisque Bouillier was only exaggerating the strength of the enemy for purposes of keeping the troops bellicose. But his remarks in 1844 concur with Valette's assessment that sensationalism provided a kind of intellectual bedrock in early nineteenth-century France and achieved the status of what might be called a vernacular knowledge[29]—that is, a set of propositions so thoroughly assimilated into the mental habits of a culture that it was accepted almost as a matter of common sense and could not be readily unseated by means of fiats delivered from the top of the political or academic hierarchies. Said Bouillier:

> In order that a new philosophy [i.e., Cousinianism] bear all its fruits, it is not sufficient that it reign among scholars. . . . , that it dethrone and topple the old philosophy. It is not even sufficient that it occupy its place uncontested. It is also necessary that it seep, so to speak, into the ideas of a large number of people, that it penetrate scholarship, literature, customs and attitudes and, finally, legislation. Now such a mental revolution can take place only slowly and cumulatively. Thus while it is very certain that, from a scholarly standpoint, sensationalism no longer exists, it is nonetheless certain that its principles and its consequences still live on. . . .[30]

That, too, was the opinion of the medical journalist Louis Peisse, a more unusual figure, sociologically speaking, who seems to have been Cousin's only conspicuous supporter in the Paris medical world of the period, a milieu dominated by a tendency to physiological reductionism. To be sure, Peisse deplored what he called "the school designated today by the name of *sensualiste*" and acknowledged that its major theorists were all dead (the dwindling of the cohort had, of course, been Daunou's problem at the time of the founding of the Academy of Moral and Political Sciences). But he nonetheless testified in 1840 to the abiding power of sensationalism over the French way of thinking. Not only did an array of sciences—the physical and natural, the physiological, even the economic and political—continue to bear its deep imprint. Peisse's claim went further. Of the several philosophical schools coexisting in France at that date, he contended, sensationalism was "certainly the largest, the most popular and, in a way, the most national."[31]

A third but effectively "closeted" Cousinian, Caroline Angebert, voiced the same opinion in a letter at the end of the Restoration. Expressing her very partisan belief that sensationalist psychology had "already [been] repulsed by the intellectual leadership," she regarded that blow as far from definitive. For instead of disappearing, sensationalism had "taken refuge" among "the masses," where it presently flourished, "still transmitted from father to son."[32] In this tacit theory of intellectual percolation, the discarded hand-me-downs of the intelligentsia were paraded as high fashion among the popular classes.

What Cousin was up against, then, was—perhaps in actual fact but certainly in a unanimously agreed upon rhetorical representation—a technically outdated but still potent psychology. As a form of vernacular knowledge able to lay claim to the attribute of "Frenchness," sensationalism would not be easy to extirpate.

Improbable Guru: Cousin's Early Career

Cousin's brand of psychology took shape and made its debut under the Empire and Restoration, the same period of rudderless intellectual flux that saw Laromiguière's influence wax, wane, and then wax again.[33]

Given the fact that he became such a permanent and imposing fixture on the nineteenth-century French cultural scene, it is striking how little is known about Cousin's background and early years. The same shreds of information are everywhere repeated, the very paucity of embellishment lending them almost mythic status. Born in Paris in 1792, Cousin was, we are told, the son of poor but literate working-class parents. His father was a jeweler (the occupation he listed on Victor's birth certificate), but accounts of Cousin's origins often represented him as a watchmaker, a variant that adds intriguing if largely inappropriate Rousseauean overtones to the story. His mother was a laundress. Although Cousin "almost never spoke of them,"[34] he did share with Jules Simon one poignant, emblematic detail: their lodgings were reached by means of a primitive contraption more resembling a ladder than a staircase.[35] That the unpropitious circumstances of Cousin's birth did not limit his social horizons was, the standard story continues, the combined result of his inherent nobility of character and a happy accident. He protected a schoolmate bullied by the other children, and the boy's grateful mother offered to subsidize his education. Hence, instead of learning a manual trade, he attended the Lycée Charlemagne, one of the best secondary schools in the capital at this date. By dint of hard work and native intelligence, he then passed the rigorous examination for the Ecole normale supérieure, the hatchery of the French professoriate and intelligentsia, in 1810 at the age of eighteen. He belonged to the Ecole's very first class after its post-Revolutionary reestablishment, and his score on the entrance examination had been the highest of all the applicants. Membership in the intellectual elite was now within his reach.[36]

Born, according to some, under the Rousseauean sign of a paternal watchmaker and compelled to lift himself by his own bootstraps, Cousin might seem to have had all the makings of a democrat. But, in fact, his developmental trajectory turned him into a liberal of a distinctly conservative stripe and a rabid antidemocrat. The "mere name of democracy never reached his ears without causing him obvious displeasure," one of his disciples remarked a few years after his death.[37] And in a letter to Royer-Collard in 1833, Cousin made much the same point when noting how the vagaries of classical Greek political practice had influenced the political philosophy of his beloved Plato. As Cousin reconstructed the linkage, Plato failed to perceive the full potential of monarchy because he was familiar only with the unpalatable example of Sparta, yet he correctly opposed democracy because he had an instance of it "right before his eyes"![38]

The milieu of Cousin's formative adolescent years, which doubled as the environment he inhabited during most of his subsequent career, helps to explain his political views. He forged his adult identity in the newly established Université, as the Napoleonic state educational corporation was called. A giant bureaucratic apparatus, pyramidal in structure, the Université aimed at providing a centrally supervised and nationally uniform system of education. At the top of the pyramid was a Grand Master, advised by the University Council; at the next level were the artificially created educational districts called "academies," each headed by a rector having his own advisory council. At both the central and academy levels, inspectors visited and reported on the component teaching institutions—the lycées, the other secondary schools, and the faculties. The Université was, in other words, a very different institutional entity from a "university," as that term was construed elsewhere in nineteenth-century Europe. Its primary purpose was teaching rather than research, the transmission to adolescents of already validated knowledge, not the production of new knowledge.[39] As the premier training institution for lycée teachers, the Ecole normale supérieure was an integral part of the structure, while the Ecole polytechnique, the Collège de France, and the Muséum d'histoire naturelle were placed outside it as loci of research.[40]

The Université also functioned as a giant meritocratic machine repeatedly skimming the cream off the student body through a series of ritualized examinations. This mechanism, so decisive a force in

Cousin's personal destiny, may have instilled his belief in a deserving intellectual aristocracy and his corresponding hostility toward the automatic all-inclusiveness of democracy. From a global perspective, the meritocratic operations of the Université can be seen as an instance of French precocity. According to Alan Spitzer's apt description, "The virtually universal pattern of the organization of higher education in the modern world—socialization and training of an elite in age-segregated institutions—had already assumed its characteristic French form" by the second decade of the nineteenth century.[41]

The Université thus additionally became the locus of the formation of generational identity. As Spitzer has brilliantly argued, it was by encountering and reencountering one another in the halls of academe that the members of a particular age-cohort acquired the sense that their shared year of birth created a bond of a special sort; they constituted a generation, or a historical entity with a distinctive outlook.[42] Insofar as it can be schematized, the defining feature of Cousin's generation was its position, both chronological and ideological, vis-à-vis the Revolution. They were, in at least two senses, post-Revolutionary: they inherited the social fluidity and career open to talent that the Revolution had secured; and they rejected as naive the political idealism that the Revolution had attempted to actualize. The decades of upheaval following 1789 had convinced them that mandates for sociopolitical change needed to be carefully evaluated and balanced by some countervailing force, be that force the partial retention of traditional arrangements that had proved their mettle over time or a mode of organic reasoning and/or feeling that could complement the corrosive effects of unmitigated analytic and critical reason. The generational concept played an important role in Cousin's success. Recognizing his message at the lectern as crystallizing their own age-based view of things, students selected him de facto as the spokesman for their post-Revolutionary generational consciousness.

The environment of the Université in its early years was not entirely inhospitable to political radicalism. The Ecole normale contributed student recruits to the Carbonarist revolt of 1820; even the young faculty member Victor Cousin may have lent a hand despite his later denials of involvement.[43] Still, it is probably not accidental that the Ecole polytechnique, existing outside the strict purview of the Université, rather than the Ecole normale, spawned the movement known as Saint-Simonian socialism.[44] And for those individuals who became professional *universitaires*—the teachers and administrators comprising the educational corporation—and who thus remained permanently within its bureaucratic carapace, the Université not surprisingly fostered an incremental attitude toward social change and a predilection for bureaucratic solutions to social problems. Certainly that was to be its long-term effect on Cousin.

Finally, as suggested in the Introduction to this book, the Université was one embodiment of the French state's post-Revolutionary mission to "produce society" in the absence of the recently destroyed corporations. By training civil servants to man the state's administrative apparatus, it also served as a major locus of production of the new post-Revolutionary social elite—the bourgeosie. As such, it formed the young working-class Cousin in an elitist bourgeois mold and, in turn, prepared him to embark upon his own chief assignment, which might be described as the pedagogical production and reproduction of bourgeois subjectivity.

The single most powerful influence on the young Cousin was a denizen of the Université. Pierre-Paul Royer-Collard not only recruited Cousin to the party of so-called Doctrinaire constitutional monarchism but also showed by his own example how effortlessly that political position meshed with an anti-sensationalist stance in philosophy. It was he who brought Cousin to the meetings of Maine de Biran's metaphysical society, thus furthering the avant-garde psychological education of his protégé. The affection and loyalty that marked their relationship can be seen in the steady stream of letters that passed between them after the aging Royer-Collard left Paris for the provinces, each man routinely addressing the other as "mon cher ami."[45] Royer-Collard had taught philosophy at the Ecole normale before moving in 1810 to the new chair in the history of philosophy at the Paris Faculty of Letters. Cousin followed him like a shadow, assuming the posts that Royer-Collard vacated and apparently finding a role model in the older man's gravitation to the sphere of educational administration. It is far from immediately obvious that Royer-Collard, who single handedly founded a new school of French academic philosophy by importing the common sense philosophy of Thomas Reid from Scotland, would have wanted to run a bureaucracy. Yet in 1815 he resigned his Sorbonne chair in practice, while retaining it in name, in order to preside over the Council of Public Instruction, a post that he held until 1819.[46] This jack-of-all-trades versatility, whereby the producer of knowledge then oversees its educational dissemination, was possible because of the rudimentary condition of the Université at this date. What made it desirable—and why Cousin would later emulate it—was the Doctrinaire understanding of the post-Revolutionary political situation of France.

A small group of engaged and, eventually, very powerful intellectuals of the post-Revolutionary generation, the Doctrinaires included from their inception Royer-Collard and François Guizot, the best-selling historian who would serve the July Monarchy as minister of public instruction from 1832–36 and, ultimately, as prime minister during the 1840s. That Royer-Collard was a Jansenist and Guizot a Protestant was of more than anecdotal significance: in the era of resurgent clericalism that followed Napoleon's repair of the breach with Rome, Doctrinaire thought was marked by its refusal to rely on the Catholic Church to organize and monitor society. The group seemed to pop up almost everywhere during the Restoration and July Monarchy, militating for reform of the penal code and for the abolition of slavery, lobbying for public hygiene, aid to orphaned children, and the establishment of asylums for the insane. Their collective name is misleading. Although they were said to employ pedantic and sententious language (the accusation from which the name derived), initially at least they lacked a highly elaborated doctrine.[47] Indeed wariness of doctrine may have been their hallmark. As Pierre Rosanvallon, one of their most recent (and sympathetic) interpreters, has pointed out, they never produced a major treatise of political philosophy, being more concerned with the day-to-day pragmatics of reconstructing and restabilizing France after its Revolutionary tumult than with abstract pronouncements about the ideal polity.[48] After all, the Revolution had offered ample evidence of the impotence of abstract political prescriptions.

As Rosanvallon restates Guizot's political position, which can roughly stand for that of the Doctrinaires as a whole, it turned on a recognition of the new, modern relationship between politics and society. Premodern power had, in Guizot's view, resided securely in specific individuals and families; modern power, by contrast, could be found "everywhere," circulating rapidly, impersonally, and almost invisibly through society and necessitating for the first time that the state actively reckon with "the masses." Hence new methods of government had to be, in Guizot's words, "internal" to society rather than "external" to it; constitutional political rulers had to busy themselves with creating "institutions, whereas despots had merely formed instruments."[49] Always at the ready, the state bureaucracy became in the Doctrinaire view the obvious means for crafting the institutions that, firmly located in society, would make modern governance feasible.[50] Chief among those institutions were the public schools that, placed under the supervision of the Université, already had one foot in the state. To produce new forms of knowledge and then disseminate them by means of the school system was thus a characteristically Doctrinaire procedure for the modernization of political power. To be sure, the trajectory of Idéologie under the Revolution had already supplied a concrete precedent in this regard. But not until the Doctrinaires was such a broad-gauged theoretical rationale for it advanced.

Guizot devised an idiosyncratic vocabulary to articulate the intimate connection that he envisioned between knowledge and political power. He spoke of the "government of minds" and of "governing by the management of minds, not by the upheaval of ways of life."[51] A disciple of Cousin expressed the same position more baldly during the 1840s. In the *Revue des deux mondes,* Jules Simon announced that the pressing problem of the day—what he called "the true social question"—was, contrary to many contemporary pundits, neither the organization of labor nor the need for electoral reform. Rather "the first and foremost question everywhere and always, but especially in those places where liberty is proclaimed as fact and as right, is education." And if education, and in particular education in philosophy, had such salience, it was because its content would eventually "penetrate to the lowest ranks of society, become the common patrimony, and give the civilization of an epoch its distinctive, historically recognizable character."[52]

In light of this Doctrinaire vision, it is clear that for Cousin the enterprise of philosophy was, at least from the moment that he fell under Royer-Collard's influence, necessarily linked to post-Revolutionary political concerns. He described in simple but revealing language the annual inspection of the third-year philosophy class at the Ecole normale, which he taught between 1815 and 1820, by the president of the Council of Public Instruction, then Royer-Collard: "As a philosopher and as a man of state, Monsieur Royer-Collard took a double interest in our work."[53] As an ally of the Doctrinaires, Cousin unabashedly avowed the connection between his philosophy and his politics, finding in that connection nothing of a dubious or compromising nature. These avowals became starker and more pointed with the passage of time. In a letter to Hegel of 1826 imploring the great German metaphysician to criticize the preface to a just-published collection of his Sorbonne lectures (the "Preface . . . alone is readable," he observed, indicating his personal hierarchization of his philosophical writings), Cousin also registered his intention to press his philosophical oeuvre into service for the political rehabilitation of France. "Be all the more pitiless," he exhorted Hegel, "knowing that, since I am determined to be useful to my country, I will always take the liberty of modifying the directives of my German masters according to the needs and condition, such as it is, of this poor country." Hegel never replied.[54]

In his celebrated lecture series of 1828, when he was allowed to return to his Sorbonne podium after eight years of silence imposed by the far-right faction within the restored Bourbon monarchy, Cousin publicly declared the formal analogies that made his philosophical system congruent with his political views. Labeling that philosophical system eclecticism and stressing its combination of the best of a variety of competing philosophical traditions, he declared that it replicated the mixture of monarchical, aristocratic, and democratic elements in the French constitution, the Charter of 1814. This striking formal analogy lent his philosophical creed additional authority. "I ask, when everything around us is mixed, complex, commingled, when all the opposites live and prosper together, if it is possible for philosophy to escape the general spirit; I ask if philosophy could be other than eclectic . . ."[55] At the beginning of the July Monarchy, when he and the other Doctrinaires had become political insiders, he proclaimed with laconic boldness in print, "My political faith conforms in every respect to my philosophical faith."[56] By that time, of course, the Doctrinaire political position had shed its earlier elusiveness and had been boiled down into a catchword that underscored its family resemblance with the eclectic philosophy: the *juste-milieu,* or the golden mean between extremes.[57]

But if Cousin could never entirely separate philosophy from politics, in his initial public incarnation during the Restoration he was perceived by his adoring Sorbonne audience far more as a pure, incandescent intellect than as a politician. That audience was dominated by young men, under the age of thirty and, although Hippolyte Taine would much later derisively describe the mature Cousinian philosophy as a "nice relaxing tepid bath into which fathers dip their children as a healthful precaution,"[58] there can be no doubt that its impact on his early audience was exactly the opposite: wildly exhilarating. Part of that exhilaration owed to the new generational consciousness that had crystallized around Cousin. Stunningly young himself—only nineteen when he became a tutor (*élève répétiteur*) at the Ecole normale supérieure and a mere twenty-three when he first mounted the podium of the Sorbonne—Cousin was disowning the putatively arid analytic style of the previous century in favor of a new, affirmative mode of thought and feeling. "The eighteenth century was the age of criticism and destruction. The nineteenth century must be that of intelligent rehabilitation," Cousin told his audience in 1817.[59]

Cousin cared too much about reason to be a full-fledged Romantic, but his recognition of the insufficiency of reason, as well as the prose style that accompanied that recognition, sufficed to qualify him as a generic romantic. At this historical juncture, Romanticism was routinely seen as an expression of youth. In *Racine et Shakespeare* (1823), his famous pamphlet on the relative merits of the classic and romantic literary modes, Stendhal recounts a conversation he (supposedly) had with a theater manager about the artistic preferences of students at the medical and law faculties and attributes to himself the following retort, "But sir, the vast majority of well-bred *youth* have been converted to Romanticism by the eloquence of Monsieur Cousin."[60] So much did the young Cousin harp on the virtues of youth that he could even get himself into a situation verging on self-parody. In December 1819, returning to his Sorbonne podium after a bout of illness, he referred to "my weak state of health" and warned his students, "No longer expect from me that ardor, that vivacity of youth that corresponds to yours; it is lost, perhaps irretrievably."[61] Cousin was at the time twenty-seven years old and would live to the age of seventy-six!

Part of the exhilaration about Cousin derived from his oratory, a talent that even his most bitter opponents grudgingly acknowledged during the 1820s. The arch-detractor Armand Marrast could not contain his perverse admiration for Cousin's stirring lecturing style. Cousin, he said, "speaks like a high priest; his rich intonation, his mobile features, his weighty and cadenced diction, the painful childbirth of a thought that seems to have gestated in his gut—everything he does favors the impression that he makes on his audience."[62] An equally fierce opponent, Auguste Comte, arrived at the same conclusion. Although Cousin offered his students an unreliable account of contemporary German philosophy, he had, according to Comte, succeeded in acquiring a fanatic following because "he possesses one of the essential skills of the Ciceronian orator—gesture and facial expression."[63] Looking back on the 1828 lecture series from the distance of almost three decades, Hippolyte Taine stressed the difference between the oral styles of Cousin and his sensationalist predecessors:

> We were all a little German ... ; we ran [to hear Cousin] the way people run to the opera; and in truth it was an opera. In the space of an hour, the impetuous orator brought onstage and paraded before us God, nature, humanity. ... ; this symphony sung by a single man inspired vertigo, and minds accustomed to the calm disquisitions of the sensationalists gave themselves over ... to the poet who populated their imaginations with such prodigious phantoms. ...[64]

Alan Spitzer has rightly noted that the excitement surrounding Cousin in the 1820s "puts a considerable strain on our [late twentieth-century] historical empathy."[65] When we read the texts of his 1828 lectures, we comprehend only with great difficulty why Cousin's original presentation of them qualified as Restoration-style media events, attracting swarms of journalists and even prompting a market-conscious publisher to hire stenographers (until then used only to record parliamentary proceedings) so that each lecture could be immediately printed and sold in pamphlet form.[66] The accumulation of documentary evidence, however, leaves no doubt that early in his career Cousin attained the status of a youth guru. For most of the Restoration, the symbiosis of power and knowledge that was later blatantly—and, to some, cynically—epitomized by his thought seems to have lingered below the surface, well out of sight. Cousin appeared as an inspired sage, not as a sordid calculator. The view from across the Channel even stressed his unworldy disinterestedness. "He has," the *Edinburgh Review* told its readers in 1829, "consecrated himself, his life, and labours, to philosophy, and philosophy alone; nor has he approached the sanctuary with unwashed hands."[67]

A *Moi* Given Whole and A Priori

As a member of the immediately post-Revolutionary generation, Cousin perceived the legacy of the Revolution as intensely problematic. In his view, the events of 1789 had overthrown tradition as the guide to social and political life and installed in its place nothing more substantial than a gamut of competing theories, leaving France threatened with perennial instability. Cousin was not inclined to join in the lament that depicted the Revolution and its sequelae as "the fault of Voltaire, the fault of Rousseau." Rather, amplifying a theme that we have already seen in Maine de Biran's journal, he preferred to assign the blame to Condillac and the sensationalist psychology more generally. As Cousin analyzed the situation, the unchallenged ascendancy of sensationalism had the disastrous effect of eroding the moral verities that must, if society is to remain stable, serve as a brake on human impulse. As he saw it, sensationalism built up a self (or more accurately, a simulacrum of a self) through the accumulation of atomistic sensations, each of which had originated as a reaction to a material stimulus and was thus essentially passive. Such a psychology could not ground a durable, unified self—one that, animated by an active spiritual principle, would bear moral responsibility both as a duty in this life and because the specter of eternal punishment deterred it from straying. The fragmented sensationalist self had instead opened the door to the exaggerated, reckless idealism and the antisocial violence that had characterized the Revolutionary decade. In the Cousinian scheme of things, as in its less militant Biranian counterpart, repairing the self by philosophical means was therefore the linchpin in the project of the post-Revolutionary stabilization of France.

That remedial project is sketched in broad strokes on the first page of the bound notebook of an obscure student who attended Cousin's Sorbonne never-published course of mid-December 1819 to mid-March 1820. The page contains a single paragraph, ascribed to "Cousin," but since the student begins his verbatim record of the actual lecture series only several pages later, the precise provenance of the paragraph in question is unclear. Perhaps the student copied it from the notes he had garnered at another of Cousin's courses. Almost certainly he intended it as the introduction to the notebook as a whole—and aptly so, for it masterfully captures the core of Cousin's philosophical message. To "Cousin" is attributed the following:

> In my view, the man of character is a man who makes himself, a man who has a will, who is his own source of life. The man of temperament is one who acts according to his passivity. Now persistent passivity does not constitute character. That is how we can distinguish the men

of antiquity from modern men. [The ancients] remained hidden for a long time, shaping themselves as they wished to be, and if they consequently appeared calm and tranquil amidst turmoil, that is because *character is unity!* The moderns are filled with anxiety because they have not made for themselves a self *(moi)* that persists. They are not themselves, they are [dispersed] in everything that surrounds them.[68]

All the basic Cousinian elements are present: the repeated jibes against sensationalism, here encoded under the words "passivity" and "modern"; the mockery of pedagogical regimens based upon it (for example, the Idéologue curriculum of the central schools), which so emphasized acute observation of the external world that, in Cousin's view, the student's personal being was vitiated, reduced to bits and pieces wantonly strewn throughout the environment; the weakness and anxiety associated with such psychological fragmentation; the high praise reserved for the unified *moi*.

Almost immediately upon assuming a public role, Cousin began to hammer out his message about the grandeur of the human *moi* and the inability of a sensationalist philosophy to provide a foundation for that indispensable entity. His fixation on the *moi* surfaced in December 1815, when he began his stint as Royer-Collard's substitute in the history of modern philosophy at the Sorbonne. His inaugural lecture had announced a course on the perception of external phenomena. However, after several classes on the declared topic, Cousin suddenly—and, no doubt, all the more memorably—reversed direction and decided to devote the entire year to the philosophical issue he regarded as "first both chronologically and in importance, that of the *moi* and of personal existence."[69] To be sure, Royer-Collard's teaching, which Cousin would later characterize in gendered language as a "manly dialectic" *(mâle dialectique)*,[70] had already gone some small distance in the direction of rescuing the self from its abject (and politically perilous) condition of sensationalist fragmentation. Relying on the Scottish common sense school of philosophy as an antidote to sensationalism, Royer-Collard had insisted on the distinction between sensation and perception. This seemingly technical point, in fact, advanced the meaning-laden argument that a passive capacity for sensory reception and an active capacity for judgment were equally constitutive of the human mind.[71] But Cousin would take this tendency much further than his mentor and eventually create a philosophical system entirely centered on an active *moi*.

With this goal already in view, Cousin's maiden course treated the history of philosophy exclusively through the lens of the vicissitudes of the self. Thus when Cousin turned to Condillac, he warned his audience not to "expect any general consideration" of that philosopher or of the eighteenth century. "I will limit myself . . . to all the passages about the *moi* that can be found in [Condillac's] writings." His criticism was harsh. Condillac, he charged, "departs from a radically defective hypothesis" and subsequently "gets lost in nihilism." He is able to make the self dependent on something as flimsy and feeble as memory only by confusing it with another concept, that of the self-identical self. After all, Cousin pointed out, "memory returns to that which was; if there is nothing prior, it is mute. It can say 'still me' only after an initial act of intelligence mingled with consciousness has said 'me.'" Cousin thus corrected Condillac by insisting, much as Maine de Biran had, that the *moi* exists a priori, that it is already there at the first sensation and the first glimmerings of consciousness. Only its absolute priority, its foundational nature, enables a more highly elaborated entity, the self-identical *moi* that endures through space and time, to come into existence at the moment of the second sensation.[72]

The *moi* is a substance, Cousin furthermore insisted, controverting Condillac; but, pace Spinoza, it is not a substance that can be defined axiomatically. "Metaphysics," Cousin stated, "is not a part of mathematics. It is instead a science of observation, like physics or the natural sciences." Hence, Cousin's eclecticism would not be a simple reprise of the seventeenth-century systems; it would return to metaphysics while inflecting it with the modality of observation emphasized by the eighteenth-century empiricists. Cousin's insistence on self-as-substance was also marshaled against Condillac's definition of the self as a collection of sensations, a collection that, Cousin said, paraphrasing Condillac, was located in an indeterminate "somewhere" and was nothing but a "logical and grammatical subject," a "sign" affixed to an assemblage of floating qualities "imagined" as a subject. By contrast, Cousin's substantial self was no nebulous, jerry-built somewhere; as "common sense and the entire human race" attested, it was a "real subject."[73]

The core of Cousin's observationally based metaphysics, of that "so sought after alliance of metaphysical and physical science," was what he called the "psychological method." Descriptions of that method lard his teaching like incantations. Here is a description from 1826:

> The psychological method consists in isolating oneself from any other world but that of consciousness in order to establish and orient oneself there, where everything is real but where the reality is exceedingly diverse and delicate. The talent for the psychological consists in voluntarily inserting oneself into this entirely interior world, in giving oneself to oneself as spectacle, and in reproducing freely and distinctly all the phenomena that, in the circumstances of ordinary life, are thrown up only in an accidental and confused manner.

The basic rule was totality: undertaken without bias, observation "must be complete, must exhaust its object, and can be allowed to stop only when there are no phenomena left to observe." No wonder, then, that there were "many different levels of depth in the psychological method," as years of practice had taught Cousin.[74]

Nonetheless, the method had led to at least one discovery of capital importance. In direct refutation of sensationalist doctrine, it had revealed that sensation and its derivatives constituted only one of the categories of the so-called real contents of consciousness. (Engaging in the same mental exercise some seventy-five years earlier, Condillac had, not surprisingly, reported exactly the opposite finding!)[75] Distinct from and "impossible to confound with" sensation, but equally incontestably real, were two additional components: volition and reason.[76] The three components operated as a seamless ensemble, but they could be teased apart by means of analysis. They were, Cousin noted in a phrase heavy-handed in its neologizing as well as in its religious reference, "a triplicity which resolves itself into a unity and a unity which develops into a triplicity."[77] Cousin considered this classification of the elements of consciousness as one of his signal contributions. "It has really caught on," he observed with evident pleasure in 1833, "for I see it reproduced in practically every work of psychology that has recently appeared."[78]

The psychological method was for Cousin the key to the philosophical enterprise not only because its supposed scientific rigor as an observational practice lent it credibility in an early nineteenth-century intellectual environment. The method also extended well beyond itself, functioning (in another of his favorite phrases) as the "vestibule" to ontology and metaphysics.[79] As Cousin said when urging Hegel to read the 1826 preface to his *Fragmens philosophiques,* that "little writing," which encapsulated his entire system, could be boiled down to: "1, the method; 2, its application to consciousness or psychology; 3, the transition from psychology to ontology. . . ."[80] To fail to make the transition was a serious defect in a philosopher. Cousin believed that his student Jouffroy, for example, had compromised his genius by shrinking from high-wire speculation. "For fear of losing his way . . . in higher metaphysics . . . , Monsieur Jouffroy enjoyed remaining on the firm terrain of psychology, in those luminous and serene regions where observation is always effective. . . ."[81]

According to Cousin, any fledgling philosopher who began by scrutinizing his own consciousness would soon learn that its so-called triplicity provided a map of the very structure of the universe. "Ontology is given to us in its entirety at the same time as psychology." The three internal elements of consciousness had their external counterparts, voluntary activity translating into mankind, sensibility into nature, and reason into God.[82] Delving deeply inside himself, then, the student of Cousinian philosophy would eventually be propelled outward and upward, arriving at an intimate conviction of certain fixed, immutable principles. According to Cousin, "We can consider as a guaranteed conquest of the experimental method and of true psychological analysis the establishment of principles that, given to us by the most certain of all experiences, that of consciousness, nonetheless have a reach beyond experience and open up to us regions inaccessible to empiricism."[83] These precious super-empirical principles concerned "the true, the beautiful, and the good," to cite the anodyne keywords of Cousin's 1818 lectures, much later transformed into his abundantly reprinted textbook of the same title.[84]

But how was the *moi* related to the three distinct elements of consciousness? Although Cousin did not pose the question so baldly in his earliest teachings,[85] by the mid-1820s he made it clear that volition was the stuff of selfhood. "The will alone is the person or the *moi,*" he announced in 1826, only to reiterate a few sentences later, "Our personality is the will and nothing more." In contrast to those "movements that external agents determine in us, despite ourselves, we have the power to initiate a different kind of movement," one that "in the eyes of consciousness, assumes a new character." We "impute [such a movement] to ourselves," consider ourselves as its cause; indeed it serves for us as the very origin of the concept of cause. Voluntary activity is that element of consciousness that we perceive as our own; it belongs to us. It exists in a "foreign world, amidst two orders of phenomena [the sensible and the rational] that do not belong to us, that we can only perceive on the condition of separating them from ourselves."[86]

The motif of belonging and not belonging was one that Cousin mined extensively. In the Fichtean language that he sometimes favored, the data about the external world that came in through our sense organs comprised the *non-moi*. And though not technically relegated to the *non-moi* (whose very name seems to connote a pariah status), reason was in Cousin's scheme also utterly foreign to the *moi*. This was the central claim of his celebrated concept of "impersonal reason."[87] As he instructed the students in his 1828 course, "Your intelligence is not free. . . . You do not constitute your reason, and it *does not belong to you*." There was nothing "less individual" or "less personal" than reason. If the products of reason were merely personal, imposing them on others "would be an exaggerated form of despotism." Instead, the "universal and absolute nature" of reason obliged everyone to bend to its dictates. We are within our rights when "we declare totally crazy (*en délire*) those who do not accept the truths of arithmetic or the difference between beauty and ugliness, justice and injustice."[88] In other words, Cousin deployed the claim that reason does not "belong to us" (but rather to God) as a powerful argument in favor of common standards and values and against the kind of social and political contestation that bred instability and revolution.

Conversely, the claim that voluntary activity, or the *moi*, did indeed "belong to us" provided Cousin with an equally powerful argument in favor of private property. It is worth noting that both Locke and Cousin provided a philosophical blueprint of the self with reference to its legal implications. Locke's forensic reference was, as discussed in Chapter 3, the criminal law. He emphasized the pragmatic need to postulate a continuous self-identical self to ensure the just punishment of wrongdoers. Cousin's forensic reference was, on the other hand, the civil law. He stressed the inextricable intertwinement of the theory of the self with the right to private property. In this regard, he may have been influenced by his informal mentor Maine de Biran, who pondered the matter in his *journal intime* in 1817. Responding to a philosophical manuscript of an old friend and colleague who grounded property in the person, which he equated with the human *organisation*—that is, its complex physiological structure—and its capacity for sensation, Maine de Biran agreed with the basic line of reasoning but faulted the definition of the person that the author was employing. "You have to know what you mean by the *moi*." To function as guarantor in such an argument, the *moi* could not originate in a "living, organized, sensing *composite*" (my emphasis) but only in a so-called "simple" entity, one not composed of parts, "that acts or creates effort while having at its disposal certain faculties lodged in the same whole."[89] This motif must have stayed with Maine de Biran because, some months later, he nearly crowed in exultation upon reaching his family estate at Grateloup in the Périgord:

> I arrive home. There I enjoy a complete sense of property. The changes that took place in my absence pique my curiosity and call me fully to the outside world [*au dehors*, a term that Maine de Biran uses as the opposite of his states of meditative interiority]. I examine each object with an attention full of attraction. Everything interests me: the least shrub, the plant that escapes other eyes elicits my glance. It is mine; it is a part of myself.[90]

Whether or not inspired by Maine de Biran, Cousin sketched out the linkage between the *moi* and private property in detail in his 1818–19 Sorbonne lectures on the history of moral philosophy. He began by declaring that the "first and most intimate development of the free *moi* is thought; all thought, considered within the bounds of the individual sphere, is sacred." Its quality of inviolability derived from the transfer to it of an essential quality of the self—that it belongs to us. Thus, in keeping with the principle that "our original property is ourselves, our *moi*," Cousin asserts that the "first act of free, personal thought is the first act of property." This rhetorical move then enabled him to make sweeping assertions about property in general. Property was not, he assured his student audience, based upon mere convention; after all, conventions could be annulled by the parties who had agreed to them. Rather it was founded on a "superior principle—that of the sanctity of liberty." Property consisted in the "free imposition of the personality," that is, of volitional activity, "on things." Once acquired, those things "participate in some manner in my personality." They obtain rights by this relationship or, what is the same thing, "I have rights in them," so that "by augmenting [my] property, [I] extend the circle of [my] rights." The natural right to property thus rested on the principle of human liberty, and that natural right, in turn, became institutionalized as a right protected by civil law.[91]

In sum, property was for Cousin not only rooted in and protected by the homologous structures of the human psyche and the universe but was also an arena of distinctly human self-development. Nowhere, perhaps, than in its gloss on property does eclectic philosophy and its conception of the *moi* appear more clearly as a justification for the bourgeois order, in both the Marxian and the ordinary senses of that term. The urgency of the eclectic need to shore up property can be seen by comparing Cousin's argument with those of his predecessors, Locke and Destutt de Tracy.

In his late seventeenth-century *Second Treatise on Government,* Locke also derived the right of private property from the contention that "every Man has a Property in his own Person." However, his understanding of the person in this context was a corporeal rather than a spiritual or psychological one ("The Labour of his Body, and the Work of his Hands, we may say, are property"), and he cast his whole discussion in terms of man's natural right to physical self-preservation. Although an unambiguous advocate of private property, Locke did not attempt to depict ownership as a spiritual desideratum, nor did he return to the issue in his *Essay Concerning Human Understanding* in order to treat it from a psychological angle.[92]

In an argument quite similar to and nearly contemporaneous with Cousin's, Destutt de Tracy did derive private property from human psychology and, in particular, from the will. But that will was itself a rather more contingent affair than it was in the eclectic system, being itself a consequence of the prior capacity for sensation. Tracy insisted that the capacity for sensation was originary. It was "that beyond which we cannot go," and as such it was "the same thing as *us*," the "existence of the *moi* and the sensitivity of the *moi*" being simply identical. Hence, to regard "one's will as the equivalent of oneself is [erroneously] to take the part for the whole." Tracy even entertained the possibility that a being endowed with sensitivity but lacking a will could have individuality or personality; but such a being, he opined, could never come up with the idea of property. On the other hand, once the sensory capacity had generated a will, the idea of property would be born "necessarily and inevitably in all its plenitude."[93] In other words, Idéologues like

Destutt de Tracy were entirely committed to the idea of private property, but they thought that idea sufficiently hardy that it did not need the fortress-like protection of an a priori *moi* nor of a tripartite division of consciousness replicated in the structure of the universe as a whole. Cousin had, obviously, more stringent requirements for order, which embraced the self and its property together.

Cousinian Introspection as a Technology of the Self

What Cousin called the psychological method undergirded more than just a philosophical system. From the perspective of the person employing it, it was a learned skill that helped to fashion a particular kind of self. As such, it qualified as a "technology of the self" in Michel Foucault's sense—one of those "procedures, which have doubtless existed in all civilizations, that are proposed or prescribed to individuals in order to fix, maintain, or transform their identities with particular ends in view" and that operate by means of either "a mastery of the self by the self or a knowledge of the self by the self."[94] Cousin's version of introspection provided adepts with both a practical mode of access to the inner life and a specialized language with which to talk about it. It shaped the self in part through the deceptively simple gesture of naming it, of affixing the label *moi* to a certain kind of mental content.

Cousin hammered home the central importance of introspection—or, as it was called in nineteenth-century France, interior observation[95]— through his representation of his personal itinerary as a philosopher. As he described his formative years in 1826 (when he had attained the ripe age of thirty-four and could apparently afford to muse on his beginnings), the driving force behind his philosophical vocation had been twofold: on the one hand, his realization of the destruction wrought by the "analytic spirit" of the eighteenth-century sensualists and hence of the urgent need for reconstruction; on the other hand, his fundamental admiration for the Baconian inductive method that those same sensualists endorsed. His philosophical breakthrough came in 1815 when he decided that the way out of his impasse was to wed Baconian observation to the metaphysics that the sensualists proscribed. Accordingly in that year, he pioneered on himself his "psychological method," which ever since had "constitute[d] the fundamental unity of my teaching." What this method owed to Maine de Biran's *méditation psychologique*, or

even whether Cousin knew of the older philosopher's habitual introspective practices, we can only speculate. In any case, Cousin's "historical consciousness"—or perhaps, more accurately, his precocious desire
for self-memorialization—spurred him on to reproduce faithfully and
"in all their weakness" his very first applications of this unusually fertile
method and to publish them under the title *Fragmens philosophiques.*
That book made available three years' worth of his "obscure and painful
labors." The "psychological details" it recorded, while "arid and lacking
in all apparent grandeur," must nonetheless, he admonished, "never be
forgotten since they form the legitimate point of departure for all the
future directions that philosophy can and should take."[96]

Cousin's whole system of eclecticism had, in other words, issued from
his heroic introspective experience of the years 1815–17. That experience had both founded the discipline of eclectic philosophy and formed
the prototype of all subsequent work in it, much as Descartes' period of
systematic doubt while living in solitude in Holland and Freud's interpretation of his own dreams in fin-de-siècle Vienna had served in a joint
foundational-prototypical capacity in the disciplines of Cartesian philosophy and psychoanalysis, respectively. Not surprisingly, then, training in Cousinian philosophy mirrored the master's development by also
featuring introspection. This was already true as early as 1815–20,
when, as *maître de conférences* in philosophy at the Ecole normale,
Cousin imposed on his students (so close to him in age that they later
became "my friends") what he called "that austere discipline . . . exempt
from all mechanical narrowness." At its heart was an effort to instill in
them "that psychological sense, that art of interior observation without
which man remains unknown to man and philosophy is only an assemblage of lifeless concepts. . . ."[97]

Outsiders likewise regarded Cousinianism as fostering introspection
among the student population of the late 1830s. One of Auguste
Comte's harangues against interior observation, and in favor of the
"positive" method of studying mental phenomena exclusively by means
of cerebral and nervous physiology, mentioned the "deplorable psychological mania that a famous sophist had momentarily succeeded in
inspiring in French youth." His listeners would have readily identified
the unnamed "sophist" as Cousin and the "psychological mania" as the
enthusiastic belief in the scientific efficacy of introspection; the adverb
"momentarily" bespoke Comte's fond wish that the vogue of Cousinian-

ism might quickly pass.[98] Stendhal also saw introspection as the hall-mark of the Cousinian teaching. To be sure, his own adherence to Idéologie committed him to introspection, but he satirized Cousin's particular variety of it mercilessly:

> Monsieur Cousin claims to have found all this out by means of what he calls a "meditative interrogation of consciousness." That is the whole secret of the new school of philosophy. If these gentlemen did not hide behind the obscurity of their style, everyone would see the inanity of their thought. While they interrogate their consciousnesses, in which they read so many fine things, they shut their eyes to the realities established by Locke and Condillac and replace facts and experiences with ideal speculations.[99]

What guidelines did Cousin offer the student embarking on the momentous journey of interior observation? The descriptions of the introspective method scattered through the master's writings hardly provide step-by-step instructions. Stendhal was not far from the mark when he acerbically summed them up as "Close your eyes and search your consciousness."[100] In fact, the very word "consciousness," a mainstay in the Cousinian vocabulary, may help to explain why the *maître* did not feel called upon to provide a lavish description of the procedure. "Consciousness," which seems to have entered the English language when Locke invoked it in the *Essay on Human Understanding* as one of the sources of personal identity, initially had no French equivalent. "We have in my view only the words *sentiment* and *conviction* which correspond in some manner to [Locke's] idea," complained Pierre Coste, the French translator of Locke's great work, and he consequently adopted the awkward neologism *con-science,* stipulating that it be both hyphenated and italicized to accentuate its Latin roots.[101] Soon standardized as the nonhyphenated and nonitalicized *conscience,* the term was, in Cousin's usage, basically synonymous with the *sens intime* of the eighteenth-century Catholic Cartesian apologists. "See 'Consciousness' (*Conscience*)," the Cousinian philosophical dictionary tells the reader who attempts to look up *sens intime.*[102] Both terms denoted the sheer obviousness, or self-evidence, of our knowledge of the self; our immediate, unshakable, a priori conviction about its existence, unity, and identity. Insofar as the act of introspection was, simply, attending to consciousness, it was hard to see how it could be analyzed, elaborated upon, or expressed as a temporal sequence.

Nonetheless, Cousin's occasional descriptions of introspection do convey some sense of the relevant procedure, as he understood it. In addition to the description, cited in the previous section, that figured in Cousin's 1826 account of the strenuous early years of his own philosophic career, there are revealing characterizations in his Sorbonne lectures of 1828:

> What is psychological analysis? It is the slow, patient, and meticulous observation, with the aid of consciousness, of phenomena hidden in the depths of human nature. These phenomena are complicated, fleeting, obscure, rendered almost indiscernible (*insaissisable*) by their very closeness. The consciousness which applies itself to them is an instrument of extreme delicacy: it is a microscope applied to things infinitely small.[103]

> There is, Gentlemen, a psychological art, for reflection is, so to speak, against nature, and this art is not learned in a day. One does not fold back upon oneself easily without long practice, sustained habit, and a laborious apprenticeship.[104]

Two motifs stand out in these accounts. First, introspection is an ascetic, almost monastic discipline tinged with heroism: it requires self-sacrifice and a long and painful tutelage, it goes against the grain, and it removes the practitioner from the reassuring world of ordinary social intercourse. Second, in epistemological terms, introspection is decidedly hybrid. At times Cousin stresses its scientificity, as when he metaphorically identifies it with a microscope or, in a passage that I have not quoted here, declares that psychology and physics are on a par as empirical sciences.[105] At other times, however, he designates introspection as an art and intimates that plying it to more than superficial effect requires a touch of genius. In thus suggesting that introspection is a combined art-and-science, Cousin clearly wants to have his cake and eat it too. A zealous opponent of the reduction of mental phenomena to biological ones, he nonetheless wants his psychology to possess all the authority that the term "science" conferred in the early nineteenth century. At the same time he appeals to the Romantic sensibilities of his audience by endowing his key procedure of interior observation with the ethos of an art capable of seizing the extremely delicate and elusive nature of consciousness as an object. In its Romantic guise, successful introspection is a feat of almost high-wire virtousity.

Cousin gives us enough information to infer such a general description of introspection but, beyond that, he has little to say about what introspection discovers. He was apparently uninterested in the texture of subjectivity, in capturing nuances of emotion or in charting the ebbs, flows, and clashes of currents of thought and feeling. Interiority was not for him a preferred locus of experience or place of refuge, although he liked to depict himself to his students as if it were. (At the opening lecture of his 1828 course, for example, he made much of the inwardness that he had cultivated during his years of banishment from teaching and worried aloud that, having become "accustomed to those forms of thought that serve well to explain ourselves to ourselves," he might have lost the knack of communicating to a large audience.)[106] Instead, interiority attracted him as a polemical resource: he sought to marshal the evidence of introspection to establish once and for all that the human subject was not passive and hence dangerously exempt from moral responsibility but active, and that a host of moral and political consequences flowed inexorably from that truth.

His polemical investment in mental activity colored his evaluations of his predecessors. Thus Maine de Biran earned the accolade of the most important of Cousin's French mentors because of the heed he paid to the phenomena of the will. "That admirable observer taught me to tease out in all our knowledge, and even in the simple events of consciousness, the role of voluntary activity, of that activity in which our personality bursts forth."[107] On the other hand, Cousin demoted Kant, finding him guilty of a "psychological error that put him en route to the abyss." By failing to bestow on "voluntary and free activity" the same care and analytic scrutiny that he bestowed on reason, Kant never recognized the special connection between will and personality.[108]

Given the primarily polemical purpose of Cousinian introspection, it is hardly surprising that its fruits were minimalist and monochromatic rather than variegated, richly textured, and elaborately patterned. Cousin never explicitly defined the concept of mental activity that functioned as his psychological holy grail. He did imply (perhaps following Maine de Biran) that it was a kind of switch point at the border between an individual's spirituality and materiality, the mental impetus within that individual whose "mysterious" property was to cause that individual's muscles to move.[109] Hence a self equated with volition or activity would probably be introspectively experienced by its possessor as a surge of absolutely unified and unmarked assertion, as an element of consciousness essentially lacking in specific content.

The quest for mental activity thus helps to explain why the Cousinian movement, for all its reliance and insistence on introspection, did not produce an introspective literature, even during the era in which the *journal intime* emerged as a genre and then flourished exuberantly.[110] Cousin and his followers wrote profusely, but they did not ordinarily cultivate the modalities of the diary, the confession, or even the autobiographical reminiscence. Cousin may have learned many things from Maine de Biran, but he evidently had no inclination to adopt his mentor's practice of keeping a daily journal replete with descriptions of his inner mental states and bouts of emotional malaise. Nor did he place a high value on Biran's own journal, or rather on what was characteristic of it as an instance of the genre: presented with it in 1843 (when Biran's son sent piles of his deceased father's papers to Paris), he opened only one of the four notebooks and, totally incurious about Biran's protracted dialogue with himself, certified its worth by observing that it contained "rather long philosophical passages."[111] The bits of autobiography that Cousin wove into the prefaces of his *Fragmens philosophiques* are much stiffer, less revelatory, more exclusively confined to professional career and public face than even what Descartes saw fit to share with his readers in the *Discourse on Method*.

In their pursuit of their own brand of reflexivity, some Cousinians went further than merely bypassing the soul-searching variety. Ernest Bersot actively deplored what he called the "demon of interior analysis," that incessant "work on [one]self" that had, in his view, been Rousseau's undoing. Instead of depicting it neutrally as a more intense form of the method of interior observation on which psychological science relied, he cast it as something radically different, indeed as the enemy of that science. In Bersot's view, such interior analysis made one prey to illusion; it roused "the sleeping chaos of feelings and thoughts" always lurking in the "depths of the soul" and caused it to assume invasive proportions. Those who engaged in this dangerously excessive self-observation would never know "true science."[112]

Among Cousin's students, I have come across a single exception to this general rule of avoidance of soul-searching introspection. Between the years 1836 and 1849 Antoine Charma kept what he playfully called a *nocturnal*—that is, a journal in reverse, a record of his mental activities at night—later using it as the raw material for a scholarly work on sleep. Charma believed, in orthodox Cousinian fashion, that sleep did not suspend the will, that "one possesses oneself while dreaming" and that, as "master of [him]self," the dreaming subject continues to deliberate. Although he thus adamantly refused to disown the self that appeared in his dreams, he nonetheless frankly recounted dreams in which his murderous rage toward an enemy and or his anxieties about saving a drowning child, and subsequent humiliation when the supposed child turned out to be an old rooster, were on full view.[113] But, as will be discussed in the next chapter, Charma was hardly the ideal type of the Cousinian and broke with the *maître* for reasons both of doctrine and of temperament.

In sum, although Cousin was, in technical philosophical terms, a zealous champion of introspection, and although in everyday terms, he placed high cultural value on a person's ability to look inward, he was not introspective in the way that we ordinarily use that term today. He seems to have utterly lacked the propensity to rummage around in his psyche or to find layers of hidden complexity in his motives and feelings. An agitated letter to the *maître* by one of his students makes this point vividly. Having reported a painful inner conflict between personal desire and professional duty, Etienne Vacherot was devastated when Cousin's advice to him acknowledged only the claims of duty. He described himself as "driven to despair" by the thought that "it would be necessary [for Cousin] to be inside myself (*être en moi-même*) to understand my position."[114] Vacherot's choice of language was telling. By admitting, as a consummate Cousinian, that he could not expect his mentor to share or even appreciate his inner state, that such "in-dwelling" exceeded the bounds of Cousin's possibilities, he inadvertently attests to the oddly abstract nature of Cousinian-style introspection. Within the total system of eclecticism, introspection served an intellectual function as a bridge to ontology and a social function as a token of cultivation. It dispensed with that attentiveness to the nuances of one's own thoughts and feelings that typically endowed an introspective individual—in the ordinary meaning of that term—with a capacity for empathy.

A Discourse of Human Difference: The Selved and the Unselved

The chief discovery that Cousin made by means of introspection was that the human personality could be identified with activity or will. However, in Cousin's canon, introspection was associated with another, equally momentous breakthrough: it revealed the axis on which the fundamental difference between human beings could be plotted. The so-called triplicity of consciousness, or the operational fusion of the three analytically distinct elements of sensibility, rationality, and will, served for some people, but not for others, as a permanent barrier to teasing out the *moi* and forcefully appropriating it for—and as—themselves. In other words, everyone had a *moi* in principle. But to have one in practice required a certain mental agility, which Cousin called the capacity for reflection. Volition may have been the content of selfhood, but without reflection that content remained largely inaccessible to its owner. At his pivotal 1828 course, Cousin expounded this theme to the students packing the hall:

> The identity of consciousness constitutes the identity of human knowledge. It is on this common base that time sketches all the differences that distinguish one man from another. The three terms of consciousness form a primitive synthesis, in which they exist in a more or less confused state. Often a man stops at that point—that is, in fact, the case with the majority of men. Sometimes a man goes further and succeeds in exiting: he adds analysis to the primitive synthesis, develops it by reflection, disentangles the complex phenomenon by submitting it to a light which, spreading successively over each of the three terms of consciousness, illuminates them reciprocally. What happens then? The man knows better what he knew already. All the possible differences between one man and another reside there.[115]

This is a slippery passage, oscillating as it does between a democratic insistence on our common humanity, save for some variations that might be merely cosmetic, and an elitist insistence on the significant intellectual superiority of a minority of the population who are able to hone the primeval mental stuff with which we are all endowed. During subsequent decades, Cousin opted for both of those readings, stressing one or the other according to the circumstances. But just as the passage quoted lavishes more attention on the mechanism of human differentiation and its hierarchical implications, so, too, did Cousin tend to favor the elitist interpretation of his text. And even at those moments when the democratic interpretation appealed to him, he managed to give it an inegalitarian twist.

The two categories of human difference that preoccupied Cousin were those, spawned by the process of industrialization, that preoccupied most early nineteenth-century Western Europeans: gender and class. By contrast, race seems to have been largely outside his ken. Despite his fascination with Asian and, in particular, Indian philosophy, he evinced no inclination to construct a racial hierarchy of human intellectual abilities.[116] Similarly, his close philosophical collaborator Jouffroy could, while a member of the Chamber of Deputies in 1840, write a detailed account of the contemporary situation in Algeria, including the diversity and mutual enmity of its three component "races"—Kabyles, Moors, and Arabs—and use the term "race" in a distinctly neutral register, synonymous with "peoples" and "populations" and lacking any pejorative connotation, biological content, or even special salience as a marker of human difference.[117] As for the otherness represented by the Jews, be it religious or in some manner racial, it seems to have struck Cousin as decidedly unproblematic. He was, if anything, philosemitic and was attacked on those grounds by the right-wing press.[118]

How then, from the vantage point of his psychological theory, did Cousin construe the inherent differences that struck him as significant, those between males and females, between the bourgeoisie and the popular classes?

Cousin's ruminations on the intellectual capacities of women and the consequent possibility of female selfhood were a basically private affair, though one prompted by his very public verbalization of the most banal prejudices.[119] During a lecture on the laws governing history that he gave as part of his 1828 course, Cousin commended his own brand of philosophy, often referred to as rational spiritualism, by depicting it as the golden mean between the materialist "philosophy of sensation" and a "sentimental and cowardly spiritualism, good for children and for women [but] fatal to science." In the very next lecture of the series, he again belittled that defective compound being, women-and-children: "There [i.e., in the domain of metaphysics], all is obscure for the senses and the imagination, for children and for women; but there, too, all is light for reflection, for he who demands of himself a manly (*viril*) accounting of his own thought."[120] The vast majority of Cousin's auditors and readers probably failed to notice these offhand comments. So unquestioned in this era were the gender stereotypes they expressed that Stendhal had even bidden his sister to conduct her reading of Condillac and Destutt de Tracy in secret because a "woman cuts the legs from under herself if she is seen studying."[121] But the aspersions cast by

Cousin provoked an autodidact bourgeois lady in her mid-thirties to write to the Sorbonne philosopher for the first time.

Already his self-described "fervent disciple," Caroline Angebert had been following his 1828 course from her home in Dunkerque (her husband was a navy officer), apparently by reading the individually published installments. She now took him to task for a denigration of the female intellect ("the disdain that you express for my sex in assimilating it to childhood!"). Such a position was, she contended, not merely insulting to women but, worse still, logically inconsistent with the rest of his system. Hadn't Cousin insisted, after all, on the common "intellectual patrimony of humanity"? Hadn't he stated that a man's mind was "composed of the same elements" as that of his wife, mother, and sister? Hadn't he maintained that a principle of intelligence existed in each of us but required development, thus implying that the present intellectual inequality between the sexes resulted from developmental vicissitude rather than inborn constraint?[122]

Angebert argued with astonishing acuity. Although self-taught, she had clearly grasped the structure of Cousin's reasoning and had intuitively zeroed in on one of his most fundamental contradictions. Let me put this contradiction in language not available to Angebert. In his quest for a unified and morally responsible *moi*, Cousin had purposely severed in his psychology the biological roots that he found so distasteful in sensationalism. He thereby denied himself a mode of argument that would have led seamlessly to the positing of an explicitly female— and inferior—mental apparatus. Out of his reach were those visceral "commotions" and those nervous vibrations accompanying menstruation that, for an Idéologue like Cabanis, interfered with the idea-generating mechanism in the adult female and inevitably beclouded female ideas.[123] The biologistic turn of Western thought at the beginning of the nineteenth century furnished powerful tools for the construction of gender inequality. But, utterly committed to mind/body dualism and to the radical disembodiment of intellect, Cousin could not avail himself of those tools. Angebert was correct: the most basic logic of his system failed to support Cousin's disparagement of women. While her arguments were more explicitly feminist, she was plowing the same furrow as the seventeenth-century *cartésiennes* who noted the advantages of Descartes' dualism for validating female intellectual pursuits; indeed, in initiating a correspondence with Cousin, she may have had in the back of her mind the famous epistolary relationship between Descartes and Elisabeth of Bohemia.[124]

Angebert and Cousin exchanged about a dozen letters between 1828 and 1832, and their entanglement was as fascinating from a personal as from an intellectual viewpoint. Although animosity always hovered in the wings, each was, for a time at least, highly motivated to maintain a cordial relationship: Angebert because she was awed by Cousin's fame and desperately wanted a supervisor for her philosophy reading; Cousin because he was loath to let go a female disciple at once so intellectually gifted and so obvious infatuated with him. The unlikely pair thus found a modus vivendi through a slightly disingenuous compromise. Begging Angebert not to "confuse a manner of speaking with the articulation of a principle," Cousin reaffirmed the fundamental universalism of his psychology.[125] For her part Angebert conceded that her characterization of his views of the female sex had been "a little exaggerated," that "I sometimes let myself be swept away by my imagination," that despite her nearly constant preoccupation with "the destiny of women, their education, their social position," he had assuaged her doubts "in a satisfactory manner."[126]

I will consider in Chapter 5 the impact of this correspondence on Angebert. As for its influence on Cousin, it seems to have left intact the basically patronizing attitude toward women and the firm identification of intellect with masculinity revealed in his 1828 lectures. As minister of public instruction in 1840, for example, he sent out a circular on the unjustified neglect of logic in the philosophy curriculum that was almost comic in its use of gendered language:

> The syllogistic art is at the very least a powerful form of fencing that gives precision and rigor to the mind. It was in that virile school that our fathers were formed; it can only be to the advantage of today's youth that we detain them there a while.[127]

What Cousin did take away from his encounter with Angebert was a tactical nicety. He learned that the internal consistency of his system required that, when speaking of women, he grant them the same intellectual potential as men. This lesson led him not to embrace gender equality as a principle but rather to shift his argument for gender inequality to new ground: the separation of the public and private spheres as a social norm.

It is that subtly inflected argument that he presents in the 1844 article on Pascal's sister Jacqueline that he addressed to a general readership. True to his first, conciliatory letter to Angebert, he noted that both sexes have the same God-given intellectual faculties and the same divinely ordained obligation to cultivate them. However, the use to which intellect might legitimately be put differed radically for men and women. By definition, men were public personages and women domestic creatures. A woman should thus take no pride or pleasure in exercising her mind but should do so only for the sake of the man in her life. She should acquire the knowledge that "permits her to enter into spiritual rapport [with her partner], to understand his work. . . . to feel his sufferings in order to soothe them." Cousin summed up his views in a laconic dictum: "I make a sharp distinction between the woman of wit and learning (*femme d'esprit*) and the woman author. I infinitely honor the one, and I have little taste for the other."[128] Women could, in other words, tastefully deploy intellect in the context of the married couple, where they played an ancillary, collaborative and, above all, inconspicuous role. But they could not attract attention as the freestanding, self-possessed authors of their own intellectual activity. For a woman to extricate her *moi* from the viscous, primitive synthesis of the elements of consciousness was, quite simply, an offensive act. No wonder that a student of Cousin making his debut as a professor of Cousinian philosophy in 1839 at the Lyon Faculty, where his lectures were open to the public, thought to tell the *maître* that "my audience differs from that of my colleagues in that there are no ladies. I chased them all away by the second lesson."[129]

As far as I know, Cousin never encountered a working-class equivalent of Caroline Angebert, though later, under the Second Republic, one of his own students would defiantly deconstruct the eclectic philosophy and seek to expose its intrinsically democratic bent (see Chapter 5). For lack of such an interlocutor, Cousin's position on the lower orders' capacity for selfhood seems to have remained constant. Like his pre-Angebert position on women, it hinged on the ability of the group in question to engage in reflection. However, with respect to the lower orders more than with respect to women, Cousin stressed the distinction between reflection and its binary opposite, something that he labeled "spontaneity." "This theory of spontaneity and reflection," he observed late in his career, "that in our eyes is the key that unlocks so many difficulties, recurs incessantly in our works."[130] The young Ernest Renan, reading and annotating in the mid 1840s an edition of Cousin's celebrated 1818 lectures on the true, the beautiful, and the good, also noted the repeated use of the reflection-spontaneity distinction but found the distinction murky and unhelpful: "mysterious" was his pejorative adjective.[131] Renan was correct. Cousin said little about the precise nature of the two mental processes except that spontaneity preceded reflection developmentally (presumably in both the biography of the individual and in the history of the human species) and that, as a form of "primitive" knowledge, spontaneity was "indistinct [and] obscure."[132] He apparently preferred to dwell on their sociology, broadly construed.

In Cousin's view, the difference between the two mental processes translated directly into the different social groups that characteristically employed them. As he asserted in 1826:

> There is in reflection nothing that is not in the [mental] operation that precedes it, spontaneity. Reflection is, to be sure, a degree of intelligence rarer and higher than spontaneity, but it is bound by the condition that it summarize spontaneity faithfully and develop it without destroying it. Now, in my opinion, *the mass of humanity is spontaneous and not reflective.*[133]

Cousin reiterated the general point two years later in his 1828 course. "I have the deepest respect for good sense, for good sense is nothing but reason itself at its lowest level, in its most popular [i.e., pertaining to *le peuple*] aspect."[134] A quarter century later, Cousin's sociology of reflection and spontaneity had even gained a rough quantitative aspect. "The child, the people, *three-quarters of the human race,*" Cousin now confidently estimated, "scarcely go beyond [spontaneous intuition] and rely on it with full, unlimited security."[135] These more ubiquitous but less potent forms of reason—spontaneity, good sense—were not, of course, capable of performing the mental gymnastics that could isolate the *moi* and render it accessible to its possessor. Hence workers were, though Cousin did not say it in so many words, unselved beings. No wonder the young Renan suspected that Cousin's frequent recourse to the spontaneity-reflection distinction covertly expressed the kind of "haughty and disdainful philosophy at which he aims."[136]

At other times, however, the psychological similarity of human beings struck Cousin as more noteworthy than their different, class-based capacities to apprehend the pure dynamism of the *moi*. One of those times was the immediate aftermath of the bloody June Days of 1848, when a working-class uprising threatened the newly proclaimed Second Republic and was, in turn, brutally crushed by the state.

Such eruptions of sociopolitical violence were exactly what Cousin had always feared for France, and in 1848 he followed his long-standing inclination to trace them to pernicious conceptions of the psyche. Writing the very first of the "little treatises" (*petits traités*) that the Academy of Moral and Political Sciences had decided to prepare for the working classes at this critical historical juncture, Cousin took up a question that might at first glance seem irrelevant to the crisis at hand: whether the people could be taught philosophy. However, that rubric afforded him the opportunity to specify the native philosophical-cum-psychological beliefs of the people and then to engage in some wishful thinking out loud, a kind of exhortation to the people to assume the traits he had already imputed to them.

Cousin insisted that all human beings had (in the manner of Rousseau's Savoyard vicar, whose profession of faith from the *Emile* formed the appendix to the pamphlet) spontaneous, unreflective knowledge of certain metaphysical truths—for example, the existence of God, the mind-body distinction, the existence and immortality of the soul. The content of this so-called popular philosophy was exactly the same as that of the learned philosophy based on the higher mental operation of reflection; the two philosophies differed only in vocabulary and style. Thus psychologically equipped (and Cousin took care to specify that the popular philosophy "has its psychology"), the people, like their social and educational betters, were and knew themselves to be morally accountable beings. Natural opponents of Locke and Condillac, they required no instruction to recognize that "man does not wholly reside in his senses."[137]

The accent of this pamphlet was thus apparently democratic. But, placed in its historical context, as well as in the full context of the Cousinian philosophy, it acquired strong hierarchical and disciplinarian overtones. The worker was psychologically constituted so as to give assent to and be hedged round by the same moral restraints as the bourgeois. If he listened to his conscience, he would, for example, know better than to subvert the social order through rebellion. If saddled with moral accountability, however, the worker was still, like the woman, excluded from the buoyantly positive side of the Cousinian doctrine. While he could and should repress wayward impulses and choose correct behavior, he could not reflect on what it meant to choose. He could never experience the thrilling sense of self-affirmation that came from disaggregating consciousness, appropriating the *moi*, and making direct contact with the self-willed activity coursing within him.

As we shall see in the next chapter, the fundamentally unselved nature of women and workers reverberated in the writings of Cousin's numerous followers and, even more important, was sealed in the arrangements for the educational institutionalization of Cousinianism. In other words, Cousin and the Cousinian movement deployed the concept of the *moi* in a startlingly literal politics of selfhood. The *moi* became a marker, both objective and subjective, that distinguished the central players in early nineteenth-century French society from the peripheral ones, the rulers from the ruled. When asserting in his 1848 pamphlet that workers could never grasp the full-strength metaphysics of the learned, Cousin nonetheless praised their diluted, popular philosophy as "serious," "grand," and eminently "male," a vast improvement over the "effeminate" pablum served up to the people by charitable do-gooders.[138] But even if the working class had a modest title to mental virility, the exclusion of both workers and women from the corridors of power was, in the Cousinian canon, a given. Or more accurately, it was a given for which Cousin had additionally supplied a psychological rationale.

The Ambiguous Gift of Bourgeois Selfhood

And what about the lucky few whom the Cousinian canon deemed to be possessors of selves? Cousin's invidious comments about women and his rudimentary sociology of spontaneity and reflection enable us to infer, by a process of elimination, that the group in question was the male bourgeoisie—defined not in a strict Marxian sense as the owners of the means of capitalist production but in a looser, more colloquial sense as the new, non-noble and frequently state-educated post-Revolutionary social elite. That identification also tallies with Cousin's strong linkage of the *moi* and private property; it will, moreover, be repeatedly confirmed in the next chapter through an examination of the state-run schools and state-approved philosophy curricula.

However, even for those so favored, the prospects were not entirely rosy. As we can extrapolate from its structural properties alone, the robust self with which Cousin had endowed these beneficiaries was also peculiarly compromised. Conceptualized as an entirely individual will and a personal principle of activity able to impose itself on inanimate matter, the Cousinian *moi* nonetheless saw its options for titanic self-making severely limited by the ontology that it generated and to which it was thus inextricably bound. Radically free and capable of profound introspection, its life journey would be one of quasi-comic deflation. For the grandiose *moi* was destined to be thoroughly unoriginal, to rediscover and take as its guide the banal verities about "the true, the beautiful, and the good" to which Cousin's ubiquitous textbook would so famously lend his name. In short, the Cousinian combination of "personal will" and "impersonal reason" flattered the possessor of the *moi* that he enjoyed a thrilling degree of individuality and efficacy yet at the same time guaranteed that he would not rock the boat.

These conflicting poles of Cousinian selfhood seem so profoundly bourgeois as even to constitute a definition of the bourgeois mentality. They mesh perfectly, in fact, with the definition offered by Jerrold Seigel, when he speaks of the "conflict that arose at the heart [of bourgeois life]: "Bourgeois progress called for the dissolution of traditional restrictions on personal development; harmony and stability required that some new and different limits be set up in their place." From this tug of war arose, according to Seigel, the prevalence in the nineteenth century of the image and practice of bohemianism: the refusal to fit in, the powerful impulse to withdraw to the margins of society. As he notes, "Bohemian and bourgeois were—and are—parts of a single field: they imply, require, and attract each other."[139] Although Cousin does not figure in Seigel's analysis, he would be eminently at home there. The conformist Cousinian *moi* is the precise antitype of the bohemian, the articulation in the language of philosophical psychology of the very forces that brought the bohemian into existence. Or, put differently, the attributes of the Cousinian *moi* refer simultaneously to the affirmative self-image of the nineteenth-century bourgeois and the risible image of that same social creature featured in the abundant antibourgeois satire of the era.

The conformity to the status quo that Cousin purposely built into the *moi* further explains the oddity of Cousinian introspection. Who, after all, knew where unsupervised, genuinely open-ended self-examination might lead? To what end were individual idiosyncrasies, discontents, and maladaptations scrutinized and magnified? Clearly such a process could end in subversion. Cousin wanted to associate his system nominally with the prestigious French "family of *méditatifs intérieurs*," as Sainte-Beuve called the tradition running from Montaigne to Pascal, Rousseau, and Maine de Biran.[140] He wanted his students to appear "deep." But he also wanted introspection to yield predictable results.

In effect, then, Cousin constructed male bourgeois subjectivity and rationalized male bourgeois power with a decidedly self-abnegating model of selfhood. The combination of volition and metaphysical limits in his recipe for the *moi* well exemplifies two related Foucauldian concepts: that of power as simultaneously creative and constraining and that of the modern subject as the locus of both autonomy and subjection.[141] A particularly good exemplar of power/knowledge, Cousinian psychology singled out bourgeois males for validation by conferring on them a literal gift of dynamic selfhood, but at the same time it restricted their sphere of thought and activity to ensure their support of the political status quo. This psychology thus suggests how a ruling class controls not only its subordinates but also its own members. It concretizes Foucault's assertions about the "anonymity" of modern power: its agents are organized in a vast machine-like network, the supervisors themselves supervised, so that "it is the apparatus as a whole that produces 'power,'" leaving no one exempt.[142]

During the period of the constitutional monarchy, then, a Cousinian *moi* was a valuable, relatively rare, and status-conferring possession. But to those on whom it was bestowed, it was a nonetheless an ambiguous, even tarnished gift.

5

Cousinian Hegemony

The enemy is disciplined. Let us discipline ourselves.
Victor Cousin, 1843

A French bourgeois household of the era of the July Monarchy might
have owned and displayed on its bookshelves the *Dictionnaire de la conversation et de la lecture,* a multivolume, all-purpose reference work
intended to serve the everyday needs of the educated middle-class family. Turning to its article, "Moi," the reader would find these remarkable
opening lines:

> That word [*moi*], which formerly belonged only to the domain of
> grammar and was nothing more than the most notable of pronouns,
> has become, after the word "God," the substantive noun par
> excellence. It now plays, and justly so, a powerful role in philosophy.
> In fact, we could say without exaggeration that it epitomizes all of
> philosophy.[1]

The *moi,* the author informs us, has acquired preeminence among the
concepts of academic philosophy. But that is not all. In its new, philosophically inflected guise—no longer merely a humble grammatical element
but an entity exceeded in ontological status only by the divinity—the
word has also entered ordinary speech. People are apparently talking
more about the self; they are taking their selves more seriously.

This brief passage from a widely consulted text of the period testifies
to the impact of Cousinianism on the general culture of early nineteenth-century France. Its author was, to be sure, a minor Cousinian
philosopher, no doubt biased in favor of exaggerating the influence of
his teacher.[2] Nonetheless, it is significant that the editors of the *Dic-*

tionnaire, who prided themselves on toeing no party line and giving voice to divergent opinions,[3] saw fit to include the rubric "Moi" in their reference work in the first place. Having once made that decision, they doubtless recognized that the entry could be consigned only to a Cousinian: while all the psychologies of the period mentioned the self, only Cousin's made the self its signature concept.

How can we account for the cultural situation that the *Dictionnaire* editors had perceived, one in which Cousinianism and its iconic *moi* had moved beyond the lecture halls of the Ecole normale supérieure and the Paris Faculty of Letters and entered the mainstream? Given the dryness and difficulty of the relevant texts, an effect of such magnitude could hardly have been accomplished by individual readers alone, by a bevy of Caroline Angeberts. More likely an institutional intervention was responsible. In fact, from 1832 on, the two institutions that had disseminated Cousinianism during the 1820s, both located in the capital, were supplemented by a third, vastly broader in scope: the entire lycée system of France. If French bureaucrats could envisage the late eighteenth-century hospital as a "healing machine,"[4] so too might the nineteenth-century state-run secondary school be justly imagined as a machine for the production of selfhood. The hegemony of Cousinianism in France, its ability to beat out its competitors and impose its concept of the self on a significant segment of the population, rested first and foremost on Cousin's capture of the lycée curriculum.

Not every supporter of Cousinianism approved of the route the *maître* had taken. At least one, Caroline Angebert, believed that his capacity to influence the future of France lay in his writing and in his personal presence at the lectern. "I never experienced a more painful feeling," she wrote him reproachfully some months after the July Revolution, "than the day I learned that you were abandoning your teaching" for a career at the Ministry of Education. No doubt he would do a lot of good there, she acknowledged, but he would not ensure the triumph of his philosophy. The bureaucracy was notoriously fickle: "another, after you, can destroy your work; another can even arrange to have you conveniently replaced." And even if he succeeded at the administrative game, he would not thereby win the battle for the hearts and minds of Frenchmen, a battle that would take place in what Angebert called society:

In order to make a philosophy dominant, Sir, does it suffice to implant it in the system of public education? Wouldn't it be like a dead language if it lacked roots in society? How many would believe in Christianity if its dogmas were taught and practiced [only] in the colleges? Social education is more powerful today. If you recognize that truth, if you want your doctrine to be propagated, how can you leave the task to someone else?[5]

But Angebert need not have worried. As a fellow traveler of the Doctrinaires and a protégé of Royer-Collard, Cousin had thrown in his lot with the expanding, post-Revolutionary state educational system with all due deliberation; moreover, he had done so precisely because he wanted to knit together government and society and see his philosophy achieve dominance through active propagation. In sum, Cousin and Angebert shared the same goals for eclecticism but, of the two, he proved to have the more up-to-date and accurate assessment of the strategic possibilities of educational institutionalization.

Institutionalizing Psychology: The Teamwork of Cousin and Guizot

Cousin's pedagogical takeover was not a purely individual tour de force. Its roots lay deep in Doctrinaire political culture, and its realization hinged especially on the long political association of Cousin and Guizot. Under the Empire, both young men belonged to the politically tinged philosophical circle around their common mentor, Royer-Collard.[6] When the Université was subjected to clerical repression in the early 1820s, the two were dramatically paired as martyred Sorbonne professors, suspended from their teaching of philosophy and history, respectively, because of their liberal ideas and the oratorical force with which they presented them.[7] When, still wandering in the political wilderness, Guizot attempted to form a small society of moral and political sciences in 1824 to keep the Doctrinaire viewpoint alive, he named Cousin, in a personal letter on the subject, as one of the founding members— although his reference to him as "Cousin" rather than by the first name he employed for others suggests that long affiliation had not, in their case, blossomed into intimate rapport.[8] And when the "three glorious days" of the July 1830 Revolution unfolded, Cousin was one of the inner circle that gathered at Guizot's apartment to plot strategy.[9]

The 1830 Revolution marked the ascension of the Doctrinaires to power and, if Guizot led that collective movement, Cousin did not lag far behind. When Guizot was named minister of public instruction in 1832, Cousin was already a member of the five-man Royal Council of Public Instruction—indeed he had received this appointment within weeks of the July Revolution. As one newspaper quipped, "It is not solely as a philosopher that Cousin has come to power but as a representative of a triumphant doctrine; that is his credential and his pitfall."[10] The primary school law of 1833, the great accomplishment of Guizot's ministry, may actually have been penned by Cousin. At the very least, it drew heavily on the data about Prussian primary education that Cousin had gathered firsthand in 1831—his trip subsidized by the government and his personal services well remunerated—and published in book form two years later.[11] The law is relevant to us here as an example of the Doctrinaire use of education as social policy, a maneuver that would figure as well in the institutionalization of Cousinian psychology. As Cousin said when he wrote to a German acquaintance in 1833, enclosing the text of the law, "[the law's] eclectic spirit will enable you to guess its author."[12]

What was characteristically Doctrinaire and eclectic about the law of 1833 was its provision for two distinct levels of primary education, the usual elementary one (the three R's plus moral instruction) and a more innovative superior one (drawing, geometry, physical science, natural history, some history, and geography). Both levels were noncompulsory and offered free of charge to those unable to pay. The purpose of the higher level—for which Cousin had found a precedent in contemporary Prussia—was to offer the popular classes a *juste-milieu* between social opportunity and social restriction. According to Doctrinaire logic, public utility required that able members of the lower classes who wished to develop their intellects not be stifled. At the same time, prudence dictated that such development be contained within appropriate limits. The talented children of the poor should have their thirst for learning satisfied among their peers in the superior primary school, an institution dedicated solely to that purpose. They should not be encouraged to enter the track of full-fledged secondary education where, mingling with the sons of the bourgeoisie, they would acquire outsized ambitions, expose themselves to disappointment and embitterment, and thus become potentially destabilizing agents in society. The superior primary school was, in other words, the translation into educational policy of the Doctrinaires' overriding fear of renewed revolution and their obsession with imposing a straitjacket of order on all manifestations of social mobility.[13]

In other ways, too, the 1833 law, called "la loi Guizot" from its inception, embodied the basic sociopolitical philosophy of both Guizot and Cousin. First, the law placed a relative emphasis on state centralization: in the requirement that more teacher training institutions, the joint responsibility of state and department, be established and in the expectation that these *écoles normales* would function as a node for the permeation of society by government in its benign, noncoercive aspect; and also in the provision for a significant component of state authority over the primary schools, an authority shared with the localities and the Church. Second, the law was noteworthy for the rigor with which it was enforced, both by Guizot during the four years of his ministry and by successive ministers following his example. A stream of decrees, circulars, and letters treating the interpretation of the law emanated from Guizot's office; the minister had all correspondence pointing out defects and omissions in the law collected and classified. It was Guizot who created the venerable French "tradition whereby the minister of public instruction concerned himself with the slightest detail of the smallest school."[14]

These features—state centralization, rigorous execution of measures enacted into law, and especially the use of educational policy to bolster social hierarchy or, at least, monitor social mobility—recurred in the institutionalization of Cousinian psychology in the lycée system.

Given the close collaboration between the two men, it is not surprising that the dissemination of a "correct" psychology interested Guizot as well as Cousin, even if the former failed to elevate that task to his life's mission. Guizot was a serious enough participant in the metaphysical society that met in Maine de Biran's home during the early years of the Restoration that his host recorded in his journal the precise views about the *moi* that the budding politician expressed on October 17, 1814—views that even provoked him to prepare a "Reply to Monsieur Guizot."[15] With Royer-Collard, Guizot edited the *Archives philosophiques, politiques et littéraires,* a short-lived journal whose dates, 1817–18, coincided with the period during which Cousin hammered out the main lines of his philosophy in his courses at the Faculty of Letters. In fact the journal's editorial board, which convened regularly and included Maine de Biran, regarded itself as the successor to Maine de Biran's metaphysical society. Calling himself the "old man of the gang," Biran agreed to collaborate in the venture (he and Cousin were its joint philosophy editors) in order to "give a moral and useful direction to psychological doctrines."[16]

As editor of and a contributor to the *Encyclopédie progressive,* a never-completed project that he began in the waning years of the Restoration, Guizot dropped hints about his familiarity with Cousin's psychology. Noting that Diderot and d'Alembert had adopted as their scheme for the classification of human knowledge in the great *Encyclopédie* the division of the human mind into the faculties of memory, reason, and imagination, Guizot stressed the arbitrariness of such a choice and enumerated alternatives. Among them, "One could find in the opposition of man and the world, of spectator and spectacle, of *moi* and *non-moi,* a principle of classification taken, like theirs, from inside ourselves and yet very different."[17] The comment implicitly called attention to two competing psychologies: the sensationalism that had dictated the shape of the tree of knowledge in the eighteenth-century *Encyclopédie,* and Cousinianism, replete with its conceptual borrowings from Kant and Fichte.

A second and less canonical article, "Abrégé," reveals more about Guizot's position on psychology. Here he addressed the question of the textual form in which different sciences could be transmitted and, by extension, who would be able to learn them. The question itself thus sprang from characteristically Doctrinaire concerns about supplying each social class with just the amount of knowledge suited to it, meticulously avoiding both insufficiency and excess.

Abrégés, a term that included summaries and concise handbooks, were proliferating, Guizot announced at the beginning of this article. Even encyclopedias such as his own were nothing but collections of such *abrégés.* Since contemporaries alternately hailed and damned this publishing trend (the sensationalists, as shown in Chapter 2, were enthusiastic advocates, who hoped to use the *abrégé* to transmit their science to the humblest citizens), Guizot sought a balanced assessment of it. On the negative side, he observed, reading a summary of a science taught a person only the results of that science, not how to think in accordance with its central suppositions or to pursue research in the same vein. In other words, *abrégés* were, in Guizot's phrase, deficient in "fecundity." But if they could not mold creative scientists, *abrégés* were, on the positive side, still useful in dispelling the ignorance of nonspecialists who encountered various sciences in their daily lives. As such they were, said Guizot, employing a key concept of Western modernity that he personally did so much to define, "a means of civilization."[18] *Abrégés* also supplied a "public" for savants, ensuring another feature of civilization: that the taste for scientific knowledge would be widespread in society instead of the monopoly of the few.[19]

Every science was not, however, equally amenable to summary. The so-called "aristocratic sciences" were, by their nature, inaccessible "to a casual attention, a curiosity without labor"; they did not "allow the crowd casually to gather their fruits." Within this category of the hard-to-get were those sciences lacking a direct practical application, such as mathematics; those that required mastery of an immense number of facts, such as philology; and those whose objects were intrinsically vague, such as psychology.[20] With respect to this last aristocratic science, Guizot cited a recently published essay by a brilliant spokesman for Cousinian-style psychology, Théodore Jouffroy. Only a few years younger than Cousin, Jouffroy had been Cousin's student at the Ecole normale supérieure, but chronic ill health prevented his entrance into an ordinary academic career. He and Guizot were bound by particularly warm ties of friendship,[21] in contrast to the pragmatic and durable but rather cool alliance that joined Cousin and Guizot.

The essay cited by Guizot was Jouffroy's long preface to his translation of the Scottish philosopher Dugald Stewart. In this text Jouffroy identified as "popular" and ascribed to "the public" the view that only those phenomena apprehended by the senses possessed certainty—once again, an early nineteenth-century Frenchman depicted sensationalism as a form of vernacular knowledge. Jouffroy went on to demur from this accepted wisdom, upholding instead the existence and absolute certainty of the non-sensory phenomena of consciousness. "Invisible to the eye, intangible to the hand, impervious to the most perfect microscope and scalpel," they were nonetheless fully "observable."[22] Still, Guizot continued, "no one can enter into possession of such a science [of consciousness] without discovering it, so to speak, himself, and in its entirety."[23] In other words, Guizot assigned a precise social location to psychology of the introspective, Cousinian variety. It utterly eluded superficial popular dissemination; it was within the grasp only of those who studied it with such thoroughness and care that they had personally reenacted the founding of the science.

Guizot had enough stake in the teaching of psychology to have kept among his papers a manuscript syllabus for the second part of a course in basic psychology. The document is written in Jouffroy's hand. Tellingly, in terms of Doctrinaire preoccupations, the absent first part of the syllabus dealt with the intellect, while the carefully preserved second part concerned moral psychology and focused on the *moi* as the "voluntary force." Inventorying the different factors that impinged upon deliberations of the will, Jouffroy's manuscript listed the pleasures and pains caused by the *moi* itself, by so-called "pure activity." He thus explicitly detailed an emotional repertory and realm of experience accessible only to the literally self-possessed elite who had successfully laid hold of the *moi:* the "pleasure derived from the consciousness of activity of the *moi,* the pleasure derived from the consciousness of easeful and full deployment of the activity of the *moi;* and the pain derived from consciousness of the difficult, incomplete, and obstructed deployment of the activity of the *moi.*" The provenance of this manuscript is unclear: since its heading says nothing about where the course was actually taught, Jouffroy may even have prepared it at Guizot's request as a kind of blueprint for a widely replicable course of the future.[24]

But the blueprint for the teaching of psychology in early nineteenth-century French schools that was in fact adopted—and, moreover, adopted during Guizot's tenure as minister of public instruction—was not Jouffroy's but Cousin's. The archives record nothing of the circumstances surrounding this quasi-event, but on September 28, 1832, the Royal Council of Public Instruction, which counted Cousin among its members, decreed an innovation in the standard philosophy course in the lycées (which were once again called by their Old Regime name, *collèges,* from the beginning of the Restoration until the Revolution of 1848).[25] A subject called "Psichologie" (sic) was to be added to the course as its first substantive section; indeed the decree spoke of the "necessity of commencing the study of philosophy by psychology." The new curriculum included learning about "consciousness and the certitude appropriate to it," understanding "voluntary and free activity" so as to be able to "describe the phenomenon of the will and all the circumstances surrounding it," and grasping the key concept of the "*moi,* its identity and unity."[26] True to form, Guizot sent out a circular to all

the rectors of the academies six months later, emphasizing the importance of conformity to the new syllabus not only in its content but also
in the order of presentation of topics.[27] The strategy for the implantation of Cousinianism must be seen very much as the combined effort of
Cousin and Guizot: unlike other prominent ministers of education during the July Monarchy, Guizot affiliated himself closely with the Royal
Council of Public Instruction (Cousin's main power base at this date),
seeing this organ of the corporate Université as his ally rather than his
rival.[28]

The two men could hardly have chosen a more conspicuous place in
the curriculum in which to insert the new subject matter. The lycée
classe de philosophie of the third and last year was universally regarded
in France as the "crown" of secondary education, a culmination that
reproduced the ontological order in the scholastic one. Philosophy
loomed so large that the entire third year of lycée instruction was often
referred to metonymically as the "philosophy class." Nor was the philosophy professor a run-of-the-mill teacher; by spending so many hours
with his students and initiating them into a type of knowledge they had
never before encountered, he was supposed to exert an extraordinary
degree of influence over them. Furthermore, this instruction was seen
as quintessentially French, an expression of the national genius,
because the French included much more intensive training in philosophy as part of secondary education than did their neighbors.[29] At the
end of the nineteenth century, when a suggestion was made that philosophy be introduced in small, preparatory doses earlier in the lycée curriculum, a retired Cousinian forcefully reiterated the mystique of the
classe de philosophie. The proposed pedagogical measure, he said,
"would be fatal to philosophy itself by removing from it precisely that
trait of novelty that brings forth astonishment [in the student] while at
the same time commanding respect and provoking attraction. What
characterizes philosophy in relation to subjects taught earlier is that it
considers thought in its nakedness. . . ."[30]

Situating psychology in the lycée also allowed that subject matter to
partake automatically of the class and gender discriminations that had
defined the lycée since its Napoleonic inception: designed to provide
civil servants for the state, the lycée would remain until the 1880s the
exclusive preserve of bourgeois males. The institutional locus of psychology thus reinforced Cousin's insistence that only a small fraction of

the population possessed the intellectual finesse necessary to seize the *moi*; it meshed as well with Guizot's identification of psychology as an elite science requiring total immersion on the part of the student and firsthand rediscovery of its basic tenets. Of course, Guizot's theory of the middle class as the universal class—the one accessible to all who had *capacité*—completed the picture. It identified intellectual talent, as measured by the ability to get rich and thus meet the property qualifications for voting under the *monarchie censitaire,* with membership in the bourgeoisie.[31] A seamless ideology, then, selected the bourgeoisie for training in selfhood.

The social-class specificity of instruction in psychology at this date was highly nuanced. Consider the posture of a minor Cousinian, A.-Jacques Matter—the same minor Cousinian, in fact, responsible for the article "Moi" in the *Dictionnaire de la conversation et de la lecture*—when writing a handbook for primary schoolteachers in the 1840s. Both psychology and its offshoot pedagogy were, he opined, indispensable preparation for the members of this occupational group. Because they needed skill in the "art of communicating" to their pupils, they would benefit greatly from familiarity with the human mental faculties and from expertise in the means of developing them. But (although Matter does not say this) primary schoolteachers were drawn from the lower middle classes and below.[32] Hence, Matter assumed that his readers would not even know what the term "psychology" meant unless he provided them with a definition.[33] Sketching the rudiments of that arcane discipline, he informed them that one of the first accomplishments of thought was to make a clear distinction between our senses and external objects. He elaborated this point with a touch of condescension:

> That is what the philosophers call "distinguishing the interior world from the exterior world, the *moi* from the *non-moi*," scientific words that I would never employ and that I would spare myself the trouble of mentioning to you if they did not figure in certain books that you might find useful. . . .[34]

In this way Matter, a representative Cousinian, finely calibrated his scientific language to the social echelon, lower than his own, from which the corps of schoolteachers was recruited. Recognizing immediately that their social station precluded lycée attendance, he took pains to specify that psychology was a subject taught in secondary school.[35] He knew that the term *moi,* construed in a technical sense, would likely be outside their ken. A more striking testimony to the social-class identity of psychology under the July Monarchy can hardly be imagined.

In its indelible association with the elite, the possession of an articulable *moi* thus began to function under the July Monarchy as a marker of social status, much like the ability to read Latin in early modern Europe. Indeed the *moi* might seem to have been the designated successor of Latinity in this regard since the same reform of 1832 which introduced psychology into the curriculum also suppressed the philosophy examination in Latin as a requirement for the baccalaureate.[36] However, the periodization is rather more complicated. During the July Monarchy efforts were made, alternately, to erode and to shore up the classical secondary curriculum (which would, in fact, not lose its privileged position until 1902).[37] When he served as minister of public education for eight months in 1840, Cousin was associated with the traditionalist position.[38] So was Guizot, who appeared on the floor of the Chamber of Deputies during his term as minister of public instruction to answer an impromptu attack on the preference his budget accorded to the classics.[39] The *moi* and classical learning thus overlapped in nineteenth-century French public education as redundant, standardized ways to distinguish the socially dominant from the marginal. What the *moi* contributed to this mechanism of distinction was a marker that dug deeper and more intimately into the individual's sense of self, one that concerned a dialogue of the self with the self.

The great bulwark of Cousinian institutionalization was the 1832 lycée curriculum in philosophy, reaffirmed in 1840 with only the most minor additions and then basically unchanged until 1874.[40] But, to be fully effective, this centerpiece required a host of supporting institutions.

During the July Monarchy Cousin furnished most of this infrastructure almost single-handedly through the venerable French practice of *le cumul*—the holding of posts simultaneously. Responding to accusations that Cousin was earning an exorbitant income by combining multiple salaries, Guizot attempted to set the record straight during his tenure as minister of public instruction (1832–36) by listing all of his colleague's appointments and the remunerations each carried. Cousin was, as already mentioned, a member of the Royal Council of Public Instruction (his main job, said Guizot, earning him 9,000 francs a year). Despite his humble birth, he had been named a peer of France and sat in the Chamber of Peers (no additional income, an "illustrious burden"); he held memberships in the Institut de France, the Académie française, and the Academy of Moral and Political Sciences ("a modest salary" for the first only). He held a chair in philosophy at the Sorbonne (negative income since he had to pay a substitute professor out of his own pocket). In his capacity as councilor of public instruction, he had since 1833 been entrusted with the general supervision of the Ecole normale supérieure, a task previously shared by all the councilors. If he received no additional financial benefit from this charge, it did offer him firm control over France's principal hatchery of philosophy professors. As Guizot noted, "Monsieur Cousin directs everything related to the philosophical sciences, and everyone has paid tribute to the strong impulsion that he has stamped on this part of public service and to the numerous improvements that he has introduced."[41]

In 1840 Cousin created the new status of *agrégé* in philosophy—that is, a mandatory certification for all who would teach philosophy at the highest level of the state educational system, the Faculties of Letters in Paris and the departments. At the same time, he added to his official titles that of president of the jury of the annual *concours,* or public competition, that granted this qualification. The influence he exercised in his new post was, he apparently believed, indispensable to the success of his educational project. "My health is miserable," he noted glumly in a letter to a former student in the summer of 1845. "But if I go to take the waters, who will pass the *agrégation?* I will remain, then, [in Paris] for the *agrégation*."[42]

The culmination of the institutional edifice of Cousinianism was the six-volume *Dictionnaire des sciences philosophiques* (1844–52), a compendium of orthodoxy produced through a collaborative effort of Cousin's disciples with some participation and oversight by the *maître.* Its editor, Adolphe Franck, reserved for himself authorship of the article "Moi," yet another indication of the utter centrality of that concept in the Cousinian worldview.[43] Curiously enough, given Cousin's loathing for the physiological reductionism prevalent in Paris medicine, it was the sixty-volume *Dictionnaire des sciences médicales* (1812–22) that provided the model for the philosophical dictionary. The former was regarded during the nineteenth century as an emblem of the boiled down, sum total of medical knowledge, as can be seen in the novel *Madame Bovary* (1857), where Flaubert's narrator enumerates the contents of the consulting room of Charles Bovary, licensed *officier de santé:* "Volumes of the 'Dictionary of Medical Science,' uncut, but the binding rather the worse for the successive sales through which they had gone, occupied almost alone six shelves of a pinewood bookcase."[44] The Cousinian reference work bore a parallel title and a parallel representation of its collective authorship ("By a Society of Physicians and Surgeons" became "By a Society of Philosophy Professors"); it was even printed by the same firm.[45]

To understand why the Cousinians chose to imitate the physicians in this way, it is useful to look at the anonymous "Authors' Preface" to the philosophical dictionary. This document, in which, according to private correspondence, Cousin himself had a hand,[46] betrayed a strong sense of embattlement. It alluded darkly to the "abundant self-interested hatreds [that] rise up against [philosophy]" and to the widespread allegations that "after three thousand years, [philosophy] can still do no more than haltingly address frivolous questions, being condemned on more serious matters to the most shameful and incorrigible confusion." But, the Preface allowed, the future looked brighter. The publication of the first volume of the *Dictionnaire* was providing the professors with the occasion for announcing that the "science" [of philosophy] had finally manage[d] to constitute itself."[47] An odd announcement to be sure, in light of the fact that the tradition of philosophy in the West went back at least to Plato. The professors obviously meant the *re-*constitution of philosophy by Cousin under peculiarly nineteenth-century conditions, when the prevailing definition of science had changed and the materialist trends associated with medicine and sensationalist philosophy had threatened to subsume mental phenomena under the laws of biology and thus to put philosophy out of business altogether.[48] The *Dictionnaire* was thus intended as a monument to the successful execution of that re-constitutive task. And however far their own epistemological commitments diverged from those of the prevailing school of medicine, the Cousinians were sufficiently savvy and opportunistic to deck out their *Dictionnaire* with all the formal trappings of the famous *Dictionnaire des sciences médicales,* thus tacitly asserting a full scientific parity between philosophy and medicine—a version of Cousin's earlier statements that his brand of metaphysics was an observational science and that his psychology possessed the same degree of scientific certainty as physics (see Chapter 4).

The Cousinian Textbook: Supplementing the Master

Max Weber's *The Protestant Ethic and the Spirit of Capitalism* contains a suggestive case study in the elaboration and dissemination of a system of ideas. Outlining Calvin's theology, Weber infers the deep anxiety that it would likely inspire in its sixteenth- and seventeenth-century adherents: for how could people who cared above all about the afterlife cope with the presumption that, by a secret and irrevocable decree, God had already sealed their eternal destiny? Weber notes that Calvin, supremely confident of his own divine election, never thought to offer his followers advice for handling the sense of helpless dread that would engulf so many of them. Instead, it fell to Calvinist ministers, who encountered the distressed parishioners face to face, to formulate that necessary, practical aspect of the doctrine. And hence it was to manuals of pastoral care that Weber turned to learn how Calvinist theology was amplified and nuanced to meet the challenges it posed for daily life—to ensure, in other words, the feasibility of its dissemination.[49]

This model has relevance for Cousinianism as well. Although the so-called psychological method was, both historically and theoretically, the linchpin of his system, and although he depicted himself as extremely proficient in it, Cousin did little to specify how this indispensable skill was to be imparted to others. Such a lacuna was a weak spot in a system of thought designed for large-scale educational institutionalization. After all, the run of middle-class adolescent males could hardly be expected to possess native introspective tendencies. Furthermore, following the Revolution of 1830, Cousin withdrew from the classroom, assuming the increasingly managerial and bureaucratic role that so dismayed Caroline Angebert. Only in 1853, when the return of Bonapartism had relieved him of these responsibilities, would he even compose a general work, suitable for student use, synthesizing his philosophical principles.[50] Nor did Maine de Biran, the unwitting progenitor of the Cousinian movement and a true virtuoso of the inner life, offer help in this regard. Nothing could have been more foreign to Biran's fiercely individualistic spirit than the project of institutionalizating the introspective method: indeed, reviewing a bill on public instruction before the Chamber of Deputies in 1817, he confided in his journal that, unlike the Doctrinaires, he found government control of education a "true intellectual tyranny."[51]

Hence, during the critical period of the July Monarchy, it fell to Cousin's disciples to figure out an effective pedagogy for the Cousinian philosophy and to use the genre of the textbook to make the practice of interior observation—or, alternatively, the fruits of that practice—accessible to the ordinary *lycéen*. What the manual of pastoral care was to Max Weber's sixteenth- and seventeenth-century Calvinists, the student textbook was to the nineteenth-century Cousinian movement.

The Idéologues had also cultivated the textbook genre. If the short life span of the central schools curtailed the circulation of Destutt de Tracy's intended textbook, the *Elémens d'idéologie,* the stylistic features of that work nonetheless expressed the group's distinctive pedagogical outlook—that is, their refusal to use schooling to indoctrinate or catechize the population, and their insistence on training students for both self-reflexivity and intellectual autonomy. Instead of presenting his material in an unambiguous, laconically authoritative manner suitable for rote memorization, Destutt de Tracy emphasized process. On more than one occasion, he showed students how he had abandoned and improved upon his initial hypothesis through correcting his mode of reasoning.[52] The Idéologue Laromiguière employed a similarly open-ended pedagogical style. As the published version of his course reveals, he invited questions and objections from his audience and composed whole lectures around them. "Gentlemen," he told his students on one occasion, "it is not I who gives this course, or at least I don't do it alone. Your reflections run ahead of mine; they carry me forward."[53]

With its celebrated linkage between psychology and ontology, Cousinianism aimed at producing self-reflexivity in the student while discouraging or, at least, severely restricting intellectual autonomy. As a result, Cousinian textbooks were more conventional instances of the genre, exuding matter-of-fact certainty.[54] Institutional forces exerted pressure in the same direction. Since all young people aspiring to the baccalaureate under the July Monarchy had to pass an examination in Cousin's philosophy—this was, after all, the brunt of the 1832 decree of the Royal Council of Public Instruction—a cottage industry in philosophy manuals rapidly sprang up. The superficiality of the early manuals led philosophy professors, concerned to prevent the degradation of their discipline, to take over the writing of these study guides from the hacks who had pioneered them and to aim their enriched contents at both students and teachers.[55] Given the dread examination that loomed large over such textbooks, their authors, unlike Destutt de Tracy, obviously strove for simple, unambiguous clarity.

I will be looking here at a group of such textbooks, all pre-1848 products of Cousin's former students-turned-philosophy-professors and each offering a slightly different variation on the basic Cousinian themes adumbated in the master's oral teaching and his published writings. Two of these textbooks demonstrated particular staying power: Adolphe-Félix Gatien-Arnoult's *Programme d'un cours de philosophie* was reprinted five times between 1830 and 1850; the much longer and more elaborate *Manuel de philosophie, à l'usage des collèges,* the joint effort of a trio of Cousinian disciples, Amédée Jacques, Jules Simon, and Emile Saisset, became something of a workhorse, going through nine printings between its initial publication in 1846 and 1883.[56]

Taken together these textbooks indicate, more often by their awkward silence than by their overt comments, the extreme difficulty of teaching introspection. All of them rehearsed, in some form or other, the Cousinian dictum that introspection is the route to psychological knowledge. But only one textbook writer, Gatien-Arnoult, saw fit to address the nagging practical issue of just how introspective capacity was to be acquired. After listing the questions about the *moi* that Cousin's curriculum required every student to answer, Gatien-Arnoult pronounced categorically, "There is but a single way to discover the true responses to these questions, *interior observation.*"[57] Yet, as he revealed in a footnote, getting his young charges to grasp the "interior reality" *(fait intérieur)* was no simple matter. Leaving class one day in 1828, brooding on what had occurred there, he recognized a curious fact: that his students' success at introspection was inversely proportional to the ordinariness and simplicity of the mental processes on which he bade them to reflect. He speculated that he might therefore elicit greater introspective prowess if he asked his students to reflect only on the extraordinary aspects of mental life, following the logic that "a pupil who mumbles when reading aloud should be given as reading material books printed in an unusual typeface or in a foreign language."[58] He did not, however, develop this point. He did, however, enumerate the many obstacles to introspection, especially for the novice, mentioning our instinctive and habitual propensity to train our attention outward, the fleeting nature of internal phenomena, and the poverty of our linguistic resources for describing them. By this device, Gatien-Arnoult apparently hoped to relieve his students' sense of frustration and personal inadequacy in face of their assigned task. He also assured them that "constant labor" and a "strong will" would eventually overcome the obstacles and open the way to a continually rewarding "conquest" of the inner realm.[59]

In addition to these tentative and disjointed suggestions about how to impart introspective skill to the average *lycéen*, Gatien-Arnoult provided a detailed account of what introspection was supposed to reveal. So, too, did the other textbook writers; indeed that account constituted the bulk of all these textbooks. Such straightforward disclosure of the results of the psychological "experiment" was, on the one hand, pedagogically necessary; even the most successful instance of student introspection could not be expected to stand on its own, without authoritative verification. On the other hand, disclosure made possible a kind of cheating. It encouraged the lazy and the obtuse simply to bypass the introspective moment, thus violating the sacrosanct principle that every student personally reconstruct the science of psychology for himself. At the same time, it offered an analogous shortcut to professors and textbook writers: how much easier to transmit secondhand the introspective discoveries of the master psychologists than to figure out how to initiate adolescent males into the mysteries of interior observation. It is in this light that we should probably interpret the suspiciously self-assured remark made by Antoine Charma when he was teaching his very first philosophy course. "I got through the psychology without a hitch," he told Cousin.[60] To judge from the textbook Charma wrote several years later, which frequently cited evidence gleaned by the self-observing consciousness, but neglected the mechanics of introspection, Charma taught psychology with ease because he gave his students the answers. He did not force them to turn inward to arrive at the answers on their own.[61]

Some of the textbook writers took up a related aspect of introspection: the problem of whether introspective capacity was evenly distributed among the population. This problem had implications both for everyday pedagogical practice and for the perennial Cousinian themes of human difference and social hierarchy. Thus Charles Mallet, whose textbook began with a discussion of Cousin's pregnant and ubiquitous distinction between spontaneity and reflection, mused, "If consciousness notifies us of everything that happens in the *for intérieur,* why are certain men so much more adept at recounting what transpires within them? That bright interior light that you call consciousness, is it brighter for some than for others?" Mallet responded to this rhetorical question by asserting the utter equality of the consciousness of everybody. As he saw it, distinctions entered the picture only in the processing of consciousness, a task that relied on the faculty of will and its derivative, attention:

> Now since men do not have the same force of will and consequently do not give the same degree of attention to what transpires within them, it follows that knowledge of internal phenomena is clearer and more complete for some than for others. Consciousness itself is the same for everyone but reflection is not, if we take reflection to mean the volontary act of the mind folding back on itself and concentrating its effort on those phenomena whose presence is attested by consciousness. Consciousness is fatal, reflection is free.[62]

Mallet here repeated the position articulated by Cousin in his 1828 lectures, but with a slight shift of accent. For Cousin, reflection—the operation able to tease out the *moi*, or will, from the primitive synthesis of the elements of consciousness—was a type of intelligence; for Mallet, reflection was itself a manifestation of will. The divergence between these positions is small and quite possibly inconsequential: both men, after all, ended up offering a psychological justification for human hierarchy. But the divergence nonetheless points to areas of ambiguity and fluidity in Cousin's doctrine and hence to the interpretive power implicitly vested in the textbook writers.

The exercise of that interpretive power proved more significant in the *Manuel* of Jacques, Simon, and Saisset. As sole author of the textbook's section on psychology, Jacques, too, addressed the politically delicate issue of differences in introspective capacity. He first broached that issue in his discussion of will—the content of the *moi* and perhaps also (if one followed Mallet) the instrument for appropriating the *moi*. Did the will, he wondered, differ in quality in different human beings? Appearances were in this case deceiving, he warned. We were accustomed to speaking of "firmness of character as unequally distributed among the different individuals of the species," and this turn of phrase usually led us to the conclusion that will, too, is unequally distributed. But, in fact, all men were endowed with an equal capacity for volition and that very equality, paradoxically, explained why some have firm characters and others weak ones. Although "[h]e who wills with force and tenacity what he has resolved passes for a man of character [while] he who wills weakly and is quickly discouraged is deemed a man lacking in will," those commonplace assessments were false. Withdrawal from the struggle was itself proof of the vigorous independence of the will, "less well employed perhaps, but as perfect as that of the man who continued the struggle." In contrast to Mallet, who postulated an equal luminescence of consciousness among men but an unequal will to undertake the difficulties of its interior observation, Jacques insisted that "men are equal only in will and hence they are absolutely (*rigoureusement*) equal. That equality, the only true kind, is also the only good kind and the only possible kind."[63]

Thus the perpetual problematic of Cousinian psychology—whether it would affirm a universal human nature or a hierarchical differentiation of people—seems to have been decided by Jacques in a fundamentally democratic fashion: if we are different, we are so by dint of the resolutions freely made by our equally powerful wills. While Jacques recognized that Nature did not create us with equivalent sensibilities (some are "exquisite" and others "dense") or equivalent intellects (some are "lively" and others "slow"),[64] these disparities in the two other faculties of consciousness did not impair our capacity to enjoy the exercise of our formally equivalent wills.

Jacques' nascent democratic tendency came through again when he described the introspection that isolates and apprehends the will. He seemed to say—though he left this detail vague, perhaps deliberately and prudently so—that any human being is capable of such introspection and self-appropriation. Here is his description of that all-important mental act. It is the nearest thing to a step-by-step guide to introspection that he provided in his textbook, and he saved it for the very last pages of the section on psychology:

> It is only a matter of collecting oneself inside oneself and for an instant cutting oneself off from the tumult of the senses, brushing aside the false glimmers of the imagination that obscure that spirit of the truth that illuminates our interior. *Whoever is capable of that effort* will soon sense that the cloud hiding his own nature from himself has dissipated, and for the confused feeling he initially had about [his own nature] will be substituted by degrees an increasingly distinct feeling

of the simplicity of what he calls the *moi;* and that feeling will ultimately take on all the persuasive force and all the clarity of a lively and luminous apperception. Thus he will have rediscovered *by reflection* the true sense of the word "I"[. . .] It only requires a little will and a moment of calm and silence. Don't reason; look, and you will feel a simple and unified power live inside you [. . .][65]

The political import of this passage turns on the meaning ascribed to the phrase "whoever is capable of that effort." Jacques' discussion of the equality of the will would seem to imply that everyone is technically capable, but that some people may freely choose to abstain from the activity of introspective self-appropriation that the passage identifies with reflection. Nor, apparently, will the group of abstainers be defined by their social-class position. For, unlike Mallet, Jacques did not reproduce in his textbook Cousin's discussion of spontaneity as the modality of the people and reflection as that of the elite.

Subtly hinted at in the *Manuel,* Jacques' particular political slant on Cousinian psychology was almost certainly invisible to the privileged students who used that book as a study guide. ("This being a purely elementary work," the triumvirate of authors pledged in the foreword, "any possibly controversial material has been scrupulously eliminated.")[66] It would be broadcast clearly only during the Second Republic, in the aftermath of a highly public *affaire.* In the end, Jacques would provide the deconstructive reading of Cousin with respect to social class that Caroline Angbert had provided—decades earlier and in the sheltered context of a private correspondence—with respect to gender.[67] Nevertheless, for all his incendiary potential, the Jacques of the 1846 *Manuel* must still be seen as one of the group of Cousinian disciples who dutifully attempted to train bourgeois male lycée students in Cousin's technology of the self.

How successful they were in teaching introspection is, of course, impossible to assess with precision, any more than we can gauge the success rate in the comparable pedagogical endeavors of their religious forebears, the monks and confessors, or their twentieth-century successors, the psychoanalysts. One factor that may have conduced to their success was that they aimed lower than these other groups. They nurtured introspective capability and knowledge not as a way of life or a means to continually unfolding self-discovery, though they did seem to prize the verbal precision that it would likely lend to the educated man's accounts of his psychic states.[68] Rather they appealed to introspection on something more akin to a "one-time" basis. Once the adept had experienced firsthand the force of the free volitional activity contained in consciousness, and had identified it with his "self," he had learned the indispensable, basic lesson. Presumably periodic reexperience would reinforce that lesson. But the manuals, geared to the statement of doctrine, did not emphasize repeated recourse to introspective practice.

Yet even if Cousinian introspection was not an ongoing process—and even if it is safe to assume that many *lycéens* failed to master it and instead memorized its supposed results—the certitude of both selfhood and membership in an elite that it provided lent it enormous cachet. Surely it is not accidental that the Cousinian philosopher Francisque Bouillier assured his students in 1844 that "psychological observation, replete with all its depths" would never spread from the elite to the multitude.[69] And in his textbook even the democratically inclined Jacques held out to his readers the promise of social superiority, observing of the Cousinian philosophy generally that "it gives the mind those virile habits that render men capable and distinguished."[70]

The Regiment

Ever the institution-builder, Cousin created at the grass-roots level a remarkably effective informal institution: the network of his former students, now inserted by his own hand in posts as philosophy professors all across France. One of his means for cementing his students' postgraduate loyalty doubles as a major source of information about the network they constituted. The students kept in touch with Cousin by mail, writing him at more or less regular intervals over the course of years or even decades. Cousin in turn assiduously preserved their letters and then, at his death, left his personal archive to the Sorbonne. Since in their capacity as letter writers the students were often loquacious, and since Cousin did not save his side of the correspondence, the historian who consults this archive has the sense of eavesdropping on interminable chatter directed at a silent and powerful interlocutor.[71] The students were doubtless giving a command performance. Although they rarely broached sexual matters, and then only with extreme delicacy,[72] their verbosity on other topics may qualify as the effect of a Foucauldian-style incitement to discourse: a forced disclosure through which they constituted their subjective identities.[73] In this case, those identities were the combined ones of philosophers, teachers, and disciples.

Textual evidence from a variety of sources indicates Cousin's role as the initiator and architect of these inevitably asymmetric epistolary exchanges: it was he who insisted upon or at least strongly encouraged the correspondence. According to an undated manuscript by Jules Simon, Cousin's "preferred followers were *authorized* to correspond with him."[74] A letter by Ernest Bersot to his family in 1844 points up the anxiety that accompanied writing to the *maître,* the uncomfortable sense that one's epistolary offerings were being appraised and graded. From his teaching post in Dijon, Bersot happily reported the testimony of a reliable friend in Paris that "Monsieur Cousin has been very pleased with my letters and speaks of me in a friendly manner."[75] And the students' letters to Cousin are voluble on the subject of their own, unspontaneous conditions of production. "I delayed writing to you, as you had requested me to do, about the *Cours de philosophie* that you wanted me to publicize at Bourges. . . ."[76] "Since you promised to write me first, I was waiting for your letter in order to write to you myself."[77] "Today I take advantage of the permission that you so kindly gave me to write to you."[78]

At the end of a long and information-packed missive, one student even brought to the fore the radically equivocal status of the letters, the uneasy space that they occupied between private and official communications. Mentioning that he had fallen short of some of his pedagogical goals in his philosophy class in Rouen, Mallet said that he would prefer to discuss the matter face to face when he saw Cousin in Paris. He would wait until Easter, even though he knew he could unburden himself immediately in the epistolary medium. After all, he remarked, "the letters that I have the honor of writing you do not exactly have an official character."[79] What did Mallet mean by this cryptic observation? That the letters were, in fact, quasi-official and hence should not include potentially damaging information about his inadequacies as a state employee? That the letters could not be farther from official, and hence should avoid overly solemn, work-related issues? Perhaps Mallet himself was unsure, the ambiguity of his meaning reproducing the ambiguity of the "scene of writing" that Cousin had created.

Cousin's strong shaping influence on the correspondence is seen in the fact that all of the letters touched on the same basic repertory of topics.

These topics may have been explicitly proposed or prescribed at the point at which the student left Paris to assume his first teaching post, or they may have been elicited by questions contained in Cousin's own letters. Some of the standard topics concerned the student's life situation: the headway he was making on the two required theses, one in Latin and the other in French; his meditations on his philosophical vocation ("I love philosophy because I strongly believe in it, and I am firmly resolved always to serve it."[80] "I would accept an administrative position only if it left me sufficient leisure for my philosophical work, which has become a need for me"[81]); his attitude toward his teaching post and, almost always, his desire for career advancement; his decision to marry, or not to marry. Other topics concerned the general progress of the Cousinian movement: the precise content of the courses the student was teaching, so that Cousin could be assured that all the critical points were being touched; the enrollment (Gatien-Arnoult triumphantly announced an audience of 500 or 600, "crammed on the benches or perched on the windows," in a room seating only 400, Charma crowed that "our psychological studies" had drawn twice as many students as the local Law Faculty, and Bouillier, who started out with a class of 200, proudly reported at the end of the academic year, "Not only did my audience not abandon me, but it has grown");[82] the relations of the student with the intellectuals and clergy in the town, and especially the sentiments expressed by both those groups toward Cousin's philosophy; the coverage Cousin received in the local press. With respect to this second set of topics, Cousin used his former students like the bureaucratic appointees they were. Scattered around the country in the venues predetermined by the structure of the French educational administration, they served as his eyes and ears in the provinces, gathering data and funneling it back to the center, managing public opinion, furthering Cousin's agenda, and defending him from attack. "Cousin is unknown in the departments," the *Gazette des écoles* had observed shortly after Cousin's 1830 appointment to the Royal Council of Public Instruction.[83] It was one of the jobs of the regiment to render that dictum obsolete.

The modes of address in these letters were, like the topics included in their contents, highly ritualized. "Monsieur" indicated a relationship with Cousin at the more distant and formal end of the spectrum. A more elaborate form of it, "M. le Conseiller" or "M. le Ministre," signaled a letter that was a vehicle for official business rather than an occasion for chitchat. "Mon cher maître" was the intimate mode of address. Students often made the transition from "Monsieur" to "Mon cher maître" (or the slightly less familiar "Mon illustre maître") when they had crossed some psychological barrier, specified or unspecified. The reverse transition was ominous, a reliable sign of a falling out.

The letters show the uniformly strong tendency of the former students to perceive themselves as belonging to a collectivity. Under a variety of names, many of them metaphorical, they refer proudly to the group, headed by Cousin, which claims them as its members. The military term "regiment," which I have used as the title of this section and by which the group was often known in the outside world,[84] was apparently of Cousin's own coinage. Thus Ernest Bersot informed his family in 1837 that he had passed his major examination with Monsieur Cousin who, at the end of a long and occasionally "terrifying" interrogation, "enrolled me in his regiment."[85] In a remarkably frank letter to Royer-Collard earlier that decade, Cousin not only indicated the ease and regularity with which he used the term "regiment" to describe the collective body of his students and clients but also laid down one of the ground rules of that informal organization. Responding to Royer-Collard's inquiry about the employment situation of a former student, he indicated that he had some time ago moved the young man from Nîmes to Grenoble ("an improvement in his situation") and had just authorized a second transfer to Angers, where he would be closer to Royer-Collard. But Orléans was out of the question, having been earmarked for another, particularly worthy "young Doctor" whose "sacrifice" to Royer-Collard's student would have been "supremely unjust." As devoted to Royer-Collard as Cousin was, there were limits to what he would do for his mentor's protégés—a point that he spelled out so explicitly that it deserves to be quoted verbatim.

> Since [this particular student] is under your patronage, invite him to do honor to [that status] by distinguishing himself from his classmates through his labors. *For I take pains to preserve in my regiment a competition (émulation) founded on the conviction that merit always determines advancement.*[86]

Despite Cousin's apparent preference for "regiment," his students employed that term rather infrequently in their correspondence with him. "Service in your regiment is perilous, especially when one has earned his stripes from you," Ernest Bersot concluded a letter from Bordeaux in 1842.[87] But other military references abounded. Francis Riaux assured Cousin from Rennes that, despite the geographical distance that separated them, he need fear no lapse in the younger man's fidelity: a "soldier feels his courage and force intensify when he knows that his general's eyes are on him." Three years later he described himself as a "grateful and loyal soldier" and depicted the Cousinian collectivity with quiet passion as "our cause," an expression also used by other students and by Cousin himself.[88] He sometimes fused the military with the literary metaphor, as when he took consolation in belonging to "that little galaxy [pléiade—a term used for the greatest of the French Renaissance poets] of young professors arrayed in the shadow of your flag."[89] The religious metaphor was also extensively mined. To Bersot, the group could be aptly described as Cousin's "flock."[90] Reminding Cousin that his discipleship dated back to 1818, Laurent Delcasso spoke of "our old cult"[91]—a phrase that, taken out of context, could easily pass for a lapsed Catholic's allusion to Catholicism. But Delcasso obviously meant it to refer to the Cousinian philosophy, whose foundations were laid in 1815–18, and to the appeal that it exercised among its faithful as a substitute religion.

The solidarity of the group was also perceived by outsiders. When, beset by rational doubt, Ernest Renan left the Saint-Sulpice seminary in 1845 after nine years' total immersion in Catholicism, many Paris intellectuals were eager to aid his reorientation to secular culture. Cousin made welcoming gestures, but Renan nonetheless regarded the philosopher as fundamentally inaccessible: "Monsieur Cousin. . . . was too surrounded by disciples for me to attempt to elbow my way through that crowd, tightly bound together by the words of the master."[92]

Although the students' letters to Cousin are far from relaxed in style, they are not always cramped or stilted. Venting anger at Cousin, while a rare occurrence, was apparently permissible and indicates the emotionally intense, hothouse atmosphere that characterized this circle—at least during the 1840s, when Cousin's political and bureaucratic power was at its peak. At the moment of an emotional outburst, the student letter writers seem to have abandoned self-censorship. Thus Jules Barni could not "get over [his] astonishment" at the harsh words that Cousin had addressed to him in front of "a third party" at what was supposed to be a pleasurable evening in the country in July 1846. "Even if your reproaches had had some foundation, which I refuse to accept, you should have delivered them at another moment and in a different tone." For the "man of conscience" he pretended to be, Cousin had treated him "outrageously." To be sure, Barni did not maintain the upper hand throughout this angry letter; his avowal of his suffering and of his sense of wounded dignity could be read as an appropriately palliative acknowledgment of his inferior status vis-à-vis Cousin. In any case, Barni's outburst seems to have been accepted by Cousin and integrated into their continuing patron-client relationship. Within twenty-four hours Cousin had dashed off a brief note to Barni, and the latter replied, regretting what he had said while under the sway of "an emotion I could not vanquish" and thanking Cousin for having relieved his heart of the oppressive weight of resentment.[93]

The outburst of Antoine Charma, on the other hand, could not be contained within the structure of Cousinian patron-clientage and was the prelude to a break with Cousin. For reasons that the correspondence does not clearly specify, Charma felt himself spurned and unappreciated by Cousin. "I could have been your favorite disciple . . . Plato would have found a Phaedo in me! Will I remain to the end lost in the crowd of your admirers, or is my period of trial finally over?"[94] The issue seems to have been Charma's desire to leave his teaching post at the Faculty of Letters in Caen, about whose lax academic standards he had earlier complained, for something more stimulating and lucrative in Paris.[95] Although his boredom in Caen was temporarily relieved by the 1836 trial there of the patricide Pierre Rivière[96]—an event made known in our own era by Michel Foucault's book[97]—he filled his letters to Cousin with grievances about life in Normandy. He spoke of his seven long years of exile, of the "too marked disparity between the theater [presumably the Faculty of Caen] and the actor [himself]," of the impossibility of providing for two children and a young wife on a provincial salary so low that he had been unable to save a single sou.[98] The letters leading up to the outburst reveal a long-simmering tension between teacher and student. One ends with an extravagant and anxious expression of attachment: "Permit me, Sir, to tell you in closing that if my letters (as your latest response has made me fear) distort me to the point of not betraying in every line my intense desire to satisfy you—you who, in truth, gave birth to my moral life—those letters lie disgracefully and I disown them."[99] The next letter pleads ill health as the reason for Charma's decision not to make his usual summer visit to Paris and adds with unintended sarcasm, "The most costly aspect of this resolution is the loss of the several minutes of time that you are so kind to give me each year."[100]

But Charma may have strained the already frayed relationship beyond the breaking point when he implicitly accused Cousin of rationalist detachment and insensitivity to human feelings, bidding him to "descend from the heights of your philosophical throne into the hardly scholarly secrets of my inner self (mon intérieur)."[101] Since, whatever his construction of the term, Cousin typically depicted himself as a virtuoso of the intérieur, this oblique attack on his professional legitimacy may have struck him as intolerable. In any event, Charma did not write his old patron again for nearly six years, and then only after Cousin had deputized another former student, Adolphe Franck, to extend the olive branch.[102] The relationship between Charma and Cousin then resumed, less intense but also less tortured and more genuinely affectionate than before. Though he never got his longed-for release from the obscurity of Caen, Charma began to address Cousin as his "très-cher maître."[103]

While still a student in Paris, Paul Janet began his correspondence with Cousin in order to apologize for an angry outburst:

> Please be so kind as to inform me of your intentions with regard to me and if I ought to construe narrowly the resolve that you expressed last night. If the sole cause of that resolve was the uncontrolled and violent words that I made the mistake of uttering, please accept on that point all my apologies. I strongly regret having failed in what I owe you, and I would be sorry if the inflamed words of a young man ruptured a relation at once so useful and so honorable to me.

The letter seems to have appeased Cousin, for Janet embarked upon a particularly long and eminent career as a representative of the Cousinian school. His next letter, written when he was about to leave Paris to take up a provincial post, gracefully alludes to their recurrent interpersonal difficulties. ("I would have wanted to have a natural disposition that would permit me to satisfy you more constantly.") However, once Janet was on his own and out of sight, peace seems to have reigned between patron and client.[104]

The correspondence also sheds light on the place of marriage in the lives of this first generation of professional, state-employed philosophers. Cousin himself never married and, although his sexual liaison with the writer Louise Colet produced a journalistic scandal in Paris in 1840,[105] his students seem to have believed, or more likely pretended to believe, that carnal passion was unknown to him. A chapter titillatingly called "The Loves" in Jules Simon's 1887 biography of the *maître* describes only the sketches of seventeenth-century women to which Cousin devoted his years of retirement. That chapter and the whole biography end with a dictum as arresting as it is false: "Into his life no woman enters—at least, no living woman; in his heart and in his talent this great lacuna remains."[106]

Cousin's bachelorhood must have lent his leadership a priestly aura. Barthélemy-Saint-Hilaire's 1895 biography declares that Cousin regretted this status, regarding the failure to marry as fundamentally antisocial behavior, and that he consequently recommended marriage to all who sought his advice.[107] But Cousin's correspondence with his former students reveals a more complicated story, as one might expect of a mentor who tended so forcefully to affirm his own personal example. Cousin was deeply ambivalent about the place of marriage in the philosophical life. So pronounced was his irresolution that he was capable of describing prolonged bachelorhood as producing "a painful void in the soul" and, in the immediately following sentences, to declare that most men lacked the "firmness of heart" that would prevent "family interests" from causing them to "falter in the exercise of [their] duties as philosophers and as citizens" and, even more stridently, that "Marriage has weakened the Université while celibacy has been a source of strength for the Church."[108]

Cousin's position on the marriage of his students seems to have been a function of his own plans for the particular student, how he intended to deploy him in the grand regimental strategy for the propagation of philosophy. He had, it would appear from the letters, no qualms at all about the marriage of Francisque Bouillier, a disciple stationed in Lyon. In January 1848, Bouillier had mentioned a rich uncle who had recently vowed to remain single until the end of his days; he would leave his entire fortune to his two nephews, in addition to providing a gift of 60,000 francs to each on his wedding day. The good news had immediately turned Bouillier's thoughts to marriage and to the salutary effect that an advantageous

Figure 4: The Maître.   This portrait of Victor Cousin, originally attributed to the photographer Nadar but now believed to be the work of Gustave Le Gray, dates from 1854–1859, when the *maître* was in his sixties—older than in the period covered in detail by this book. Cousin's grave countenance accords well with the concept of the self he promulgated, although here it may convey his suspicion of the time-consuming photographic process that was fixing his image for posterity. His slightly disheveled look (note his wrinkled clothing and the bit of patterned fabric peeking out between his vest and trousers) befits his status as an aging bachelor. (The J. Paul Getty Museum, Los Angeles © The J. Paul Getty Museum)

match would have on the political career that, already a municipal coun-cilor in Lyon, he envisioned for himself.[109] Cousin apparently could not contain his curiosity about his student's marital aspirations, for some two months later Bouillier wrote to him, "You've expressed so much interest that I feel obliged to announce my coming marriage. I am already engaged. . . ." His betrothed was twenty years old and had an aristocratic particle in her name. "It is a rather fine marriage," Bouillier opined, "with respect to the person, the family, and the fortune."[110] Soon he was taking vacations on the landed property of his wife's grandmother and, coining a memorable phrase, he epitomized his lifestyle there as one in which he divided his time "between Cartesianism and hunting."[111] Bouillier's mar-riage was clearly a vehicle for his social and possibly political advance-ment, enhancing his influence as a proponent of Cousinianism; and if for no other reason Cousin seems to have approved of it.[112]

However, the case of Vacherot shows that, where the marriage of former students was concerned, Cousin had more than one string to his bow. He felt, in short, free to meddle. In an emotional letter that went straight to the point, Vacherot began, "I have suffered a great deal and I will continue to suffer for a long time still from the service you have rendered me; yet my reason still acknowledges that service and is deeply grateful to you for it." Apparently Cousin had talked Vacherot out of getting married or, at least, had persuaded him to refrain from doing so in the immediate future.

> I ought not think of marrying right now. I have as yet done nowhere near enough for the science to which I belong entirely. You had real grounds for doubting my philosophical vocation, seeing me thus inclined to lull myself prematurely in the bosom of family life. But I hope to prove to you that even if philosophy is not my soul's only need, it will always be its premier need.[113]

Vacherot later reversed his principled decision to remain single, impressed by the continued devotion of his jilted fiancée and by her parents' generous promise to aid him in discharging his obligations to his own family. But at the moment of reversal, he again emphasized how heavily Cousin's opinion had influenced his earlier resolution to break off the engagement.

> Here is my position. Eight months ago I renounced a marriage advantageous in every respect. I did so not because I believe marriage

irreconcilable with the functions of the sacred philosophical calling (*sacerdoce philosophique*) but only because I feared the loss of your trust.[114]

He even tried in another letter to persuade Cousin that his very desire to marry was evidence of the strength of his philosophical vocation. "I have never liked *le monde* [the world of polite sociability], and that is why I sense that marriage is necessary in my case. I want to live with Philosophy as my goal and have recourse to family affection to refresh and distract me."[115]

As one attempts to decipher Vacherot's letters, always hampered by the absence of Cousin's, it appears that Cousin had tied Vacherot's proof of his so-called philosophical vocation to his willingness to leave a teaching post in the familiar environment of Versailles (where both his family and fiancée lived) for a far more difficult one at a *collège* in the intellectual backwater of Caen. There he would be perpetually on the front lines, attempting to persuade hostile Catholic parents that Cousinian philosophy was good for their children. He had, in other words, to be willing to sacrifice his personal happiness for the good of the movement. But whatever the details of Vacherot's case, one fact is clear: Cousin was fully capable of invoking the quasi-priestly ideal of vocation (*sacerdoce*) as an argument against the marriage of a professor of Cousinian philosophy.

And indeed the correspondence reveals a distinctly ascetic streak in the culture of Cousin's regiment, the kind of tendency that would, after all, make reference to the philosophical calling an effective rhetorical strategy. Vacherot, for example, noted that he tried hard to "spark a vocation" in appropriate students, not only because it was his duty to do so but because it gave him an "ineffable happiness." He furthermore described the student with vocational potential as one "who puts to the service of his philosophical studies an impartial mind and especially a pure heart."[116] He also recounted instructing his charges in Normandy that happiness was not tantamount to pleasure. "I have wiped out the egoistic principle from the moral law. . . . What is most difficult to transmit to the minds and hearts of our young people is the conviction that no one has the right to complain of the distribution of rewards and punishments on this earth, and that happiness (*but not pleasure*) is the lot of every virtuous man."[117] Newly stationed in Tours as a young philosophy professor, Vapereau reported that he "mingled in society only as much as was necessary to avoid being treated as a misanthrope." He attributed his unworldly, ascetic habits to Cousin. "My thought and my feelings have a higher goal, and I owe to my education, and to the influence that you spread about you, that I prefer the satisfactions of study to a frivolous vanity."[118]

An aspect of this asceticism was the widely shared belief that great shows of emotion—including the occasional angry outbursts that Cousin seems to have both provoked and selectively tolerated—were self-indulgent, that rationality ought to contain emotion. Thus, after sharing with Cousin his complicated feelings about marriage, Vacherot began his next letter with an apology. Ever since Cousin had honored him with admission into his "philosophical intimacy," the younger man had, at least when "constrained by necessity," also confided to him about "personal matters." He was now contrite: "I know very well that you have the right to expect something else entirely from a philosophy professor."[119] The same ethos of containment of unruly passion by rationality can be seen in Mallet's analysis of the suicide of a fellow student, Bach. In a discursive move reminiscent of the eighteenth century, Mallet finds the source of Bach's tragedy in an overactive imagination. "There is a letter in which he speaks of an interview he had with you, Sir, around the middle of August. Bach's imagination was so quick and far-reaching that he stretched the meaning of your promises to cover things they couldn't possibly have included. That's what ruined him." We know from Mallet's comments earlier in the same letter exactly what imagination connotes to him. Bemoaning the relatively little "aptitude for philosophical studies" that he has found among his students in Rouen, he observes that most of them are "no more than sixteen or seventeen, still at an age more favorable to the exercise of the imagination, than to that of reflection and reason."[120]

The correspondence also provides vivid accounts of the sometimes brutal conflict that broke out between the local clergy and the young Cousinian professoriate newly arrived from Paris. These accounts make clear both the institutional function of the regiment to disseminate Cousinianism in the provinces and the extreme discomfort entailed for the loyal soldiers by the lopsided way that Cousin occupied his position of middlingness. Cousin confronted his enemies to the left—those who reduced mind to matter, tolerated psychological fragmentation, and supported political and social democracy—head-on and without apology. But he attempted to appease his already powerful clerical enemies to the right, hoping to persuade them that there was nothing in his philosophy fundamentally inimical to Catholicism. He moreover enrolled his former students in this work of appeasement. Thus the Cousin disciple Emile Saisset wrote a pair of articles in the *Revue des deux mondes* in the mid-1840s arguing that the intelligentsia should studiously avoid anticlericalism and embrace the representation of Cousinianism as a "conciliatory spiritualism" capable of harmonizing philosophy and Catholicism.[121] As the student correspondence reveals, the daily, face-to-face labor of persuading influential Catholics that Cousinianism posed no threat fell to the new graduates whom the *maître* had assigned to the provinces.

The otherwise put-upon Vacherot offers a vignette of himself engaged in this labor in Caen in 1836, duly uttering doublespeak. The superior of the local seminary has paid him a call, apparently for the purpose of discussing Cousin's philosophy. He tells the young man that he finds Cousin's system "admirable" insofar as it stays within its proper sphere, aloof from matters of religion. Such separation is, in his view, the key to peace between religion and philosophy: "Each in its own house," and war can no more break out between them than between religion and physics. Called upon to reply, Vacherot becomes mealy-mouthed. He neither "accepts nor refuses [the] compromise settlement" proposed by his visitor but instead changes the subject, a strategy of evasion that he characterizes as "remaining faithful to the fatherly advice that you [Cousin] gave me." It is not that Vacherot is intellectually undecided about the matter at hand; rather, following Cousin's own views ("this flag of independence that you have planted in the French philosophical community"), he abhors the cleric's position: "Science cannot accept such a compromise settlement without mutilating itself by its own hand . . ." Vacherot devises a neat formula to sum up his complex social performance: "I said nothing that I didn't believe to be true; but I didn't say everything that I believe to be true." Both pride and shame seem to inhere in his account of the episode. He has obediently followed Cousin's bidding, but he has also manifested a calculated disingenuousness.[122]

If Vacherot experienced vague moral unease at the mediating role foisted upon him by Cousin, Ernest Bersot's suffering was more intense.[123]

The young philosopher was initially delighted with his appointment to Bordeaux in autumn 1840, recognizing that in bestowing it upon him Cousin had violated his basic principle, identical to that of the Old Regime state bureaucracy, of not placing functionaries in the geographical regions where they had familial roots. He fully knew "what gratitude you expect of me" for such bounty, and he regretted not having requested from his patron pre-departure "instructions for comporting myself in the city." He soon announced to his students that he would "profess eclecticism"—a risky avowal, since this was a region in France in which people quipped that "Catholic doesn't rhyme with eclectic" and in which they knew little about Cousin's doctrine except that it was subversive: "When they don't laugh at it, they put it on the Index." By November Bersot described his "position in the city," by which he meant his reception by the clergy, as a difficult one. The archbishop "and his party" regretted that, unlike his "devout" predecessor, Bersot was "simply religious" and was also "bringing your philosophy into the diocese." Cousin had apparently prepared his disciples for such sticky situations, for Bersot pledged, "If I am attacked, I will not reply, following your counsel." Happily and not unexpectedly, his relations with state appointees at the level of the department were smoother: "I spent the evening at the home of the Prefect, who lavishly praised your administration [as minister of public instruction, a post Cousin had lost just the month before]."[124]

Bersot apparently stayed out of trouble for more than a year. However, in March 1842, perhaps lulled into a false sense of security, he called attention to himself by writing two articles criticizing the liberal Catholic Lacordaire, then preaching at the cathedral in Bordeaux, for dismissing philosophy as powerless and irrelevant.[125] The clerical machinery now began to intrude on Bersot's life in earnest.

> The Rector [of the Faculty of Letters] has stopped greeting me, and the day of the college holiday the assistant chaplain . . . delivered in front of the rector, the archbishop, the professors, the pupils and myself a sermon against philosophy in which I was personally heckled in such a scandalous manner that all the pupils turned around to look at me. His gentlest words were, "Reply obscure metaphysicians, frivolous psychologists, futile thinkers."

Still, a petition demanding Bersot's revocation from his post that was circulated among the parents of his pupils (presumably by his clerical enemies) received insufficient support and never saw the light of day. "I have not lost a single pupil, and they are all devoted to me."[126]

Two days later, however, Bersot began his letter with a cry for help ("If you abandon your protection of me, soon—perhaps in a few days— I will no longer belong to the Université") and proceeded to give Cousin a detailed account of the "incredible" events that had just transpired. His pupils were scheduled for their Easter examinations, ordinarily given by a state bureaucratic official, the inspector of the Academy, as the local unit of the state's educational administration was called. Departing from standard practice, the rector asked that the pupils be examined by a professor of the Faculty—in fact, by none other than Bersot's "devout" predecessor, who had been supplied beforehand with a detailed syllabus of Bersot's course. In the presence of the rector and the headmaster, this Professor Ladévi-Roche questioned the pupils about two points in the syllabus that he had earmarked as seditious: the theory that language was of human rather than divine origin and the existence of a faculty of will also called the *force motrice*. In their responses, the pupils dutifully presented Bersot's views on the topics at hand, causing the rector and headmaster to indicate "their repulsion for my doctrines by their shrugs of the shoulders and signs of impatience." When Ladévi-Roche presented his own opinions, the same two authority figures nodded and exclaimed with pleasure. An ugly scenario at best: Bersot submitted to official scrutiny through the medium of his pupils and in his pupils' presence. The examination culminated in the rector's tirade against the *force motrice*.

> Then the Rector, furious, cried out, "I must protest publicly and energetically against such pernicious doctrines. What we have here is atheism. What is this *force motrice*, this material soul? It is a newfangled power that may or may not obey the orders of the will. When I plunge a dagger into a man's heart, it is not I who does the plunging, it is the *force motrice*; I'm not responsible, it is. Neither crimes nor virtues exist any longer. It is a doctrine of pure materialism."

By following Cousin's advice about self-control under pressure, Bersot effectively got the last word. When the rector turned toward him, awaiting his response, "I was the master of myself (*maître de moi*) and replied calmly, 'Sir, I will give my pupils an example of respect and obedience by being silent.'"[127]

In these tense circumstances, Bersot continued to be *maître de moi* (a term he seems to have favored, perhaps because of its distinctly Cousinian ring). But the tension had produced what he recognized as psychosomatic symptoms:

> I am very nervous, very irritable, and *my body is taking its revenge.* That same evening [after another confrontation with the Rector], I had a fever; M. Bazin [his friend the zoology professor] put me to bed; I fought it for several days and finally last Tuesday decided it was necessary to find someone to take over my class temporarily; it was a true malady of nerves."[128]

Cousin protected his outspoken client. When, at the rector's insistence, the minister of public instruction was called in to mediate the conflict, Bersot remained secure in his post. The state inspectors who evaluated his teaching later that spring found in his favor and at the same time indicated to him that they were firmly under Cousin's thumb. As Bersot reported gratefully to Cousin, "Instead of the severe admonition with which I had been publicly threatened, I found benevolence, minds already turned *by you* in my favor.[129] But neither had Cousin given Bersot carte blanche. In a private letter whose confidentiality he underscored, he admonished Bersot to withdraw from the debate over Lacordaire, indeed always to take pains to represent himself publicly as absolute in his respect for religion. Thus Cousin's desire to conciliate the clergy not only produced psychosomatic ailments in Bersot but necessitated that the younger man curtail his freedom of expression.[130]

Although Bersot's trials were particularly flamboyant, he was not alone among Cousin's soldiers in receiving unkind treatment from the local clergy. Jules Simon reported from Caen "a sort of conspiracy on the part of the clergy to prevent my marriage, and you will be sad to hear that it is my status as a pupil of Monsieur Cousin that has rendered me suspect to these gentlemen."[131] Like Bersot in Bordeaux, Bouillier in Lyon immediately announced his affiliations. "I was at once proud and moderate, as you recommended. I emphasized eclecticism, the Ecole normale, [apparently virtually synonymous with eclecticism] and the independence of human reason." True to his expectations, he was soon attacked in the legitimist press, especially after he expressed the opinion that "Spinoza was not an atheist and was even an extremely honorable man." In Bouillier's case, it was the political right, rather than the clergy, that came forth to torment him, although the grounds for criticism were the same. He mentioned some of the pamphlets newly circulating in Lyon: "One of them accuses you in bold letters of having taught Jouffroy not to believe in God; in another a criminal making a confession admits that reading your books led him to murder his benefactor, etc." Bouillier's relationship with the local clergy was, by contrast, cordial if intrinsically unstable. "I am on good terms with abbé Noirot, thanks to the questions that we have put aside and tacitly agreed not to speak about. I nonetheless suspect that he wasn't pleased by everything I said in my inaugural lecture."[132]

As the copious ethnographic detail cited in this section has shown, the members of Cousin's regiment ended up embracing Cousinianism not merely as an intellectual doctrine but as a way of life, one with its own customs, rituals, value system, career trajectory, and automatic set of friends and enemies. Grafted onto the formal institution of the Université, this highly elaborated informal network helped provide the infrastructure for Cousinian hegemony.

Internalizing the Cousinian Self (1): Men

In making the claim that the Cousinian movement defined and inculcated the nineteenth-century French bourgeois self, it would be gratifying to be able to cite numerous first-person testimonials to the experience of self-discovery under the aegis of Cousinian pedagogy. But the young bourgeois men for whom that pedagogy was designed have not, apparently, obliged the historian in this regard. Their virtual silence, rather than undercutting my claim, probably indicates a certain redundancy of that pedagogy where they were concerned: they had not, to be sure, previously possessed a technical language to articulate their selfhood, but the conception of themselves as inherently active, willful beings would have come as no surprise. In their case, training in Cousinian psychology confirmed a truth already implicit in their social position; introspective knowledge solidified and shaped a preexisting, informal sense of self rather than measurably transforming them.

What the early nineteenth-century beneficiaries of Cousinian instruction have left behind for the historian are some of their school examinations and compositions. Probably because the Restoration education ministry was closely monitoring philosophy instruction at the Ecole normale supérieure—it would decide to close that headstrong institution between 1822 and 1828—the Archives Nationales contain a full set of graded examination papers from the year 1820.[133] The date places these papers at the end of the foundational period of Cousinian philosophy, before it had been disseminated throughout France but when it was already firmly entrenched on the Rue d'Ulm. The students sitting for this particular examination were queried about the fundamental tenets of philosophical dualism: "What are the foundations of the belief that there exist not only an indefinite number of substances but also substances of different natures? How are we led to recognize that we are ourselves composed of two distinct substances, one material and the other immaterial, and what are the essential characteristics of these substances?" By their diversity of approach, the responses to these questions indicated that the students were not simply repeating formulae supplied by their professors but that they had to some degree integrated Cousinian philosophy into their own mental frameworks. They could pick and choose among its elements. They could speak Cousinian.

One student, the recipient of the highest grade, answered the question by offering a macrocosm-microcosm analogy and casting himself as the active, very impressionable investigator of both worlds. After surveying the material bodies that constituted the larger world and inferring from their order and regularity the existence of a divine spiritual substance, he turned his attention to the microcosm, the individual human being. In his excited involvement in this exercise, he even erred grammatically by switching from the first-person plural to the first-person singular midway through the argument:

> The same phenomenon that *astonishes us* in the universe and shows us an immaterial substance—one, intelligent, and volitional—animating this great whole and lending it in some way a more noble and majestic life, *strikes us again* when we return our gaze to ourselves. We first see our body, which lives only the ordinary life, which is born, develops and declines like other beings. But I hasten to perceive that, like the universe, I am double. My body gets weak and demands food, and I refuse it. Time and again I make light of its needs and its pains. I examine this *strange part of myself* that so often struggles against what I believe myself to be entirely; I soon perceive that it [the strange part] is everything and that my body is almost nothing. I pursue my research, and this is what I discover. . .

The student tells us little about how he pursued his research; he does not, in other words, describe an introspective process. But he does say that, having nearly fallen himself into the trap of overestimating the importance of human corporeality, he can now understand the foibles of the "philosophers of the last century [who] could, by taking activity away from thought, reduce man to a sensitive being." And he concludes his essay with a flourish that makes use of a bevy of Cousinian key-words: "Unity, Simplicity, Identity, Liberty—all those ideas are resolved into that of Personality. And there you have it: the essential characteristics of the substance of the human *moi*."[134]

The less fluent, third-ranking student took a completely different approach, stressing the relationship of the material and immaterial substances to the different stages of the human life cycle. "The child thinks only of what he sees around himself; he exercises his powers of observation only on the external world." But once he becomes a man, this need to observe turns him in a "new and more noble" direction. His observation

> takes another route and folds back entirely upon itself internally in order to show him to himself for what he is. He no longer sees but he feels, and as he feels only because there is something that he can feel, he concludes that there exists within him a second substance, of a nature different from the first, capable all by itself of movement—that is, immaterial—and whose existence is as well-proven as that of his body.

Unlike the first student, then, this one treated the question as an invitation to describe, as best he could, the elusive process of introspection.[135]

The second-ranking student took yet another tack, introducing into his examination paper a Romantically tinged reminiscence—a stylistic gesture that might have been more typical for French philosophy students in 1820 than it was during the July Monarchy. He began by invoking an "autumn day when I was wandering in the country plunged into my customary reveries." Nevertheless, his unfocused, Rousseauean dreaminess quickly gave way to the acute rationalism prized by the Cousinian school. Coming upon a peasant plowing the fields, he engaged him in conversation and made the classic Cousinian discovery about the lower orders: "I soon saw that he was not lacking in good sense *(bon sens).*" This realization inspired in him the desire, as he put it in a mixture of inductive and deductive vocabulary that well-expressed the Cousinian ethos, "to conduct an experiment in metaphysics on him."

"Do you believe," I say to him, pointing to the stone that marks the limits of his field, "do you believe that stone exists?" "Why, yes, I believe that." "But how do you know that it exists?" "Because I see it." "Couldn't you be mistaken?" My man thinks a few moments while rubbing his brow. "I am no more mistaken than I am when I believe that I exist." "You also believe that you exist then?" "Good Lord, yes! I've never doubted it, nor has my priest. I feel it, that's all." "But," I continued, "do you exist in the same way the stone does?" "Well, I have a body and a soul. My body is made of matter. My soul . . ." He hesitated and I continued to interrogate him. "My soul," he added, "is how I sense that all this exists." "Your soul is not made of matter then?" "No." "Then what is it?" "I don't know. But I sense that it is not like that stone nor like my body." "You are right," I tell him. I take my leave and, after a few paces, turn my head and see my laborer looking pensive. But soon I hear him whistling as he goes back to his furrows.

As the student sums up this excruciatingly condescending encounter: "Thus all men, *even the most ignorant,* believe in the existence of body and soul. It is only the philosopher who doubts and who seeks to delude himself about the beliefs held in common by humanity as a whole."[136]

This examination paper is a particularly telling historical document. It shows how Cousinianism linked philosophical dualism to a particular set of social attitudes, and it suggests how readily students grasped and internalized that linkage. In the rough-hewn, good-tempered, church-going, and eminently sensible peasant who submits to his questioning, the philosophy student has created a stereotype of the man of the people: a gracious subordinate of the man equipped with a lycée education and a natural ally of Cousinianism. The villain of the piece is the "philosopher," which in 1820 still meant the Enlightenment philosophe espousing sensationalism. The student takes as given that the Cousinian insistence on self as spiritual substance entails an entirely patronizing bonhomie toward the lower classes.

Some of these same social attitudes come through in the essay of the fourth-ranking student. That essay ends with a description of the *moi* that, although couched in abstract philosophical vocabulary, speaks passionately, almost brutally, about hierarchies of power and their justification. The rulership inherent in selfhood is this student's theme:

I name "self" (*moi*) that force that matter obeys, a force about which matter can do nothing. I do not know its nature, but I sense that it is always acting, while matter is lifeless if that force does not animate it. I sense that the one is always producing, while the other, sterile by nature, can only passively receive either impressions from outside or commandments from that other substance which, in its liberty, obeys only itself or a power that it chooses to recognize.[137]

An 1833 composition by Emile Saisset, then a *normalien*, that Cousin preserved among his own papers presents in more decorously measured language a similar enthusiasm for the unconstrained force of volition that is the core of the Cousinian self. Setting as his task to "inquire of consciousness what the 'I' is in the ordinary propositions 'I will,' 'I think,' 'I sense,'" Saisset concludes that the first proposition is unique among the three for only in that case does the 'I' immediately cause what it perceives. Thought and sensation are not products of the *moi*, although they exist for us only insofar as the *moi* spotlights them with an act of attention. Volition is, however, a direct and exhilarating self-affirmation. Saisset experiences it as something akin to the ego trip of late twentieth-century American slang:

I will. Doesn't that mean "I produce," "I cause a volition"? Of my accord, without being constrained by anything at all, I make up my mind to act in such and such a way? Isn't that irresistible evidence for me that that resolution, that willing, is an effect of which I am the cause?[138]

Internalizing the Cousinian Self (2): Women

If the bourgeois male lycée students have left evidence of their internalization of the Cousinian language of the self mainly in the papers they were forced to write, the female outsiders, whose acquisition of Cousinian philosophical knowledge was never intended by the state educational system, comment more explicitly on its transformative impact. The exemplary case is Caroline Angebert who, as described in Chapter 4, wangled a correspondence course from the *maître* himself. Angebert's sense of exclusion from the male enterprise of philosophy was acute. Visiting Paris in the autumn of 1829 (her official purpose was to intercede at the Naval Ministry on behalf of her husband, who had received an unwanted posting), she asked "everyone [she] met whether women could attend" Cousin's Sorbonne lectures. She also made a Sunday "pilgrimage to the Rue d'Enfer," where Cousin lived, and enacted the role of outsider by virtually pressing her nose against the glass. "I stopped for several moments in front of your door, and there I saw you in my imagination, surrounded by [male] disciples who were much happier but no more loyal than I."[139]

Once the *maître* had yielded to her entreaties and inducted her into his psychological method, Angebert gratefully provided him with detailed, exuberant accounts of her introspective experience. In January 1830 she reported, "I have [now] done enough to convince myself that psychology is neither cold nor arid; on the contrary, I feel that I will be strongly attached to it and that it is very fruitful."[140] Several months later she told him that "my psychological ardor has . . . taken me into depths where I have trouble seeing clearly and can hardly recognize myself." Psychology, she eventually concluded, was a terrain intrinsically alien to women:

> I am, and with good reason, much more fearful when I speak to you in the name of those great truths that we all carry within ourselves. It is far easier for me to follow you headlong into ontology, whose most sublime roads are now and then accessible even to the weakest woman, than to approach you on the thorny path of psychological science.

That women in general should feel more comfortable with the impersonal and imposing truths of pure being than with the intimacy of psychology may seem counterintuitive to us. Nevertheless, Angebert explains quite convincingly why Cousin's psychological method presents her sex with the stranger, more unaccustomed experience. In the case of ontology, she could, in her words, ascend "on [Cousin's] wings," thinking that the great principles she encountered were "made to be obeyed" and that "one would always work out a suitable accommodation to them." Never had she dreamed that the ground rules of psychology would be so different, that they would entail actively "coordinating" great principles and "verifying them in my own mind." Thus she concludes: "Almost everything in psychology was new for me."[141]

Angebert's comments testify to the efficacy of Cousinian psychology as instruction in selfhood, as a kind of intellectual exercise in which one not only learned the arcane truths arrived at by others but vividly experienced one's self as an autonomous source of truth. At first the techniques of introspection made Angebert feel like a "poor little thing," alone on "an immense sea of time and space"; later she learned to "steer my little boat myself." To be sure, Angebert sometimes expressed doubt about Cousin's exclusive reliance on introspective data and informally tested his psychology against her own observations of young children. How, she wondered, could he seriously believe that consciousness of the *moi* preceded that of the *non-moi* when a child obviously "gives himself over so passionately to the objects which entice him. . . . Isn't his mind more attached to the butterfly, to the bird he pursues than to the mental operation occurring within himself?"[142] But in general, she applauded the instruction she received in the self-evidence of consciousness. Precisely because Angebert was not entitled to this instruction—indeed was officially debarred from it by the conventions and policies of the day—she noticed and recorded its impact on her. Unlike the bourgeois male lycée students, for whom Cousinian psychology was the required, crowning moment of a long, informal education in self-worth, Angebert experienced that psychology as bolt from the blue and a revelation.

While not as dramatic as the case of Angebert, that of Pauline Franck also illustrates the impact of Cousinianism on a female outsider. Franck, an autodidact Jewish governess and a woman of bold intellect, came by her Cousinianism with considerably less effort than Angebert. She married Adolphe Franck, the Cousinian disciple who would later edit the *Dictionnaire des sciences philosophiques* and become (under Cousin's patronage) the first Jew to be elected to the Institut de France.[143] During their long engagement (1831–38), when Pauline was in eastern France and Franck held teaching posts in various provincial and Parisian lycées, the two exchanged frequent letters, of which only Pauline's seem to have survived.[144] Such preconjugal correspondence was part of the ritual of nineteenth-century French bourgeois marriage, a delimited space of mutual seduction in which the already committed couple expressed their desire to be together.[145] Although Pauline the letter writer routinely belittled her own mental powers, Franck consistently treated her as a worthy interlocutor and eagerly shared his intellectual life with her. Both motifs are evident in this passage from one of her letters of 1833:

> You have given me a very keen pleasure, my friend, by explaining to
> me the philosophical principles that you want to develop in your

book. No doubt you have taken care to descend to my level because I found nothing unintelligible or obscure in your language. . . .[146]

A similar letter from 1836 indicates that Franck had been regaling her with his work on psychology—weeks earlier she had even referred to "our psychology lessons"[147]—and that Pauline lacked enthusiasm for this subject matter:

> You honor me more than I deserve, my friend, by asking my opinion of your philosophical style, and I disclaim all competence, stranger that I am to philosophical language generally. All that I know is that I understand you and find you extremely clear. I confess, however, that I preferred your letters from Douai: you were then discussing moral philosophy, which interested me much more than the principles of psychology. And if I didn't fear being deceived by a preference of taste, I would say that you are more in your element when you treat the part of philosophy that teaches us the duty and destination of man.[148]

But Franck, a student of Gatien-Arnoult,[149] whose textbook expressed such concern about transmitting the capacity for introspection, had obviously given his fiancée solid instruction about the central place of psychology in Cousin's system. For she immediately qualified her negative opinion by adding, "I nonetheless understand very well how important psychological investigation is; it is the base that sustains the edifice."[150]

Whatever Pauline's views of psychology in the Cousinian mode—and, as we will see, they vacillated during the years of her engagement to Franck—her fiancé seems to have involved her in affectionate verbal play about the *moi,* egged on in this regard by her repeated gestures of self-deprecation. Asked her opinion of the post that Gatien-Arnoult had offered Adolphe, for example, she declined to reply on the grounds that "your will shall always be my own."[151] When Adolphe entreated her to include in her letters less about him and more about herself, she countered:

> You have thus reminded me that there was a difference to be established. But I have always found that talking about you is the same as talking about myself. For, my friend, a woman who lives entirely in her loved object regards her own existence as merely secondary.

Continuing in this vein, she criticized women with intellectual and literary aspirations. "To shine, that is always their goal, as if it were not a thousand times sweeter to love and be loved, as if we needed to be embellished by any glory other than that reflected from a beloved countenance."[152] In the intellectual relationship between Pauline and Adolphe, then, the roles of Caroline Angebert and Victor Cousin were reversed. Instead of claiming her equality, Pauline held fast to her subordinate, feminine status and, in response, Adolphe seems to have pressed selfhood upon her.

That pressure is evident in her explicit responses to his requests that she be more present in her letters and in the way that she uses the word *moi,* underlined in the standard philosophical style:

> It is not to assuage your anxiety that I am writing to you today . . . ; nor is it to compensate for my long silence. It is simply the inevitable *moi* that makes me pick up my pen. I am so happy while writing, such a sweet quietude comes over me in our amicable chats.[153]

> During the interval that passed after my writing was interrupted, I received a letter from my brother. And since it is for *moi* that I am writing this time, you will know that it is still for *moi* and not for you that I take pleasure in transcribing the following passage. . . .[154]

> I needed that little worry to balance the state of unaccustomed quietude in which I have been for some time now. I am sometimes tempted to wonder if I am really *moi*. What has become of all those bursts of imagination, those fevers of hope and expectation, those youthful daydreams that used to consume so many hours?[155]

At the end of 1835, Pauline's appreciation of the science of psychology apparently reached a zenith. Finding herself gripped by melancholy although her external situation had in no way changed, she wondered aloud to her fiancé why "the same causes subsisting, we are more keenly affected by them at one moment than at another." Displaying her newly won sophistication, she immediately put this curiosity into a formal scientific frame: "Is it for psychology or for physiology to resolve the problem?" There was, she opined, doubtless a physiological component: the "mobile [physiological] organization of a woman" encouraged a quick succession of moods. But she came down on the side of the explanatory power of psychology. Significantly, for our purposes, she stressed the aspects of her self that she had been able to appropriate only under Franck's tutelage in that science:

In wondering how many of my faculties would have remained forever unknown to me without you, how many were perhaps stifled at their birth by the persistent anxiety that clouded my youth, I am led to conclude that psychology is a very vast and very difficult science. For isn't it true, my gentle master, that it must provide us with an analysis of the human mind (*âme*)?

Equally significant was Pauline's partial dissent from Cousinian psychological orthodoxy in this same letter. Perhaps as a result of her deeply imbued, conventional nineteenth-century female modesty, she could not accept that any individual *moi* was sufficiently grand to generate all of psychology. "Who would dare to give his *moi* as the rule without fearing to narrow [that science]? Who has lived so expansive an existence that he would have been able to feel every type of emotion?" Hence, while affirming the introspective method in psychology, she—much like Caroline Angebert—also wished to supplement it. "I believe, then, that psychology cannot be studied completely in the interior (*foyer*) of a single consciousness, that it needs to progress from observation of the individual to that of the thousands of varied phenomena that take place outside us." Still, she ended her discussion by declaring her gratitude for Franck's psychology instruction. "I should have begun by telling you that your lessons will never tire me," in part because of the personal bond between the two of them, in part "because the science you treat has a marvelous attraction for me."[156]

Barely six months later, as we have seen, Pauline reported a decided lack of interest in psychology. Yet that pronouncement should be taken with a grain of salt, for subsequent developments would show that psychology was not something that she could easily let go. A letter from 1837 reveals that she has acquired an interest in disciplined introspection: she had talked to Adolphe of keeping a journal, writing in it each night, and sharing the contents with him. Ashamed that she has not yet done so, she speaks wryly of her inner life. "*Raconter son âme*—that would doubtless be very fine and pleasant for both of us, but to this narration is attached an indispensable condition: that of having an *âme*." Her own spiritual substance is, she confesses, only sporadically in residence. "The noble inhabitant of my poor envelope makes frequent disappearances, goes off, and comes back without my being able to explain either its departure or its return." Its absences produce what she calls "my vegetative period[s]." Reverting to her familiar posture of self-deprecation, she then jokes that God may have made only one soul for every two female bodies, indeed that Adolphe may regard this calculation as overly generous. Then, adopting a feistier tone, she hazards a guess that the percentage of men with spiritual substance is even lower, that "among the men themselves, Sir," many of the "most gilded, most titled, most admired . . . haven't the slightest divine spark!"[157] Unlike Caroline Angebert, Pauline Franck had neither actively sought instruction in Cousinian psychology nor experienced it as a force comparable to conversion. She did continue to experiment with it—perhaps more accurately to toy with it—throughout the 1830s. It became part of her intellectual repertory, a linguistic medium for self-reflexivity and for musing on the differences between men and women.

Extending the Cousinian Self: Guizot's Theory of History

That the *moi* was not only an interior space but also an entity thoroughly implicated in the outside world was, of course, a Cousinian axiom. It was the point that Cousin made repeatedly when he called psychology the vestibule to ontology and mapped all of reality onto the three distinct elements composing consciousness (see Chapter 4). Hence it is hardly surprising that Cousin and his followers used his psychological doctrine to illuminate the objective world. The *maître* adumbrated the possibilities of such a project in his 1828 lectures when he interpreted the science of political economy in terms of the interaction between the *moi* and the *non-moi*: as the study of human industriousness, it treated "man metamorphos[ing] things" and "put[ting] on them the imprint of his personality, elevat[ing] them into simulacra of liberty and intelligence."[158] Some Cousinian textbooks explicitly articulated an imperialist agenda for introspective psychology. The preface to Damiron's *Cours de philosophie* expressed the hope that a total, unified system of knowledge encompassing man, nature, and the divinity would one day be built on its foundation.[159] In his introduction to the multi-author *Manuel,* Amédée Jacques likewise saw Cousin's psychology as the master human science ("the science of God is called Theodicy, and the science of man Psychology") and stated that rhetoric, history, politics, and jurisprudence all derived from a prior knowledge of human nature and the human mental faculties; "if they are not supported by psychology, they are built on sand."[160] An exhaustive study of what might be called "applied Cousinianism" is beyond the scope of this book. Having described elsewhere the place of the *moi* in Jouffroy's aesthetic theory,[161] I will confine myself here to the incursions of Cousinian psychology into Guizot's extraordinarily popular and influential historical lectures, the *Histoire de la civilisation en Europe* (1828).

As a text proclaiming an optimistic faith in progress and identifying the bourgeoisie as a principal instrument of that progress, the *Histoire* was a natural candidate for colonization by Cousin's bourgeois *moi*. Guizot's stated goal was a grand narrative of the development of European civilization (a term that he was helping to invent), predicated on the assumption that, despite national variations, and French superiority, a basic unity obtained in the civilization that had taken root in Europe after the fall of the Roman Empire.[162] Such a narrative had, in his view, to be permeated by philosophy. In part this philosophical element owed to the very definition of civilization that Guizot was employing: that which simultaneously advances the "development of man himself, as an individual" and advances "his visible condition, [his] society." In order to make such value-laden assessments, Guizot recognized, he would have to tackle "the largest questions of moral philosophy." Second, an "inevitable alliance between philosophy and history" was a characteristic, perhaps even the essential characteristic, of "our epoch." Unlike all previous epochs, the one following the French Revolution was obliged to consider "science and reality, theory and practice" in tandem instead of allowing those two "powers" to go about their business separately.[163]

Guizot did not specify the philosophy that he would bring to bear on his history but, not surprisingly, given the author's background, a generically Cousinian strand can be discerned in the mix. One of the great themes of Guizot's history is the transfer of power to the bourgeoisie. While this process culminated conspicuously in 1789, Guizot traced its roots back to the twelfth century when the burghers of certain communes wrested autonomy from the tyranny of the feudal seigneurs.[164] Because he regarded the inner development of the individual as an intrinsic part of civilization, Guizot's sociopolitical history necessarily contained an important psychological element. One of the questions implicitly raised by his narrative was how the bourgeoisie could have acquired the psychological strength they needed to confront their betters and, eventually, to assume power.

Guizot found the answer to that question in the long-term historical development of the *sentiment de la personnalité,* or feeling of person-hood: he used both the precise Cousinian expression[165] and variants on it that highlighted the typically Cousinian theme of free volitional activity. As he saw it, the barbarian warriors who conquered the decaying Roman Empire brought an essential component to the evolving European *sentiment de la personnalité.* To be sure, barbarism connoted the very opposite of the civilization that Guizot was tracing. He nonetheless believed that the barbarians' "pleasure in individual independence, pleasure in playing, with [their] power and liberty, amidst the opportunities of the world"—the brief description evokes a joyousness rare in Guizot's repertory—was the precious germ of a developmental principle and sequence culminating in civilization.[166]

The feudal seigneur, a subsequent incarnation of the barbarian, retained that germ and added to it the sense of importance accruing to him as "property-owner, head of family, master." These two psychological attitudes together produced in him a "feeling of immense superiority, a very particular superiority different from the ones found in [the elites of] other civilizations." Roman patricians, for example, derived, indeed "borrowed" their social superiority from their corporate existence: they wielded political power as members of the senate. Similarly, their power to officiate in religious ceremonies was delegated to them by the gods. But the possessor of a fief experienced his personality in a different register; his "grandeur" was "purely individual; he held nothing from anyone; all his rights, all his power came to him from himself alone." Guizot regarded this proud and even "insolent" sense of self as one of the defining marks of feudalism (*féodalité*) and, eventually, one of its central contributions to European civilization. "Individuality, the energy of personal existence, such was the dominant fact among those who conquered the Roman world. The [historical] development of individuality thus had to result, above all, from the social order founded by and for them." Or, even more pointedly, several lessons later:

> The feudal regime gave to all who participated in it the continual example of resistance. In no way did it present to the mind the idea of an organized, imposing government capable of regulating everything, of subduing everything solely by its intervention. *On the contrary, what it provided was the unending spectacle of individual will refusing to*

submit. . . . The feudal regime rendered this service to humanity: to demonstrate unceasingly individual will deploying itself in all its energy.

The burghers of the towns were, as early as the tenth century, the beneficiaries of this great lesson. "Despite their weakness, despite the prodigious inequality of condition between them and their feudal overlords, the towns rose up everywhere," obtaining charters that granted them, at least on paper, a sphere of autonomy.[167]

The *sentiment de la personnalité,* Guizot continued, assumes a causal role in history—or, in his phrase, it serves as one of the "two sources from which can flow, in the political realm, greatness of ambition and firmness of purpose." The first of these sources is social power, wielding actual influence over people on a vast scale. The second is subjective and psychological power: "bear[ing] in oneself an energetic feeling of complete individual independence, certitude about one's own liberty, the consciousness of a destiny foreign to every other will but that of the man himself." His account of how the bourgeoisie acquired their particular brand of that compelling *sentiment,* how they become in their turn world-historical actors, is complicated, indirect, and never fully articulated. It is not a story of simple imitation of the feudal seigneur. There are setbacks: the twelfth century saw the crystallization of the traits of timidity, humility, fearful modesty—paradoxically amidst "steadfast conduct"—that the burghers would pass on even to their distant descendants. There is inevitable domestication: the "soft activity of modern times," as opposed to the perilous and bellicose life of earlier eras, resulted in the loss by the bourgeoisie of that rough-and-ready "male character" and "obstinate energy" that characterized their medieval forebears. At the same time there emerged the *sentiment de la personnalité* in the more abstract, bourgeois, but also universal form characteristic of modern civilization: "the full consciousness of the grandeur of man as man *(l'homme en tant qu'homme),* of the power that belongs to him if he is capable of exercising it."[168] Guizot's definition is strikingly similar to the one that Habermas would offer a hundred and a fifty years later of the brunt of the Enlightenment and the conceptual apparatus that made a public sphere possible: the discovery of "pure humanity, of "the "human being as such," unmarked by particular social qualifications.[169]

In sum, it is possible to read Guizot's *Histoire de la civilisation en Europe* as the working out of Cousinian psychology on a historical canvas. Such an interpretation is not only textually grounded but also bolstered by Guizot's involvement, almost from its inception, in the project of constructing a non-sensationalist form of philosophical psychology. By twists and turns, Guizot asserts, the raw *sentiment de la personnalité* of the feudal seigneur developed into the more intricate one of the medieval burgher and then into the appreciably tamer, less vibrant one of the sedentary nineteenth-century bourgeois. Guizot's crisp description of the *sentiment* in question—one of independence, willfullness, experiencing oneself as a cause in the world—corresponds perfectly to the attributes of the *moi* in the Cousinian psychology that was taught in every nineteenth-century French lycée after 1832. Furthermore, his specification of a modern decline from the titanic energy of the founders corresponds to Cousin's metaphysical move of imposing on the *moi* conformity to the most prosaic of value systems. His characterization of the nineteenth-century form of the *sentiment* as simultaneously universal and class-based corresponds, finally, to Cousin's perpetual waffling about everyone's possession of a *moi* in principle and only the elite's possession of one in practice. That Guizot enlisted the psychological concept of the *moi* to recount the historical rise of the bourgeoisie confirms yet again the bourgeois nature of that self. That he did so in a book repeatedly reprinted during the course of the nineteenth century was yet another manifestation of Cousinian cultural hegemony.

6

Religious and Secular Access to the
Vie Intérieure: Renan at the Crossroads

The travails of the Cousinian regiment in the provinces, as described in the previous chapter, make plain the frictions between eclecticism and Catholicism that could intrude into everyday life during the 1840s—frictions summed up in the contemporary Bordelais quip that "Catholic doesn't rhyme with eclectic." But, confined to institutional politics and suffused with a sense of raw urgency, the accounts provided by Cousin's former students are necessarily limited in scope. Especially conspicuous from the vantage point of this book, they fail to probe the relationship between the two doctrines at the phenomenological level. How did Cousinian philosophical psychology and Catholic piety compare as alternate mid- nineteenth-century modes of access to an interior life? Were the clergy who "persecuted" the teachers of eclectic philosophy correct in their assessment that the kind of interiority encouraged by Cousin was inimical to their own, religious project? Did Catholic belief stand as a barrier to the appropriation of a Cousinian *moi* among men whose elite social status otherwise qualified them for that endowment?

An account of the rise of Cousinian-style selfhood cannot easily ignore such questions. Traditional religious discourse served, after all, as a basis of self-understanding for many nineteenth-century Frenchmen, and hence the way Catholicism articulated with an increasingly ascendant Cousinianism requires investigation. Obviously, however, the questions cannot be posed with respect to Catholicism *tout court*, which existed in myriad nineteenth-century varieties and was held as a belief with many different degrees of intensity and rigor. But the questions become manageable when they are directed to a single, well-situated

233

figure—a microhistorical approach that allows at least an informed approximation of the broader and more general answers.

In the 1840s the young Ernest Renan happens to have occupied a strategic position just at the intersection of the Catholic and Cousinian currents. Fortunately for our purposes, the young man who would later become a cultural figure of towering proportions—the positivist pioneer of the French historical criticism of the Bible, the philologist who helped to construct the fundamental (and fateful) opposition between Semites and Aryans, the theorist of nationhood[1]—was also a natural virtuoso of the inner life. At the age of twenty, for example, he wrote to his sister that "careers entirely filled with exterior occupations repel me; they do not allow a person to live with himself, they prevent reflection, they make you a stranger to yourself." He regularly found, he added, consolation in the thought that a "man always possesses one sure resource—to take refuge in himself and there to avenge, through sheer enjoyment of himself, all external servitude."[2] Some eighteen months later, again addressing his sister, he disparaged the sort of people who sought out social intercourse for no other reason than as an "occasion to exit themselves and [thereby] to stifle the boredom [that is for them] inseparable from reflection on the *moi*."[3] By using the young Renan as a case study, this chapter will attempt to discern the similarities and differences, as they were lived by practitioners, between the Cousinian psychology and one of its Catholic counterparts.

The Breton-born Renan had been drawn to a religious vocation from an early age. The son of a ship's captain who died at sea leaving his family in genteel poverty, he attended the Paris seminaries of Saint-Nicolas du Chardonnet, Issy, and Saint-Sulpice on a scholarship and went so far as to accept preliminary (and still revocable) ordination as a priest. But doubts about the compatibility of Catholic dogma with rational-scientific procedures of inquiry assailed him, and he departed Saint-Sulpice definitively in 1845, at the age of twenty-two, to pursue a career as a secular scholar. Chiefly responsible for corroding his faith was the taste for philosophy Renan had acquired while in the seminary itself, during the two years of mandatory instruction in that subject at Issy.[4] As he recounted to his mother at the time:

> My studies hold an ever greater attraction for me. I have recovered all
> my old appetite for mathematics. . . . As for philosophy, I'm a bit more
> of a novice, but I get as much pleasure from it as from math, all the

more so since we have as yet encountered nothing very difficult in it. It is incomparably the finest thing to study and the one most worthy of man.

Going on to say that he derived particular pleasure from philosophical argument, he described the intense and aggressive culture that had developed around that activity at the seminary. "Two pupils tackle each other hand to hand on a question, then engage in a duel to the death," all metaphorically, of course, since the weapons employed were words. Nevertheless, the sport continued ruthlessly until one of the combatants was forced to concede defeat. "Every Sunday we do this in public, and every day seven or eight of us get together to do it privately."[5]

Exactly when and how Renan encountered the Cousinian brand of philosophy is unclear. Piecing together the sometimes contradictory evidence in the manuscripts of his youth and in his retrospective autobiographical work, the *Souvenirs d'enfance et de jeunesse* (initially published in installments between 1876 and 1882), it appears that Renan first learned about Cousin's philosophical psychology from the detailed and energetic Catholic refutations of it that were standard fare at the seminary, especially the 1840 work of the abbé Henry Maret, *Essai sur le panthéisme dans les sociétés modernes.*[6] Around the time that he left the seminary, Renan grappled with Cousin directly, undertaking a close reading of a published version of the master's foundational 1818 Sorbonne course on the true, the beautiful, and the good.[7] His abundant notes on that text both summarized its contents and subjected them to strenuous criticism, revealing that the independent-minded Renan would toe the line neither of the reigning philosophical *maître* nor of his theological detractors. In any event, the text seems to have left an indelible mark on its young reader. In the jottings he made during his summer vacation of 1845, while in the throes of his agonizing decision to leave the seminary, Renan depicted the introspective modality featured in Cousin's philosophy as nothing less than the central symptom of modernity:

> What characterizes the modern era is radical reflexivity, the folding back on oneself. In the realm of philosophy, psychology is everything. (V. Cousin, 1818, Lesson 1). In literature, we no longer tell stories in the manner of Homer and the Bible; instead we paint the impressions and sentiments suppressed by the ancients, who assumed that such things went without saying. There are works devoted to nothing but

that—epistolary novels, etc. . . . For us, . . . there is no longer anything pure, as there is in the naive and popular sensibility. I have experienced it a thousand times. When I love, when I suffer, when I think, I have a model in mind or, at least, if my sensibility runs ahead of me, I reflect [afterward] and I am pleased to see that it conforms to that model. Everything begins with: I think, therefore I am.[8]

The notebooks he kept from mid-1845 until the end of 1846 mention Cousin nearly twenty times[9] and, at the beginning of his academic career, he became a contributor to the Cousinian encyclopedia project, the *Dictionnaire des sciences philosophiques*.[10] Some years later, when Renan published an article on Cousin in the *Revue des deux mondes,* he remained adamant about the enduring cultural legacy of the founder of eclecticism. The man had possessed the boldness, he now exclaimed, to create the philosophy imposed by the Université on all of France; he had single-handedly determined what young Frenchmen would be taught "about God, the universe, and the human mind!"[11] And in 1885, reviewing a new book about Cousin, his comments took on a more personal, nostalgic coloring. He remembered his first reading of Cousin's 1818 lecture course four decades earlier: "Its impact on me could not have been more profound. I knew those wingèd phrases by heart; I dreamt about them. I am aware that some of my mental frameworks come from [that source]."[12]

If, in young adulthood, Renan had an accurate appreciation of Cousin's looming historical importance, and had even been caught up in his spell, he was remarkable in keeping that factual assessment and that personal impressionability separate from his always cool appraisal of the intrinsic intellectual quality of the man's work. Both tendencies are evident in his letters to his sister in the early 1840s. On the one hand, he was happy and proud to lean on Cousin's authority to bolster his own contention about the high intellectual calibre of his seminary education: "The seminaries of Saint-Sulpice and Issy are directed by a congregation of priests free of episcopal control who have always been known for moderation [in their interpretation of dogma]. Monsieur Cousin has just published a work in which he lavishes deserved praise on them."[13] However, a couple of years later he described "Monsieur Cousin and eclecticism" in disabused fashion as an "imitation" of the contemporary German philosophy that he was then reading in the original and "very pale" by comparison.[14]

At some point in the early 1840s Renan made a deliberate decision between Catholic orthodoxy and the rational critical faculty, a decision that implicitly entailed a comparable choice between the versions of interiority offered by the priests of Saint-Sulpice and by psychological scientists like Victor Cousin. Apparently he came to regard the latter as the more factually accurate and emotionally congenial of the two options. Renan's choice did not immediately affect his long-standing tendency to gravitate to the inner life. But he now elected to conduct his interior explorations in a secular register—much as his eighteenth-century predecessor at Saint-Sulpice, the religiously tone-deaf and less fully introspective abbé Sieyès, had done (see Chapter 3). This chapter will attempt to reconstruct how Renan navigated his passage from the religious *vie intérieure* to its scientific-psychological counterpart and to indicate what was at stake in such a choice. Unlike the lycée students routinely initiated into Cousinian psychology, who had little to say about its impact on them, Renan sought out the Cousinian *moi* and was consequently well aware that it made a difference.

The Religious Inner Life, or Mediated Introspection

The category of a religious inner life is not, with respect to Renan, a historian's methodological construction. In the notebooks he kept in the immediate aftermath of his departure from Saint-Sulpice, Renan used precisely that expression, beginning a paragraph with the pregnant sentence, "Here is my fundamental principle of the religious inner life (*vie intérieure religieuse*)."[15] And indeed the same expression, in slightly abbreviated form, figures in the title of the basic seventeenth-century work of Sulpician piety, the *Catéchisme chrétien pour la vie intérieure* (1656), composed by the abbé Jean-Jacques Olier, the founder of the order. Renan knew this text well, calling it "among the most extraordinary of books, full of poetry and somber philosophy."[16] His frequent references to it in his autobiography show that he viewed it as a kind of metonym for the traditional Sulpician belief structure, and that he moreover regarded that belief structure as still vital during the first half of the nineteenth century.[17] The actual publication history of Olier's *Catéchisme*, with its abundant early nineteenth-century reprintings, confirms Renan's sense of its continued relevance.[18] So does Renan's description of the ambience of the seminary he entered in 1841: "What struck me upon arriving here is the tenacity with which customs are maintained. . . . The times have changed, but Saint-Sulpice is still the same as in the days of Monsieur Olier."[19] More recently, historians have discerned a distinct revival of Olier's brand of spirituality at Saint-Sulpice in the decades following the fall of Napoleon.[20] Hence, despite its composition nearly two centuries earlier, Olier's *Catéchisme* can provide us with an idea of how the concept of the *vie intérieure* was understood by Renan qua seminarian as well as by a whole group of early nineteenth-century French Catholics.

What it discloses is not, of course, necessarily applicable to all French Catholics of the era. Olier's religiosity was, as Renan aptly depicted it, of a highly specific sort: on the one hand "mystical" and on the other so gloomy in tone as to make Calvin's seem "almost optimistic."[21] Although Renan does not supply its intellectual genealogy, it belonged firmly to what would later be called the French school of spirituality or, alternatively (and perhaps more accurately), the Bérullian school.[22] According to the standard narrative, Pierre de Bérulle laid down the basic and enduring lines of this counterreformation current in order to reinvigorate the piety of both clergy and laity and thus to protect them against the temptations of Protestantism; Olier was a major contributor to the movement's second generation and, by some accounts, its master popularizer.[23] Often described as theocentric, Bérullianism recommended awe as the appropriate human posture before a glorious, all-powerful God and insisted that human beings, mere creatures of God, accordingly recognize themselves as utterly nothing: this latter axiom constituted the movement's signature gloominess.

Most important for us here is the strong emphasis on the psychological domain that derived from and to some extent alleviated the movement's pessimistic anthropology. Bérullian spirituality held out to the faithful the possibility of bridging the ontological abyss that separated the divine and the human, of communing intimately with God, especially by identifying with and conforming to the "states" (*états*) of Jesus—that is, the interior dispositions by which God's son had lived out the mysteries of his incarnation, passion, death, and resurrection. As one modern commentator has schematized this spiritual modality, it moves back and forth between two poles: a "mystical pole," which is the believer's ecstatic "life in Christ," and a "pole of Christian ascesis," or of rigorous personal discipline that, in this case, takes the striking form of a "death to oneself."[24] Given this schema, it is hardly surprising that the Bérullian movement invented and injected into Catholic discourse a whole vocabulary of interiority, featuring such terms as "états de Jésus" and "intérieur de Jésus."[25] The embrace of the psychological was one of the most distinctive traits of Bérullianism and a key difference between it and one of its main competitors, the Jesuit version of French Catholicism. As the historian Henri Bremond puts it, "While Saint Ignatius makes us contemplate the 'deeds' of Jesus especially, Bérulle makes us contemplate his 'states.'" Correspondingly, the follower of Ignatius poses the "moral problem" by asking himself what course of action he should follow—remaining in the world or quitting the world, keeping his fortune or distributing it to the poor. The Bérullian by contrast asks, "'What is my share of Christ's heritage? Which of his 'states' am I particularly called upon to reproduce, apply, and link myself with henceforth?'"[26]

At the point in his development at which Renan encountered Olier's brand of Bérullian religiosity, its psychological orientation must have harmonized well with his temperament. By all indications, he had a decidedly introspective bent long before he came to Paris, for he recounts in his autobiography that as a young boy in Brittany he conducted his "examinations of conscience" with such energy that he even anxiously inquired of his confessor if he might unwittingly have committed the mysterious sin listed in his manual: simony by trafficking in benefices![27] One institutional consequence of Olier's psychological sensibility was the centrality given to the work of the *directeur spirituel* in the formation of Sulpician priests; as part of the nineteenth-century revival of Olier's theology at Saint-Sulpice, his manuscript fragments setting forth his techniques for the guidance of souls were finally published for the first time in 1831, just a decade before Renan's enrollment at the seminary.[28] Renan obviously found this kind of spiritual exercise congenial. In 1841 he wrote happily to a boyhood friend that the "choice [of a spiritual director] is of the greatest importance here [at Issy]; the director is everything for each student."[29] It was thus a source of pain to him that the gentle Father Gosselin, whom he had carefully selected as his director, failed to see within his soul accurately enough to detect the crisis of faith that was brewing there and that another priest at the seminary, who had viewed him only from afar, instead "delivered a thunderbolt into my consciousness . . . and with a brutal hand tore off all the bandages by which I hid from myself the wounds of an already ailing faith."[30]

This general outline of Bérullian spirituality can help us to make sense of Olier's *Catéchisme*, to pinpoint its doctrinal particularities and, most important for purposes of this chapter, to understand the experience of interiority it held out as a model. Whether Renan actively sought to cultivate a religious inner life on this model while at Saint-Sulpice is unclear.[31] But we can say with assurance that he knew what the model was and appreciated the authority that it commanded within the walls of the seminary.

In at least one salient respect Olier's text was generically and universally Catholic: it stressed the dependence of the believer on a process of mediation. More specifically, the *vie intérieure* mentioned in its title was not immediately accessible to the individual consciousness. In fact, that sought-after inner life was nothing but the *vie intérieure de Jésus-Christ*, defined as a condition of mind and heart that, when residing in an individual, entitled that individual to the name of Christian. Olier's Bérullian specificities emerge as he enumerates the key features of this interior domain. Beginning with the generically Catholic features, such as "its religious attitude toward God, its love of its neighbor," he proceeds to the characteristically Bérullian ones: "its annihilation of itself (*anéantissement envers soi-même*), its horror of sin, and its condemnation of the world and its maxims."[32] From a secular standpoint, it is certainly a very strange form of interiority indeed that is predicated on obliterating all traces of the self! This annihilation is recognizable to us as the pole of ascesis that leads the Bérullian believer to ecstatic union with the divine. Recalling the hatred of the mundane self ("le moi est haïssable") enshrined in the writings of Pascal (see Chapter 3), Olier's formulation thus starkly underscores the difference between one Catholic version of interiority and the Cousinian version; it brings home the long intellectual distance that had to be traveled to arrive at the Cousinian valorization of the *moi*. It also disqualifies Bérullian interiority as an experiential source of what, in this book, I am calling self-talk.[33]

Olier's treatment of the will similarly contrasts to Cousin's. Postulating both a fallen will that came into being with the transgression in the Garden of Eden and a regenerate will made possible by Christ's death and resurrection, the *Catéchisme* expresses strong disapproval of the former. "Yes," agrees the respondent in the question-and-answer format,

"the will is called flesh when it adheres to the movements of the flesh."
But divine grace, the respondent declares many lessons later, changes
that lamentable situation. "We have no use of our powers—no illumina-
tion by the mind, *no movement of the will*—except insofar as we acquire
them from Jesus Christ. Because of Adam's sin, we deserved to lose
everything. But what we lost we have recovered in Christ."[34]

The regenerate will bears little resemblance to its natural counterpart.
Instead of being, as Cousin would have it, our primal, originary property and thus the very essence of human personhood, it is noteworthy
for being not exactly our own. This regenerate will and, indeed, the
entire regenerate soul *(âme)* are "deiform"—that is, congruent with the
soul of the resurrected Christ which, having "entered into [God's] interior and intimate states," has itself assumed a "total resemblance to [that
of] God his father."[35] Let me attempt to make explicit the assumptions
implicit in the *Catéchisme*. The bifurcated nature of human existence—
that is, the stark duality between the fallen and the regenerate conditions—explains why we can, in a Catholic register, probe our inner lives
only in mediated fashion. What we fallen creatures are seeking when we
seek our inner life is, after all, intimate contact with our pre-lapsarian,
"deiform" selves, with the still retrievable traces left on us by our divine
Creator before we perversely chose to mar His handiwork. Access to
that lost but ultimately authentic *vie intérieure* is not possible through
immediate introspection: such futility is the very definition of the fallen
condition. Access becomes feasible only through identification with the
external reference point that God has provided for us in the earthly
manifestation and the sacrifice of Christ.

According to the *Catéchisme*, the new, regenerate, and timeless
human soul is still "able to see outside itself, to see its 'old man,' its flesh
that continues to change and to alter." However, because its viewing
position is now "always *intime*, always interior to itself," its fleshly
incarnation takes on an alien cast and no longer poses serious temptations. The regenerate, deiform self "remains firm," refusing to "demean
itself" by reverting to corporeal ways.[36] From that position of interiority,
the individual can presumably assess the degree of incursion of unruly
fleshly impulses on the serenity of his "new man." That is, we can surmise that the achievement of religious interiority also entails a degree of
attentiveness and access to that secular, fallen psyche that the scientific
discipline of psychology takes as its sole object of investigation. But

unlike its secular counterpart, religious interiority is inconceivable without God and inseparable from knowledge of God. It requires not merely the split subject of secular introspection (the subject that both observes and is observed) but God as a third, mediating term.

The conception of religious interiority as knowledge of the Divinity who inhabits the psyche of the regenerate individual had certain very practical consequences for the conduct of life. For example, according to an 1841 biography of Olier with which the young Renan was familiar, Olier and his successors never made appeals or solicitations to individual young men to enter the seminary of Saint-Sulpice. Persuading individuals to bend their wills in a certain direction, influencing a personal process of decision-making, was thoroughly irrelevant to the Sulpician recruitment effort. The members of the order believed instead that the true religious vocation was the work of God within the individual and hence that qualified seminarians would hear an unequivocal inner call and spontaneously identify themselves to the superiors of the order.[37] The same motif can be seen in Renan's vocabulary when he was in the throes of uncertainty about whether to go through with the rite of tonsure. To make the decision, he did not seek to fathom his own desires, needs, and preferences or to make contact with his own personal will; or at least he refrained from publicly representing himself as engaged in such activities. Rather, he pledged to "neglect nothing [that would] indicate to me the will of God on this point."[38] Or, in another formulation some six weeks later after he had achieved greater clarity on the issue: "Never have I felt with more profound inner conviction, never have my superiors assured me more unanimously, that the will of God was that I be a priest."[39]

With greater instructional precision than Cousinian philosophy professors could ever muster with respect to the immediate introspection they demanded of their pupils, the Sulpicians offered methods for the attainment of the religious inner life. Their technology of the self included concrete procedures, sometimes even paraphernalia. Thus the entire second half of Olier's *Cathéchisme* was devoted to "a principal means of acquiring and retaining" that conformity with the inner life of Christ that was synonymous with "the Christian spirit."[40] The means in question was prayer, itself an activity totally dependent on supernatural grace.[41] In order to annihilate the natural self (the locus of what Olier called *amour-propre*) in preparation for the admission of its regenerate counterpart, a specific posture, both physical and emotional, as well as specific words of self-abnegation, were recommended. "Placing yourself on your knees, entirely covered with shame because of your internal wickedness, you will first say . . . 'My God and my all, I renounce myself and the sinful inclinations with which I am filled. . . .'"[42] Olier also recommended that the seminarian keep a written record of his lapses so that they would remain fresh in his memory.[43]

Another practice of Sulpician interiority still alive and well in the 1840s was a negative one, a performance of the annihilation of the worldly self designed to foster, through the creation of a void, the mystical infusion of the life in Christ. Renan reports in his autobiography that, to avoid all possible celebrity, "the rule of the Sulpicians is to publish nothing except under the veil of anonymity" and even then to write using the most bland and pallid literary style.[44] Recognized authorship, that peculiarly modern Western form of selfhood and self-assertion, was expressly forbidden.[45]

Olier took pains to cultivate religious interiority not only among the priests he trained in his seminaries but also among his most humble and untutored parishioners. For this latter group, access to the *vie intérieure* was to be doubly mediated: they could most easily make contact with the divine spirit that constituted their regenerate selves not through Christ directly but through Christ as found in the Virgin Mary. The sensuous immediacy of pictorial images was, moreover, to aid the people in this process of religious self-discovery. Olier commissioned engravings of two drawings by Charles Le Brun, the Court painter to Louis XIV who frequently served at Saint-Sulpice as the imagistic translator of the founder's religious thought.[46] These reproductions were then distributed widely among the families of the parish. ("Hardly were they made known before a multitude of pious souls wished to have them [continually] before their eyes.") The first, the more relevant to us here (see Figure 5), was additionally reproduced on one of the stained glass windows of the Church. Called the "Intérieur de la Vierge," and depicting the "life of Jesus in Mary," it showed the Virgin

> in the clouds, her hands crossed over her chest, where the Spirit of Our Lord in the form of a dove spread all the riches of his grace. The eyes of this divine Mother were raised to heaven and fixed on the monogram of Jesus, Savior of Man. This signified that if the Holy Spirit was always the principle of her actions, as represented by her hands,

L'INTERIEVR DE LA S.ᵉ VIERGE

Benedic anima mea Domino; Et omnia Interiora mea nomini Sancto eius.

PER MARIAM, CVM MARIÂ, ET IN MARIÂ.

Le Brun In. Morincourt Scul.

Figure 5: A Technology of Religious Interiority. Le Brun's late seventeenth-century etching of "The Interior of the Holy Virgin" was designed to aid the laity and, later, the clergy in the cultivation of the religious inner life through a double mediation: by identifying with Mary's inner states, believers would gain access to those of Jesus and finally catch a glimpse of their own prelapsarian selves. Renan may well have encountered the etching at the seminary of Saint-Sulpice in the 1840s and may even have attempted to use it for this purpose. (Bibliothèque Nationale de France, Cabinet des Estampes)

the love of Jesus and the salvation of souls were always the goal of those actions. Below appeared the words, which functioned as *an invitation to the viewer to be united with* [*the Virgin's*] *interior dispositions:* "With her, by her, and in her."

According to the author of a nineteenth-century work on Olier's cult of Marian devotion, or the "inner life of the Very Holy Virgin," Olier's disciples generalized the cult after his death, making it applicable to clerics as well as to the laity. An annual service "in honor of the inner life of Mary" at all the seminaries of Saint-Sulpice, and especially that of Paris, was still ongoing and vital in Renan's day. It functioned at its inception as a "new means of aiding aspirants to the priesthood to *form inside themselves the interior of this divine Mother*"—that is to say, as a means of cultivating, through double mediation, their own religious inner lives.[47]

Catholic Objections to the Cousinian Self

The fundamental difference between immediate and mediated introspection suffices to explain the hostility that many Catholic leaders felt toward Cousin's teaching. For while God was the absolutely indispensable element of the Catholic *vie intérieure,* Cousinian psychology happily opened up an inner space without Him. It postulated—indeed it prodded the initiate to experience at firsthand—a faculty of volition that, while purely human, was not contemptibly mired in the flesh but was as fully free, active, and even awe-inspiring as its divine equivalent. Not only did Cousin's psychology go about its business without reference to God. Since it was, in Cousin's celebrated phrase, the "vestibule" to ontology and metaphysics, the Cousinian *moi* served as the epistemological grounding for the existence of God and for the role of God in history rather than vice versa. A mere glance at Cousin's 1832 philosophy *programme* or at any Cousinian textbook exposed this topsy-turvy (from the Catholic standpoint) order: psychology was, emphatically, the first branch of philosophy to be treated; it was followed by logic, then by morals, and finally by theodicy. Cousin did not, to be sure, go anywhere near as far as his defiantly blasphemous German contemporary, the Young Hegelian Ludwig Feuerbach, who in his *Essence of Christianity* (1841) depicted God as the creation of a self-deceived, self-alienated humanity. Nevertheless, he could legitimately be read—as he was by many Catholics—as tacitly asserting either a parity between the human and the divine or, worse still, the primacy of the human.

Cousin's precise "intentions" in this regard, even if they are regarded as the appropriate object of a historical investigation,[48] can probably never be known. Since his working-class childhood is shrouded in obscurity, so too are his early religious education and the subsequent development of his religious beliefs. He has left behind a few shreds of information in the form of references to the piety of his mother and to the "naive faith" that she had imparted to him but that he had failed to carry into adulthood.[49] It is clear that the adult Cousin wanted, for pressing political reasons, to develop an anti-sensationalist psychology friendly to religion. However, by all indications, the religion he had in mind was more akin to a minimalist, rational deism than to Catholicism, with its demands for faith in revealed truth and submission to clerical authority.

In a seemingly candid and surprisingly affectionate exchange of letters with his liberal Catholic adversary, the abbé de Lamennais, in 1825–26 (the two men compared notes on their physical ailments and fretted about each other's health), Cousin argued for the possibility of reconciling their apparently antithetical views. But in this endeavor he always described himself and his philosophy as "Christian," never as "Catholic." "You see, Sir," he pointed out to Lamennais, "that I am a Christian requiring indulgence but, I repeat to you, seriously, my philosophy is Christian." A month later he announced, "I kneel down before catholicism," using a lowercase "c" and indicating that he took the word to mean a universal criterion for truth, rather than the doctrine of the Roman Catholic Church. "But it is in Christianity especially that I seek it," he continued, "although it may be elsewhere as well. In a word—and I speak to you from the bottom of my heart—I am or at least would like to be a Christian philosopher."[50] Yet, even in this modest depiction of his religiosity, Cousin may have been less ingenuous than he sounded. Maine de Biran, for one, characterized Cousin's personal religious beliefs as just barely deistic. After a "good philosophical conversation with the young professor Cousin" in 1821, he noted matter-of-factly in his journal, "Professor C., who knows no other revelation than that of reason, denies the present influence of a higher intelligent force on our spirit (âme)."[51]

The image of Cousin as a thinker who irreverently aggrandized the human at the expense of the divine could not have been one he sought.

It derived from his failure to control all the implications of the complex philosophical system he set in play, even as it may have accurately represented personal convictions that he would have done better to hide. In any case, it was an image that Cousin frequently tried to dispel.

The 1840 work of the abbé Maret, *Essai sur le panthéisme dans les sociétés modernes,* is a typical expression of Catholic outrage at Cousin's philosophy, if one that sparked an unusual amount of interest. Its author was a young priest who had "just emerged from his humble cell at Saint Sulpice" (he would later be appointed to the Faculty of Theology at the Sorbonne—an act of calculated contrition by none other than Victor Cousin as minister of public education!—and would rise in the clerical hierarchy to become an archbishop). Maret's nineteenth-century biographer tells us that all the educated classes in France, both clerical and lay, avidly read the *Essai* as soon as it appeared. Its first printing sold out within weeks, and a second followed before the end of the year. The book also had an international resonance and was quickly translated into German and Italian and, somewhat later, into Spanish and Polish.[52] As already mentioned, it functioned among the seminarians at Saint-Sulpice, including Ernest Renan, as the principal, authorized conduit of information about Cousin's philosophy. Hence it has particular value for us here, revealing not only what Renan initially learned about the secular psychology of the Sorbonne *maître* but also what he, as a priest-in-the-making, was supposed to find distasteful about it.

The success and wide readership of Maret's book no doubt owed to its broad scope, the general cultural criticism in which it embedded its specific, religious criticism of Cousin. The book's preface began by granting the contemporary ascendancy of Cousinianism and its apparently salutary implications for Catholics. The fact that "philosophy [had] entered a spiritualist path" could only be seen as a happy turn of events against the background of the antireligious tendencies of the eighteenth-century Enlightenment. But, Maret continued, the current vogue of spiritualism was in fact illusory, a kind of reassuring window dressing. In the absence of a vital belief in the Christian God—an aspect of the contemporary situation to which the Cousinians neither paid heed and nor devoted rehabilitative efforts—a nominal spiritualism had actually turned into the most arid materialism. As Maret analyzed this transformation, souls deprived of a divine object "fall back on themselves" and "finding there neither power nor consolation, cravenly descend again [i.e., as in the eighteenth century] into enslavement by the senses." Perversely, the high-minded nineteenth-century spiritualist philosophy had thus produced nothing but "egoism, thirst for gold, love of material comfort, and weak character."[53]

This widely unacknowledged devolution of spiritualism was more complex and pernicious still. For in the place of an evacuated God, nineteenth-century thinkers had installed man. They sought "man's law in himself," depicted humanity as "inspired and infallible," and believed that the inexorable progress of the human spirit was "the sole and necessary revelation of God." Such maneuvers, which a religious idiom would have pejoratively identified as pridefulness, were instead endorsed as "science." Maret reversed this evaluation, branding the putative science of the development of humanity over time a heretical "pantheism." By this he seems to have meant that, defying the Bérul-lian postulation of a chasm between divine omnipotence and human nullity, the so-called science of man distributed the qualities of the divinity so wantonly among mundane phenomena that it obliterated the fundamental Christian distinction between God and His worldly creation. The chief formal property of this new scientific pantheism was, Maret observed, the "desire to embrace everything, to explain everything" by reference to some newly discovered law—an astute characterization that fits many nineteenth-century intellectual systems. But despite this wildly ambitious goal, continued Maret, these sciences of man actually explained nothing at all because they pointedly failed to invoke God as an explanation, subordinating Him instead to human causes.[54]

Maret instantiated this general thesis with respect to many nineteenth-century thinkers, but he focused on Cousin. Having subjected Cousin's philosophy to serious study, he had, he reported, become "convinced that it is, at bottom, nothing but pantheism." Maret's use of "pantheism" as a smear word crystallizing Catholic objections to Cousin soon became standard in French polemics.[55] Outside Catholic circles, however, the term seems initially to have sounded as curious as it does to us now. When, in 1844, the Chamber of Peers was debating the moral implications of teaching the Cousinian philosophy in the state secondary schools, one legislator marveled at the "strangeness" of the "reproach" that had been routinely leveled against it.

What to say about the invention of this word "pantheism"? Pantheism is an opinion that has existed for a long time, for some twenty centuries, but I thought it existed in India rather than in France. I will not discuss here what pantheism is. The way in which that term has been invoked makes it impossible not to see it as one of those partisan slurs *(mots de parti)* whose meaning is not understood even by those who use it. What relation is there between the professor of our era, of our country, and the . . . Brahmans of India who went off into the ancient forests to admire nature and ended up fusing themselves with it, forgetting all terrestrial ideas? That portrait resembles no contemporary philosopher. [Laughter][56]

The legislator, of course, exaggerated the exoticism of the term, which was not only applied by Europeans to Vedic religion but also had been used, at various moments throughout the history of Christianity, to label a type of heresy.[57] Still, he justly underscored its bizarre novelty in a nineteenth-century political context as well as its status as a *mot de parti,* valued more for its slanderous effect than for its precise content.

Taking Cousin's 1828 Sorbonne course as his text, Maret presented several interlocking arguments to support his allegation of pantheism. He faulted Cousin for making inferences about the nature of divine reason on the basis of his findings about human reason, a procedure that assumed the complete parity of the two. He called Cousin's theory of God an "anthropomorphism . . . full of errors and blasphemies" because it ascribed a "human life" to God—that is a movement, which Cousin had also described in human reason, limited to the dispersion of unity in multiplicity and the bringing back of multiplicity to unity, a movement which contained only the three terms of finitude, infinity, and their relationship. And he was especially incensed that Cousin identified this "triplicity," ultimately rooted in the human psyche, with the dogma of the Trinity. His "strange theology" thus denied the true, Catholic version of the same dogma, which postulated a "divine life absolutely separate from all contact with the created, the contingent, the finite."[58]

Another strategy for demonstrating Cousin's displacement of the divine by the human occupied Maret in the *Essai* and, more especially, in an influential pamphlet of 1845 that examined Cousin's doctrine of the relationship between religion and philosophy.[59] Here Maret's criticism turned on Cousin's distinction between spontaneity and reflection, the same bedeviled distinction that, as discussed in Chapter 4, Cousin enlisted to give his philosophy its strong social-class bias. According to Maret, Cousin consistently found the source of religion in a "natural faculty... common to all men" called spontaneity. Classified in the Cousinian system as the "first form and manifestation of reason," this faculty produced an instinctive perception of divine truth accompanied by enthusiasm that the Sorbonne *maître* identified as religion. Maret leapt on this account, viewing it as a powerful example of Cousin's anti-Catholic impulse "to reduce Christian mysteries to psychological phenomena (*faits psychologiques*) [and] purely rational conceptions ... to eliminate every superhuman or incomprehensible element from mystery."[60]

Cousin exhibited this same impulse even more baldly, Maret contended, when he considered the higher manifestations of human reason, especially reflection. In Cousin's system, "human consciousness under the eye of its own reflection" constituted philosophy. Now the content of spontaneity and reflection were the same—a Cousinian credo that we have already encountered. The two differed only in form, spontaneous religion presenting certain truths as "poetic image[s]" or "venerable symbols," and reflective philosophy presenting those same truths as "intelligible ideas, purely rational concepts." In the present historical condition of humanity, certain groups, such as "the people" and "children," were capable of apprehending the truths in question only in their religious form. But philosophers, who were (in Maret's snide paraphrase of Cousin) the "elite of the human species, the aristocrats of thought," could remove the "veils and clouds" from religion so as to "seize in itself" the rational truth thereby concealed. They could consequently "do without the religious form ... divest themselves of it like a threadbare garment." According to the Cousinian philosophy of history, mankind progressed in the direction of including increasingly more philosophers in its ranks. The ideal, though probably unattainable goal of history would thus be the total obsolescence of religion, the transformation of its content into a rational form accessible to everyone. Nowhere more than in this Cousinian utopia did Maret see proof of Cousin's perverse drive to naturalize religion, stripping it of the mystery so integral to Catholicism.[61]

In sum, Maret regarded the nominal presence of the Christian God in the Cousinian philosophy as entirely misleading. For in this system no appropriately hierarchical distance separated man from God. In the final analysis, the divine attributes depicted by Cousin were indistinguishable from those of the human psyche, just as Christian mystery was identical to rational philosophy. Cousin's heresy was, according to Maret, twofold: equating the status of Creator and creation, and reducing religious mystery to psychology. As we will see, Renan would eventually embrace Cousin's second heresy—having perhaps, ironically, learned about it from Maret.

Mid-Nineteenth-Century Seminary Psychology

Since Cousinian psychology was off bounds for Catholics, one might assume that a great nineteenth-century seminary such as Saint-Sulpice would either dispense with psychology entirely, or teach some medieval version of it, or perhaps press into service Bishop Bossuet's *De la connaissance de Dieu et de soi-même* (1st ed., 1722) which, as its title plainly indicated, had the distinctly Catholic virtue of tying human self-knowledge inextricably to knowledge of God. The first strategy was rejected. As Renan described the seminary curriculum in a letter to a boyhood friend in the fall of 1841, "In the first year we have logic and theodicy, together with mathematics; in the second, psychology *(la Psychologie)* and morals, together with physics."[62] To some degree, the last strategy was followed. The older generation of teachers at Saint-Sulpice, who had studied theology at the pre-Revolutionary Sorbonne, were so steeped in Bossuet that the young Renan could almost believe that they had once literally sat at the Bishop's feet.[63] Renan himself read avidly in a nineteenth-century edition of Bossuet's *Oeuvres* and in his notebooks exclaimed, "God, what a psychologist that man was!"[64]

More surprising is the additional reliance of certain Catholic educators, like those at Saint-Sulpice, on the so-called Scottish common-sense psychology of the eighteenth century represented by Thomas Reid and Dugald Stewart. By the 1840s, such educators even had at their disposal new editions of the works of these thinkers produced by a devout translator, the abbé Pierre-Hippolyte Mabire. There is clear symbolism in the fact that Mabire's translation of Dugald Stewart's moral philosophy, which Renan used (and copiously annotated) while at Issy, as well as his book of excerpts from Thomas Reid, redid the earlier, pioneering translations of a Cousinian, Théodore Jouffroy.[65] Mabire explicitly presented them as such, and the Catholic press crowed that the good abbé's translations, while fully as accurate and elegant as those of Jouffroy, offered an important additional advantage: because of an apparatus of notes signaling and countering doctrinally impure assertions in the original text, they could be "placed in the hands of young people without the slightest danger." Furthermore, continued the *Ami de la religion,* Mabire's introduction to his translation of Stewart's *Outlines of Moral Philosophy* stood in stark opposition to Jouffroy's famous long 1826 introduction to his translation of the same work, an introduction that had (as seen in Chapter 5) served as a kind of primer of the new Cousinian philosophy for many contemporaries. Whereas Jouffroy had tacitly presented philosophy as the only available source of ultimate truth (in a work officially adopted for use in the elite state secondary schools, no less!), Mabire stressed that philosophy could never entirely supplant Christian revelation.[66] By latching on to the Scottish common-sense philosophy, in other words, French Catholics were simultaneously rejecting Cousinianism and appropriating for their own ends a type of psychological thought that had been an indispensable way station en route to Cousin's eclectic synthesis. How can this seemingly anomalous Catholic preference be explained?

The role of Scottish common-sense philosophy in the genesis of Cousinianism is well known. Cousin's mentor Pierre-Paul Royer-Collard is supposed to have happened upon the work of Thomas Reid when, in the aftermath of the Revolution, he was seeking to replace the then prevalent sensationalism with a philosophy conducive to political stability. Reid qualified for this purpose because he explicitly denied the sensationalist trope depicting mind as a tabula rasa imprinted by sensory experience; instead he contended that, independently of experience, mind was always already equipped with certain structures that formed the basis of our reasoning processes. These he labeled common sense, a term intended to have both a technical and a vernacular meaning. From Royer-Collard's perspective, Reid thus restored the immateriality of mind and all the salutary moral consequences that flowed from it; and, since the common sense he postulated was possessed by all, he also supplied an a priori basis for social consensus that would, in the nature of things, militate against revolutionary upheaval.

Although Cousin applauded the gains made by Reid and his Edinburgh colleagues and acknowledged their superiority to the sensationalists, the Scots had not, in his view, gone far enough. Their work urgently needed the supplement of German idealism. "The Scottish philosophy will prepare you for the German," Cousin told his Sorbonne audience in 1829.[67] Psychology was not, in other words, a self-sufficient discipline for Cousin. As we have seen many times, its great advantage was its capacity to function as the stepping stone to ontology and metaphysics, thereby placing the sociopolitical order on the most solid of possible foundations. By the 1840s, when his philosophy was under heavy fire from Catholics, Cousin reiterated this position with a slightly new accent. "The fundamental idea on which my friends and I rely [is] the following: that the light of high metaphysics is in psychology." One could embrace a "deep psychology" such as his own and use it as a point of departure to reach "a great moral and religious philosophy liberal in orientation." Or one could embrace a "superficial psychology" such as sensationalism that, inimical to metaphysics, would produce "atheism." Or one could, like the German idealists, adopt no clearly articulated psychology at all, and thus end up mired in cloudy speculation, in a "hypothetical metaphysics," as Cousin discreetly called it.[68] In other words, it was necessary to supplement the Scottish philosophy by the German, rather than adopting the German directly, because that path alone ensured arrival at a metaphysics that, by dint of being grounded in psychology, far surpassed its German counterpart.

At Saint-Sulpice in the 1840s, the Scottish philosophy was also prized for its stance on the immateriality of mind, but it otherwise occupied a rather different niche than it did in the Cousinian canon. Its resident purveyor was the abbé Jacques-Alexis-Augustin Manier, who served as philosophy professor at the seminary from 1835 to 1848. As affectionately described by Renan, Manier had gravitated to the Scottish philosophy because of its unexpected harmony with his religious faith. Indeed he recommended it on that account to the scrupulous and perplexed young Renan. "'Scotland reassures [rational minds fearful of straying from religious doctrine] and leads to Christianity,' he used to say to me, pointing out that the good Thomas Reid was at the same time a philosopher and a minister of the Holy Gospel." Although an otherwise logical thinker, Manier resisted the recognition that his embrace of the Scots conflicted with the rest of his belief structure. He simply pretended not to notice that the Scottish postulation of common sense as the innate given of humanity flew in the face of the Sulpician belief in the depravity of man's fallen condition. He bolstered his fondness for the Scottish position by reference to the text from the Book of Job that credited God with having "put wisdom in the entrails of man." Through his long, habitual commerce with the Scots, he had even, Renan observes, acquired their "great aversion to metaphysics."[69]

Indeed, if the antimetaphysical impulse of the Scottish philosophy was its chief deficit from Cousin's viewpoint, the lacuna that cried out for German supplementation, the very absence of metaphysics seems to have been one of its chief recommendations for French Catholics. As the abbé Mabire wrote in his introduction to his translation of Dugald Stewart:

> We have had one idea constantly in mind while translating the *Esquisses*. Philosophy can never in itself constitute a *complete science* [emphasis in the original]. It is our wish that it come closer to theology, neither fearing nor suspecting it. The two are noble sisters, both daughters of heaven, heiresses to that same celestial patrimony—the truth—which they share and of which each possesses only a part.[70]

By refraining from metaphysical speculation, then, the Scots seemed to a cleric like Mabire to offer a philosophical psychology that could be treated as an up-to-date and circumscribed field of specialized knowledge. Thus safely enclosed and decidedly incomplete, it was authoritative within its own boundaries and, at the same time, invited collaboration with Catholic metaphysics. Mabire's obvious, if unnamed, point of comparison was the Cousinian variety of psychology, which made a virtue of overflowing its boundaries and, by generating a metaphysics, seemed to style itself as competitor to Catholic theology.

Inculcating the traditional *vie intérieure religieuse*, Renan's seminary education did not, then, deprive him of all training in secular psychology but instead equipped him with some of the very tools that Cousin had used to construct his own psychological doctrine. While forbidding Cousinianism, it gave its pupil a surprisingly thorough introduction to it.

Renan Adumbrates a Secular Interiority

It was against the background of the vociferous Catholic polemic against Cousin that the young Renan struggled privately to find a suitable language for conceptualizing and organizing his inner life. During the years 1843–45, when he was simultaneously studying at Saint-

Sulpice and worrying about his commitment to the Church, his copious personal jottings demonstrated a striking proclivity to use the word "psychologie" and its derivatives, "psychologique" and "psychologiste"—a relatively unusual idiom for his day and one that he had almost certainly picked up from the abbé Manier's psychology course as well as from his indirect exposure to the philosophy of Cousin. Renan pointed to Cousin as one of his likely sources for the idiom when, finally reading his 1818 course, probably in 1845, he noted, "A remarkable thing about the method of Monsieur C. is that he always remains within the psychological viewpoint. . . ."[71] "Psychologie" did not have a stable meaning for Renan at this transitional moment. He seems rather to have been experimenting with all its possible meanings in a double quest: to augment the available modes of articulating his own mental and emotional experience; and to develop a new category of scientific analysis that he could apply to the external phenomena of language, culture, and history.

A key text for demonstrating Renan's fixation on the domain of the psychological during this period and for attempting to fathom his definition of that domain is a notebook from the end of 1843 and the beginning of 1844 that he entitled "Observations et faits psychologiques" (Psychological Observations and Phenomena). The expression "fait psychologique" is repeatedly used in the notebook as well as in Renan's other manuscripts of the period, becoming a signature concept much like "méditation psychologique" in Maine de Biran's journal. Renan is given to beginning notebook entries with the formula, "It is a very remarkable [or very important, or very singular] psychological phenomenon that . . ." So routine does this formula become that he even places under the rubric "a very remarkable psychological phenomenon" his observations about the strategy of the French clergy in their fight against the educational monopoly of the state: that they have done an ideological about-face and have availed themselves of "liberal ideas."[72]

A proponent of Baconian induction, Renan has numbered the entries in the notebook, and consequently the *faits* they contain, to enable easy comparison between the data he has gathered. Thus, "Monsieur Billion [one of Renan's fellow seminarians] observed in himself a phenomenon (*fait*) analogous to that in #17."[73] Renan seems to have hatched the plan for an exercise in concerted and documented self-observation while reading Dugald Stewart and, for purposes of his notebook, to have extended that initial plan to include observation of the behavior of other people.[74] That Manier's psychology course included both the "rational" and "experimental" varieties—the former defined as treating the nature, origin, and ends of the human mind (âme) by means of deduction from self-evident principles and the latter as treating the faculties of the human mind (âme) by means of observation—suggests how indebted to the seminary curriculum were, ironically, Renan's earliest scientific-psychological researches.[75]

The "faits psychologiques" lumped together in the notebook under that single, all-purpose rubric are, in fact, of very disparate sorts. At the one end of the spectrum are manifestations of the link between the mental and the physical in a single human organism and, at the other, mental traits ascribed to whole peoples or historical periods. Attempting to impose on them a taxonomical clarity that Renan himself found unnecessary or actively resisted, I came up with the following provisional list of his different types of faits psychologiques, arranged in ascending order from the biological to the historical:

(1) Psychosomatic reciprocity, or, as Renan puts it, the "astonishing" impact of a psychological state (état psychologique) on the body—For example, Renan notes that a good mood invariably manifests itself by a relaxed upper lip, a bad mood by a tightened one; when he wanted to hide a feeling of elation from others at the seminary, he was annoyed that, unable to control the musculature of his upper lip, he willy-nilly divulged his inner state.[76]

(2) Dreams and the thin line between dreaming and wakeful consciousness—For example, Renan notes that one morning when he overslept, he awoke fully only after the church bell had stopped ringing; for the duration of the ringing he was unsure whether he was dreaming of the sound or actually hearing it.[77]

(3) Proofs of the applicability of a sensationalist or common-sense faculty psychology to the phenomena of everyday life—For example, Renan decides that the efficacy of scratching as an antidote to itching can be explained by the displacement of the faculty of attention onto the new, deliberately added sensation. He similarly concludes that one's capacity to feel a throbbing in a body part chosen at random is due not to the faculty of will moving the blood there (his earlier hypothesis) but to a focus on that body part by the faculty of attention, which is normally absorbed with external stimuli rather than with the throbbing of

blood that is in fact occurring at every moment everywhere in the body. He chalks up to the sensationalist principle of the "association of ideas" the observed fact that the assembled seminarians of Saint-Sulpice laughed at a tale of a philosopher of antiquity who threw his money into the sea as symbol of his intention to devote himself to the pursuit of wisdom. Had another chain of associations been tapped, Renan opines, the story would have provoked a different response: "If a saint doing the same thing had been described, we would have been filled with admiration."[78]

A significant subcategory of these applications of psychological theory concerns the power of habit, a phenomenon well studied by both sensationalist and Scottish common-sense psychologists.[79] Renan notes that the habit of maternal love has become so ingrained in his own mother that it "overflows its natural objects," causing her reliably to single out little children from a perceptual field in which there are "a thousand things to notice." An incident in which a sailor bursts out in anger against Renan for having tossed a stone in the direction of a boat (not the sailor's own) provokes a meditation on the attachment of workers to the tools of their trade, an attachment rooted in the habit of long, repeated use.[80]

(4) Collective psychology of small groups—While most of Renan's examples concern the individual, and a great many concern himself taken as a valid representative of the human species,[81] he also speculates occasionally on what might be called small-group dynamics. Thus, for example, he ponders a remark of Bossuet to the effect that the rule of silence in certain religious communities facilitates fraternal feeling among the members. He notes that he has more affection for some of his own condisciples when he speaks infrequently to them and explains this "very remarkable psychological phenomenon" by the fact that people living in such close proximity easily get bored with one another and need, paradoxically, to maintain distance in order to preserve their ties. He begins to wonder about the implications of this finding for "ordinary life" outside of the cloister, where keeping to oneself would be seen as a sign of indifference.[82]

(5) At the far end of the spectrum are those phenomena to which Renan gives the label *psychologo-historique*. Thus, he identifies three features of the "barbarism of the Middle Ages" that distinguished Western Europeans of that era from "other barbarous nations" and presaged

their later progress. These three are the rational spirit of the scholastics, which entailed a "prodigious extension given to the faculty of deduction," and the central place accorded two ideas: that of law and that of loyalty and honor.[83]

Thus classified, Renan's *faits psychologiques* offer an informal inventory of the various meanings of the psychological in the early 1840s. It is the last meaning that Renan would mine most intensively in his subsequent professional career. As Pierre Janet codified the received wisdom at the beginning of the twentieth century, (using as his vehicle a lycée manual of philosophy that went through numerous editions), the mature Renan sought to ground a science of psychology not in introspection but, following positivist principles, in the observation of external phenomena. Yet unlike Auguste Comte, who identified the relevant external phenomena as the anatomical and physiological features of the brain, Renan identified them in cultural terms, as the language and history of peoples.[84] It is this meaning of the psychological that Renan was already developing in his 1845 "Essai psychologique sur Jésus-Christ," an early sketch for his pioneering *Vie de Jésus* (1863). The title of the 1845 essay is somewhat misleading for those who do not share Renan's capacious definition of the key word: the psychology in question is not the personal one of Christ in his human incarnation but that of the historical period from which he sprang. ("History is, in effect, only the psychology of humanity," Renan declared in this manuscript.) How, Renan wanted to know, could the sublimity of the Gospel have arisen from the same morally debased Judaic culture that produced the Talmud? Since ordinary "psychological laws" could not explain such an anomalous outcome, he solved this puzzle by resorting to what he called "extraordinary psychological laws."[85]

Although Renan's mature position on the constitution of a psychological science would thus reject introspection as its appropriate method, it is clear that, at least at the critical juncture when he transferred his religious vocation to the scientific pursuit of truth, introspection was still his natural medium and an essential part of his daily life. An entry in his notebooks from the period June 1845-December 1846 attests quite powerfully to that introspective proclivity and to the multiple purposes it served:

> Strange phenomenon, that shows that we measure time by internal memory. When I listen, when I attend a course, for example, the professor will sometimes stop speaking and my reflections will rapidly

pursue some object during his brief silence, so that when he resumes speaking, it seems to me that I have been awakened and that he was silent for a long time. I measure the time elapsed by the thoughts that have filled the interruption.

He then caps this self-reflexive maneuver with a reflection on the fact that he is engaging in it. "It is a consolation for me to notice that, amidst the cruel circumstances that torment me"—he is referring to his recent departure from the seminary—"I still have enough courage and enough faith in science to pursue my speculative line of thought so dispassionately."[86] Not only, then, does Renan have a natural inclination to turn inward. He also uses his observations of his own mental processes as grist for psychological theorizing, a disciplined scientific endeavor that in turn (to adopt a psychoanalytic idiom) acts as a defense against the tumult of his emotions. Interestingly, Renan's own note to this journal entry indicates that it was written in the context of his attendance at the course of the generically Cousinian philosopher Adolphe Garnier.[87] Renan was, then, the ideal type of the Cousinian pupil, actively constructing a psychological science on the basis of his own interior observation.

During this fluid, transitional period, Renan's psychological researches were not wholly secular. He still allowed himself occasional recourse to religious explanation, to an introspection mediated, in classical Catholic fashion, by reference to supernatural entities. Thus at one moment he expressed the view that, in a world without divine grace, the study of human psychology would be doomed to futility from a practical standpoint. "Necessity of grace. To cure man's heart, one would have to cure his reason, and to cure his reason, one would first have to cure his heart. Impossible to exit from that [vicious] circle without external help."[88] At another moment, a "psychological phenomenon that I have experienced for a long time" convinced him of the existence of "the devil" as an entity affecting the human psyche. When distracted during an "exercise of piety," he always found the source of the distraction to possess an "inexpressible charm, oh! but inexpressible." Yet if he returned to it at a moment when involvement in it was licit, he found it utterly lacking in appeal. "That seems entirely inexplicable to me on natural grounds, and I see in it one of the strongest proofs of the Christian religion, as an induction made from the existence of the devil and of the devil's repugnance for the practices of that religion."[89]

A striking feature of this heady, still unorganized mix of psychological theorizing is the absence of self-talk. Renan introspected in a fundamentally pointillist manner, registering and explaining discrete psychological phenomena; he showed no interest in that bounded totality called the self. As we continue to follow the path of his psychological speculation, we will want to find out how he reacted to the Cousinian concept of the *moi*. We will also want to find out if he sought a systematic reconciliation of the secular and religious versions of interiority, in place of the simple commingling of the two that seemed to satisfy him initially, and whether Cousinianism was useful to him in that task.

Rendezvous with Cousin

Cousin's doctrine was part of Renan's intellectual universe even when he knew it only from secondhand accounts. Already in the notebook entitled "Observations and faits psychologiques," he announced that "Monsieur Cousin [had] well analyzed the progress of the human mind in the search for truth"; he had correctly asserted that "it proceeds from an exclusive view of one aspect of the truth, bracketing the rest," and eventually arrives at a *juste-milieu* taking into account all aspects. Mulling over this Cousinian proposition, Renan deemed it valid when applied both to the individual intellect and to the mental development of humanity in general. As usual, he reasoned from introspection: "I have experienced it in myself." He analogized the mental process to the physical oscillations of a pendulum: "From one extreme it passes to another extreme, less distant from the middle; from that extreme to the opposite one, less distant still. . ."[90]

When, around 1845, Renan finally read Cousin's 1818 course, its "wingèd phrases" transported him considerably less than his fond remembrance of the event four decades later would suggest. Judging from his copious notes, reading Cousin inspired no epiphany in him: in all likelihood, long prior familiarity with the basic outlines of the philosophy made his encounter with the actual text anticlimactic. Perhaps, too, the exalted nature of his expectations—this was, after all, an author banned by his seminary teachers!—inevitably produced disappointment and hence an accentuation of what he perceived as Cousin's failings.

Thus, he played down the novelty of Cousin's views, frequently assimilating them to the insights of the Scottish common-sense philosophers. He complained that some of Cousin's criticisms of the Scots did not hold water, and he reserved the colorful outburst "Charlatanism!" for a place in the text where he believed Cousin to be following the Scots even as he pretended to be improving on their allegedly flawed position.[91] We can assume, given this fondness for the Scots, that he sided with the conception of Reid and Kant as represented by Cousin— "they create the world by the *moi*"—against that of Locke and Condillac—"they create the *moi* by the world."[92] Yet he took pains to observe that Cousin's anti-sensationalist arguments were not in themselves convincing: "The proofs he adduces against Locke are of an almost comical inexactitude and vagueness."[93] His response to Cousin's religious positions was no more favorable. On the issue of pantheism, he shared Maret's opinion that this label suited Cousin's philosophical doctrine: "Pantheist ideas very evidently come through in this lesson. . . . He who does not know the pantheism of Monsieur C. lacks the key to his ideas." Unlike Maret, however, Renan apparently did not think that this pantheism fully discredited Cousin's philosophy, making its every aspect worthless or dangerous. What seemed to bother him more was the cynicism with which Cousin vehemently denied the charges of critics like Maret and his imagined readiness to "mock [in private] those who believe his protestations [that his philosophy is not pantheistic]."[94] In addition, steeped in the latest philology and Hebraic studies, Renan took pleasure in pointing out that Cousin, lacking such erudition, erroneously repeated the old saw that Christianity grew out of the culture of Greek antiquity. "The Greek spirit contributed nothing to the birth of Christianity but a good deal to its development. The root of Christianity is solely in Judaism. That is a fact, and the assertions of this entire century will do nothing to change it."[95]

Faced with Cousin's novel psychological propositions, however, the otherwise prickly Renan became oddly phlegmatic. In a two-part format divided into a summary of each of Cousin's lectures and a list of his own rejoinders to the arguments presented, he duly recorded Cousin's doctrine of the *moi* and its distinctive identification of selfhood with free activity and will. As we know well, this aspect of Cousin's philosophy was hardly anodyne. So offensive, in fact, did Catholic critics find it that, accusing the Sorbonne *maître* of deifying the human self, some even referred sarcastically to his entire oeuvre as the "philosophy of the *moi*."[96] Renan, by contrast, said nothing; he failed to respond to the doctrine in either positive or negative terms.[97] To this strange silence must be added his equally peculiar reaction to one of Cousin's related claims: that the idea of cause originates in the *moi* and, specifically, in the individual's introspective awareness of the free activity of his own will. Renan did not comment on this claim either. But instead of merely ignoring it, he seems to have displaced his curiosity about it onto the psychohistorical plane. Prodded by Cousin's thesis, he pondered not the human will but its divine counterpart:

> It would be intriguing to examine psychologically in what sense Christianity made us aware of the idea of cause through its dogma of providence and its precept of submission to the will of God, such as the saints have practiced it. To do so it would be necessary to study intensively the lives of the saints, which in fact form an invaluable repertory for the psychologist. . . .[98]

It is hard to believe that Cousin's theory of the *moi* held no interest for Renan. A far more probable interpretation of his silence in the one case and his deflected response in the other is that they expressed anxiety rather than indifference. Certainly some comments of his older sister Henriette tend in this direction. When Ernest began to confide in her his still tentative plans to leave the seminary, she wrote to him from Poland (where she had gone to serve in the household of a nobleman who had promised that the job would provide her with time and resources for study): "You suffer, my Ernest, in discovering personhood [*personnalité*, the term that Cousin used as a synonym for the *moi*] and ambition where your righteous and pure heart dreamt only of abnegation and devotion."[99] And as his determination to renounce his religious vocation grew stronger, she wrote that his most recent letter had given her "great joy because I see in it a finally emerging resolve, I find in it traces of that energy, of that *force of will* that I have so much desired for you and without which we remain all our lives only overgrown children."[100]

It is, then, Henriette rather than her brother who gives voice to the idea that part of Ernest's crisis of vocation is a conflict between two opposing psychological modalities: bending to the will of God, or cultivating one's own, human will. It seems safe to accept the accuracy of Henriette's observations in this regard. Sharing, by his own testimony, Ernest's "strong disposition for the *vie intérieure*,"[101] her close relationship to her brother gave her privileged knowledge of him; moreover, she selflessly poured support, advice, and tenderness into her younger sibling as into a work in progress.[102] On the basis of her remarks, we can only assume that Cousin's concept of the *moi* aroused enormous ambivalence in the young Renan. It was easier for him to apply the Cousinian philosophy at a safe distance to the psychohistorical meaning of the Christian doctrine of the divine will than to apply it at close range to himself—and this despite the fact that he habitually looked to his own case as verification for the propositions of psychological theory.

Occasionally during this period of his life, Renan does speak of the self, even of his own self, in the egoistic manner so dear to Cousinian philosophy and so inimical to Bérullian Catholicism. In the *fait psychologique* cited earlier concerning the sailor's anger at Renan's tossing a rock at a boat, Renan goes on to explain that oddly strong reaction in a way consonant with, but much more Cousinian than, his initial explanation in terms of habit. A worker, he suggests, grows attached to the tools of his trade not only because of his habitual use of them but also because of a psychological mechanism whereby he identifies them with himself. In language reminiscent of Cousin's justification of private property by the a priori existence of the *moi,* Renan speaks in this context of the "principle that identifies us with our *property*" (emphasis in the original). "We regard it as an extension of ourselves, and that is what binds us to it so powerfully."[103] Another of these rare instances of a *fait psychologique* recorded by the young Renan that muses on selfhood occurs in his notebooks from his Breton summer vacation of 1845, when his decision-making about his future connection to the seminary had come to a head. Encountering a small child that people say looks the way he looked at that age, he notes in one entry, "Ah, my nice past, I will never renounce you. That little child has had more effect on me than ten volumes of philosophy." A few entries later he returns to the episode to theorize it further in terms of the self, to make an admission that might seem obvious but that is quite unusual and even a little shocking for Renan who, for all his introspection, does not often dwell on or even acknowledge the self. "Strange psychological phenomenon, that singularly lively affection that I felt for that small child, who is, it is true, quite good and sweet. But the true reason for my affection, I imagine, is that people say that he resembles me when I was his age. Upon hearing that, I assimilated myself to him, identified with him; and what I love in him is my past. . ."[104]

During the critical period 1843–46, then—and this chapter is concerned only with those years—Renan seems to have been poised or suspended between self-abnegation and willfulness and, at the same time, between a religious and a secular *vie intérieure*. This liminal position accorded well with the pattern of life he adopted immediately after leaving Saint-Sulpice: although he would no longer devote his life to the Church, but rather to secular science, he had not ceased to be a practicing Catholic and still took the sacraments, noting the "very striking psychological phenomenon" that he "literally could not imagine" that the host was ordinary bread.[105] He frankly viewed the faculty psychology of the common-sense school that he had learned at the seminary and that formed a large part of the conceptual scaffolding for his secular introspection as unable to accommodate the transcendent. He seems, in fact, to have reached the same impasse with respect to the Scottish psychology that Cousin had reached several decades earlier—that is, finding it wanting by dint of its inability to accommodate a metaphysical dimension. He expressed this insight in his own variant on the vocabulary of square pegs and round holes:

> The faculties that constitute our mind are like little boxes, molds of a certain shape—square, I suppose; and truths are bodies, also of certain shapes, that must be stuffed into these molds. But these truths are of all sorts of shapes, of completely distinct orders, square, round, etc. Now it is very evident that only the square ones will fit. The others, impossible! The square ones are phenomena, the round ones are metaphysical truths and mysteries.[106]

Awareness of the tension between his religious and secular psychological modalities led Renan to try out, during the pivotal year 1845, at least two different strategies of integrating them. One such experiment took the form of a manuscript entitled "Psychologie de la confession," probably prepared in March as a response to Michelet's just published, attention-getting *Du prêtre, de la femme et de la famille*.[107] Michelet's book contained a virulent attack on confession, which it depicted as a cynical mechanism for the maintenance of Church power, a preying on the sensibilities of women (who chiefly availed themselves of this sacrament) to insinuate clerical influence into the heart of what should have been a patriarchal household. Renan, in turn, vigorously defended confession but, enacting the extreme ambivalence he felt toward the Church at this date and expressing his heartfelt desire to reconcile religion and science, he did so by using the tools of scientific psychology, including the Cousinian variety.

Thus Renan's essay never even employs the term "sacrament." Casting itself as a *vérification psychologique* of a traditional Church teaching (Renan has here adopted the very sort of analysis that Maret labeled as heretical in Cousin), it audaciously defines sin in Cousinian vocabulary as the revolt of the finite against the absolute, an error of a *moi* which, believing itself fully autonomous, neglects to regulate its actions according to the dictates of impersonal reason. The essay tacks back and forth between introspective data and psychological theory. With a richness of detail that could only be autobiographical in origin, Renan notes the extreme psychological "rigidity" of the sinner, the haughty inflexibility that renders him immune to self-reform. Only confession before one's fellow man has the force to assail this posture; the humiliation that it brings about entails "a sort of heat that softens [the soul] and makes it more susceptible to the impressions of virtue." An agonistic encounter occurs in the confession box: "Shaken in its pridefulness . . ., [the soul] vacillates, awaiting an impulsion that will determine the side to which it will fall. It is then that, one-on-one with the virtue and reason that speak to it, it opens itself of its own accord to their blows and astonishes itself by yielding to their attacks . . ."

Renan goes on to invoke Dugald Stewart's theory of the association of ideas to explain the implications of this intense experience for personal development over time. "Nothing is more tenacious, as we know, than these associations when they are formed in circumstances where the soul is disposed to receive strong impressions. . . . Hence, among persons accustomed to confession, [one finds] a certain modesty that holds them back before the mere idea of great wrongdoing." The sequence of confession-humiliation-reform achieves its psychological efficacy, according to Renan, not only by the stick but also by the carrot. Indeed the two are linked, in the positivist terminology Renan favored, by a psychological law. It is "one of the most remarkable laws of the human affective life to be able to taste no lively joy without having first purchased it through a painful preparation." Thus the pain of confession produces a divine balm: an "inexpressible sweetness" such that "all who have tasted it attest without hesitation [that it] is worth more than anything."[108]

Renan may have been personally satisfied with this syncretistic attempt to justify an orthodox religious practice with a scientific method. But whatever pleasure he took in his work was severely diminished when he exposed it to the evaluation of a superior at the seminary. A comment penciled at the top of the manuscript in handwriting not Renan's own declared: "Basically good. Too much pretension at depth, producing some false and extravagant consequences."[109] We know Renan's response to this dismissive criticism because he wrote about it, and apparently about a subsequent conversation with the same superior, in his private notebook:

> A curious fact to relate in the history of philosophy: in the middle of the nineteenth century, the use of the psychological method has been accused of "pretension at depth" and of ridiculous neologizing, at the Seminary of Saint-Sulpice, in Paris. One must acknowledge that the circulation is quite slow in certain parts of the human body.[110]

The sardonic, almost mock-heroic tone of this entry is noteworthy (the commas before and after "at the Seminary of Saint-Sulpice" modulate the pace, making each successive revelation more incredible) as is the fact that Renan has chosen to characterize his essay as a "use of the psychological method" *tout court*. Renan, we can surmise, experienced this rejection bitterly, and he summoned all his artfulness to protect himself, even implicitly analogizing the Church to an atrophied limb of an otherwise vital social organism. What he had offered his superior was, after all, not an idle speculative exercise but an urgent attempt to reconcile the two institutions to which he was most committed—the Church and science—and, related to them, the two different modes of access to the *vie intérieure* to which he had become accustomed.

In the summer or fall of 1845, he made another attempt at integration in the notebook entry beginning with the arresting sentence quoted earlier in this chapter: "Here is my fundamental principle of the religious inner life." That entry, like much of the material in Renan's youthful manuscripts, is neither crystal clear nor fully worked out. Tellingly for our purposes, it is shot through with references to Cousin, who is, moreover, represented with the blatant inconsistency that befits a highly charged object. Renan alternately blames the Sorbonne *maître* for demoting the religious to an isolable aspect of human nature and praises him extravagantly for having devised a system in which the apparent opposition between the secular and the religious is erased. The passage, a self-contained paragraph for which Renan supplied no context, deserves to be quoted in its entirety:

> Here is my fundamental principle of the religious interior life. The religious is not a faculty apart, a separate compartment or pigeonhole in man (as Cousin and [the abbé] Bautain seem to construe it, Cousin by smothering it under the others, Bautain by smothering the others under it.) It is rather a facet of everything, of all duties, of every exercise of the faculties, etc. If the first point of view is admitted, what is called for is the theory of our harshest mystics, of Monsieur Olier, etc. Cut up, slice the human being and leave only the religious elements. For the rest not being religious, and only the religious having real value, what remains is futile. Once these principles are admitted, it is only superficial people who could possibly cultivate science, the mind, take an interest in life, etc. The mystics regard them with pity and rightly so: for [this way of life] augurs in them a weak head, little rigor, a spineless moderation. But, according to the other viewpoint, everything in man must be cultivated and conserved, nothing *renounced,* but everything raised to the level of the religious. At this point, the sacred and the profane disappear. The distinction has meaning only for limited minds. Everything is sacred in one facet, in every facet, if you wish, profane in another. (See Cousin, Course of 1818, towards the end) The science of phenomena could correspond to the profane, and philosophy to the sacred, but it would be better to say that the two words lack meaning, like all words that express unreal distinctions.[111]

As Renan prepared to leave organized religion behind, he apparently sought reassurance, even ultimate answers, from Cousin's philosophy. He construed it as providing a warrant to believe that he did not have to choose between the traditional *vie intérieure religieuse*—here represented, not surprisingly, by Olier—and an inner domain produced solely by secular processes of introspection. Rather the distinction between the two could be dissolved and the pair magically reconciled by Cousin's Gallic version of Hegelian *Aufhebung.* The reader of this ardent passage cannot help but feel that Renan was engaging in a bit of self-deceptive casuistry in his final hour and that, by identifying the sacred with philosophy, he had already thrown overboard the religiosity of his seminary years.

This chapter has traced Renan's pathway from the effaced or even completely "annihilated" Bérullian self ("The principle the [Sulpicians] preached the most was never to have oneself spoken of and, if one had something to say, to say it simply, as if hiding oneself," Renan remarked retrospectively);[112] through empirical self-observation under the aegis of the Scots, which served him in a transitional capacity; to something akin to a Cousinian self—secular-scientific, highly valorized, and willful enough to authorize a fundamental life decision. Renan did not, at least in 1845–46, live out that valorization of self directly. Rather he embraced the "psychological method" that he ascribed to Cousin, a method which made the workings of the self the primary level of reality and the one to which all the others could be legitimately reduced. The chapter has suggested the paradoxical relationship between Cousinian and Catholic interiority. On the one hand, true Catholic belief was incompatible with the Cousinian *moi* and could thus place Catholics outside the reach of the Cousinian hegemony that prevailed in secular society. On the other hand, Cousin's metaphysical impulse could, as clerics feared, smooth the way from Catholic orthodoxy to the embrace of a garden-variety secular bourgeois self.

7

A Palpable Self for the Socially Marginal: The Phrenological Alternative

I make no appeal to 14 in this country [France]. Here one is polite, social, agreeable, but we must not expect 14.

J. C. Spurzheim to George Combe, 1824

At the end of November 1839, an infernal machine—the same kind of device that had been used several years earlier in Fieschi's attempted assassination of King Louis-Philippe—mysteriously exploded in the center of Paris, destroying a wall on a street adjacent to the Palais-Royal. The police soon decided that the crime had been politically motivated, the work of a left-wing secret society hostile to the July Monarchy. They based this conclusion on the fact that their chief suspect, whose tiny rented room in the Marais was found to harbor a cache of explosives, had previously been sentenced for placarding the city with "seditious" posters. The suspect was Antoine-Pierre Béraud, a young man of twenty-two enrolled at the Paris Law Faculty. The arrest of Béraud proved to be a colorful affair. According to the *Gazette des tribunaux*, a police officer successfully recognized him at night even though he was "decked out in a workingman's smock and was wearing a flowing blond wig to hide his close-cropped black hair." Resisting arrest, he "pull[ed] up his smock with one hand [and] tried to arm himself with the pistol and kitchen knife tucked into his belt." A crowd gathered, illuminated by gaslight, and "as was usual for the public" in such situations, cheered him on in his defiance of authority; only the arrival of other police offic-ers sealed his fate.[1] Several years later, after imprisonment for the infernal

269

machine episode had converted him to more pacific ways, Béraud turned up in Moulins, a town in the Auvergne. There he petitioned the local authorities for permission to teach a public course. The French bureaucracy operated with admirable efficiency, and a letter dispatched to Paris soon brought word that the request was to be denied, in part because the petitioner had a criminal record, in part because the proposed course, though "more or less scientific" in nature, was known to have "baneful tendencies." What was the subject that Béraud wanted to disseminate among the Auvergnats? It was phrenology.[2]

Though rebuffed in his pedagogical mission in Moulins, Béraud did succeed in propagating phrenology under more informal auspices. During the next five years, in visits to Burgundy, the Loire Valley, Alsace, and especially the West, he staged demonstrations of his phrenological skills, "eager," as he put it in his handbill, "to spread with all our strength a science as great as it is useful" and "happy to offer our enlightenment to persons who wish to submit their heads to us."[3] In the revolutionary year of 1848, he published a long book on the applications of phrenology to philosophy, morals and, most significantly, socialism.[4]

As curious and marginal a character as Béraud may seem, he was, in fact, entirely typical of the leadership of early nineteenth-century French phrenology. Other influential phrenological advocates had remarkably similar profiles. They hailed from petit bourgeois or working-class backgrounds (Béraud was the son of a Lyonnais grocer),[5] had sought but not obtained professional credentials, and were activists in or sympathizers with the left-wing opposition to the July Monarchy.

Thus, like the failed law student Béraud, Auguste Luchet dropped out of the Paris Medical Faculty.[6] The grandson of a Paris carpetmaker and the son of a Paris clerk, he subsequently pursued a career as a publicist, playwright for the boulevard theater, and author of popular novels, larding his literary and journalistic productions with references to phrenology and Fourierist socialist theory. He had his own brush with the law. In 1837 he was hauled before the royal court of the Pas-de-Calais on a press violation: the state's prosecutor charged that an article on phrenology that Luchet had contributed to the *Almanach populaire de la France* "incited hatred among the different classes of society."[7]

Pierre Dumoutier, the son of a decorative craftsman in the Marais, first enrolled at the Paris Medical Faculty in 1814. He never received certification as a physician, but neither did he give up the quest: he took his first examination for the medical doctorate in 1836, when he was almost forty, and his fifth and last examination when he was almost sixty, but he apparently ran out of steam before writing the required thesis.[8] Calling himself an "anatomist," Dumoutier was a founding member of the Paris Phrenological Society and, during the 1830s, a well-known instructor of phrenology in the capital giving public courses unaffiliated with the state educational system. He seems to have been less politically radical than the others, or at least more intent on keeping his political views hidden from the authorities, for (in what must have been the pinnacle of his career) he was invited to take part in a government-sponsored voyage to the South Seas as the ship's resident phrenologist in charge of observing the cranial configurations of primitive peoples.[9] Despite this moment of glory, Dumoutier remained sporadically employed and decidedly marginal; some of the phrenological manuscripts in his hand that I have come across are written on the backs of unpaid bills.[10]

To be sure, other noteworthy proponents of phrenology in this era were of bourgeois origin and regular enough in their habits actually to complete the professional training they started; but they, too, connected their advocacy of the new science to left-wing politics. Perhaps the most famous of this group was Ange Guépin, the democratic socialist from Nantes. While a beginning medical student at the Paris Faculty in the early 1820s, spending "four hours a day with my hands and nose in a cadaver," Guépin was introduced to phrenology—not as a part of the official curriculum but as one of the extracurricular student enthusiasms of the day. Classmates brought him to the private course of Franz-Joseph Gall, the Viennese refugee living in Paris who had founded phrenology. A fascinated Guépin attended the course faithfully, every Thursday evening and Sunday afternoon, and reported to a boyhood friend that Gall put to the class such audacious questions as "Is there a separate cerebral organ of marriage?" and "Is marriage a purely civil act or a natural institution?"[11] By the opening years of the July Monarchy, Guépin was using his post at the Nantes medical school to propagandize for phrenology, suggesting that schoolteachers aim their instruction at the "anterior lobes of the brain" in order to "render sociable the individuals who are today being led by our educational institutions into the debasement of egoism."[12] His adherence to phrenology would continue for the rest of his life.[13]

The art critic Theophile Thoré, best known for his discovery of the seventeenth-century painter Vermeer, also falls into this category. The son of a well-to-do merchant, he received a law degree in Poitiers but abandoned his legal career in disgust ("never will I accept a life stupidly spent among stupid people") to fight for radical political causes and to live by his pen in Paris. He construed journalism in lofty democratic terms as a kind of secular priesthood in which he would serve as an "intermediary between [abstract] thought and the people." Living in a garret, he formed a close friendship with Dumoutier, and the two young men companionably studied phrenology together. He instructed his mother to sell his neglected magistrate's robe for cash; whether or not she complied, it was the money she periodically sent him that enabled him to make ends meet. Partly as a potboiler, partly as a labor of love, he wrote a *Dictionnaire de phrénologie* in 1836 for a publisher who offered him an advance of 600 francs and a second 600 francs if the sales reached 2,000 copies.[14] The carefully crafted entries indicate the connection of phrenology to both his aesthetic theory and his politics. They included one that identified Gall's science as the "first element of art" because it revealed the "direct and constant relation between the inner life and the visible manifestation," and another that grounded private property in the brain organ of acquisitiveness but nonetheless questioned the validity of the capitalist property sanctioned by nineteenth-century law codes.[15]

As the exploits of this motley crew suggest, phrenology was a psychological discourse contemporaneous with Cousinianism but very different in every other respect: intellectual content, political affiliations, institutional organization, audience, and rhetoric. Where Cousin insisted first and foremost on the immateriality of mind, phrenology embedded mind in brain. Where Cousinian psychology supported constitutional monarchy, limited suffrage, and a middle-of-the-road politics that made stability its highest priority, phrenology typically allied, during the period of the July Monarchy, with republican and socialist movements intent on overturning the political status quo. Where Cousin's psychology became entrenched, comfortably and powerfully, in the state educational system, phrenology hovered hungrily on the sidelines of the establishment. Where Cousinianism took all the male lycée students in France for its captive audience and soberly initiated this bourgeois elite-in-the-making into the arcane language and practices of introspection, phrenology used makeshift settings and a simple, swift, and graphic pedagogy in an effort to win over the popular classes, who had been deliberately excluded from the lycées and hence from training in selfhood. Where Cousinians defined psychology as an exclusively male enterprise and debarred the female population from official instruction in the *moi*, phrenologists welcomed women into their courses. In terms of the sociology of its dissemination, phrenology was a decidedly compensatory psychology, offering its particular version of selfhood to those whom the Université had disdained.

Small wonder, then, that the appearance on the scene of an active phrenological movement prompted the Cousinians to redefine their enemy or, at least, to define it more capaciously than before. In the same letter of 1829 in which Caroline Angebert called to Cousin's attention the continued vitality of sensationalist psychology among "the masses" after its abandonment by the intelligentsia (see Chapter 4), she also warned of a fresh peril, bearing a family resemblance to the first. "Grafted by physiology onto the *sensualisme* of the previous century, a new materialism is advancing. It has for leaders and auxiliaries men of action, stirring up the crowd, which finds their principles as easy to grasp as their doctrines are easy to put into practice."[16] Left unnamed by Angebert, that new enemy was subsequently identified and scrutinized by other Cousinians in prominent, published texts. Adolphe Garnier's 1839 *La psychologie et la phrénologie comparées* grew out of the author's dialectical position that responsible adherence to any scientific theory required thorough examination of the theories opposed to it. Hence, Garnier told his readers, as a strong partisan of Cousin and Jouffroy he had no choice but to treat "the doctrine of Gall and his successors, a doctrine that, under the name of phrenology, has attained the highest celebrity, that has its own journals, its savant societies, its public courses. . . ."[17] The manual of Cousinian philosophy coauthored by Amédée Jacques showed that, by 1846, the new dialectical couple had become standard pedagogical fare. In fact, Jacques' textbook contrasts sharply with the master's own writings in that sensationalism, Cousin's Other par excellence, has been fundamentally displaced by this relative newcomer, equally inimical to the Cousinian project:

> In what secret recess of matter, in what obscure cranny of the brain, will the physiologist go to grasp foresight, memory, reason and, more generally, thought, which has neither shape nor form? Still, some

physiologists have pretensions to accomplishing just that, and, under the time-honored (sic) title of *phrenology*, they have instituted a science destined to supplant psychology by substituting for the direct study of the intellectual and moral faculties of man [by means of consciousness] the easier and clearer description of their organs.[18]

Rudiments of the Scientific Theory

From the beginning, phrenology was a theory of cerebral localization possessing a strong semiotic component. Like the physiognomy of the Swiss pastor, Johann-Caspar Lavater, also in vogue in the early nineteenth century (and with which it was often coupled, or even confused),[19] it emphasized the possibility of divining internal psychological traits through the semiotic exercise of scrutinizing external physical morphology: facial features in the case of physiognomy, and skull conformation in the case of phrenology. A "psychological hieroglyphic," one late eighteenth-century German admirer of phrenology called the skull.[20] But unlike physiognomy, which offered no explanation for the correspondences it registered between faces and personalities, phrenology based its reading of skulls on a full-fledged theory of the relationship between mind and brain.

Its founder, the Baden-born physician Franz-Joseph Gall, had, by his own account, embarked upon his career as a phrenologist with an accidental observation of a generically physiognomical sort: as a schoolboy and again as a university student, he noticed that those of his classmates who had extremely good memories, and thus typically bested him in scholastic examinations, also had prominent eyes.[21] For Lavater, such a finding would have been an end in itself. But Gall probed further, seeking the cause of the phenomenon, and indeed of all particularly well-developed mental faculties, in cerebral structure. Working in Vienna with a young collaborator, the medical student Johann-Caspar Spurzheim, he hammered out his theory during the last decade of the eighteenth century. He posited that, far from being composed of homogeneous tissue (as was generally thought at this date), the human brain was divided into discrete organs, each controlling a single intellectual attribute or affective propensity. The volume of each of these so-called brain organs in a given individual was, according to the theory, responsible for the degree of strength of the relevant mental traits in that individual. Brain-organ volume could be discerned indirectly through an examination of the surface contours of the skull that housed them: hence Gall's innovative procedure of making plaster casts of the skulls of his research subjects. It could be directly verified by a postmortem dissection of the brain itself, one conducted according to Gall's distinctive procedure of respecting the natural folds of that organ instead of cutting it into parallel, geometrically regular sections.[22] The relation between brain configuration and personality could then be corroborated by external evidence of the subject's behavior in social situations, by tracing what would come to be called the subject's "phrenological biography."[23]

Gall thus thoroughly integrated mind and brain, and the religious implications of this theoretical move soon excited controversy. Adversaries labeled his doctrine "materialist and fatalist," a shorthand term of opprobrium that meant that, by situating human mental processes in brute, organic matter (the "materialist" maneuver), a given philosophy or science subsumed them under the determinist laws that governed all matter (the "fatalist" consequence). Moreover, these same critics charged, the philosophy or science in question denied the existence of the free will that God had bestowed upon human beings; in effect it threw up its hands helplessly in the face of human conduct, adopting the position that people had no choice but to be and do what they were and did.

Once applied to Gall's doctrine, this double allegation inspired political sanctions. The Hapsburgs had initially supported Gall's research, granting him privileged access to the state-run prisons and insane asylums where he avidly palpated skulls, molded them in plaster, and inquired into the social conduct of the persons to whom they belonged. Yet in 1802 Emperor Francis II sharply revised his opinion of his scientific client. He forbade Gall to continue to offer private courses in the realm, citing the tendency of his doctrine to subvert religion and morality. In response, Gall and Spurzheim took to the road with their large collection of plaster casts, lecturing their way across Western Europe and arriving in Paris toward the end of 1807. The freedom of instruction they enjoyed in the French capital prompted them to settle there, even though their teaching, which won numerous converts, soon gave rise in certain quarters to the same allegations that had been its undoing in Vienna.

The Checkered Fortunes of Phrenology in France

The scientific marginality that phrenology eventually acquired under the July Monarchy and the affiliation with the popular movement that became an element of its identity were not foreordained. They resulted instead from a set of highly contingent circumstances. In fact, the fortunes of phrenology alternately waxed and waned in France after Gall's arrival there; at times, victory seemed within its grasp.

Effectively exiled from Vienna, Gall was understandably eager to win legitimacy for his science in Paris. However, he found his quest thwarted not only by the irreligious connotations of phrenology but also, it seems, by the swift and effortless entrance of phrenology into popular discourse and the comic potential of its signature act of skull palpation. The arrival of Gall and Spurzheim in Paris immediately produced a wave of parodies. For example, a one-act comedy of 1808 called *Monsieur Têtu* (French for "stubborn," with an obvious play on *tête*, or head), subtitled *La Cranomanie* (skull-mania), presented the story of the aptly named bourgeois paterfamilias Monsieur Dujour who, having long tried the patience of his family and servants with his enthusiastic adherence to all the scientific fads of the day, outdoes himself when he makes the choice of his daughter's marriage partner dependent on a phrenological reading.[24] Against the no doubt disheartening background of such parodies, many of which placed Gall in the same ignominious line of seductive charlatans that included Mesmer,[25] he and Spurzheim actively sought the imprimatur of official science in 1808 by submitting a memoir on the anatomy of the brain to the Academy of Sciences.

The commission charged with assessing it, headed by Georges Cuvier, dealt the phrenologists an oblique but nonetheless forceful blow. They generously acknowledged the experimental contributions of the two researchers, especially their demonstration of an uninterrupted connection between the spinal cord and brain. Nevertheless, they hastened to add that this laudable anatomical finding had no bearing on Gall's much better known doctrine of cranial bumps or, as the report referred to it in more dignified fashion, "the physiological doctrine that [Gall] espouses on the special functions of the different parts of the cerebral organ." Indeed the commissioners simply placed that latter doctrine outside their purview, declining to comment on it at all. They held that its validity ultimately depended on "observations about individuals' moral and intellectual dispositions" which, they noted disparagingly, "assuredly fall within the competence of no academy of science." The degree to which the public was cognizant of Gall's findings was repeatedly mentioned by the commissioners, as if popularity in itself militated against scientific accuracy and respectability. Whereas, they said, Gall's research remained as yet unpublished (a criterion for assessment by the Academy), the extent of his "oral teaching" had given it a degree of "publicity" comparable to that of a printed text. Certain aspects of it had even become "a topic of passionate discussion among people of all stations" and had thus "rendered [Gall's] name popular."[26]

Deprived of validation by the Academy, but not censured either, Gall continued to lecture at the Athénée de Paris, an "anomalous" and "amateur" private institution (the characterization is that of a late twentieth-century historian of science) that had recruited him almost immediately upon his arrival in the French capital. Long associated both with political opposition and with a commitment to the technical application of science, the Athénée, founded toward the end of the Old Regime, was in the early decades of the nineteenth century enjoying a period of particular vitality and prestige. It was at the forefront of such new disciplines as physiology and political economy.[27] It catered to a relatively affluent lay public, who purchased subscriptions for the privilege of attending its courses. It also had a reputation for philosophical materialism. After attending an evening physiology lecture there in January 1817, Maine de Biran noted in his journal that the speaker's ramblings had received the "applause of the multitude." Referring to the philosophical underpinnings of the lecture, he then asked acerbically, "What value can be attached to the approbation of ignorant men who let themselves be captivated exclusively by their senses?"[28]

During the two decades that he lectured at the Athénée, Gall was much in demand by the fashionable upper classes of the capital for private consultations. He and Spurzheim quarreled around 1810 or 1811, for reasons that one historian has characterized as "less intellectual than emotional," and parted ways soon after.[29] Each man continued to devote all his efforts to the development of phrenology—the name for their science that Gall, disliking neologisms, always refused but that Spurzheim embraced.[30] (Gall also adamantly rejected the name "cranioscopy" as focusing too exclusively on skull semiotics and glossing over the portion of the science concerning the anatomy and physiology of the brain.)[31] In 1821, revealing his still unappeased longing for acceptance by the establishment, Gall submitted his candidacy for membership in the Academy of Sciences, but obtained only a single vote.

When the Restoration monarchy moved into its intensely clerical phase after the accession of Charles X in 1825, the prospects for phrenology dimmed drastically in France. As the peripatetic Spurzheim (who had already spent some years in Britain and would eventually leave for the United States) wrote in a personal letter from Paris in June 1825 in his imperfect but serviceable English, "Priesthood gaining every day more ground and authority in France, my exertion for Phrenology will be less and less appreciated there, nay my powers would be paralyzed. I therefore must think again of England."[32] Or, mulling over the same problem even more pessimistically and with greater resolve a year later:

> I come now to my plan as intended for the future. It was necessary for me either to give up lecturing on Phrenology and to stick to my practice of Medecin (sic) in Paris, or to give up my practice in Paris and to lecture in England. The happy period to unite both sorts of occupations is over in France and will not return in our days, the things growing worse every day and the spirit of Jesuitism spreading. . . .[33]

Gall died in Paris in 1828, having lived out his final years in a political environment officially hostile to his creation. Nevertheless, contrary to Spurzheim's forecast, the future soon brightened for phrenology in France. The Revolution of 1830 installed a liberal regime that was, at least at the outset, undaunted by phrenology's materialistic taint and strongly inclined to exploit the potential of the young science for political benefit. Expectations ran high, almost absurdly so, one might say with the benefit of hindsight. In 1832 a bureaucrat in the Ministry of Commerce wrote to the French consul in London requesting, for purposes of comparison, information about the status of phrenology in Britain. Describing phrenology as a science that had in France already merited the "attention of our scholars and engaged the interest of the government," he predicted extravagantly that its "results [could], in time, have an influence on societies as direct and not less profitable than that of the science of political economy"! Reflecting the famously French étatist bias, he inquired particularly into the steps that the British government had taken to foster the development of phrenology on the other side of the Channel.[34] This functionary did not indicate exactly what "results" he expected phrenology to produce, but his analogy to political economy, as well as the fact that he served in the Ministry of Commerce, suggests that he envisioned an increase in the productivity of the French labor force once individuals had been set to work in the areas for which they possessed innate talents. For its part, the French diplomatic corps in Britain began collecting the desired data almost immediately.[35]

By the time this letter was penned, a Paris Phrenological Society had already been formed, its founding members obviously emboldened by the Revolution of 1830 to bring into the open a scientific association that had for years been informal and partly subterranean. As early as October 1830, just months after the change of regime, a group of "medical and other gentlemen" approached Spurzheim about their intention to form a phrenology society, causing him to observe with evident relief, "There is now something to be done in Paris for phrenology."[36] In April 1831, the Ministry of Commerce responded promptly and affirmatively to the request of the Society for authorization to hold meetings, and in February 1833 the Ministry of Public Instruction responded similarly, and with similar alacrity, to the additional request that one of its members, Pierre Dumoutier (the superannuated medical student whom we encountered at the beginning of this chapter), be allowed to give a phrenology course, open free of charge to the general public.[37] The Society, which counted 145 members at its inception in 1831, grew to 206 by 1834.[38] No formal professional credentials were initially required for membership, although by 1843 candidates needed to submit a "work on phrenology or its applications" whose merit would be evaluated by a committee report and a vote of the plenum. The resultant inclusion of amateurs in the Society—which contributed to the pervasive image of phrenology as a popular endeavor—led one commentator to quip that anyone with "twenty-four francs [the annual dues] in his pocket could join."[39] Indeed, the "unlimited" number of members specified in the original regulations prevented the group from being officially recognized by the government as a savant society.[40] Nonetheless, within a year the Society had spawned a journal devoted to its activities.[41] So giddy were hopes for the institutionalization of Gall's science at this juncture that rumors circulated about a plan afoot at the Ministry of Public Instruction for the imminent creation of a phrenology chair.[42]

Ripples of the post-1830 liberation of phrenology were felt in the provinces as well. In the town of Troyes, for example, a certain Dr. Patin had received permission in 1828 to teach a free public course in popular hygiene. About a year later, however, a colleague denounced him to the prefect as an affiliate of the "Jacobino-liberal party" who, under the innocuous cover of hygiene, had been teaching elite youth the "absurd and pernicious doctrines of materialism"—especially the "system of Gall," according to which "all vices and crimes [are] excused, even justified, as the inevitable effects of individual physical organization." When other citizens, including the mayor, joined in the denunciation, the state authorities closed the course. But in December 1833, an unbowed Dr. Patin again requested and received authorization for this same pedagogical endeavor. From the perspective of the July Monarchy, a supporter could now characterize the earlier incident as pure and simple "harassment" carried out by those "enemies of all social improvement who, unhappily, had too much credibility under the Restoration."[43]

That the founding of the July Monarchy had given the green light to phrenology was also seen in the conduct of Gall's young widow. Though her husband had left her nearly destitute when he died in April 1828, she waited a full three years, until May 1831, to request a pension from the French state in return for her single valuable property: the large collection of skulls (600 items, 50% human, 25% mammalian, and 25% avian) that Gall had amassed over some three decades. The government referred the matter to the Muséum d'histoire naturelle, which in turn appointed a commission composed of three prestigious zoologists and comparative anatomists—Geoffroy Saint-Hilaire, Blainville, and Cuvier— to study Madame Gall's offering and assess its worth. Although agnostic on the subject of the ultimate validity of Gall's controversial theory, the three unanimously favored acceptance of the gift, describing it as an abundance of carefully chosen material evidence supporting phrenological claims and, as such, worthy of being "deposited intact in a public institution"; the pension requested by the widow Gall was, moreover, a fair price for it.[44] At the beginning of the July Monarchy, then, phrenology was taken seriously both by the government and by the most eminent naturalists in France.

However, even when its fortunes were in the ascendant, phrenology was dogged by its propensity to pass rapidly and uncontrollably into popular culture. Properly managed, such popularization could be useful, or at least benign. By 1837, when Gall's collection was already on display at the Museum, a pocket guide for visitors to the Jardin des Plantes (the location of the Museum) included a long section describing the skulls in detail, thus recognizing their iconic status for a curious public.[45] But popularization could also have a distortive and damaging effect. Writing in the Society's journal in 1837, Charles Place decried the "Phrenological and Physiognomical Consultation" that had just sprung up on the well-trafficked Boulevard Saint-Martin. Situated behind a drop cloth featuring a "large and inane countenance drawn according to the phrenological topography of I don't know who," it bore the authentic phrenological slogan, "The external man is the projection of the internal man." All manner of charlatans had previously occupied the very same location, exhibiting such wonders as the "Skeleton Man" and the "Mechanical Man." Thus, in Place's view, did the unwitting enemies of phrenology "pollute public opinion" by informing the "credulous" popular classes that "this science, which is truly a science" was instead a "mumbo jumbo." They did a disservice both to phrenology and to the people, pandering to the latter's "faculty of marvelousness" (one of the phrenological brain organs) instead of instructing them to "moderate [their marvelousness] with the most severe rationality."[46]

That even the educated classes had a highly ambiguous conception of phrenology during the first decade of the July Monarchy can be seen in a curious case heard by a Paris criminal court in November 1836: a defamation suit brought by the heirs of a deceased woman against two physicians for the phrenological opinions they had announced after an autopsy of her brain. The use of phrenological experts in Paris police matters was not unusual at this date. Dumoutier, for example, was summoned to neighborhood police headquarters in 1833 to examine the skull of a woman believed to have committed suicide and to give his opinion about her propensity for such a drastic act. He found, among other anatomical features illuminating her character, a weakly developed organ of *biophilie*—a sure mark of a vulnerability to taking one's own life in times of stress.[47] But the respect for the scientific status of phrenology that the Paris police evinced in this instance was hardly universal.

In the 1836 case, the widow Chéron, a well-to-do *rentière*, had been murdered at her home near Versailles two years before, at which time the judiciary had ordered a routine autopsy of her body. One of the physicians engaged for this purpose decided to seize the opportunity to "submit the head [of the deceased] to the examination of a phrenologist" and thereby to "confirm the value that phrenological science could have for forensic medicine." He chose a certain Dr. Leroi of Versailles and, to authenticate the experiment, even arranged to have it witnessed by two other physicians and by some medical students serving as interns in the local hospital.[48] Dr. Leroi's findings were hardly flattering to the widow Chéron. Presented only with the head of a woman, and denied all information about her, he identified her dominant traits as ruse and love of money. Happily for the phrenological enterprise, if unhappily for the widow and her descendants, these derogatory pronouncements were then amply confirmed by acquaintances of Madame Chéron.[49] Pleased with his own performance, Dr. Leroi hastened to report it to the Paris Phrenological Society, of which he was a member. The secretary of the Society then communicated the news in the report of the year's activities that he presented at the annual meeting, in the presence (according to one source) of five or six hundred people.[50] From there it was picked up by the newspaper *Le Messager des Chambres*, which, for purposes of its feuilleton, seems to have embroidered the story by depicting the widow Chéron as a notorious moneylender and miser.[51] The newspaper thereby earned itself inclusion in the defamation suit.[52]

Our appreciation of the significance of this "bizarre"[53] case is unfortunately hindered by the paucity of documentation. Not only, as is standard for Paris trials of this era, did the judicial dossier perish in 1871 in the fires of the Paris Commune, but the harsh press law of 1835—a mark of the regime's retreat, in the face of left-wing opposition, from its initially liberal commitments—even prevented newspapers from offering full coverage of the judicial proceedings. Thus, we will never know what the lawyers and judges had to say about the complex "questions of morality, jurisprudence, and science" with which the suit confronted them.[54] However, we can infer from the wording of the accusation, and even more emphatically from the fact that the Paris judiciary agreed to hear the case, that it was perfectly acceptable in educated circles at this date to assume that phrenology lacked scientific content. Note that while the heirs were objecting to the publicity given the phrenological reading, they were not citing a failure to keep the "medical secret"—a failure actionable under Article 378 of the Napoleonic penal code. A suit under Article 378 would have been based on a presumption of the real expertise of the physicians who had characterized the widow Chéron's condition and hence of the veracity of their comments; its point would have been to preserve the right of an individual or family to keep knowledge about a medical condition scrupulously private.[55] The heirs' charge of defamation instead suggested the probable falsity of the phrenological opinion, and hence its "insulting" nature and capacity to "undermine the honor and esteem that rightly belong to the family."[56]

The case thus effectively put phrenology itself on trial and, more generally, seemed to engage the judiciary in the dubious business of distinguishing legitimate scientific hypotheses and conclusions from malevolent slander. As such, it became a *cause célèbre,* drawing crowds of lawyers, law students, scholars, and ordinary Parisians to the courtroom. Not surprisingly, organized phrenology was also well represented among the spectators at the trial. A request by the Paris Phrenological Society for a large number of tickets had gone unanswered, but the followers of Gall and Spurzheim made a point of arriving early enough to claim unreserved seats.[57] One commentator alleged that enthusiasts of the "phrenological cause" had so thoroughly packed the chamber that they had to be forcibly restrained.[58] That the Chéron case also had a civil libertarian and hence, under the July Monarchy, a political dimension was seen in the fact that the two physicians had chosen as one of their lawyers Alexandre-Auguste Ledru-Rollin, the future Minister of the Interior of the Second Republic whose republican sentiments had already been made known when in 1834 he criticized the Guizot government for carrying out the massacre on the Rue Transnonain.[59] Nor was the trial without comedy: the speech of the lawyer for the *Messager* (of which no record has survived) was said to have "provoked in the audience a hilarity that all the gravity of the judges was not always able to forbid."[60]

In the end, the judge handed down a compromise verdict that avoided the larger, jurisprudential issues of the case and focused on technicalities. The memory of the dead ought to be respected, he said, and hence the heirs had justly protested the "flagrant insults" directed against the deceased. On the other hand, the physicians had evinced no malicious intent—they had been motivated instead by what the judge called an "indiscreet zeal for the scientific system they profess"—and hence the charge of defamation was inapplicable to the facts. The judge cautiously neglected to commit himself one way or another on the issue of whether that "system" was genuinely "scientific" or, if it was, whether it warranted special, free speech protection. He did, however, cite in favor of the plaintiffs that the phrenological reading of Madame Chéron's character had been "contradicted in an authentic manner" during the course of the trial by the attestations of the authorities of the commune in which she had lived. The judge declared himself incompetent to decide whether the phrenologists therefore owed the heirs monetary damages and, in Solomonic fashion, he divided the cost of the judicial proceedings between the parties.[61] It was, in short, neither a victory nor a defeat for phrenology, but rather a marker of its liminal status even in the best of times.

Also in 1836, the institutionalization of phrenology in France reached its zenith. The venerable if controversial Dr. F.-J.-V. Broussais, who had "converted" to phrenology shortly after 1828,[62] was allowed to give a public course on that subject at the Faculty of Medicine of Paris, where he had held a chair in general pathology since the 1830 Revolution. The course, it must be stressed, was not integrated into the regular medical school curriculum but was classified as a form of supplementary, elective instruction for which the Faculty had made available one of its amphitheaters. Nonetheless, the mere fact that phrenology had (literally) gotten its foot in the door—that, again, it had achieved liminal status—was a momentous occasion at the time.

Contemporary accounts of Broussais' lectures invariably stress the excitement of the large crowd in attendance, estimated as 3,000 strong by one horrified Cousinian.[63] A police report described the "noisy" audience as composed not merely of medical students but of students of all sorts who came to hear Broussais "combine political teachings with the principles of the purest materialism"; it went on to note that the professor's interactive style—he invited questions during his presentation—gave rise to nonstop interruptions and other such disorders.[64] The audience proved to be too excited for its own good, for its uncontrollably effervescent behavior resulted in the closing of the course after only three sessions, all of them held in the space of a single week. As Broussais memorably described the debacle in a personal letter, the students had, by the second session, taken to "invading" the preceding class in order to be assured a seat at the phrenology lecture; they made such a racket while waiting that they prevented the professor from giving his lesson. By the third session, the administration had, not inappropriately, locked the doors of the preceding class and posted guards both outside and inside. But, not to be deterred, the aficionados of phrenology carried off the guards and battered down the door. Broussais then conferred with the dean of the medical faculty and, in light of "these encroachments on the premises and this violence," temporarily suspended the course with the assurance that another, off-campus site would be found for it. However, when approached by the dean, the professors of the Jardin des Plantes refused to lend their facilities to Broussais. The medical students then raised a subscription to rent a private hall. But now the Paris Prefect of Police intervened, refusing to give Broussais the necessary authorization to teach a public course. He explained his position by characterizing Broussais' phrenological doctrines as "incendiary" and (here Broussais is probably embellishing the actual statement) "dangerous for a group of young people who are ardent, materialist, atheist, Anabaptist, anarchist, in a word, bad." At the very moment that phrenology was acquiring a significant token of official acceptance, its perceived political and religious radicalism once again consigned it to exclusion.[65]

In fact, phrenology was not necessarily out of tune with the socioeconomic biases of the July Monarchy. Just as it was construed in the opening years of the regime as fostering bourgeois political economy by pointing the way to a more efficient division of labor, one that scientifically matched workers' native talents to their jobs, so too the semiotic abilities it imparted were seen as aiding the bourgeoisie (and others) in navigating the increasingly anonymous environment of the nineteenth-century metropolis. In the full printed version of his abortive phrenology course, Broussais observed that the "art of dissimulating has been carried so far in our present state of civilization" that the experience through which we gradually learn the true character of another person almost always comes too late. Phrenology could, however, substitute for hard-earned experience, alerting us to and deciphering the "external, positive signs" of our fellows' mental makeup before we entered into friendships or business contracts.[66] Thus a standard application of Gall's science in this period was the hiring of domestic servants. A popular

Figure 6: Phrenological Self-Exploration through Palpation. Daumier's cartoon, which appeared in *Le Charivari* in March 1836 and was (untranslatably) entitled "Le Cranioscope-Phrénologistocope," captures the bewilderment of the French layman confronted with the new social expectation that he achieve scientific self-understanding. This bourgeois, wearing the black frock coat that was the sign of his class, seems to have purchased study aids: a treatise of phrenology as well as two porcelain models of the cranium indicating the position of the brain organs. The year 1836 marked the high point of phrenology's respectability in the eyes of the French scientific establishment; hence, Daumier's choice of a bourgeois rather than a working-class devotee is especially appropriate. Daumier's antic caption reads: "Yes, that's it. I have the bump of ideality, of causality, of locativity. It's a prodigiosity." (Benjamin A. and Julia M. Trustman Collection, Brandeis University Libraries)

phrenology manual written and illustrated by Spurzheim's son-in-law offered a visual image of the kind of woman who should *not* be employed as a nanny: one whose cranial conformation (large and nearly round) announced, even beneath her coiffure, "secretiveness" and "acquisitiveness" as well as a marked insufficiency of the requisite protuberances for "kindness" and "love of children" (*philogeniture*).[67] Reflecting the situation of the bourgeoisie after the abolition of the corporations, the same manual mentioned the workshop manager (*chef d'atelier*) as someone who could make good use of phrenology because his occupation required him to choose his employees from among strangers.[68] Insofar as phrenology offered a guide to those areas of nineteenth-century activity once safely regulated by corporate and community ties but now left to the forces of the market, it could readily serve practical, everyday bourgeois needs.

Yet the embourgeoisement of phrenology, which took place in early nineteenth-century Britain (where it then ushered in a strong, second-phase phrenological movement among the working classes),[69] never occurred in France. The letters of French phrenologists to George Combe, the Edinburgh lawyer turned leader of British phrenology, are peppered with laments about the comparative status of phrenology in the two countries. "Now I do not know that [any] French man has paid particular attention to Phrenology in order to establish this science. It is the greatest effort in them to allow its existence and importance. Be certain, you and your countrymen will be the best defenders and members of phrenology." Or, of a text by Combe just translated into French by Giovanni Fossati, an Italian-born phrenologist living in Paris: "It is a very strange thing that an elementary work on phrenology is, in France, the work of a Scot and an Italian, in France, I say, where Gall and Spurzheim, Germans, published their first and most important works. But in this country our science still encounters a mass of powerful adversaries. . . ."[70] One major factor that seems to have obstructed the implantation of phrenology among the French bourgeoisie was the quasi-hegemonic power to define the bourgeois psyche that Cousinianism acquired after 1832 by means of France's centralized system of secondary education, which had no analogue in Britain. Certainly, the increasing conservatism that characterized the July Monarchy after the working-class uprisings of the early 1830s played a role in placing phrenology out of bounds. In addition, the gravitas and high-flown dignity of the Cousinian *moi* must have made the comic aspects of popular phrenology all the more dissonant for potential consumers of Gall's science among the French middle classes.

The Imperative of Popularization

The double accusation "materialist and fatalist" routinely leveled against phrenology by its detractors was only half justified. While the first part of the accusation had a certain plausibility and could be honestly debated, no careful reader of Gall and Spurzheim could have seriously categorized their doctrine as fatalist. Early nineteenth-century phrenology never recommended passivity in the face of information about one's cerebral constitution. Rather, it taught that brain organs, though innate, were malleable to a limited but nonetheless meaningful degree. If people were born with certain talents and propensities, and if these could be revealed through scientific investigation, then the responsibility fell to those people, or to their parents, or, perhaps, to society as a whole to tailor a suitable education for them: one that encouraged the growth and expression of the brain organs controlling positive, socially useful traits and inhibited the growth and expression of those controlling negative, socially harmful ones. Phrenology was, in other words, a passionate summons to educational activism. Gall even identified it as such in the opening lines of the inaugural lecture he gave in Paris in 1808, shortly after his arrival in the French capital. The whole purpose of advancing scientific knowledge of the human race was, he said, "to give a clear direction to education" and "an appropriate impulsion to the different passions in order to make them the instruments of the particular happiness of the individual and of the general good of society."[71]

Hence, the idea that phrenology needed to be both popularized and applied to concrete, ameliorative projects was integral to the theory. Béraud expressed that ethos succinctly in 1848. "Phrenology," he said, "consists wholly in its practical application."[72] Decades earlier, Spurzheim's letters to his British counterpart George Combe revealed an almost obsessive concern with propagation. "I am very much obliged to you for the kindness of letting me know the various circumstances which may have some influence on the propagation of the doctrine," he writes on one occasion.[73] On another, "I am actually

[Spurzheim's Franglais for 'currently'] delivering a course of lectures, and I am much pleased with my auditors. They are gentlemen from all countries, and I am certain they will become disciples who will feel inclined to propagate phrenology."[74] Spurzheim championed the writing of phrenological case histories less from scientific considerations than from tactical ones connected to the central task of propagation:

> The knowledge of Phrenology, if true, must increase; it is, however, important to awake constantly the public attention. It is not necessary to write long articles. I wish the friends might begin to describe cases, just as is done with other branches of knowledge, medicine for instance, or surgery. *The common reader wishes to be amused with anecdotes.* Each fact is more convincing than all details of principles in my book.[75]

After the death of his wife, he rededicated himself to the phrenological cause: "Having lost her with whom alone and for whom alone I could have lived, I shall employ my whole mind to the propagation of phrenology."[76] The same ethos was expressed by a fictional phrenologist in a boulevard melodrama of 1834 coauthored by Auguste Luchet. Chided by friends for "killing himself" with long hours of public and private teaching, he rejoins, "Everyone on earth has his mission . . . Mine is to continue the work of my illustrious master, Gall; mine is to popularize with all my strength the admirable science that makes the good and bad penchants of a man legible on his head." What fuels his zeal is his belief that phrenological knowledge can reclaim society's outcasts. "Education must take hold of the dangerous child, combat his baneful penchants and neutralize their power by developing opposing penchants."[77]

To the meliorist commitment that formed an internal, logical reason for the phrenologists' support of the popularization of their science was joined an equally powerful sociological reason: if they were excluded from official science and from the state educational establishment, they would have to look downward in the social scale and find their allies among the people.

In opting for such a strategy, the phrenologists had before them the example of a fellow traveler, Auguste Comte. A staunch supporter of phrenology by the early 1820s and a founding member of the Paris Phrenological Society in 1831, Comte even adopted phrenological language in calling the type of government he envisioned the "organ" of the common good.[78] After attempting unsuccessfully to persuade the establishment of the truth of his positive philosophy, he decided that the political transformation he envisioned—that is, the transfer of the functions of government to a scientifically informed body that would expertly manage affairs for the good of society as a whole—instead required an appeal to the working classes. The workers had, after all, escaped the intellectual deformation effected in the privileged and powerful classes by the vicious educational regimen of the day, one that not only emphasized metaphysical philosophy and imaginative literature but also encouraged a narrow specialization that prevented an apprehension of the interconnectedness of all knowledge. The workers qualified, in other words, as the collective tabula rasa on which the positive philosophy could be readily imprinted.[79] Hence, beginning in 1830 and throughout the years of the July Monarchy, Comte gave a Sunday morning course in "popular astronomy" free of charge to the working classes of the third arrondissement of Paris; comprised of some two dozen weekly sessions, it was serious fare for such an audience as well as substituting for the Catholic Mass as a Sunday morning activity.[80] Whether deliberately or not, phrenologists gradually adopted a roughly Comtean model of propagation.

The Laudable Superficiality of Phrenology

Guizot's 1826 article "Abrégé" (see Chapter 5) had explicitly placed psychology in the category of sciences unsuited for popularization. Psychology of the introspective variety—the only variety Guizot recognized—could not, he argued, be adequately represented or communicated by a succinct account of its conclusions. It instead required the student to rediscover those conclusions personally through his own essays in interior observation, through a sounding of the depths of consciousness that could occur only at the end of a long period of formal schooling. Phrenologists, however, tended to make the opposite claim for their psychological science. Its insights, they said, were readily available to every comer. Easy-to-use visual abrégés of the doctrine—in the form of diagrams of the brain or plaster casts of the skull indicating the location of the different cerebral organs—were its stock in trade. Phrenology excelled in the production of "immutable mobiles," those enduring yet portable inscriptions that, according to Bruno Latour, both readily convey knowledge and persuade audiences of its scientific worth.[81] If the Cousinians emphasized mysterious depth (though never depth that precluded consciousness) as the salient characteristic of their psychology, the phrenologists almost boasted of superficiality: the surface of things, highlighted in the procedure of cranial palpation, announced the most valuable knowledge.

Claims about the ease of acquiring phrenological competence abound in the writings of advocates of phrenology. Years before Gall arrived in Paris, Charles Villers, who had translated Kant into French and was committed to informing the French about advances in knowledge on the other side of the Rhine, published a sympathetic account of phrenology in the form of an open letter to Georges Cuvier. It was not, he said, that Gall's research was the most significant of recent German scientific endeavors. He had singled it out, rather, because of its extraordinary potential for popularization. "The new theory is easily understandable, even among the least educated of people."[82] In the early 1820s, Ange Guépin described Gall's "system" to a boyhood friend as "entirely new yet very simple."[83] Calling on artists in 1829 to apply craniology to drawing and painting, Dr. Fleury Imbert, a Lyonnais phrenologist who had married Gall's young widow, anticipated the objections of his audience: "How to acquire all the details [of this science] if one hasn't studied it with undivided attention? . . . Aren't brain organs as numerous as shades of color? How to distinguish among them? How to become familiar with them? It's a Chinese alphabet." But he then went on to dismiss such worries out of hand. "It's only a question of some general data furnished by observation, only facts that everyone can, *without study*, verify everyday."[84] Most phrenologists were not as cavalier as Imbert, but they still believed that their science could be very readily absorbed and that simple pedagogical techniques would speed up the process.

Thus Spurzheim was pleased to report to Combe in 1831 that he had supervised the development of a phrenological study aid: a set of sixty plaster phrenological "specimens" that its manufacturer sold for two guineas. Spurzheim envisioned that it would find a market among those "auditors [of courses in phrenology] who complain that they have no opportunity of exercising their phrenological skill." Such a person might "study at home and exercise his eyes in seeing differences of size and form." The kit would also be useful in giving "private instruction in phrenology to children in families, as it is done with geography. . . ."[85]

Similarly, acknowledging his nomination for honorary membership in the fledgling Paris Phrenological Society in September 1831, Combe had words of advice for its secretary, Casimir Broussais. The "first care" of the Society should be "to accomplish the instruction of their members in the organology of the science." He spoke from personal experience, he assured Broussais *fils*. He had in Edinburgh "put skulls in the hands of the members and engaged them in writing down the development" (a term of art for the relative size of each brain organ). "They were astonished at first at the extent of their ignorance but *after some weeks of practice* were delighted in the progress they made in acquiring positive ideas."[86]

In sum, unlike Cousinian psychologists, phrenologists were committed to demystifying their special knowledge. They boiled it down for ease of transmission and emphasized its broad accessibility.

Channels of Popularization: *Cours libres* and *Almanachs populaires*

How could the advocates of phrenology bring their science to the people? Even after 1830, the French government posed obstacles to the dissemination of what one bureaucrat nervously described as a science "that so closely touches the principles on which society rests."[87] Keeping phrenology out of the official curricula of state-run institutions was only the government's first line of defense. A Napoleonic decree of 17 March 1808, still in force throughout the whole period of the *monarchie censitaire,* required authorization from the Ministry of Public Education for any so-called *cours libre*—that is, any lecture series taught in a public venue outside the state educational system. This requirement was, as the opening paragraph of this chapter has shown, the snare that kept Béraud off the podium. The Ministry's archives concerning early nineteenth-century petitions for *cours libres* are spotty; some phrenology courses that I have seen mentioned in printed sources have left no archival trace. Hence these archives cannot be trusted to tell us much about the absolute magnitude of phrenology instruction. But they do indicate the possibilities for government meddling: bureaucrats reviewed course petitions with considerable care and, in the end, had an arbitrary power of refusal. I will limit myself to just a few examples of petitions, both granted and rejected, from this period.

Two requests by physicians to teach phrenology courses free of charge in Lyon in 1844 were granted swiftly and straightforwardly. Both petitioners were well known to the local authorities; one practiced medicine on the outskirts of the city, the other was Fleury Imbert, a major figure in the French phrenological movement who, at the time of his petition, held a professorship at the city's Ecole de médecine. Back in 1829, Imbert had even won a concours for the position of chief surgeon at the Lyon hospital despite accusations that his well-known advocacy of phrenology necessarily identified him as an atheist.[88] What expedited decision-making on the 1844 petitions was the existence of criteria established by the medical school. It had explicitly adopted the liberal principle that instruction in all the branches of medicine ought to be made available to its students as long as unofficial courses were neither taught on its premises nor at hours that conflicted with the official curriculum.[89] But elsewhere clear guidelines of this sort seemed to be lacking.

In 1846, for example, a certain Dr. Funel petitioned the minister for permission to open a free public course in phrenology in Rouen. His request had already been favorably received by the mayor of the city, who had, in turn, referred him to the higher reaches of the bureaucracy for definitive approval. The minister requested a background check on Funel from the rector of the educational administrative district of Rouen, who discovered that the young doctor had only recently settled there and was "known by no one." The rector thus summoned Funel before him to gather the relevant information face to face; he learned that Funel had studied law before deciding to obtain a degree in medicine, that while attempting to set up a medical practice in Marseille he had taught phrenology for three years at the municipal school there, that he had relocated to Rouen to take up a post as physician to the English workers building the railroad between that city and Le Havre, and that he now wished to gain a local reputation by means of a course that would "pique the curiosity of the public." Grilled by the rector on how he intended to present "so delicate" a subject matter as phrenology, Funel was extremely forthcoming. He volunteered that the "reserve" he had shown in drawing out the implications of phrenological theory when teaching in Marseille had brought him "much praise from religious persons." That he hastened to name names, without knowing what kinds of connections the rector might have among the Marseille "notabilities," convinced the rector of his candor. He concluded that

Funel should be allowed to teach phrenology in Rouen because he would do so with due respect for "elevated questions of civic and religious morality." After all this labor on the part of his subordinate, the minister nonetheless decided not to grant the authorization, and he conveyed that information without any explanation whatsoever.[90] We can only assume that he was less sanguine than the rector about the lack of moral danger entailed in Funel's teaching.

Advocates of phrenology who were denied authorization to teach *cours libres* still had recourse to itinerant demonstrations of their craniological skills. They could also reach a popular audience by means of articles inserted in almanacs. "A thorough history of almanacs since the discovery of printing could be an excellent introduction to the use of books for the instruction of the most numerous classes." So began the entry on almanacs in a left-leaning encyclopedia published during the July Monarchy. The entry went on to say that this genre, originally the work of astrologers offering meteorological predictions and physicians peddling hygienic advice, had assumed a decidedly partisan cast and a new role in early nineteenth-century France. "Today it can be said that almost every almanac circulated among the poor is under the influence of a religious, philosophical, or political opinion." As such, almanacs had become the auxiliaries of newspapers; they were "arms of propaganda that each system, each party, annually sends out across France, beyond the habitual circle of traffic in books."[91]

The *Almanach populaire de la France,* where (as mentioned in the opening section) Auguste Luchet's attention-getting article on phrenology appeared in 1837, was one of the most notorious instances of the genre. Its editor, the ex-Carbonaro Frédéric Degeorge, was a provincial journalist, vigorous defender of the freedom of the press, and republican activist with a network of contacts in Paris. He introduced the *Almanach populaire* in 1836 as a national and far more politically outspoken version of his earlier, local creation, the *Almanach populaire du Pas-de-Calais.* For the first four years of its existence, the *Almanach populaire* was unceasingly pursued by the government for its seditious content: the seizure of all extant copies and the indictment of editor, printer, and contributing authors on press violations became something of an annual ritual.[92] Bureaucratic memoranda concerning the 1837 edition convey the alarm that this little publication inspired in the authorities. A letter of the Paris Prefect of Police to the Minister of

Justice described "several articles that engender in the minds of readers sentiments hostile to the government and that excite in the lowest classes of society animosity against the classes that are above them by dint of function or fortune." The *Almanach populaire* was a "scurrilous lampoon" *(libelle),* a "dangerous work poisoning the capital." Its large print run and modest cost per copy (50 centimes) enhanced the threat it posed.[93] In Lyon, recently the scene of the silkworkers' uprising, the attorney general used lurid language to announce the confiscation of a shipment of the *Almanach populaire* at a local bookstore "to which it had been sent to infest our working class."[94] In the fall of 1837, a police chief in the Ministry of the Interior anxiously reported an article in the *Bon Sens,* a newspaper edited by Luchet. It had announced provocatively that, far from being deterred by government harassment, Degeorge had already sent the next year's edition of the *Almanach populaire* to press.[95]

Anxiety emanated from other sectors of French society as well. Reviewing the latest edition of the *Almanach populaire,* a newspaper with religious sympathies sternly specified the features that made that publication unsuitable for its working-class readers: the utter absence from its pages of references to the Christian faith or to such moral virtues as temperance, thrift, patience, and resignation. While writing for *le peuple* was, said the reviewer, a "sacred calling" in principle, the *Almanach populaire* failed the avid mass audience that had bought 50,000 copies in 1838 and double that number in 1839. "It reminds the people of their rights but not of their duties." Happily, continued the journalist, a new instance of the genre, the thoroughly Christian *Almanach des Bons-Conseils,* would soon challenge its dominance.[96]

The government carried out its seizure and destruction of the 1837 edition of the *Almanach populaire* so effectively that my search of Paris libraries and archives failed to turn up a single copy of it. But Degeorge reprinted Luchet's phrenology article in the 1838 edition, which was apparently less thoroughly extirpated by the police and which additionally contained the text of Luchet's (successful) self-defense before his accusers at the criminal court of the Pas-de-Calais. So celebrated had the whole affair become that an advertisement for the 1838 edition announced Luchet's speech in bold type and endorsed his original, inflammatory article.[97]

Entitled "A Word on the Direction to Give to the Teaching of Phrenology," Luchet's article called for the shift in the audience of phrenology that would soon occur in fact. It argued that phrenology was by its nature an "entirely democratic science" whose "future [and] triumph" lay in its implantation among the people. "To wish to limit phrenology, as has been done until now, to the supposed instruction of rich and well-bred people . . . is to throw before swine the pearls of the legacy of Gall." The rich, presently cosseted by society, had no incentive to appreciate Gall's message about the essential cerebral equality of mankind:

> You will never persuade a *juré censitaire* [a man whose high tax payment qualified him for service as a juror under the July Monarchy], living in perpetual terror of the possible unleashing of base passions, that he, a notable, a member of the electorate, who has never lacked bread, would have been able to become a criminal—just like the accused man he is about to condemn—if one day poverty shook up certain of his cerebral forces. . . . How would you ever get into the head of a cabinet minister or a king the smallest grain of sympathy for phrenology, for a science that recognizes no privilege of heredity or caste, that banishes crowned foolishness from the throne and replaces it with the intelligence of commoners?

In Luchet's implicit scenario, then, phrenology might teach a rich man willing to listen that he possessed a large bump of theft and that the only reason that he was more law-abiding than his poor counterpart was not because of his intrinsic moral superiority but simply because his cerebral constitution had never been tested by hunger. It might teach a king or cabinet minister willing to listen that his intellectual faculties were inadequate for his position and that he ought to step down in favor of a humble but intellectually gifted man. But what rich man or king or cabinet minister would be willing to listen?

Hence Luchet concluded, "The time has come for phrenology to construe its mission in a completely different way," to seek an audience among workers rather than elites. The poorest classes had "a sole and precious capital" of which they could not be despoiled: intelligence. Phrenology would teach them to "make use of [this] power which, appropriately exercised, can replace and surpass all other powers." Once "applied to the instruction, to the consolation of the people"— consolation because it would show them that they were not, as they thought, devoid of resources—phrenology would have "prodigious results": "What colossal reform, what immense transformation! Nothing, it seems to me, can give an adequate idea of the energetic, invincible development of this innumerable mass of intelligences and wills magically awakened from their mortal torpor."[98] The rendition of phrenology Luchet presented here thus largely ignored Gall and Spurzheim's precise physiological and craniological teachings. It stressed politically charged themes: the malleability of our cerebral endowment by means of education; the democratic distribution of both positive and negative traits throughout all classes of society, so that no class could claim intrinsic moral or intellectual superiority.

Other popular almanacs also disseminated information about phrenology. The *Almanach prophétique,* a creation of the 1840s, told readers about Dumoutier's phrenological museum in Paris, describing it reverently as a place of "calm and silence, [where] everything invites contemplation and meditation." In the course of reviewing the plaster casts of famous heads displayed there, it articulated the educational credo of phrenology, regretfully exclaiming about one notorious criminal of the day, "Lacenaire, whom society repelled from its bosom when it could have made a useful man of him."[99] But as befit its name, it more typically (if completely improperly) conflated phrenology with the occult arts of prediction that were the traditional stuff of almanacs.[100]

Far more explicitly political and far more thorough in its account of phrenology was the *Almanach de la communauté* of 1843, condemned by the government and then reincarnated in 1844 as the otherwise identical *Almanach de l'organisation sociale.* Its title page bore the inscription "by various communist writers," and the principal force behind it was Théodore Dézamy, a self-proclaimed communist who had earlier served as secretary to the theorist of utopian communism, Etienne Cabet. Dézamy was frankly materialist. When the 1844 *Almanach* was successfully prosecuted for press violations, among the offensive passages cited was: "We are not among those who hope for happiness beyond the grave. Happiness is on earth. . . ."[101] The *Almanach de la communauté* contained a long article, "Phrenology: A Chapter on the Physics of the Human Mind," by the Belgian phrenologist Napoléon Barthel, a corresponding member of the Paris Phrenological Society.[102] The article was intended as an *abrégé,* a succinct introduction to Gall's science, emphasizing its development after Gall and describing the purview of each of the brain organs.[103] Since Dézamy and his fellow editors announced the "vulgarization of social science" as the primary goal of the *Almanach,* it is clear that phrenology was their preferred scientific account of the domain of human mental life and the one they regarded as suitable for life in a communist society.

The Company It Kept

Nothing better shows the left-wing political identity of phrenology under the July Monarchy than the company it kept—that is, the cluster of radical pedagogical schemes that tended to gravitate toward it or to which it extended its hand in fellowship. Although these schemes and phrenology sometimes conflicted in their details, they all belonged to a common universe of discourse that featured some combination of physiology, political opposition, and pedagogical reform for the betterment of the working classes. All participated in a veritable ferment of utopianism that marked the French public sphere in the decades leading up to the 1848 Revolution, when highly inventive blueprints for nonviolent social change, usually claiming scientific status, vied for the attention of likely constituencies and potential benefactors. The Saint-Simonians wished to abolish inheritance, place productive forces in the hands of those best qualified to exploit them maximally, and in addition "emancipate the flesh"; the followers of Cabet wished to establish a perfectly egalitarian community of a million inhabitants called Icaria, where property and dwelling places would be collective, industry planned, and money banished; the Fourierists wished to make all aspects of life, especially work, sensually pleasurable and to reorganize society and economy into small, autonomous communities called phalansteries. Though phrenology contained no explicit social doctrine, contemporaries were inclined to perceive and cultivate its affinities with pre-Marxian socialism.

Since Fourierism derived from a theory of "passional attraction" conceived on the Newtonian model, Fourier's disciples seemed automatically to assume that phrenology disclosed the specific brain physiology undergirding the founder's social ideas. "The points of agreement are numerous," wrote Charles Pellarin in a detailed, two-part article in 1833. "What is initially striking about Gall's enumeration of the faculties is that the first three, whose location is the best documented, are also those that Monsieur Fourier has so well defined and even hierarchized among themselves: love, familial feeling, friendship."[104] Fourier, in turn, wrote a long, testy response to Pellarin, "protest[ing] against any agreement" between his incontestable and lasting discoveries and "these [other] doctrines temporarily in vogue." For one thing, phrenology situated all the passions in the brain, thus "dethroning" what Fourier regarded as their true seat, the heart. For another, phrenologists failed to recognize that the evaluation of any individual passional constitution was primarily a function of the prevailing social order: whether it was the repressive "civilization" of Fourier's own era or the "harmony" that would be inaugurated in the phalanstery, an institution devoted to permitting the full expression of its members' natural passions while providing a scientifically engineered social context in which those passions would necessarily be harnessed for useful ends. Once human social life had been relocated to the phalanstery, observed Fourier, there would be "no disadvantage in discovering that a child possesses instincts that would lead, *in civilization,* to theft or murder," for those same instincts would be safely rechanneled in a socially beneficial direction. Fourier assumed that "in civilization"—which was, after all, the social milieu of phrenology—a comparable discovery would have punitive or exclusionary consequences: he envisioned the preemptive hanging of an honest man displaying the cranial protuberance for murder, or the cancellation of the wedding when the fiancée was found to possess an outsized bump of coquetry.[105]

Thus, like many of his contemporaries, Fourier ignored the profoundly meliorist orientation of phrenology, mistaking it for a fatalistic doctrine. But when we add this meliorism to the equation, we cannot help but be struck, pace Fourier, by the important similarities between Fourierism and phrenology. Both sought to know people's innate passional givens and to use them as raw material susceptible of deliberate transformation. Not surprisingly, then, adepts moved back and forth over the boundary between the two doctrines, as through a porous membrane. In Lyon, for example, the supporters of phrenology, including their leader, Fleury Imbert, were largely "physicians who had grown up in Saint-Simonian or Fourierist milieux."[106] In 1836 Imbert even published an open letter to Victor Considérant, Fourier's chief disciple, urging that phrenology and Fourierism join forces; it ended with the rousing prediction, "You will be a phrenologist."[107] The republican socialist Ange Guépin, introduced to phrenology (as we have seen) while still a medical student in Paris, went on to embrace Fourierism in the early years of the July Monarchy.[108] He would later scold Fourier for failing to use extant science in his laudable project of creating a social science, a failure exemplified by his "substitution of a new psychology for that physiology known today as phrenology."[109] Charles Pellarin himself was, in 1833, simultaneously writing for a Fourierist journal and, as a naval doctor, attending Broussais' clinical visits at Val-de-Grâce and accompanying the celebrated physician to the dissection theater where, "infatuat[ed] . . . with phrenology," he measured and weighed brains.[110] Prosper Dumont, the French translator of Combe, told the Scotsman that Fourier's ideas so thrilled him when he first encountered them in 1832 that he immediately began to "verify [them] by phrenology."[111]

Two visionary pedagogical schemes of the day were also linked to phrenology. One was the "positive education" of the man known simply as Colonel Raucourt. A graduate of the Ecole polytechnique and a state engineer of bridges and roads, Raucourt had the classic background of a Saint-Simonian, but instead of joining that movement, he struck out on his own. Social change, he decided, could be achieved only by exerting transformative pressure on the individual worker, to whom it was "indispensable to teach the art of knowing and commanding oneself." Like Comte, Raucourt installed himself in the *mairie* of the third arrondissement—a neighborhood apparently favored by utopian pedagogues—where he offered the working class a "free course in positive education"; having been approached by a benevolent manufacturer, he also taught workers privately in a Paris atelier.[112]

Phrenology soon reached out to positive education. Luchet began his article on phrenology in the 1837 edition of the *Almanach populaire* with a long quote from Raucourt, treating him as if he were a phrenologist and concurring that the use of a scientific form of pedagogy to educate the people was the key to all desirable social and political change.[113] Also in 1837, Broussais presented a long report on Raucourt's project to the Paris Phrenological Society, emphasizing its many parallels with Gall's science. Raucourt's pedagogy was based, he told his audience, on a rudimentary physiological conception of the five senses and a sixth, called *entente*. This additional sense was basically equivalent to the faculty of comparing and judging "to which we assign a particular organ in the brain." The colonel inculcated a modality of *savoir-choisir* in his pupils which, Broussais noted, affirming a stereotype of the working class, was directly opposed to their natural psychological habits:

> *Savoir-choisir* consists in. . . . disentangling the consequences, either for the external world or for themselves, of all the impulses that move them to act. Far from seeking to dissimulate, or to keep awareness of these impulses from themselves, *as is customary among the people,* Monsieur Raucourt trains his pupils to uncover them. The consequences are each day more strongly felt, and the motivation to repel certain suggestions [of the impulses] and to listen to others continually acquires additional weight.

Raucourt thus engaged his pupils in a "constant struggle of intelligence against instincts," a struggle familiar to applied phrenology as well. Nor was this struggle coded in religious terms; its goal was "neither to please the divinity nor to make oneself worthy of the blessings of a future life." Hence the adjective "positive" that Raucourt aptly gave to his pedagogy, which was truly founded "not on fictions but on facts that are within the reach of the senses." The pedagogy's secular orientation accorded fully with that of phrenology.

Broussais also noted divergences. Raucourt lumped all the impulses together under the name "animality," which he situated not in the brain but "in the manner of Cabanis . . . in the heart, stomach, and sexual organs"; his physiological theory thus lacked the analytic precision afforded phrenology by its large repertory of specific brain organs. Furthermore, Raucourt had devised a "philanthropic" pedagogy useful to the working classes but not to the higher classes of society. Its goal was to silence the visceral, pleasure-seeking impulses in those whose material circumstances could not, realistically, satisfy them. It failed to recognize the just claims of "our physical organization" and offered no useful guidance to those in a position to follow the biddings of the impulses and to seize wealth, honors, and power. Phrenology was, by contrast, a psychology suited for all classes of society.[114]

Responding to Broussais in print, Raucourt politely demurred from some of the physician's conclusions, especially those concerning the antireligious bent of positive education. But like Broussais, he wanted to minimize the quarrel and emphasize the strong family affinity between their two doctrines. The Paris Phrenological Society, he said warmly, followed the "scientific method that is ours"—that is, "simple observation of the phenomena of nature." Their differences in "viewpoint and language" paled before their common commitment to fact and to the "social sciences."[115]

Another, more radically egalitarian pedagogical movement of the 1830s was Joseph Jacotot's "intellectual emancipation," which held that master and pupil were equally ignorant but could nonetheless engage in fruitful mutual instruction.[116] Jacotot gave the name "degradation" (*abrutissement*) to the belief in one's own intellectual superiority, which he defined as regarding oneself able to judge other people while refusing to submit to their judgment. The remedy for *abrutissement* was the procedure followed in his educational institutions, where the would-be judge received the following admonition: "Sir . . . sing your little song; the child will sing his, and you will judge one another."[117] Jacotot intended his pedagogy as an antidote to the loathsome intellectual hierarchy that reigned in the state educational system. In his antic, somewhat opaque prose style, he made that point by mentioning both Victor Cousin and the teaching of philosophy in the lycée:

> At first I sensed that a father, however ignorant he was himself, could educate his son. I imagined how much furor that revelation would have to arouse in all the employees of the Université, from the professor of the sixth [i.e., the lycée philosophy class] to the Grand Master. Picture Cousin, the chief boiler-maker (*père chaudronnier*), meeting by chance Monsieur Villemain and wanting to persuade the director of public instruction that each of them could teach music to their children even though the director was as ignorant of music as the boiler-maker. . . .[118]

Given the shared oppositional credentials of phrenology and intellectual emancipation, it is not surprising to learn that Jacotot received a visit from Broussais,[119] who subsequently urged the founder's physician son to attend the meetings of the Paris Phrenological Society. Dr. H.-V. Jacotot instead read the Society's journal and was dismayed by the phrenologists' axiomatic acceptance of intellectual inequality, the diametric opposite of the Jacotists' own belief in what they called *homophrénie*.[120] But that the two doctrines agreed in spirit and could be combined in practice is seen in the case of Ange Guépin. The socialist politician from Nantes who permanently embraced phrenology lent his enthusiastic support to Jacotot's intellectual emancipation, or the "new method," as he called it. He went so far as to liken the "old method" to the use of swaddling clothes for infants. "In the time of our fathers, swaddling clothes produced the most baneful results. They killed the weakest and crippled many; only the hardiest escaped."[121]

Women as Consumers of Phrenology

The physiological basis of phrenology offered potential resources for a conception of women that accentuated their difference from men and could therefore argue easily for their inferior abilities. But, as the story of Cousinianism has abundantly shown, the internal logic of a psychological theory does not necessarily predict the uses to which that theory will actually be put in a specific historical context. Just as a theoretically gender-neutral Cousinianism excluded women from possession of a *moi,* so a phrenology seemingly prone to invidious gender distinctions tended, at least in the context of early nineteenth-century France, to be welcoming to women. This attitude was primarily a function of phrenology's Enlightenment belief in improvement through education, which led its supporters to envision a progressive integration of women into the public sphere. It was additionally a consequence of phrenologists' genuine open-mindedness and empiricist curiosity, their sense that their infant science as yet knew little about the relative mental strengths and weaknesses of the two sexes. For example, musing on the faculty of "concentratedness," which manifested itself in "stick[ing] to an object," Spurzheim asked Combe, "Do you think that the female sexe (sic) has this power stronger?" He himself thought so "as to their feelings" but doubted that "it is also the case as to their intellectual faculties." Despite the stereotypical nature of his hunches, he ultimately suspended judgment until more data could be collected, admonishing his colleague, "[L]et us listen to observation."[122]

Phrenology's welcoming attitude toward women resulted, finally, from its failure to win official acceptance: its own outsider status induced it to throw in its lot with that of society's marginal groups.

Thus, while Caroline Angebert doubted that she would be admitted, even as a one-time auditor, to a Sorbonne lecture by Cousin, phrenologists typically went out of their way to make their public courses accessible to women. At the Athénée de Paris, where Gall and then his disciple Fossati taught phrenology, women's attendance was encouraged by reduced subscription fees.[123] When in 1808 Gall, still smarting from the accusations of corrupt morals he had received in Vienna, asked his female auditors to absent themselves from those of his lectures treating the phrenology of sex, a woman protested the exclusion in the pages of the *Journal des dames et des modes.*[124] From phrenology's first introduction in France, then, women seemed to regard instruction in it as their due. In Metz, where in 1834 Dr. Scoutetten gave a course on phrenology to an overflowing crowd in the largest meeting room in the city hall, women showed up in significant numbers. He noted with pleasure: "Once again the phrenology course has been the scene of a new phenomenon in the provinces, one that holds the greatest interest for the civilization of the future: the appearance of ladies. At several lectures more than a hundred of them were counted."[125] When Dumoutier opened a phrenological museum in 1836 as the arm of the Paris Phrenological Society devoted to propagating Gall's science among the laity (it permanently displayed a collection of two hundred skulls and was the locus of free courses on phrenology throughout the school year), the invitation to his inaugural lecture explicitly noted, "Seats will be reserved for ladies."[126]

The media of the period depicted women as eager consumers of phrenology. In Luchet's boulevard melodrama, *Le brigand et le philosophe,* two guests at a party argue about the validity of phrenology. Among those in attendance, it is a flock of women who follow the debate most closely. "Ask Magnus [the philosopher-phrenologist of title]," the hostess urges them, and then, turning to Magnus, she adds, "These ladies absolutely want to know." He then explicates Gall's science "to the ladies who surround him."[127] During its inaugural year of 1832, the *Journal des femmes,* written by and for women and dedicated to female emancipation through education, included a long quasi-fictional article called "The Phrenology Lesson." It opens with one bourgeois lady bursting into the bedroom of a friend. From beneath the cashmere shawl that envelops her, she removes "a plaster head covered with numbers and criss-crossed with lines." The friend responds with a fit of giggles. Far from being perplexed by the strange object, she picks up a copy of the *"Manual of Phrenology* of Dr. Spurzheim, which was on her dressing table," and hands it to her visitor. She then goes over to her glass-enclosed armoire and takes out a similar plaster head. Each woman has been pursuing, on her own, the study of phrenology.[128]

Can Phrenology Ground a Self?

Like sensationalism, phrenology posited a material substratum of mind that was not only logically divisible by dint of its sheer materiality but also explicitly plural in fact. The bevy of discrete, atomistic sensations that came together to constitute mind in Condillac's theory had their counterpart in the multiplicity of brain organs in Gall's. Neither theory possessed an obvious means to overcome the plurality it posited nor to convert that plurality into the unified entity commonly referred to as the self. But the phrenologists went further along this continuum than did their sensationalist predecessors. While Locke and Condillac insisted, with varying degrees of zeal, on the capacity of their psychological theory to ground a unitary self, French phrenologists tended to doubt that such a self was either necessary or useful. That shockingly heterodox position—and one senses a certain delight that accompanied their articulation of it—marked yet another area in which they differed from the Cousinians, the masters of self-talk.

Among the supporters of phrenology, Auguste Comte presented the phrenological doctrine of the self in its bluntest and broadest form. In Lesson 45 of his *Cours de philosophie positive*, written at the end of 1837, he railed against "psychology," his name for the would-be science that he conspicuously omitted from the complete catalog of positive sciences presented in the *Cours*. Psychology, as Comte understood the term, attempted to investigate mind by using the method of introspection. But that method was inherently defective and self-contradictory. As Comte had argued in the opening lesson of the *Cours,* any essay in interior observation bogged down in the merging of subject and object; the *moi* could not simultaneously act and see itself acting, suffer and contemplate its own suffering. As soon as observation began, the fleeting phenomenon it sought to pin down disappeared, replaced by the very act of reflection. Only the observer remained; there was nothing left to observe.[129] An inevitably futile psychology had, in Comte's view, been recently supplanted by phrenology, which exteriorized mind in brain, thus rendering it genuinely observable and the proper object of a positive science. Moreover, within Comte's three-stage theory of conjoint epistemological and social progress, psychology was mired in the second, metaphysical stage, which had simply substituted abstractions for the divinities of the theological stage while persisting in the childish habit of explaining the world by reference to unknowable ultimate causes. Phrenology renounced such childishness and maturely contented itself with the kind of limited explanation offered by the discovery of lawful regularities among phenomena.

Within this schema, Comte regarded the self (*moi*) as a creature of psychology and of the discredited metaphysical stage. It was little more than a variant on the theological "soul," duplicating the latter's mysterious immateriality and perfect unity. But positive scientists were, he noted, under no obligation to carry around the old theologico-metaphysical baggage. Able "to see, unhindered, the true state of things and to reproduce it in their theories with scrupulous exactitude," they recognized that, "far from being single, human nature is in reality eminently multiple." By "multiple" Comte meant (as he put it in one of his typically tortured and ungainly phrases) "almost always solicited in different directions by several very distinct and fully independent powers among which equilibrium is very painfully established since in most cases none of them is pronounced enough to acquire spontaneously a high degree of preponderance over all the others." Given the multiply importuned brain-and-nervous-system that he equated with the human mind, Comte concluded that the "famous theory of the *moi*" represented a "purely fictive condition."[130]

But where did the pervasive fiction of the self come from? Comte believed that it originated in the experience, subsequently abstracted and reified by the metaphysicians, of periods of harmony among the competing forces in a healthy organism. Thus modestly and realistically defined as a transient period of organismic accord, the self belonged to lower animals as much as to human beings—despite the claims of its metaphysical proponents that it was the infallible mark of human personhood. A cat, observed Comte gravely, very likely possessed such a self: "without knowing how to say 'I,' [it] does not habitually mistake itself for another"! The same was true of a host of other vertebrates of a lesser complexity than man. (When one descended far enough down the zoological scale, however, animals lacked the nervous capabilities to produce and experience the *sentiment composé* associated with the self.) In fact, certain higher animals might well have an even stronger "feeling of personhood" than humans do "because of their more isolated mode of life." Rather than being a badge of superiority, in other words, a self simply translated the lack of an organized social life—the social life that would, in Comte's theory, characterize humanity once the positive stage of history had been ushered in and sociology had for the first time been constituted as a science.[131]

Thus phrenology perfectly suited the future social state that Comte heralded. The brain organs and their correlative mental traits concretized the so-called multiplicity of human nature. They enabled the individual to operate not as the enclosed subject of rights featured in liberal political thought (which, after all, only epitomized the fallacies of the metaphysical stage of history) but instead as a loose and versatile assemblage capable of dispersion through a network of duties to and functions in society. Finding only merit in the fragmentation of the entity commonly known as the self, phrenology used the discrete pieces to construct a truly social human being.

Comte took up this theme again in the opening lecture of his *Traité philosophique d'astronomie populaire,* the published version of his course for workers in the third arrondissement of Paris. Here he argued that the "positive spirit" was "alone susceptible of directly developing the social sentiment." Those who remained trapped in the metaphysical worldview might bemoan the egoism of the age, but they could only reinforce it, given the "necessarily personal nature of such a philosophy." The chief categories by which these metaphysicians organized the world were the *moi* and the *non-moi.* (Without explicitly identifying them, Comte thus pointed to the Cousinians as a chief instance of the guilty party.) The *non-moi* was the negative name "confusedly" given to the "vague ensemble" of everything other than one's own self, even other humans. In such an impoverished conceptual universe, "the notion of the 'we' (*nous*) can find no place." What the positive philosophy sought, said Comte, purposely playing on the Cousinian term for individual consciousness, was to familiarize people with the "*sentiment intime* of social solidarity."[132] Positivists and phrenologists, who did not regard saying "I" as an especially worthy goal, apparently knew how to say "we."

Other proponents of phrenology expressed a view of the *moi* similar to Comte's but lacking his strong social accent. Writing the article "Phrenology" for a household encyclopedia in the 1830s, Dr. Fossati immediately noted his disinclination to personify the mind. He preferred to consider *esprit* as a "collective noun, the conventional term for expressing the ensemble of brain functions or, if you will, the unknown cause that makes the brain . . . capable of manifesting this or that qual-ity." But, he warned, if we "personify this word or this unknown cause" and assign to it attributes other than simple organic functions, we enter on the false path followed by "our predecessors in philosophy, who got lost in abstract reasoning instead of setting their course by observation and induction." Among the benighted personifiers of the mind, it turns out, are those contemporaries of Fossati's who take the *moi* as a central category and treat it as a "real being." Such a *moi,* he noted in an arrest-ing metaphor, "has the effect on us of a marionette in a comedy for overgrown children."[133] Only children, or adults who clung to out-moded childish beliefs, could take a puppet—or the patently fictive concept of the *moi,* its strings pulled by such invented metaphysical abstractions as Liberty and Free Will—for a real being.

François Broussais also considered the *moi* from a phrenological per-spective in a long paper delivered before the Academy of Moral and Political Sciences in 1838. Given the formal setting, it is not surprising that the paper lacks the polemical bite of Comte's comparable state-ments. But, apart from the missing social dimension—more a function of Broussais' way of thinking than of the circumstances of presenta-tion—the content of the paper is as consistent with Comte's views as the style is different.

Like Comte, Broussais wants to grant something like a self to all ver-tebrates, not just to human beings. "[F]earing to profane [the] word [person] by applying it to animals," however, he ascribes to lesser verte-brates not the feeling of personhood of Cousinian fame but a more mor-ally neutral "feeling of individuality." He cites in favor of this view his own observations of cats and dogs in front of a mirror: at first they take their reflections for another animal of the same species and attempt to engage it in play, but after meeting with repeated failure, they lose inter-est in the reflection, "which seems to indicate that they have recognized themselves in it." Dubious logic, perhaps, but it does show that Brous-sais shares Comte's inter-species democratizing impulse with respect to the self and agrees that one cat is unlikely to mistake itself for another.[134]

Decorously reserving the terms *moi* and *sentiment personnel* for humans, Broussais marks his distance from the Cousinians in every other way. He denies that the *moi* is innate, citing empirical evidence to argue that it is instead a child's gradual acquisition. (A child "designates himself by the name that others give him. He will not say, 'I want bread' but rather 'Paul, Charles, [or] Ernest wants bread.'") He denies that the *moi* exists a priori, asserting that it develops in dialectic interaction with the outside world: people with impaired sensory organs have less experience of the external world and hence a weaker sense of self. He warns against personifying it as an independent agent. He chides those who "dematerialize" it. He refuses to adopt toward it the reverential attitude of the introspective psychologists. Classifying it as merely one faculty among many, he reserves his reverence for the organized matter that makes up our bodies:

> Let us cease being astonished at the wonders of the *moi.* The other faculties are no less wondrous. Do we think that one of our faculties is any more explicable than another? That would be a grave error. For us, incomprehensibility resides in nervous tissue. . . . It is there that all miracles happen, starting with that of sensibility, which has no need of the *moi,* nor of the feeling of personhood, nor even of the feeling of individuality, to manifest itself to us plainly.

And if the *moi* is only one faculty among many, it is neither a hierarchically superior one nor a directing force. "It is not then possible to establish a central *moi* within the group of our faculties," Broussais asserted. The mind contained no central deliberating agency that took in data from the external world, combined them with mental contents, and then issued "orders for execution." Broussais repeated the dictum: "[There is] no unique central point, but an ensemble . . ."[135]

The phrenologists thus demoted the self, according it none of the grandeur that it had within the Cousinian system. To be sure, both Cousinians and phrenologists treated the mind as a microcosm of the larger world, but they understood the analogy in different ways. The Cousinians projected the three elements of consciousness upward and outward onto a metaphysical canvas where sensibility corresponded to nature, will to mankind, and reason to God. Mankind, or human society, was composed of active and willful selves, each complete within itself. The phrenologists, and most explicitly the Comteans among them, omitted the metaphysical dimension altogether and conceived of the mind as directly analogous to society, and in particular to a society formed by the division of labor. This functional connection of the two divisions of labor—the mental and the social one—was evident in phrenological discourse, which routinely mentioned the scientific determination of job aptitude as one of the major social applications of phrenology. Thus Thoré: "By indicating the capacities of each person, phrenology will enable society to direct all its members toward their specialties." No longer will paternal fiat or the privileges of birth serve as an "obstacle to this normal and salutary [occupational] classification" according to aptitude.[136] Or Béraud: "How many young men are thrown into a career where their faculties, which would elsewhere make them superior, leave them mediocre and incapable!. . . . It is particularly in education, then, in choosing a career for children and even remaking adults, that phrenology is truly humanitarian."[137] When mapped onto the larger society, the multiplicity of brain organs and their tasks illustrated the mechanism of social solidarity through specialization of function as well as the fitness of unselved human beings for the social state.

Phrenological Subjectivity

As in the case of sensationalism, paucity of self-talk did not prevent phrenology from furnishing the conceptual basis and the language for a distinctive experience of interiority. That it did so was somewhat ironic for, while sensationalists frankly availed themselves of interior observation to obtain psychological knowledge, phrenology was supposed to operate only by observing objects (cranial protuberances and dissected brains), never by inhabiting the position of subject.

Nevertheless, phrenology could not entirely dispense with introspection. One of the more thoughtful critiques of Gall's science offered by a Cousinian made that point persuasively. In a book of 1839, Adolphe Garnier argued that a major difficulty in carrying out the phrenological project—a difficulty that typically fomented conflict among practitioners—was the identification of the brain organs: how many there were, what the scope of each consisted in. Garnier noted that the challenges inherent in this task concerned more than objective questions of cerebral localization. "Before assigning the seat of a faculty, one must . . . confirm the existence of the faculty by purely mental observation—that is to say, one must have a psychology." Even though phrenologists professed disdain for introspection, the founding fathers, Gall and Spurzheim, had surely been "endowed with a very high degree of psychological acuity."[138]

Spurzheim's long correspondence with George Combe offers rich evidence both of the problems entailed in identifying brain organs and of Spurzheim's own psychological flair. It also reveals the kind of fragmented or punctuated subjectivity-without-selfhood that adherence to phrenological principles encouraged.

In a letter of 1819, Spurzheim ruminated on the changes in the system of brain organs that he had introduced after his break with Gall some eight years earlier. Those changes were partly quantitative: where Gall had named twenty-seven organs, Spurzheim's list contained thirty-five. But writing in his somewhat awkward English, Spurzheim, who had grouped the organs into the affective and the intellectual, noted that principles of classification were also at issue:

> I am sorry to say that Dr Gall will not admit the ideas I have conceived since I left him. He continues to prefer a nomenclature according to the actions, to reject the difference between feelings and intellectual faculties, to attribute inquiry and judgment to the feelings; in short to speak of the doctrine as he did 10 years ago. . . . He admits still negative faculties, fear, for instance, as absence of courage. He attributes justice to benevolence. . . .[139]

A not insignificant portion of the Spurzheim-Combe correspondence consisted of give-and-take between the two men about how to define a brain organ. Combe had lighted upon an especially valuable specimen, the shoemaker Spence, much touted at the time for inventing a putative perpetual motion machine. A phrenological reading of his skull revealed a prominent organ of constructiveness. Spurzheim was at pains to specify the abilities that this organ controlled and those that it did not. He made the discrimination by means of the affect-intellect dichotomy that governed his scheme for classifying the organs. "Constructiveness does nothing but construct, and it can build what the other powers suggest, the model of a shoe, a loom, a wheel, &c . . . [It] may execute a model but it will not invent it. The purpose of its activity indicates the other powers which employ it. . . ."[140] He returned to this theme several months later. "You think that constructiveness implies a power of forming ideas of the thing to be constructed. I do not think so, the idea of the thing to be constructed is the result of intellectual faculties which desire also but whose characteristics are *to know.*" Constructiveness was an impulse without a specific object, he insisted, just as amativity "excites to love" without "determin[ing] us to prefer a fine figure to an ugly one."[141]

When Spurzheim turned to describing his own actions or states of mind, or (more often) those of others, he did so by pinpointing the particular brain organs that, according to his version of phrenological theory, had contributed to the outcome in question. He typically referred to these organs by number, thus highlighting the fragmented approach to mental life to which phrenology conduced. On one occasion he tried, citing "8" (acquisitiveness) and "10" (self-esteem), to help Combe decipher the motivations behind a slight he had received from Gall. The resulting analysis sounds odd and comic to the uninitiated:

> I do not think that Dr. Gall has not answered your invitation from the motive you have mentioned. I think it is mere idleness assisted by 10. Should his 8 have gained by it, then he would have taken the trouble of answering. For in the combat of 10 & 8 this commonly gains the victory. If 10 be alone, he forgets to answer the letters he receives.

Spurzheim's hostility toward his former mentor comes through in this letter even before he adds, slightly ungrammatically, "We both are no longer on friendly terms. . . ."[142] On another occasion, he complained about the behavioral norms of the French scientific community. Its members typically criticized phrenology in public while simultaneously pilfering phrenologists' ideas, using them without proper attribution. He ascribed this situation to the French national character, which he depicted numerically as insufficient in "14" (veneration, respect): "I make no appeal to 14 in this country," he concluded with disgust. "Here one is polite, social, agreeable, but we must not expect 14."[143]

Sometimes, in such analyses, the brain organs were named rather than numbered. "My little marvellousness was quite astonished to see Deville's collection," Spurzheim exclaimed, referring to the brain organ that occupied the eighteenth position on his list. "No other indeed can be compared to it."[144] Whatever his cerebral givens, viewing collections of skulls and plasters seems to have frequently brought Spurzheim's emotions to a high pitch of intensity. In 1822 he viewed the collection of a Monsieur Royer in Paris and confessed to Combe, "I must plead guilty for having taken from him several heads, particularly of monkies (sic), he had destined for your Society. I thought them necessary to me, and I could not help saying: charity begins at home." Now, by way of explaining his conduct, he invoked his wife's phrenological interpretation. She had zeroed in on the eighth organ. "Mrs. Sp. was with me to pick them out. She accused me that she had never seen my covetousness or bitter acquisitiveness so active as at that moment."[145]

A similar if more amateur use of phrenology can be seen in the copious personal jottings of the early nineteenth-century sculptor Pierre-Jean David, called David d'Angers. A specialist in busts of living celebrities, and an ardent republican in politics, he turned to phrenology (Gall's version of it) to aid his eye in seizing on the cranial characteristics that expressed personality traits.[146] For example, meeting the novelist Eugène Sue in the early 1830s, he noticed an absence of the "bumps" for music, construction, and poetry, only mediocre development of the bump of comparative discernment (*sagacité comparative*), and very prominent bumps for distinction and physical love. Sue's bump of "ideality" (Gall's term for the synthesizing power of imagination) combined its force with those for ruse, perseverance, and cruelty. David summed up these visual findings in a highly derogatory vignette: "This man is cruel, inflexible; he obviously relishes depicting human suffering, he eats human flesh, so to speak . . ."[147]

David turned the same phrenological eye on himself. A railway trip in 1840—surely a quintessential early nineteenth-century experience—caused him to ruminate on the brain organ of *sagacité comparative* and to locate in it an essential rational capacity of human beings:

> When one travels by railroad, the horses on the plain seem not to be moving even though they are. When one is in a stagecoach the horses regain—or at least seem to regain—their real movement. It is by comparison that we perceive life. The bump of *sagacité comparative* is the one that completes man. Without it, he is deficient. He is almost always prey to all sorts of aberrations. He is the slave of his senses, the plaything of all his illusions. He can have wit but never genius.[148]

Sometimes this kind of self-reflection emphasized even more the fragmentation of subjectivity attendant on a phrenological perspective. In a passage written in 1832, David attributed to the discernibly corporeal exertions of a single brain organ what another person might well describe and analyze as a complex experience of intellectual inspiration. "When an idea comes to me and moves me strongly by the enthusiasm that it procures for me, I feel very factually (*positivement*) an itch, a fire, in the spot of the bump of exaltation."[149]

Turns of phrase of this sort could sometimes have a tautological quality, even as they indicated a propensity to understand one's states of feeling in phrenological terms. Thus, describing his life as an impoverished journalist to his mother in 1835, Thoré substituted for the fact of his hearty appetite the brain organ presumably controlling it. "It is necessary to eat, and I have the misfortune of possessing a very developed organ of alimentivity."[150] The bachelor Prosper Dumont, Combe's French translator, demonstrated a more complex and artful manipulation of phrenological language in a letter to Combe's unmarried niece. Remembering the pleasant hours he had spent with her in Edinburgh, he said that he often vowed to visit her again. "You know that I love voyages," he continued, "and that *my organization* should lead me back frequently to that idea. For more than a year I have never desired any other voyage but that to Edinburgh."[151] Dumont achieved a fine compromise. It was in his organization—that is, his cerebral constitution, his complement of brain organs—to crave travel. But if that craving was a given for him, its object was not. In the elective sentimental preference for Miss Cox that gave form to Dumont's diffuse, constitutionally determined impulse to travel lay a touch of phrenological romance.

As these examples suggest, phrenology readily lent its initiates a mode of constructing their subjectivity. Like phrenological doctrine itself, the subjectivity produced was pointillist or punctuate. It focused on the discrete contributions of separate cerebral organs and, for better or worse, omitted any image of the whole.

Banishing Self-Talk

The trajectory of phrenology in France shows once again—this time in reverse—the strongly bourgeois affiliation of the unitary *moi*. Gall's disciples attempted to turn phrenology into a mainstream French doctrine, one that would minister to the needs of the country's elite, serve the growing industrial economy, and win institutionalization in the state educational system. That attempt failed and, by default, phrenology found a niche as an oppositional doctrine promoting the improvement of the condition of the working class. It advanced the argument that the lot of the individual worker would improve once he submitted to a cranial reading in order to learn, first, his mental aptitudes and hence his optimal location in the division of labor and, second, his dangerous tendencies, which could then be neutralized by a special educational program drawn up for him by the phrenological experts. Self-knowledge was thus the key to improvement. Encouraging self-scrutiny through a simple, graphic technology, phrenology clearly offered the worker a particular version of subjectivity. It offered him a self in the sense of that term I have used in this book: the individuated mental stuff and the individual's own representation of it.

But while valorizing the psychological dimension and providing a language for speaking about it, phrenology shunned self-talk per se. It distanced itself from the *moi* of the Cousinians and everything that the *moi* stood for: the sacralized quality of an immaterial self, the obscurity of the procedures for accessing the portion of consciousness that qualified as the self, the rigid principles of social hierarchy associated with selfhood. The Cousinians, of course, had thoroughly affirmed the *moi*. For them, it was a source of human efficacy and moral responsibility in the world and a point of connection between the human and the divine. The phrenologists saw it in wholly negative terms. One republican socialist close to phrenological circles put it memorably. Of the unhappy bourgeois whose meager aptitudes matched neither his elite education ("he studied in a *collège royal* [the name given to the lycée during the period of the constitutional monarchy] and emerged stuffed with scraps of Greek and Latin") nor his high place in the social division of labor, he said, "This man oozes the *moi* and the greed for gain from every pore."[152]

Epilogue

> When you have just taken the *bachot* at the age of seventeen with the
> "I think, therefore I am" of Descartes as your text and you open *The
> Psychopathology of Everyday Life* and you read the famous episode of
> Signorelli with its substitutions, combinations and displacements,
> implying that Freud was simultaneously thinking of a patient who had
> committed suicide and of certain Turkish mores, on so on—when you
> read all that, your breath is simply taken away.
>
> *Jean-Paul Sartre*

With the marginalization of phrenology in the late 1840s, and the
strong reaffirmation of the unitary *moi* that it represented, we come to
the end of our principal story. But to tie up some loose ends and grasp
more fully the significance of Cousin's project, we need to look ahead
into the latter half of the nineteenth century. This epilogue will consider
three aspects of the post-1850 history of Cousinian self-talk, all hinted
at in the body of the text: the fate of the internal contradictions of Cousinian psychology with respect to its denial of selfhood to workers and to
women, respectively; and the remarkable longevity of Cousinianism, or,
more precisely, of certain of its signature psychological elements, in the
philosophy curriculum of the lycée. Finally, turning to a theme that I
have not yet touched upon, I will briefly sketch out the implications of
the nineteenth-century contest of psychologies for its much more
famous successor, the so-called discovery of the unconscious that took
place at the fin-de-siècle.

Vindicating the Workingman: The *Affaire* Jacques

As Chapter 4 has shown, nothing in the internal logic of Cousin's psychology compelled his exclusion of certain large groups, notably workers and women, from the capacity for reflection required to disaggregate

316

the three primordially fused elements of consciousness (sensation, reason, and will) and to appropriate the will for and as one's self. That exclusion, stated often and unapologetically in Cousin's public rhetoric, was rather an independent policy choice. Stemming from the Doctrinaire vision of the class and gender hierarchies required in a fragile, post-Revolutionary society, it was subsequently overlaid on a psychological theory not especially well suited to support it. Another Doctrinaire desideratum—an unimpregnably unified and morally accountable self—did, to be sure, flow inexorably from Cousin's spiritualist postulates. But criteria for human difference did not. Cousin, however, presented the exclusion of workers and women from selfhood *as if* it were a logically necessary corollary of his psychological theory. He then reinforced that exclusion by inserting training in psychology into a state system of lycées where attendance was restricted to the male bourgeoisie.

Among Cousin's regiment, it was Amédée Jacques who, in the standard philosophy manual that he coauthored with two other Cousinian disciples in 1846, came closest to exposing the internal contradiction thinly papered over by the *maître*. As indicated in Chapter 5, Jacques argued for the "scrupulous" equality of the power of volition in everyone and furthermore insinuated that the individual appropriation of that power as the *moi* depended on a willed effort rather than on an act of (unequally distributed) intelligence. By implication, then, those who failed to take possession of the *moi* were not constrained in this regard by inbuilt impediments but had freely chosen to do so. Jacques advanced this argument in an unprovocative, indeed, semi-covert manner: he left aspects of his position fuzzy, did not label the position as a criticism of Cousin, and included it in an elementary textbook that explicitly declared its aloofness from controversy. But with the Revolution of 1848 and the establishment of the Second Republic, his posture gradually changed. Either he grasped for the first time the fundamental challenge to the Cousinian status quo contained in his own arguments or, more likely, he was emboldened by the political climate to proclaim as subversive what he had earlier presented as thoroughly innocuous.

Jacques had always been something of a fair-haired boy of the Cousinian regiment. Admitted to the Ecole normale supérieure in 1832,[1] the young Parisian, the son of a painter of miniatures, passed the *agrégation* qualifying him to teach philosophy in the lycée in 1835 and the much more selective *agrégation* qualifying him to teach philosophy at the

Sorbonne in 1843. At the time of that latter triumph, Cousin's published account of the concours (which he proudly likened in intellectual quality to the philosophical disputations of the seventeenth century and Middle Ages!) indicated that, of the seven candidates, the two winners—Jacques and his classmate Emile Saisset—had consistently outshone the others. All the candidates, Cousin observed in passing, were doctrinally correct, a remark that would no doubt come back to haunt him.[2] Failing a vacancy at the Sorbonne after the concours, Jacques was promoted from the lycée in Versailles to the prestigious Lycée Louis-le-Grand in Paris, where the inspectors noted the excellence of his pedagogy and his capacity to attract the brightest pupils to his classes.[3]

Exactly what happened in 1847 and 1848 to derail the apparently conformist, prudent, and career-oriented Jacques can only be surmised from the various textual remains of his activities. In the waning days of the July Monarchy, as demands for the expansion of the suffrage intensified, Jacques founded a journal, *La Liberté de penser*, sympathetic to the left-wing opposition to the regime but without more precise political affiliation, leery of clerical intervention in the public sphere, and primarily concerned to ensure the free circulation of philosophical ideas.[4] After the February Revolution, the journal declared its democratic republicanism. At this stage, its attitude toward Cousinianism was quite benign, even moderately favorable. Jacques did not think that philosophy instruction should "belong to" anyone, "neither to Plato, Aristotle, Descartes, Locke, Laromiguière, nor to Monsieur Cousin." Nonetheless, he regarded as an unambiguous good the "stamp of spiritualism and elevation" that Cousin had placed on that instruction. He waxed eloquent about the "inviolability" of the "free personality." He warned against charging religion exclusively with the task of inculcating morality. ("The *obligatory* teaching of moral philosophy in the institutions of secondary education must and can be one of the foundations of the moral unity of the society of the nineteenth century.") He believed in the fundamentally mind-altering power of philosophy. ("We call on anyone who has attentively followed an officially sanctioned philosophy course. Has he not felt his intelligence created, so to speak, for a second time?") Apart from denying Cousin ownership of academic philosophy, Jacques' initial platform had only one plank to which the *maître* could object: a commitment to democracy—always Cousin's nemesis—including an assertion that philosophy was its natural ally.[5]

With the passage of the Falloux Law in March 1850, the Second Republic took a sharply conservative, pro-clerical turn. That law ended the monopoly of the Université, facilitated the creation of private, church-run schools, and gave the clergy a larger voice in the public secondary education administered by the state. At this juncture, the politics of *La Liberté de penser* became more strident and more risky, for the journal, always suspicious of Catholic influence, now found itself on the wrong side of the regime. In April Jules Simon, a future founder of the Third Republic and Jacques' collaborator both on the Cousinian *Manuel de philosophie* and on the journal, cautiously quit the journal's editorial board for political reasons.[6] Continuing on his collision course with the regime, Jacques began to write and to publish in the journal a series of "Essays in Popular Philosophy." The first two installments, which served as the introduction to the whole, were rabidly anticlerical, attempting, for example, to prove that the standard Catholic catechism, far from providing wholesome pedagogy for children, stupefied and ultimately corrupted them.[7] In February and March 1851, the Council of Public Instruction, citing these two articles, removed Jacques from his teaching post at Louis-le-Grand and barred him from all future employment in the state educational system. The membership of the Council that delivered this harsh verdict included two archbishops, a bishop, and two priests; but, much more personally relevant to Jacques, it also included Victor Cousin and Adolphe Franck.[8]

While it was Jacques' anticlericalism that brought upon him the wrath of the state—a state that was nominally republican and democratic but was in fact headed for imminent conversion into a Bonapartist empire—it is another aspect of "The Essays on Popular Philosophy" that principally interests me here. In these essays Jacques finally carried to its logical conclusion the democratic critique of Cousin present in germ in the 1846 *Manuel*. He finally, in effect, deconstructed the wholly external bias against *le peuple* that Cousin had imposed on his psychology.

Jacques began this task in the second of the introductory essays—that is, in one of the pieces that Cousin read and sat in judgment on at the Council of Public Instruction. We must recall that the term "popular philosophy" had a decidedly Cousinian ring at this date. The *maître* had just written a pamphlet of that title in 1848, the first in a series of *petits traités* that the Academy of Moral and Political Sciences had sponsored after the June Days for the purpose of soothing the insurrectionary mood of the people (see Chapter 4). Cousin's point had been that the popular classes had a native, intuitive philosophy, rather like the natural religion of Rousseau's Savoyard vicar, that provided all they needed to know about morality, God, and the immortality of the soul; they did not require the specialized vocabulary and arcane techniques of academic philosophy. Without mentioning Cousin's pamphlet, Jacques made precisely the opposite point early in 1851: the people needed to be taught philosophy because cultivated rationality was an indispensable accoutrement of freedom. Withholding such instruction, he implied, was an intentional strategy to keep the people in their place and to mark them as inferior. His "Essays" would thus draw up, on the basis of his "eighteen years . . . of practice of secondary instruction," a formal philosophy curriculum geared to an audience of workers and peasants. It would not replicate the Cousinian curriculum neither because Cousinianism was too difficult for the popular classes nor intrinsically rotten—"one can take this word [eclecticism] in a good sense"—but because its own founder had, over time, corrupted it:

> I detest and I reject with all my force what the most illustrious representative of contemporary eclecticism has accumulated under that rubric. It has now come to signify . . . in politics the preference for expedients over principles, for fact over right; in everything, the study and the restitution of the past in place of the concern and preparation for the future. It signifies still worse: an impossible alliance between faith and reason—that is, an inexplicable compromise between slavery and freedom, a perpetual capitulation of conscience.[9]

One indication of Cousin's corruption of eclecticism was his exclusionary educational policy, his reservation of instruction in psychology to the social elite. On this subject, Jacques' revulsion spilled over:

> The education of the young bourgeoisie is in fact a thankless job. The terrain where only the counsels of interest grow is worn-out, sterile, and arid. I know them, these children of the bourgeoisie: youth is on their faces but not in their hearts. . . . What they seek least of all is the beautiful and the true; they are impervious to the charm of letters and the enlightenment provided by the sciences. Their ambition focuses them wholly on obtaining a university degree, which will open for them what is conventionally called *a career.* . . .[10]

According to Jacques, the content of Cousin's own philosophy, if properly construed, undermined the policy that restricted training in it to the bourgeoisie. In the substantive installments of his "Essays," Jacques reiterated, almost verbatim, the argument for the equality of wills he had inconspicuously tucked away in his 1846 *Manuel*. But now, by its presence in a philosophy course addressed to *le peuple,* that same argument took on the attributes of fiery political rhetoric. "The liberty to will," wrote Jacques, "that is our true property. Only that do we absolutely possess; but that, at least, we possess entirely, without reserve, without limit." Furthermore, he continued, "that liberty is equal in all men; only in that [dimension] are men scrupulously equal among themselves." Wealth was the most unequally distributed of human resources; physical strength also varied considerably from one person to another, as did intelligence. "But all are equal by an equal liberty to will." Finally, the equality of wills meant for Jacques the equal accessibility of selfhood to all. "The will, the free force that produces [our resolutions], is not only ours, it is us, and it alone is us. It is what we designate when we say 'I' or 'me' *(moi)*."[11]

In these journal articles Jacques developed a model philosophy curriculum for the workingman, one that followed generally Cousinian lines with respect to substance but sharply diverged from Cousin's arbitrary practice of excluding the larger part of humanity from the ranks of the selved. Had historical circumstances afforded him the opportunity to carry out his pedagogical program, he might have ended up cutting the tie between the Cousinian self and the bourgeois mode of being in the world. But Jacques' program never advanced beyond the planning stage. Not only had he forfeited his hard-won academic credentials, but Louis-Napoleon's successful coup d'état later in 1851 drove him into exile in South America; he died in Buenos Aires in 1865 at the age of fifty-two.[12]

A Female Cousinian-Style Self?

Jacques did for workingmen what Caroline Angebert had done for women: both laid bare not so much the injustice as the sheer logical inconsistency of Cousin's denial of selfhood to an unprivileged group. But even if Jacques' intervention came relatively late (Angebert began badgering Cousin before the Revolution of 1830) and was ultimately inefficacious, he at least made his case in a public forum. Angebert had confined hers to private correspondence with the *maître,* and in the end she requested instruction in philosophical psychology only for herself, not for women in general.

If a public vindication of the female capacity for Cousinian-style selfhood was ever going to occur, surely the opportune moment for it would be the founding of the national system of lycées for girls under the early Third Republic. Since the lycée class in philosophy had, by the 1880s, already been the locus of training in the *moi* for several generations of young Frenchmen, it is easy to imagine a republican educator speaking out on the importance of providing comparable training for their female counterparts. Even if these educators made no direct connection between academic philosophy and selfhood, they were certainly aware of the incomparable prestige that philosophy enjoyed in the secondary school curriculum and some, at least, must have been eager to see young women partake of its intellectual riches and even its cachet. But in fact, far from being spokesmen for female selfhood, or even for female training in philosophy, the educators of the early Third Republic took pains to keep the philosophy class out of the reach of their newly invented creature, the *lycéenne*.

The parliamentary commission that prepared the legislation on the new lycées excluded philosophy from the curriculum on the grounds that "all the philosophic knowledge usefully taught to girls is already included in moral instruction, in history, or in literary history." From the rather telegraphic minutes of their proceedings, we can infer that they meant by this pronouncement, first, that girls simply had less practical use for "philosophic knowledge" because their future vocation lay in being "mothers and housewives" rather than *savantes*. But the commissioners gave a second meaning to the lack of "usefulness" of philosophy for girls, a meaning imbued with the anticlerical aims that shaped so many late nineteenth-century French government policies on women. At their private meeting, Paul Bert proposed that the curriculum for girls be headed by "moral instruction"; this abbreviated version of the traditional rubric "moral and religious instruction" would, he argued, "indicate from the outset the spirit informing this new education." In response, Camille Sée urged that the term "philosophy" be included in the formula as well, but Bert—whose viewpoint eventually ruled the day—warned against the employment of a term that had already given rise to "so many objections."[13] If we attempt to decode this cryptic interchange, it appears that Bert believed that suppressing the phrase "religious instruction" would send to parents and clerics the entirely accurate message that the Third Republic, committed to laicization, intended to remove religious training from the state schools and relegate it to voluntary, extra-curricular settings. But he also apparently believed that replacing "religious instruction" with "philosophy" would be an excessive provocation. Because the clergy and its sympathizers had long alleged philosophy to be a subject matter corrosive of religious faith, such nomenclature would identify the new curriculum not merely as religiously neutral but as actively antireligious. The female lycées would thus certainly attract a barrage of clerical hostility.

In other words, *lycéennes* were to be deprived of a philosophy class in part because a prudent anticlerical politics dictated that the state accord a measure of respect to the long-standing bond between the Church and the female sex and that it not appear to be embarking upon the aggressive dechristianization of women. The conflation of the commissioners' two meanings tempered the discriminatory nature of the policy: girls were to be taught only a smattering of philosophy not because they were intellectually incapable of absorbing more but because philosophy—and especially philosophy for girls—was a red flag to influential segments of the public. Bert and his colleagues have here presented a typical instance of early Third Republican reasoning on women's questions, with anticlerical requirements entering the picture as a justification for antifeminist policy decisions. In much the same way, for example, many republicans later refused to support women's suffrage, not because of any intrinsic deficiency of women but because the female vote would, they contended, vastly expand the political power of the clergy.[14]

The decision to omit a full-fledged philosophy course from the new lycées translated in practice into a course in morals that began in the third year and met a mere hour a week; in the fifth and final year it was devoted to a consideration of "Elements of Psychology Applied to Education." The applied rather than pure nature of this instruction was thought to suit young women because, by dint of the domestic authority they would one day wield, they were fated to be "always educator[s] in fact." A pathetically watered down version of the psychology given pride of place in the Cousinian *programme*, this psychology course for girls contained a brief mention of "Voluntary activity: liberty and personality" under an unintentionally comic heading that included such other forms of "activity" as the "instinctive" and the "gymnastic." There was no mention of the *moi* or of introspective technique.[15]

Nor can the omission of the *moi* be regarded as accidental. More than a decade after the creation of the new curriculum, one philosopher-educator regarded as a champion of women felt obliged to state—it was apparently not obvious to his audience—that women were persons. "Whatever history, physiology, and psychology can teach us about the weaknesses and miseries of women," said Henri Marion, "nothing will prevent her from being, in our eyes, *a person* (italics in the original)— that is, a being responsible in the same way a man is, having a destiny to fulfill freely."[16] Truncating the philosophy curriculum in the female lycées may have been a prudent way to navigate the treacherous political shoals of the early Third Republic. But we can only conclude that what, in particular, was removed faithfully reflected the fact that, in the discourse of the Université at the end of the nineteenth century, female selfhood was far from axiomatic. Throughout the nineteenth century the Cousinian-style *moi* thus preserved the exclusively masculine character that, according to prevailing stereotypes, suited its core definition as willed activity in the world.

A Long-Lived *Programme*

As I have often noted in this book, the chief source of the broad cultural influence exerted by Cousinian psychology was its national institutionalization in the *programme,* or syllabus, of the lycée philosophy class. That institutionalization, which initially occurred in 1832, reflected Cousin's explicit tailoring of his intellectual creation to the political needs of the July Monarchy. But what is most interesting, because perhaps most unexpected, was the persistence of the Cousinian *programme* long after the July Monarchy had passed from the scene.

Between its 1832 implantation and the end of the century, Cousinianism was in retreat for only a period of a dozen years at the beginning of the Second Empire. Soon after Louis-Napoléon's coup d'état at the end of 1851, the lycée *classe de philosophie,* now officially labeled "sterile or dangerous," was abolished outright and replaced with a far more restricted course in logic.[17] In an era in which French elites had again embraced traditional religion as an instrument of social peace, the government clearly intended to rid secondary instruction of that heretically tinged, anthropocentric Cousinian psychology that had always irked the Church. But by the second decade of the Empire, when liberalization was the political watchword, this extreme, pro-clerical measure had outlived its usefulness. Immediately upon his appointment as minister of public education in 1863, and to "signal clearly the turn my administration was going to take," Victor Duruy rescinded it in favor of a version of the old Cousinian philosophy course. He had been appalled, while inspector-general of the Université some years earlier, to witness the degradation of philosophy at the hands of the clerical reaction; attending the logic class at a provincial lycée, for example, he found the professor "tiring his pupils and himself by presenting the forty or fifty forms of the syllogism that medieval scholars had enjoyed studying in order to avoid thinking about more serious things." Duruy construed lycée instruction in philosophy—full-fledged philosophy, not its reduced form as logic— in the same elitist terms as Cousin. Because France was, he opined, the "true moral center of the world," and because it had been under a regime of universal suffrage since 1848, it needed an "aristocracy of intelligence" specifically fortified by philosophy to serve as a "legitimate counterweight to a boundless democracy."[18]

The early Third Republic *programmes* of 1874, 1880, and 1902, the last of which continued in force until 1925, all retained what is for our purposes the essential Cousinian innovation: the commencement of philosophy education by the study of psychology, a subject matter which included, in some form or other, the tenet of the unity of the self. To be sure, these successive *programmes* diverged in certain respects from the Cousinian template. The one of 1874, promulgated when the nominal Republic sought to enforce a conservative "moral order," substituted the old-fashioned term *âme* for that of *moi;* it insisted on the unity of the faculties of the *âme* as constitutive of the "human personality." The one for 1880 placed the *moi* under the rubric of intellectual rather than volitional activity and included the study of mental phenomena outside the purview of ordinary consciousness: sleep, dreams, somnambulism, hallucination, madness. The one for 1902 referred to such extraconscious mental events more laconically under the rubric "psychological automatism" and then accentuated "the personality, the idea of the *moi*" by listing it as the conclusion of the entire section on psychology.[19]

Even the 1925 *programme,* the first curricular innovation in more than two decades and one that might have reflected the profound dislocations of the First World War, represented no fundamental overhaul of the entrenched pedagogy. As one textbook writer observed, it differed from its predecessor "only in appearance and especially in the order of the questions. . . ."[20] That Cousinianism continued to be a live reference point, even if no longer an orthodoxy, can be seen in this question from the 1929 baccalaureate examination in philosophy: "The school of Victor Cousin held that psychological consciousness is infallible. What do you think of such a postulate?"[21]

From a historical perspective, the staying power of Cousinianism had been put to a particularly stringent test in the 1880 *programme*, to which fell the assignment of harmonizing the lycée curriculum with the ideals of the newly republicanized Republic. Given the positivist bent of that Republic, and given the traditional role of the Cousinian *moi* as a jumping off point to metaphysics, one might have reasonably expected the *moi* to disappear from the curriculum at this date. Yet, while absent from the syllabus of the new female lycées, it maintained its old centrality in the training of young men. Some contemporary commentators alleged that it had undergone an important, if subtle, epistemological mutation. Because the scientific wisdom of the latter nineteenth century prescribed that psychology be freed from its earlier metaphysical trappings, "[t]he idea of the *moi*, the idea of the external world, and the idea of God are no longer [in the new curriculum] laid down a priori, but are set forth simply as the products of intellectual activity. One will no longer be spared the task of seeking to explain, if one can, how these ideas are formed, modified, corrected."[22] Others, however, persuasively argued that the new *programme* represented continuity far more than change, and they adduced in support of this assertion that its chief author was none other than Paul Janet, "former secretary of Monsieur Cousin, very attached to the traditions of the [Cousinian] spiritualist school though . . . open to new ideas."[23] (We first encountered Paul Janet in Chapter 5 when, still a student member of Cousin's regiment, he was given to angry outbursts against the *maître*. By the time of the republicanization of the early Third Republic some thirty-five years later, he held one of the three philosophy chairs at the Sorbonne, presided over the jury that certified candidates for university posts in philosophy, and had attained the status of representative par excellence of a still surviving Cousinianism.)[24]

This debate over the precise significance of the 1880 reforms is not of great moment for the thesis I am setting forth here. Even if the *moi* presented to *lycéens* in the late nineteenth century required some active fashioning on the part of its possessor and hence was no longer as fully anchored in the nature of things as its pure Cousinian precursor had been, the critical fact for our purposes is that all *lycéens* were still receiving serious instruction in the *moi* and that the *moi* was still being depicted as one of the components of a tripartite (Cousinian) universe divided among mankind, God, and the external world. A glance at a philosophy manual geared to the 1880 *programme* finds the key Cousinian concepts very much intact, if clothed in slightly altered vocabulary. "Activity is thus the master faculty of the human mind." Or, under a heading proclaiming the object of consciousness as "knowledge of the *moi*": "The consciousness that we have of our energy—one, indivisible, and distinct—will allow us to refute materialism. . . ."[25]

How can we account for the stunning longevity of Cousinianism? Surely bureaucratic inertia—the continuity of personnel in the state educational administration, which had been amply stocked with Cousin's disciples during the heyday of the *maître*—provides a partial explanation. But given that the *programme* was periodically revised, and that proposed changes often provoked bitter and tumultuous quarrels, its fundamentally Cousinian shape could not have endured without a broad cultural consensus in its favor. The consensus may have been largely negative, a tacit agreement that Cousinianism was the best available option under the circumstances, the least of evils. As John Brooks has argued, the capaciousness of late nineteenth-century Cousinianism gave it "an important advantage over its more exclusive opponents, particularly Catholicism and positivism. However much these two schools disliked eclecticism, they disliked each other more."[26] But it seems clear that republicans placed a positive value on the basic contours of Cousinianism as well. Even in the 1890s and beyond, an era in which social solidarity began to be held up as a dominant republican value, the official culture needed to police the boundaries of that solidarity to prevent its sliding over into socialism.[27] What better protection than to reaffirm institutionally a key element of garden-variety bourgeois belief: the free, unified, and morally accountable self?

Rethinking the Discovery of the Unconscious

We are now in a position to revisit the quotation from Sartre that figured in the Introduction and that serves as the epigraph to this Epilogue. In that passage and the surrounding text, Sartre describes himself as astounded and repelled by his first encounter with the Freudian theory of the unconscious, which (extrapolating from his 1905 birth date) occurred in the early 1920s. A mind characterized by fault lines, fissures, and repressed contents was, he tells us, unthinkable to him as brilliant young product of the French lycée education of that era.

From the vantage point of this book, Sartre's reaction is doubly noteworthy. First, Sartre offers himself as additional evidence of the fundamentally Cousinian shape that the lycée philosophy curriculum maintained well into the twentieth century. Although, as we have seen, material on sleep, dreams, somnambulism, hallucination, and madness—the very stuff from which anti-Cousinian psychologists constructed the concepts of multiple personalities and unconscious mental processes[28]—had been added to the *programme* as early as 1880, the idea of a unified self still dominated the French philosophy classroom. If mental unity was the unambiguous message the seventeen-year-old Sartre took away from his philosophical studies a few years after the end of the First World War, we can safely assume that his less gifted classmates likewise failed to perceive the threat to the Cartesian-Cousinian *moi* contained in the supplementary material on altered states of consciousness. Even for Sartre, a sustained reading of a Freudian text for its own sake was required to bring that subversive point home.[29]

Nor is it difficult to see how philosophy instruction managed to neutralize, almost trivialize such material in the service of the old doctrine of the unified *moi*. From 1880 on, philosophy textbooks propounded the doctrine that such a *moi* was not simply given a priori, as Cousin and his school had insisted. It was instead a psychological accomplishment, the result of a conscious mental process that the 1902 *programme* called *synthèse*. Such mental synthesis, resulting in the possession of a whole and unified *moi,* was the normal human condition; the domination of the psyche by unconscious modalities, and hence its fragmentation, was pathological. Consciousness was, in the standard vocabulary of the philosophy curriculum, a "superior" mental power, unconsciousness (or psychological automatism) an "inferior" one.[30] In light of this carefully crafted doctrine, even a Sartre could emerge from the lycée in the 1920s with no inkling that the Cartesian cogito, or its successor the Cousinian *moi,* was under siege. As a philosophy textbook published in 1929 confidently proclaimed: "The personality is the most perfect form of unity."[31]

Second, the history that I have recounted in this book was obviously unknown to Sartre. He rehearsed what has become the canonical modernist narrative of the fin-de-siècle discovery of the unconscious: that the theories of Freud and of Frenchmen like Henri Bergson, Gustave LeBon, and Pierre Janet came as a breathtaking bolt from the blue, unheralded and unprecedented, threatening the apparently eternal verity (elegantly theorized by Descartes) of a whole and unified self.

But from the perspective of the protracted contest of psychologies I have described here, the so-called discovery that occurred at the end of the nineteenth century takes on a very different aspect. Situating it in a *longue durée*—one that begins as far back as the reception of Locke's *Essay on Human Understanding*—considerably lessens its shock value. The fragmentation of the self appears as a more ordinary condition. Even if, to use the terminology I developed in the Introduction, the horizontal fragmentation exemplified by sensationalism and phrenology differs qualitatively from the vertical fragmentation exemplified by Freudianism and other theories of the unconscious, both types of fragmentation concur in producing perilously decentered selves: ones lacking, in the eyes of their critics, a firm unitary center that can make decisions, galvanize the whole to action, and take responsibility for that action. Within this *longue durée* Cousinianism appears as an extended and studious effort to ward off, in the name of bourgeois social order, the forces for psychic fragmentation inherent in biologistic modes of reasoning about mental life. The nineteenth-century unitary self appears perennially beleaguered. Vertical fragmentation appears as a latter-day variation on the theme of horizontal fragmentation.

From this defamiliarizing perspective, the question for the historian becomes not so much why the self shattered at the fin-de-siècle (pointing the way to even more radical, structuralist and post-structuralist claims about the death of the subject) as why the unitary self became so tenaciously implanted during the nineteenth century that even the young Sartre could mistake it for a given, a fact of life. This book has suggested an answer to that question.

Notes

Abbreviations

AN   Archives Nationales, Paris

BN   Bibliothèque nationale de France, Paris

Introduction

1. The idea that Greeks of the Homeric age had no coherent concept of the self was famously argued by Bruno Snell, *The Discovery of Mind in Greek Philosophy and Literature* (2d German ed. 1948), trans. T. G. Rosenmeyer (New York: Dover, 1982), chap. 1, and later developed by A. W. H. Adkins, *Merit and Responsibility: A Study in Greek Values* (Oxford: Oxford University Press, 1960) and *From the Many to the One: A Study of Personality and Views of Human Nature in the Context of Ancient Greek Society, Values and Beliefs* (Ithaca: Cornell University Press, 1970). Adkins also used the term "shame culture," meaning a culture whose ultimate sanction is overtly "what people will say," to refer to pre-Socratic Greece. Insofar as shame culture is seen as precluding moral autonomy, Socrates' principled adherence to a moral code at odds with the socially accepted one in classical Athens has been viewed as the historical birth of conscience and therefore personhood.

2. The Stoic practice of *askesis*, sometimes translated as "care of the self," has recently attracted attention, leading some commentators to locate the birth of a certain kind of self in Stoicism; see, for example, Pierre Hadot, *Philosophy as a Way of Life: Spiritual Exercises from Socrates to Foucault* (1st French ed. 1981), trans. Michael Chase (Oxford: Blackwell, 1995), and Michel Foucault, *The Care of the Self,* vol. 3 of *The History of Sexuality* (French ed. 1984), trans. Robert Hurley (New York: Vintage, 1990). As Charles Taylor notes, the Stoic injunction to take care of oneself "calls us to a reflexive stance" and is, he implies, the historically first philosophical system to do so; see his *Sources of the Self: The Making of the Modern Identity* (Cambridge, MA: Harvard University Press, 1989), p. 130.

331

3. See, e.g., Colin Morris, *The Discovery of the Individual, 1050–1200* (1972; repr. Toronto: University of Toronto Press, 1987) and Caroline Walker Bynum, "Did the Twelfth Century Discover the Individual?" in *Jesus as Mother: Studies in the Spirituality of the High Middle Ages* (Berkeley: University of California Press, 1982), 82–109. For a novel approach to the same thesis that focuses not on religious practice but on the use of seals, see Brigitte Miriam Bedos-Rezak, "Medieval Identity: A Sign and a Concept," *American Historical Review* 105 (2000): 1489–1533.

4. This was the position put forth in Jacob Burckhardt's *Die Cultur der Renaissance in Italien: Ein Versuch* (Basel, 1860); for a recent revision of the position, see John Martin, "Inventing Sincerity, Refashioning Prudence: The Discovery of the Individual in Renaissance Europe," *American Historical Review* 102 (1997): 1309–1342.

5. Marcel Mauss, "A Category of the Human Mind: The Notion of the Person; the Notion of the Self" (1938), trans. W. D. Halls, in *The Category of the Person: Anthropology, Philosophy, History,* ed. Michael Carrithers, Steven Collins, and Steven Lukes (Cambridge: Cambridge University Press, 1985), 1–25, quotation on p. 3. Another version of this claim comes from Clifford Geertz, "'From the Native's Point of View': On the Nature of Anthropological Understanding," in *Local Knowledge: Further Essays in Interpretive Anthropology* (New York: Basic Books, 1983), p. 59: "some sort of concept [of person], one feels reasonably safe in saying, exists in recognizable form in all social groups."

6. The reference is to Friedrich Nietzsche, *The Birth of Tragedy,* trans. Walter Kaufmann (New York: Random House, 1967), e.g., pp. 35–36, 39–40. (I have preserved Nietzsche's use of the Latin *principium individuationis* because, as discussed in Chapter 3, below, Locke used it as well.) Even the belief systems, such as Buddhism, that call the self into question assume its existence. See, e.g., Bernard Faure, *The Red Thread: Buddhist Approaches to Sexuality* (Princeton: Princeton University Press, 1998), pp. 31–32: "In spite of the dogma of no-self, Buddhist ascetics, like Indian yogis and Greek Stoics, seem to have conceived the self as a citadel besieged by the external world."

7. Jean-Paul Sartre, "An Interview," *New York Review of Books,* 26 May 1970, p. 23.

8. Mauss, "Category," pp. 4–17, quotation on 17.

9. See, e.g., Norbert Elias, *The Civilizing Process* (1st German ed. 1939, 1st English ed. 1982) and, for a focus on the psychological dynamics of Louis XIV's court at Versailles and their later impact on non-elite groups, Roger Chartier, "Trajectoires et tensions culturelles de l'Ancien Régime," in *Histoire de la France,* ed. André Burguière and Jacques Revel, 4 vols. (Paris:

Seuil, 1989–93), 4: 307–92, esp. 315–32. A similar argument is made for Renaissance monarchies in Martin, "Inventing Sincerity," p. 1322.

10. Jean-Jacques Rousseau, *Les Rêveries du promeneur solitaire* in *Oeuvres complètes,* ed. Bernard Gagnebin and Marcel Raymond, 4 vols. (Paris: Gallimard/ Pléiade, 1959–69), 1: 1047.

11. See George Chauncey, "Après Stonewall, le déplacement de la frontière entre le 'soi' public et le 'soi' privé," *Histoire et sociétés: Revue européenne d'histoire sociale* 3 (2002): 45–59. I am following Chauncey's use of the term "segmentation" here.

12. Quoted in Martin Filler, "Ghosts in the House," *New York Review of Books,* 21 October 1999, pp. 10–15, quotation on p. 10.

13. See Charles Landesman, Jr., "Consciousness," in *The Encyclopedia of Philosophy,* ed. Paul Edwards, 8 vols. (New York: Macmillan and Free Press, 1967), 2: 191–95, esp. 192, and Eric Lormand, "Consciousness," in *Routledge Encyclopedia of Philosophy,* ed. Edward Craig, 10 vols. (London: Routledge, 1998), 2: 581–96, esp. 590.

14. This analytic distinction is much in the spirit of the model of the self that William M. Reddy has proposed in *The Navigation of Feeling: A Framework for the History of the Emotions* (Cambridge: Cambridge University Press, 2001). Not unlike the deemphasized self of the sensationalists, Reddy's "disaggregated self" (p. 95), always faced by an excess of activations requiring translation, lacks inherent unity and can achieve only a provisional integration.

15. This is one of the central arguments of Keith Michael Baker, *Condorcet: From Natural Philosophy to Social Mathematics* (Chicago: University of Chicago Press, 1976).

16. Pierre Rosanvallon, *L'état en France de 1789 à nos jours* (Paris: Seuil, 1990), pp. 95–99, 108–10. Rosanvallon calls the state in this capacity the "instituteur du social," the title he gives to Part 2 of the book.

17. In this respect, my argument is not dissimilar from that of Sarah Maza, *The Myth of the French Bourgeoisie: An Essay on the Social Imaginary, 1750–1850* (Cambridge, MA: Harvard University Press, 2003), pp. 129–30, 196–97, despite Maza's provocative assertion of the nonexistence of the French bourgeoisie and her call to historians to proscribe the term.

18. See my summary of his arguments in Jan Goldstein, "Foucault and the Post-Revolutionary Self: The Uses of Cousinian Pedagogy in Nineteenth-Century France" in *Foucault and the Writing of History,* ed. Jan Goldstein, (Oxford: Blackwell, 1994), 99–115, esp. 108–11.

19. For his definition of a "technology of the self," see his obligatory summary of his course at the Collège de France in the academic year 1980–81 reprinted in Michel Foucault, *Résumé des cours, 1970–1982* (Paris: Julliard, 1989), esp. pp. 133–34.

20. See Foucault, "On the Genealogy of Ethics: An Overview of Work in Progress," in *The Foucault Reader,* ed. Paul Rabinow, (New York: Pantheon, 1984), pp. 340–72, esp. 371–72.

21. I earlier noted and attempted to explain this discrepancy between Foucault's dictum and my findings; see Goldstein, "Foucault and the Post-Revolutionary Self," esp. pp. 111–15.

22. On Foucault's lack of interest in the events of political history, see Keith Michael Baker, "A Foucauldian French Revolution?" in *Foucault and the Writing of History,* ed. Goldstein, pp. 187–205, esp. 187–89. On "micropower," see Michel Foucault, *Discipline and Punish: The Birth of the Prison,* trans. Alan Sheridan (New York: Pantheon, 1977), e.g., p. 222.

23. See François Azouvi, *Descartes et la France: Histoire d'une passion nationale* (Paris: Fayard, 2002), pp. 168–82, esp. 170–71.

24. Taylor, *Sources of the Self,* esp. p. 131.

25. Ibid., chaps. 8 and 9, esp. 163, for "bewitchment." Taylor does not, of course, contend that Descartes and Locke arrived at the same objectified mental apparatuses.

26. The locus classicus of this argument is, of course, Jacques Derrida, *Of Grammatology* (1st French ed., 1967), trans. Gayatri Chakravorty Spivak (Baltimore: Johns Hopkins University Press, 1976), esp. pt. 1, chaps. 1–2.

1. The Perils of Imagination at the End of the Old Regime

For the source of the epigraph, see note 38.

1. *Journal de Paris,* 8 January 1789, p. 39.

2. Etienne Bonnet de Condillac, *Essai sur les origines des connoissances humaines,* in *Oeuvres philosophiques de Condillac,* ed. Georges Le Roy, 3 vols. (Paris: Presses universitaires de France, 1947–51), 1: 30.

3. "Powerful cabal" is the phrase attributed to Fabre by L. Thiessé, "Notice sur Fabre d'Eglantine," in *Oeuvres choisies de Fabre d'Eglantine* (Paris: Dabo-Butschett, 1824), p. 10. The term "cabal" was a mainstay of late eighteenth-century disputes about theatrical merit and the propriety of audience behavior; see, e.g., Jeffrey S. Ravel, "Seating the Public: Spheres and Loathing in the Paris Theaters, 1777–1788," *French Historical Studies* 18 (1993): 173–210.

4. Saint-Marc Girardin, "Collin d'Harleville et Fabre d'Eglantine," *Essais de littérature et de morale,* 2 vols. (Paris: Charpentier, 1845), 1: 124–43, esp. 124.

5. Fabre memorialized the episode by indicating on the title page of the published play both its partial suppression in January 1789 and its successful full performance 13 months later; see the 1790 edition (Paris: Prault). By

contrast, Collin's *Châteaux en Espagne* was well-received before the outbreak of the Revolution; see the review of its premiere in *Journal de Paris*, 21 February 1789, pp. 236–37.

6. "Lettre de M. Fabre d'Eglantine à Monsieur De ***** relativement à la contestation survenue au sujet du *Présomptueux ou l'heureux imaginaire* et *les Châteaux en Espagne*" (n.p., n.d.). The first page of the pamphlet dates the letter 12 January 1789. For the quotations from this pamphlet in the next several paragraphs, see pp. 4–9.

7. See Montaigne, *Essais*, 3 vols. (Paris: Garnier, 1952), 1: 28–30.

8. Lettre de M. Fabre d'Eglantine à Monsieur De *****, p. 9, italics in the original.

9. For this characterization of the play, see Laurence Hervey Skinner, *Collin d'Harleville, Dramatist, 1755–1806* (New York: Publications of the Institute of French Studies, 1933), p. 94.

10. Collin d'Harleville, *Les Châteaux en Espagne, comédie en cinq actes, en vers,* Act 1, Scene 1 in *Théâtre et poésies fugitives,* 4 vols. (Paris: Duminil-Lesueur, 1805), 1: 238. All subsequent citations to Collin's play refer to this edition.

11. The matter is somewhat more complex and whimsical. As soon as he announces his plan to become a sober landowner and husband, d'Orlange once more begins spinning daydreams of his future life. Hence the valet observes at the play's closing that his master "no longer wishes to but still builds castles in Spain." Act 5, Scene 10, p. 346.

12. All citations from Fabre's play are from Philippe François Nazaire Fabre d'Eglantine, *Le Présomptueux, ou l'heureux imaginaire, comédie en cinq actes en vers* (Paris: Prault, 1790).

13. See, e.g., Act 1, Scene 3, pp. 22–23.

14. Jean le Rond d'Alembert, *Preliminary Discourse to the Encyclopedia of Diderot* (1751), trans. Richard N. Schwab (Indianapolis: Bobbs-Merrill, 1963), pp. 49–51, quotation on p. 51, my italics.

15. Ibid., p. 50.

16. See, for example, the sprawling, influential series edited by Pierre Nora, *Les lieux de mémoire,* 7 vols. (Paris: Gallimard, 1984–92); Yosef Hayim Yerushalmi, *Zakhor: Jewish History and Jewish Memory* (New York: Schocken, 1989); James E. Young, *The Texture of Memory: Holocaust Memorials and Meaning* (New Haven: Yale University Press, 1993); Alain Finkelkraut, *La mémoire vaine: Du crime contre l'humanité* (Paris: Gallimard, 1989); Henry Rousso, *The Vichy Syndrome: History and Memory in France since 1944* (Cambridge, MA: Harvard University Press, 1991), which is the English translation of a work that lacks the word "memory" in the original French title; Daniel J. Sherman, *The Construction of Memory in Interwar*

France (Chicago: University of Chicago Press, 1999); Alon Confino and Peter Fritzsche, eds., *The Work of Memory: New Directions in the Study of German Society and Culture* (Urbana: University of Illinois Press, 2003); and Stéphane Gerson, *The Pride of Place: Local Memories and Political Culture in Nineteenth-Century France* (Ithaca: Cornell University Press, 2003).

17. See, for example, the two-part essay review by Frederick Crews, "The Revenge of the Repressed," *New York Review of Books,* 17 November 1994, pp. 54–60, and 1 December 1994, pp. 49–58, which discusses no less than six recent books devoted to that subject.

18. The standard source on this subject is Frances A. Yates, *The Art of Memory* (Chicago: University of Chicago Press, 1966); the exportation to China of Western mnemotechnics by a late seventeenth-century Italian Jesuit is the subject of Jonathan D. Spence, *The Memory Palace of Matteo Ricci* (New York: Viking Penguin, 1984). As Yates notes, the art of memory dwindled among Renaissance humanists with the invention of printing but at the same time flourished in occult and magical form among the followers of the Hermetic tradition; *Art of Memory,* pp. xii, 368.

19. See Ioan P. Couliano, *Eros and Magic in the Renaissance* (Chicago: University of Chicago Press, 1987), chap. 9, esp. p. 193.

20. See "Mémoire (Métaphysique)" in *Encyclopédie, ou dictionnaire raisonné des sciences, des arts et des métiers,* ed. Denis Diderot and Jean Le Rond d'Alembert, 17 vols. (Paris, 1751–65), 10: 326–28. The first line of the article, developed in every one of its subsequent paragraphs, reads: "Il est important de bien distinguer le point qui sépare l'imagination de la *mémoire*" (italics in the original).

21. This entire paragraph and the previous one, beginning with the discussion of Aristotle, rely on Yates, *Art of Memory;* see pp. 32–33, 71, 155–57, 202, 224, 230, 241, 372–73.

22. Condillac, *Essai in Oeuvres philosophiques,* 1: 15.

23. Ibid., pp. 15–16, 19–22.

24. Ibid., pp. 27–30.

25. Ibid., pp. 30–31.

26. Nicolas Malebranche, *De la recherche de la vérité* (1674), ed. Francisque Bouillier, 2 vols. (Paris: Garnier, [1880]), 1: 136–37.

27. Ibid., pp. 164–83. As late as 1802, the physician-philosopher P.-J.-G. Cabanis refused either to affirm or deny the belief and asserted that there was much empirical evidence in support of it; see his *Rapports du physique et du morale de l'homme* in *Oeuvres philosophiques de Cabanis,* ed. Claude Lehec and Jean Cazeneuve, 2 vols. (Paris: Presses universitaires de France, 1956), 1: 605. For a study of this theme from the Renaissance to the Romantic period, see Marie-Hélène Huet, *Monstrous Imagination* (Cam-

bridge, MA: Harvard University Press, 1993) The medical belief in at least an *indirect* power of imagination on the fetus persisted into the nineteenth century; see the subsequent expansion and reprinting by one physician of his 1807 memoir, J.-B. Demangeon, *De l'imagination considérée dans ses effets directs sur l'homme et les animaux et dans ses effets indirects sur les produits de la gestation,* 2d ed. (Paris: Rouen frères, 1829), and, under an altered title, *Du Pouvoir de l'imagination sur le physique et le moral de l'homme,* new ed. (Paris: De Just Rouvier et E. Le Bouvier, 1834).

28. Malebranche, *De la recherche de la vérité,* 1: bk. 2, pt. 3, pp. 233–80.

29. "Imagination," *Encyclopédie,* 8: 560–63, esp. 561.

30. "Songe," *Encyclopédie,* 15: 354–57, esp. 355. The article was drawn from Formey, *Mélanges philosophiques,* 2 vols. (Leyden: Impr. d'E. Luzac fils, 1754), 1: 174–204, esp. 180.

31. Formey, *Principes de morale, déduits de l'usage des facultés de l'entendement humain,* 2 vols. (Leyden: Durand, 1762), 1: 131. The word in the text is "courtier" but the references in the passage to fields and bridles, as well as the fact that *coursier fougueux* is a standard locution of the period, suggest a typographical error or an eighteenth-century variant on the modern spelling.

32. See Paul Robert, *Dictionnaire alphabétique et analogique de la langue française,* 6 vols. (Paris: Société du Nouveau Littré, 1965), 3: 127.

33. These linguistic clusters demonstrated a remarkable staying power. In late nineteenth-century French psychiatry, the propensity to embark upon purposeless *fugues* was theorized as a traveling neurosis, and one to which Jews, by definition deracinated, were especially susceptible. See Jan Goldstein, "The Wandering Jew and the Problem of Psychiatric Anti-Semitism in Fin-de-Siècle France," *Journal of Contemporary History* 20 (1985): 521–52.

34. Formey, *Principes de morale,* loc. cit.

35. Ibid.

36. La Fontaine's *Fable de la laitière et le pot au lait,* which Collin D'Harleville used as the epigraph for his play *Les Châteaux en Espagne,* begins with the couplet, "Quel esprit ne bat pas la campagne?/Qui ne fait châteaux en Espagne?"

37. "Remontrances sur l'édit supprimant les jurandes et les communautés d'arts et métiers," 2–4 March 1776, in *Remontrances du Parlement de Paris au XVIIIe siècle,* ed. Jules Flammermont, 3 vols. (Paris: Impr. nationale, 1888–98), 3: 309–10.

38. "Lit de justice pour l'enregistrement de l'édit . . . supprimant les jurandes," 12 March 1776, in ibid., p. 346.

39. Jürgen Habermas, *The Structural Transformation of the Public Sphere: An Inquiry into a Category of Bourgeois Society,* trans. Thomas Burger

(Cambridge, MA: MIT Press, 1989), p. 29 for the quotation and pp. 28–29, 43–51.

40. "Observations des maîtres-gantiers," B.N. Manuscripts, Collection Joly de Fleury (henceforth, BN MSS, Coll. Joly), vol. 596, fol. 114.

41. The term "existence" may also have a material, economic meaning in this text; but that is not the meaning the glovemakers highlight. Instead, existence as "knowability" and as "subjectivity" are given primacy; and insofar as it appears at all, the economic meaning—the ability to earn a livelihood—flows from those "existential" attributes. For a very similar use of the term in the context of a post-Napoleonic call to restore the guilds, see Louis-Pierre De Seine, *Mémoire sur la nécessité du rétablissement des maîtrises et des corporations comme moyens d'encourager l'industrie et le commerce* (Paris: Impr. de Fain, 1815), p. 9: "What does one see in Paris and through all of France? Men whom nobody knows, who have no existence (*aucune existence*) in society, and who nonetheless open commercial establishments."

42. *Réflexions des maîtres tailleurs de Paris,* printed brochure dated 17 February 1776, p. 3, in BN MSS, Coll. Joly, vol. 462, fol. 173(1).

43. See "Mémoire pour la communauté des maîtres boulangers," handwritten, n.d., BN MSS, Coll. Joly, vol. 462, fol. 105v; and "Observations . . . des Maîtres blondiniers, boutonniers de Paris, handwritten, BN MSS, Coll. Joly, vol. 462, fol. 108; "A nosseigneurs de Parlement par le gardes visiteurs actuels du corps des horlogers," BN MSS, Coll. Joly, vol. 462, fol. 125.

44. *Réflexions sur l'édit concernant la suppression des jurandes par les maîtres et marchands tissutiers-rubanniers et frangers,* printed brochure dated 21 February 1776, p. 8 in BN MSS, Coll. Joly, vol. 596, fol. 98(3).

45. "A nosseigneurs du Parlement par les maîtres savetiers," BN MSS, Coll. Joly, vol. 462, fol. 148. Conversely, critics of the trade corporations vilified the gaze of the *jurés*. An anonymous and undated "Mémoire sur les communités d'arts et métiers," apparently written in the early 1770s, described that gaze as an "inhuman and revolting inquisition" which "ceaselessly violates the interior of the establishment." BN MSS, Coll. Joly, vol. 1729, fol. 141.

46. *Réflexions des six corps de la ville de Paris sur la suppression des jurandes,* BN MSS, Coll. Joly, vol. 462, pp. 12–14 (fols. 155/1–155/2), my italics. The *six-corps* were the drapers, grocers, mercers, furriers, hosiers, and goldsmiths engaged in large-scale, long-distance commerce.

47. "Mémoire pour la communauté des maîtres boulangers," fols. 106–7, my italics.

48. Bibliothèque municipale de Besançon, Fonds de l'Académie de Besançon, vol. 12, fol. 202. My thanks to Cynthia Koepp for supplying me with this citation.

49. I learned of the Bonafon affair, and of the prominence of the category of "imagination" in the police interrogation of the accused, in Lisa Jane Graham, *If the King Only Knew: Seditious Speech in the Reign of Louis XV* (Charlottesville: University of Virginia Press, 2000), chap. 2, esp. 68–69. I subsequently consulted the original sources; see Archives de la Bastille 11582, Premier Interrogatoire fait . . . à la Dlle Bonnafons, 29 August 1745, fols. 55v, 56v, 57; and Second Interrogatoire, 4 September 1745, fol. 80v. My interpretation follows Graham's.

50. I am grateful to Ken Alder for calling this example to my attention. Alder includes a discussion of the school and its founder in his *Engineering the Revolution: Arms and Enlightenment in France, 1763–1815* (Princeton: Princeton University Press, 1997), pp. 143–46.

51. Arthur Birembaut, "Les écoles gratuites du dessin," in *Enseignement et diffusion des sciences en France au 18e siècle*, ed. René Taton (Paris: Hermann, 1986), pp. 441–76, esp. 445.

52. [Bachelier], *Discours sur l'utilité des écoles élémentaires en faveur des arts mécaniques: Prononcé par M. B*** à l'ouverture de l'école royale gratuite de dessin, le 10 septembre 1766* (Paris: Impr. nationale executive du Louvre, 1792), p. 6.

53. Barnabé-Farmian de Rosoi, *Essai philosophique sur l'établissemen des écoles gratuites de dessin pour les arts mécaniques* (Paris: Impr. de Quillau, 1769), pp. 63–64, esp. 75–76.

54. The earliest listing of the Ecole in the *Almanach royale,* that of 1769, notes that the bureau overseeing the operations of the school includes a "Rector of Studies for Geometry" (p. 547).

55. See [Bachelier], *Mémoire concernant l'Ecole gratuite de dessin* (Paris: Impr. royale, 1774), esp. pp. 28–31 and the copy of the admission certificate opposite p. 38.

56. See J. G. A. Pocock, *The Machiavellian Moment: Florentine Political Thought and the Atlantic Republican Tradition* (Princeton: Princeton University Press, 1975), esp. pp. 450–51, 453–54, 459, 466; and "The Mobility of Property and the Rise of Eighteenth-Century Sociology" in *Virtue, Commerce, and History* (Cambridge: Cambridge University Press, 1985), esp. pp. 110–13.

57. "Remontrances sur l'édit supprimant les jurandes," in *Remontrances du Parlement de Paris*, 3: 296.

58. John Locke, *An Essay Concerning Human Understanding*, ed. Peter H. Nidditch (Oxford: Clarendon, 1975), bk. 2, chap. 11, para. 13, p. 161.

59. London: J. Roberts, 1721. I learned of this title from a footnote in Roy Porter, "The Rage of Party: A Glorious Revolution in English Psychiatry?" *Medical History* 27 (1983): 35–50. The pamphlet is in the Goldsmiths'-Kress collection, which I consulted on microfilm.

60. Midriff, *Observations*, pp. 1–2, 19–20.

61. For this description of Law's system, I am relying heavily on a modern economist's account, Peter M. Garber, "Famous First Bubbles," *Journal of Economic Perspectives* 4 (Spring 1990): 35–53, esp. 41–42.

62. On this point, see Thomas E. Kaiser, "Public Credit: John Law's Scheme and the Question of *Confiance*," *Proceedings of the Western Society for French History* 16 (1989): 72–81.

63. For adherents to bullionism, *écus*, the standard denomination of specie, were infinitely preferable on notes to *livres*, the fictitious money of account in which prices were legally stated. A note holder had the assurance that a note in *écus* could be exchanged for a fixed and exact quantity of specie. See Thomas E. Kaiser, "Money, Despotism and Public Opinion in Early Eighteenth-Century France: John Law and the Debate on Royal Credit," *Journal of Modern History* 63 (1991): 1–28, esp. 10.

64. "Remontrances sur l'affaire de la refonte des monnaies," 27 June 1718, in *Remontrances du Parlement de Paris*, 1: 83. My account here relies heavily on Kaiser, "Money, Despotism, and Public Opinion."

65. Quoted in Kaiser, "Money, Despotism, and Public Opinion," p. 12, from a source in the Archives Nationales, Paris.

66. *Le secret du système de M. Law dévoilé. En deux lettres écrites par un duc pair de France et un mylord anglois* (The Hague, 1721), pp. 13–14, 26, 29, my italics.

67. The "Fragment of an Ancient Mythologist" is part of Letter 142; see Charles de Secondat, baron de Montesquieu, *Lettres persanes* (Paris: Garnier, 1960), pp. 307–10. I have in general followed the translation of J. Robert Loy, Montesquieu, *The Persian Letters* (Cleveland: Meridian, 1961), pp. 258–59.

68. "Idée générale du nouveau système des finances" (1719 or 1720) in John Law, *Oeuvres complètes*, 3 vols. (Paris: Sirey, 1934), 3: 75–97, esp. 84–86.

69. See *Lettres sur le nouveau système des finances* (n.p., 1720), which the catalog of the Bibliothèque Nationale de France ascribes to the abbé Terrasson. Each of the three letters is separately paginated; the quotations come from the second letter, dated 11 March 1720, pp. 13–14, 30–32, my italics.

70. On the *disette d'argent*, see Thomas M. Luckett, "Credit and Commercial Society in France, 1740–1789" (Ph.D. dissertation, Princeton University, 1992), and "'There is No Money Here': Money Famine and Tax Revolt in

Early Modern France," in *Money: Lure, Lore and Literature*, ed. J. L. Di Gaetani (Westport, CT: Greenwood Press, 1994), pp. 77–85.

71. Michel Foucault, *The History of Sexuality*, vol. 1: *An Introduction*, trans. Robert Hurley (New York: Vintage, 1980), p. 104. On the anonymous *Onania* and the *Onanisme* of Dr. Tissot, see Théodore Tarczylo, *Sexe et liberté au siècle des lumières* (Paris: Presses de la Renaissance, 1983) and Antoinette Emch-Dériaz, *Tissot, Physician of the Enlightenment* (New York: Peter Lang, 1992).

72. See Thomas W. Laqueur, *Solitary Sex: A Cultural History of Masturbation* (New York: Zone Books, 2003), esp. pp. 210–22, 317–20. For more on the joint theme of masturbation and the imagination, see Vernon A. Rosario II, "Phantastical Pollutions: The Public Threat of Private Vice in France," in *Solitary Pleasures: The Historical, Literary and Artistic Discourses of Auto-Eroticism*, ed. Paula Bennett and Vernon Rosario II (New York: Routledge, 1995), pp. 101–30.

73. Rousseau, *The Confessions*, trans. J. M. Cohen (Harmondsworth: Penguin, 1963), p. 26, my italics; for the original French see Jean-Jacques Rousseau, *Oeuvres complètes*, ed. Bernard Gagnebin and Marcel Raymond, 4 vols. (Paris: Gallimard/Pléiade, 1959–1969), 1: 16.

74. Rousseau, *Confessions*, Eng. ed., pp. 108–9; French ed., pp. 108–9.

75. See Philippe Lejeune, "Le 'dangereux supplément': lecture d'un aveu de Rousseau," *Annales E.S.C.* 29 (1974): 1009–22, esp. 1020; the exchange of letters took place in 1762.

76. Jaucourt "Roman," *Encyclopédie*, vol. 14: 341–42, quotation from p. 341.

77. Pierre-Daniel Huet, *Traité de l'origine des romans* (1670) (Paris: N.-L.-M. Desessarts, Year VII), pp. 109–10. On Huet's anti-Cartesianism, see Nicholas Jolley, "The Reception of Descartes' Philosophy," in *The Cambridge Companion to Descartes*, ed. John Cottingham (Cambridge: Cambridge University Press, 1992), pp. 393–423, esp. p. 409.

78. Nicolas Lenglet du Fresnoy, *De l'usage des romans* (Amsterdam: De Poilras, 1734), pp. 2–3.

79. Armand-Pierre Jacquin, *Entretiens sur les romans* (Paris: Duchesne, 1755), pp. 128–29.

80. On these two originary versions of French literary history—the one excluding and the other admitting women novelists into the canon—see Joan DeJean, *Tender Geographies: Women and the Origins of the Novel in France* (New York: Columbia University Press, 1991), chap. 5. DeJean does not, however, note the corresponding positions of the two camps on the issue of imagination.

81. This thesis is put forth in Rolf Engelsing, *Der Bürger als Leser: Lesergeschichte in Deutschland, 1500–1800* (Stuttgart, 1974). For critical commen-

tary on it, see Robert Darnton, *The Great Cat Massacre and Other Episodes in French Cultural History* (New York: Basic Books, 1984), pp. 249–51; Roger Chartier, *Lectures et lecteurs dans la France d'Ancien Régime* (Paris: Seuil, 1987), pp. 201–3; and James Smith Allen, *In the Public Eye: A History of Reading in Modern France, 1800–1940* (Princeton: Princeton University Press, 1991), p. 17.

82. Archives de la Bastille 11582, Premier interrogatoire, fols. 55 and 55v.

83. See Chartier, *Lectures et lecteurs,* pp. 199–200.

84. Rousseau, *Confessions,* Eng. ed., p. 48; French ed., p. 41.

85. Michael Fried, *Absorption and Theatricality: Painting and Beholder in the Age of Diderot* (Berkeley: University of California Press, 1980), chap. 1.

86. *Rapport des commissaires chargés par le roi de l'examen du magnétisme animal* (n.p., 1784), pp. 39–42, 46, quotation on p. 39. See also my discussion of the *Rapport* in Jan Goldstein, "'Moral Contagion': A Professional Ideology of Medicine and Psychiatry in Eighteenth- and Nineteenth-Century France," in *Professions and the French State, 1700–1900,* ed. Gerald L. Geison (Philadelphia: University of Pennsylvania Press, 1984), pp. 181–222.

2. The Revolutionary Schooling of Imagination

1. "De la fête de la raison," *Les Révolutions de Paris* 17, no. 215 (23–30 brumaire Year II): 210–18, quotations on pp. 214–15.

2. Ibid., p. 211, my italics.

3. Ibid., pp. 211, 215.

4. Already sanctioned by Enlightenment epistemology, neologism became a particularly common practice in France during the Revolution, when national regeneration seemed to require it; see, e.g., Charles-Frédéric Reinhard, *Le néologiste français, ou vocabulaire portatif des mots les plus nouveaux de la langue française . . .,* (n.p., 1796), Avant-Propos. For the distinction between its good and bad forms, called *néologie* and *néologisme,* respectively, see L.S. Mercier, *Néologie, ou Vocabulaire des mots nouveaux . . .,* 2 vols. (Paris: Moussard, Year XI-1801), 1: vi–vii. See also Sophia Rosenfeld, *A Revolution in Language: The Problem of Signs in Late Eighteenth-Century France* (Stanford: Stanford University Press, 2001).

5. "Avis de l'éditeur," in François Quesnay, *Dialogues sur le commerce et sur les travaux des artisans* in *Discussions et développemens sur quelques-unes des notions de l'économie politique* (Leyden: 1757), pp. 237–38.

6. Quesnay, *Dialogues,* pp. 251–53 and "Avis de l'éditeur," p. 239.

7. Quesnay, *Dialogues,* pp. 373, 375, 377, 379.

8. The text of *Les mannequins, conte ou histoire, comme l'on voudra* can be found in Louis-François Métra, *Correspondance secrète politique et littéraire,* 18 vols. (London: J. Adamson, 1787–90), 3: 87–110.

9. Ibid., pp. 92, 94, 96.

10. Marquis de Rangoni to Condillac, 9 October 1776, in Jean Sgard, ed., *Corpus Condillac (1714–1780)* (Geneva: Slatkine, 1981), pp. 154–55.

11. Condillac, *Le commerce et le gouvernement,* in *Oeuvres philosophiques de Condillac,* ed. Georges Le Roy, 3 vols. (Paris: Presses universitaires de France, 1947–51), 2: 332–35.

12. Keith Michael Baker, *Condorcet: From Natural Philosophy to Social Mathematics* (Chicago: University of Chicago Press, 1975), pp. 111–12.

13. See the editor's note to the "Discours préliminaire," *Cours d'études pour l'instruction du prince du Parme* (1775) in *Oeuvres philosophiques,* 1: 397 n. 1.

14. *Oeuvres philosophiques,* 2: 242 n.

15. Ibid., 2: 402.

16. Ibid. On "epistemological modesty" see Baker, *Condorcet,* chap. 2.

17. *Oeuvres philosophiques,* 2: 402.

18. Ibid., p. 403, my italics. For more on error in Condillac, see David W. Bates, *Enlightenment Aberrations: Error and Revolution in France* (Ithaca: Cornell University Press, 2002).

19. "De la fête de la raison," p. 214.

20. See Guillaume-François Le Trosne, *De l'intérêt social, par rapport à la valeur, à la circulation, à l'industrie et au commerce intérieur et extérieur* (Paris: Debure, 1777), p. 75–77, 80; and Nicolas Baudeau, "Observations économistes à M. l'abbé de Condillac," *Nouvelles éphémérides économiques,* April–May 1776; reprinted in Auguste Lebeau, *Condillac économiste* (Paris: Guillaumin, 1903): 422–45, esp. 436, 438–42.

21. Baker, *Condorcet,* pp. 114–22, esp. p. 121, quotation on p. 122.

22. See Steven Kaplan, "Les corporations, les 'faux ouvriers' et le faubourg Saint-Antoine au XVIIIe siècle," *Annales E.S.C.* (March–April 1988): 353–78.

23. AN: F12 654, "Mémoire des gardes de la communauté des teinturiers en soie, laine et fil de la ville de Rouen," 13 October 1778; and "Extrait des avis . . . sur un mémoire qui a pour objet d'établir un système d'administration intermédiaire entre la stricte exécution des ancien règlemens et la liberté générale et indéfinie," MS pp. 16–17. I learned of these archives in William M. Reddy, "The Structure of a Cultural Crisis: Thinking about Cloth in France Before and After the Revolution" in *The Social Life of Things: Commodities in Cultural Perspective,* ed. Arjun Appadurai (Cambridge: Cambridge University Press, 1986), pp. 261–84.

24. *Mémoires de Condorcet sur la Révolution française,* 2 vols. (Paris: Ponthieu, 1824), 2: 37–42, quotations on 40, my italics, and 42. On the career of Suard, see Robert Darnton, "The High Enlightenment and Low-Life of Literature in Pre-Revolutionary France," *Past and Present* (May 1971): 81–115, esp. 82–85.

25. Honoré-Gabriel de Riquetti, Comte de Mirabeau, "Considérations sur l'ordre de Cincinnatus," in *Oeuvres de Mirabeau,* 8 vols. (Paris: Lecointe et Pougin, 1834–35), 3: 323–426, esp. 326 for the quotation, 333, 336.

26. Ibid., pp. 339–40, 342–43.

27. Mirabeau, *Travail sur l'éducation publique trouvé dans les papiers de Mirabeau l'aîné,* ed. P.-J.-G. Cabanis (Paris: Impr. nationale, 1791), pp. 82–83.

28. Ibid., pp. 75, 81, 85, 97, 99.

29. "Avertissement," in ibid., p. 3 n. 1.

30. These tallies come from the ARTFL database.

31. Jean-Jacques Rousseau, *Emile, ou de l'Education,* in Jean-Jacques Rousseau, *Oeuvres complètes,* ed., Bernard Gagnebin and Marcel Raymond, 4 vols. (Paris: Gallimard/Pléiade, 1959–69) 4: 303–5, quotation on 305.

32. Ibid., p. 384.

33. See Madame de Genlis, *Adèle et Théodore, ou Lettres sur l'éducation,* 6th ed., 4 vols. (Paris: Lecointe et Durey, 1822) 1: 117, 191. My thanks to Julia Douthwaite for calling this text to my attention; she discusses it in her *The Wild Girl, Natural Man, and the Monster: Dangerous Experiments in the Age of the Enlightenment* (Chicago: University of Chicago Press, 2002), pp. 145–50.

34. *Emile,* pp. 488, 502–3, 506, 517.

35. Ibid., pp. 645, 647, 860, my italics.

36. Mirabeau, *Travail sur l'éducation publique,* p. 76.

37. Louis Joubert (de l'Hérault), *Opinion sur le projet . . . sur l'organisation des écoles primaires* (Paris: Impr. nationale, Year VII), p. 3. The whole quotation appears in italics in the original.

38. The path-breaking work on the festivals is Mona Ozouf, *Festivals and the French Revolution* (Fr. ed. 1976), trans. Alan Sheridan (Cambridge, MA: Harvard University Press, 1988). On these points of chronology, see esp. pp. 61, 106.

39. See Alain-Charles Gruber, *Les grands fêtes et leurs décors à l'époque de Louis XVI* (Geneva: Droz, 1972), esp. pp. 149–57.

40. Ozouf, *Festivals,* pp. 129, 200.

41. Raymond Barennes, *Opinion sur la résolution du 6 thermidor, relative aux fêtes décadaires* (Paris: Impr. nationale, Year VI), pp. 5–6.

42. For the first quotation, see François-Antoine Boissy d'Anglas, *Essai sur les fêtes nationales, suivi de quelques idées sur les arts et sur la nécessité de les*

encourager (Paris: Impr. polyglotte, Year II), p. 37; for the second, see Joubert, "Opinion," pp. 3–4. For a similar view, see Joseph Eschassériaux l'aîné, *Réflexions et projet de décret sur les fêtes décadaires* (Paris: Impr. nationale, Year III), p. 2.

43. Antoine-Christophe Merlin (de Thionville), *Opinion sur les fêtes nationales* (Paris: Impr. nationale, Year III), pp. 19–20.

44. AN: F 1C V Seine 1, "Rapport au nom du Comité des besoins," in *Conseil général de la Seine, Procès verbaux, an VII–an XI*, pp. 164–201. See the section entitled "Des fêtes nationales et de ce qu'il conviendrait de faire pour leur imprimer un plus grand caractère . . . ," pp. 188–96, esp. pp. 188–90.

45. See Henri Grégoire, "Rapport sur la nécessité et les moyens d'anéantir les patois et d'universaliser l'usage de la langue française," presented to the Convention on 16 prairial Year II; reprinted in Michel de Certeau, Dominique Julia, and Jacques Revel, *Une politique de la langue: La Révolution française et les patois* (Paris: Gallimard, 1975), pp. 300–317, esp. 304–5 and, for citation of Condillac, 314.

46. Grégoire, *Rapport et projet de décret . . . sur les costumes des législateurs et des autres fonctionnaires publics* (Paris: Impr. nationale, Year III), pp. 7–10.

47. Ibid., p. 2. Grégoire's bill is discussed in the context of general Revolutionary policy on clothing in Lynn Hunt, *Politics, Culture and Class in the French Revolution* (Berkeley: University of California Press, 1984), pp. 77–80.

48. Grégoire, *Système de dénominations topographiques pour les places, rues, quais, etc. de toutes les communes de la République* (Paris: Impr. nationale, n.d.), pp. 2–4, 10. See also James A. Leith, *Space and Revolution: Projects for Monuments, Squares and Public Buildings in France, 1789–1799* (Montreal: McGill-Queen's University Press, 1991), pp. 120–21 and chap. 7, and Priscilla Parkhurst Ferguson, *Paris as Revolution: Writing the Nineteenth-Century City* (Berkeley: University of California Press, 1994), pp. 26–30.

49. Leith, *Space and Revolution*, pp. 27–30. See also Teisserenc, *Géographie parisienne, en forme de dictionnaire* (Paris, 1754).

50. Fabre d'Eglantine, *L'Etude de la nature: Poème à M. le comte de Buffon* (London, 1783), pp. 1–2.

51. Report of Philippe Fabre d'Eglantine, 24 October 1793, in *Procès-verbaux du Comité d'instruction publique de la Convention nationale*, ed. J. Guillaume, 7 vols. (Paris: Impri. nationale, 1891–1959), 2: 697–706, esp. 697–701.

52. Maximilien Robespierre, "Report on the Principles of Political Morality," in Keith Michael Baker, ed., *The Old Regime and the French Revolution* (Chicago: University of Chicago Press, 1987), pp. 368–84, 369 for the quotation.

53. "Discours préliminaire" to *Cours d'études pour l'instruction du prince de Parme*, in *Oeuvres philosophiques*, 1: 398.

54. R. R. Palmer, *The Improvement of Humanity: Education and the French Revolution* (Princeton: Princeton University Press, 1985), pp. 242–43.

55. On this leitmotif, see L. Pearce Williams, "Science, Education, and the French Revolution," *Isis* 44 (1953): 311–30, esp. 314–18.

56. AN: F17 1341B, letter of Guilliot, professor of drawing at the central school of the Pas de Calais, 24 floréal Year VII.

57. AN: F17 1344/28.

58. The name resurfaced in scholarly discourse when Michel Foucault, relying heavily on the textbooks of the central schools, used it to mean the codification of the characteristic attitude toward language and knowledge of the so-called classical episteme of the seventeenth and eighteenth centuries. See *The Order of Things: An Archaeology of the Human Sciences* (New York: Vintage, 1973), pp. 81–92.

59. AN: F17 1344/2, response of Antoine Magin to question 9 of the ministerial circular.

60. AN: F17 1344/2, response of Joseph Cazalis to the ministerial circular, pp. 3–4.

61. See, e.g., AN: F17 1344/8, Dossier, Hautes-Alpes, letter of 13 brumaire Year V.

62. See, e.g., AN: F17 1344/2, Labbey, "Cours de grammaire-générale," MS dated 8 brumaire Year VIII; letter of Gattel to minister of interior, 15 vendémiaire Year VIII; letter of Descoles to minister of interior, 1 prairial Year VII.

63. AN: F17 1344/3, Thiébault, "De l'Enseignement de la grammaire générale dans les écoles centrales," MS pp. 2–3.

64. AN: F17 1344/2, Gattel to minister of interior, 1 prairial Year VII. On Gattel as teacher of Stendhal, see Stendhal, *La vie de Henry Brulard,* in *Oeuvres intimes,* ed. V. Del Litto, 2 vols. (Paris: Gallimard/Pléiade, 1981), 1: chap. 22, "Ecole centrale," esp. pp. 741–430.

65. See AN: F17 1339, "Réponses à la circulaire du 20 floréal Year VII, Cours de grammaire générale." Many said nothing at all about their sources, and some mentioned other authors—especially Locke, Court de Gébelin, Dumarsais, Bauzée, and Sicard—in addition to or instead of Condillac. For purposes of this tally I excluded those departments outside the hexagon that had been annexed to France during the Revolutionary wars.

66. Ibid., Entry #60 for the Department of the Seine; the remark was made by Duhamel, professor of general grammar at the Paris central school of the Pantheon.

67. AN: F17 1344/2, reply of Durand (Department of the Ain) to the ministerial circular.

68. AN: F17 1339 Dossier 20, "Extrait du procès verbal du Conseil d'instruction publique, 18 thermidor an VII," p. 11, discussion of one Citizen Duret.

69. AN: F17 1344/3, reply to the ministerial circular of the Year VII; printed poster entitled "Département de Maine-et-Loire. Ecole centrale: Cours de Botanique"; and letter of Merlet-Laboulaye to minister of interior, 29 vendémiaire Year VIII.

70. See L. W. B. Brockliss, *French Higher Education in the Seventeenth and Eighteenth Centuries: A Cultural History* (Oxford: Clarendon Press, 1987), pp. 215–16.

71. On these points, see Palmer, *Improvement of Humanity*, pp. 15, 25, 49–51, 106–7; and Jean de Viguerie, *Une oeuvre scolaire sous l'Ancien Régime: Les Pères de la Doctrine Chrétiennes en France et en Italie, 1592–1792* (Paris: Publications de la Sorbonne, 1976), pp. 559–64, 630.

72. AN: F17 1344/3, response of Ortolan to the ministerial circular of the Year VII and a large printed poster entitled, "Prospectus. Ouverture d'un cours privé de langue française et italienne," also dated Year VII.

73. AN: F17 1344/2, response of Magin to the ministerial circular of the Year VII.

74. Stendhal, *Vie de Henry Brulard*, in *Oeuvres intimes*, 1: 738, 742.

75. Claude Désirat and Tristan Hordé, "La fabrique aux élites: théories et pratiques de la grammaire génerale dans les écoles centrales," *Annales historiques de la révolution française* 53 (1981): 61–88.

76. Destutt de Tracy, "Observations sur le système actuel d'instruction publique" (1801). Reprinted in *Elémens d'Idéologie*, pt. 3, vol. 2 (Paris: Lévi, 1825), 331–82, quotation on p. 378.

77. Palmer, *Improvement of Humanity*, p. 248. This is Palmer's conclusion on the basis of sporadic data. It is notable, for example, that the prize winners at the central school of Besançon included the sons of a hairdresser, a locksmith, and a carpenter.

78. AN: F17 1344/2, letter to minister of interior dated 1 prairial Year VII.

79. AN: F17 1344/3, poster cited in n. 72, earlier.

80. AN: F17 1344/3, letter to minister of interior.

81. Destutt de Tracy, "Observations sur le système actuel d'instruction publique," pp. 378, 381. There would be, Destutt opined, not only a dilution in the subject matter but also a time lag (while the knowledge was being perfected and the *abrégés* drawn up) before the poor were instructed in it.

82. This handbill is bound together with the BN copy of F. Pinglin, *Nouveau cours de logique, ou l'art de raisonner réduit à un seul principe, et mis à la portée de tous les âges, et de tous les esprits* (n.p.: Impr. du Journal, n.d.).

83. See "Prospectus" to *L'Ami des campagnes, par une société de gens de lettres et rédigé par F. Pinglin*, bound in the BN copy of vol. 1 (15 prairial Year

VIII-15 frimaire Year XI). Installments of the sensationalist treatise, "Education intellectuelle: Premiers développemens de l'esprit," appear in 1: 65–67, 73–76, 129–31, 137–40, 161–62, 176–79, 193–95, 225–27, 377–80, 392–96, 433–34. Like Pinglin's *Nouveau cours,* this text contains areas of dissent from Condillac.

84. Pinglin, *Ami des campagnes,* vol. 1, no. 9.

85. Laurent-Pierre Berenger, *Esprit de Mably et de Condillac relativement à la morale et à la politique,* vol. 2:, *Esprit de Condillac* (Grenoble: Le Jay, 1789).

86. Citoyen B***, *L'Esprit de Condillac, ou principes de raison et de morale extraits des ouvrages de ce philosophe* (Paris: Chez les marchands des nouveautés, Year III).

87. For that wish, see *Esprit de Condillac,* "Notice sur M. l'abbé de Condillac," p. 4; on Berenger, see the *Dictionnaire de biographie française.*

88. AN: F17 1344/9, Dossier: Ariège, printed letter, "L'Administration centrale du département de l'Ariège à ses concitoyens," dated 16 germinal Year VI, my italics.

89. Thiébault, "De l'enseignement de la grammaire générale," MS pp. 4–5.

90. Dieudonné Thiébault, *Grammaire philosophique, ou la métaphysique, la logique et la grammaire, réunies en un seul corps de doctrine,* 2 vols. (Paris: Courcier, Year XI-1802), Preface, 1: iii–iv.

91. AN: F17 1344/2, Magin, professor of general grammar at the central school of the Ardennes, "Compte rendu pour l'enseignement du cours de grammaire génerale pendant l'an sept," my italics.

92. Jean-Louis Viefville des Essars, *Discours et projet de loi pour l'affranchissement des nègres, ou l'adoucissement de leur régime, et réponse aux objections des colons* (Paris: Impr. nationale, n.d. [1791]), pp. 30–31.

93. Condorcet, "Sketch for a Historical Picture of the Progress of the Human Mind," in Keith Michael Baker, ed., *Condorcet: Selected Writings* (Indianapolis: Bobbs-Merrill, 1976), 210–82, quotations from pp. 223, 265–66, my italics.

94. Pinglin, *Nouveau cours,* no. 1., pp. 1–2. The same relation between dupery and misanthropy is sketched out in F. Pinglin, *Cours de logique à l'usage des écoles nationales, ou l'art d'éviter l'erreur, mis à la portée du plus grand nombre* (Paris: Huzard, Year VI), p. 18.

95. Louis-Marie Reveillière-Lépaux, *Réflexions sur le culte, sur les cérémonies civiles et sur les fêtes nationales* (Paris: Jansen, Year V), pp. 4–5, my italics.

3. Is There a Self in This Mental Apparatus?

The epigraph is from AN: 284 AP 2/1, "Moi" (note on a loose sheet of paper, dated 1773). My thanks to Jacques Guilhaumou for providing me with his transcription of the original text. "Le passage difficile est d'en venir à former *le moi.*"

1. Dieudonné Thiébault, *Grammaire philosophique, ou la métaphysique, la logique et la grammaire, réunies en un seul corps de doctrine,* 2 vols. (Paris: Courcier, Year XI-1802), Preface, 1: p. xx for the quotation, pp. xx–xxx for Thiébault's involvement with Frederick the Great.

2. Charles Taylor, *Sources the Self: The Making of the Modern Identity* (Cambridge, MA: Harvard University Press, 1989), p. x.

3. Louis-Marie Reveillière-Lépeaux, *Réflexions sur le culte, sur les cérémonies civiles et sur les fêtes nationales* (Paris: Jansen, Year V), pp. 33–34.

4. *Mémoires de Lareveillière-Lépaux publiés par son fils,* 3 vols. (Paris: Plon, 1895), 1: 10–13.

5. Ibid., 2: 161, my italics.

6. *Le rouge et le noir* (1831), bk. I, chap. 7; for this interpretation of the passage, see Robert M. Adams, trans. and ed., Norton Critical Edition of Stendhal, *Red and Black* (New York: W. W. Norton, 1969), p. 34 n.1.

7. Stendhal, *De l'amour,* ed. V. Del Litto (Paris: Gallimard, 1969) bk. 1, chap. 24, p. 67, for *mouvement machinal;* bk. 1, chap. 3, p. 29, asterisked note, for *livre d'idéologie.*

8. On the centrality of the sensationalist model of mind to Stendhal's novelistic vocation and technique, see Harry Levin, *Gates of Horn: A Study of Five French Realists* (New York: Oxford, 1966), pp. 101–4.

9. This generally overlooked feature of the sensationalist self has a decidedly contemporary ring, inviting comparison with the postmodern self; see D.W. Murray, "What Is the Western Concept of the Self? On Forgetting David Hume," *Ethos* 21 (1993): 3–23. While not subscribing to a postmodern epistemology, William M. Reddy similarly proposes a "disaggregated" model of the self in *The Navigation of Feeling: A Framework for the History of the Emotions* (Cambridge: Cambridge University Press, 2001), p. 95.

10. E. J. Lowe, *Locke on Human Understanding* (New York: Routledge, 1995), p. 102. For additional highly technical, late twentieth-century philosophical debate on this same point, see the essays collected in Amélie Oksenberg Rorty, ed., *The Identity of Persons* (Berkeley: University of California Press, 1976).

11. *The Correspondence of John Locke,* 8 vols. (Oxford University Press, 1976–89), 4: 647–51, esp. 650 (Letter 1609).

12. See Henry E. Allison, "Locke's Theory of Personal Identity: A Re-Examination," in *Locke on Human Understanding: Selected Essays,* ed. I. C. Tipton (Oxford: Oxford University Press, 1977), pp. 105–22, esp. 106 and 106 n. 3. For Locke's stipulation that all our ideas are furnished by "SENSATION" and "REFLECTION" (his capitals), see John Locke, *An Essay Concerning Human Understanding,* ed. Peter H. Nidditch (Oxford: Clarendon, 1975), bk. 2, chap. 1, p. 105.

13. Locke, *Essay,* bk. 2, chap. 27, para. 9–10, pp. 335–36.

14. Ibid., para. 20–26, quotations on pp. 344, 346. It should be pointed out that Locke does not assimilate madness to drunkenness and somnambulism. In his view (pp. 342–43), madness qualifies both as a valid legal reason for exemption from responsibility for a criminal act and as an instance of "duplication" of the self.

15. See Allison, "Locke's Theory of Personal Identity," p. 112.

16. David Hume, *A Treatise of Human Nature,* ed. L. A. Selby-Bigge and P. H. Nidditch, 2nd ed. (Oxford: Clarendon, 1978), bk. 1, pt. 4, esp. pp. 251, 252, 259 for the passages quoted.

17. See Jørn Schøsler, *John Locke et le philosophes français: La critique des idées innées en France au dix-huitième siècle* (Oxford: Voltaire Foundation, 1997), p. 13. On this theme more generally, see Fernando Vidal, "Brains, Bodies, Selves, and Science: Anthropologies of Identity and the Resurrection of the Body," *Critical Inquiry* 28 (2002): 930–74, esp. 950–52 on Locke's *Essay,* which specified that the selfsame person would be resurrected though possibly in another body.

18. On this point, see the excellent discussion in R. R. Palmer, *Catholics and Unbelievers in Eighteenth-Century France* (Princeton: Princeton University Press, 1947), chap. 6.

19. Jean-Nicolas-Hubert Hayer, *La spiritualité et l'immortalité de l'ame,* 3 vols. (Paris: Chaubert, 1757), 2: 1–3.

20. Ibid., pp. 6–7. Hayer also offers a spiritualist response to Locke's argument about the discontinuity in the self introduced by deep sleep; see pp. 13–18.

21. Joseph-Adrien Lelarge de Lignac, *Le témoignage du sens intime et de l'expérience opposé à la foi profane et ridicule des fatalistes modernes,* 3 vols. (Auxerre: Fournier, 1760): 1, Preface, n.p. On Lignac, see Francisque Bouillier, *Histoire de la philosophie cartésienne,* 2 vols. (Paris: Durand, 1854), 2: 616–22.

22. Lignac, *Témoignage du sens intime,* 1: 392–96. In my effort to clarify Lignac, I have explicitly identified the Lockean tenets with Locke's definition of reflection (which Lignac does not do) and have thus arrived at a simple contrast between Locke's reflection and Lignac's key term, the *sens intime.*

23. *Essai sur l'origine des connoissances humaines,* pt. I, section 1, chap. 1, para. 15, Condillac, in *Oeuvres philosophiques,* ed. Georges Le Roy, 3 vols. (Paris: Presses universitaires de France, 1947–51), 1: 14.

24. Le Roy, Introduction to Condillac, *Oeuvres philosophiques,* 1: xv.

25. *Traité des sensations,* pt. 1, chap. 6, in *Oeuvres philosophiques,* 1: 238–39. It should be noted that while this chapter includes the word "moi" in its title,

the *moi* is treated in the *Essai* in a chapter which, implicitly denying the importance of that concept, is called "De la perception, de la conscience, de l'attention, et de la reminiscence."

26. In an 1816 Sorbonne lecture, Victor Cousin would regret that it had taken so long for Hume's corrosive argument against the sensationalist self to reach France; in that year, there was still no French translation of Hume's *Treatise*. See Cousin, *Premiers essais de philosophie*, 3d ed. (Paris: Librairie nouvelle, 1855), pp. 57–58. To be sure, Hume's briefer *Enquiry Concerning Human Understanding* (1748) was available in eighteenth-century French translation; see Baker, *Condorcet*, pp. 139–40; but it omitted the critical argument on personal identity.

27. "Lettre de M. l'abbé de Condillac à l'auteur des lettres à un Amériquain," reprinted from the *Mercure de France*, April 1756, and bound with the BN copy of Condillac, *Traité des animaux* (Amsterdam, 1755), quotation on p. 10.

28. See Hume, *Treatise of Human Nature*, bk. 1, pt. 4, section 6, p. 253: "The mind is a kind of theatre, where several perceptions successively make their appearance; pass, re-pass, glide away, and mingle in an infinite variety of postures and situations."

29. Georges-Louis Leclerc, comte de Buffon, *Discours sur la nature des animaux* in *Oeuvres philosophiques de Buffon*, ed. Jean Piveteau (Paris: Presses universitaires de France, 1954), pp. 317–50. Working from a very different text of Buffon, the "Essai d'arithmétique morale" (1777), Lorraine Daston has also noted the psychological accent of Buffon's work—in this case, his probability theory; see her *Classical Probability in the Enlightenment* (Princeton: Princeton University Press, 1988), pp. 93, 95.

30. Buffon, *Discours sur la nature des animaux*, pp. 323, 328–29, 332–33.

31. Condillac, *Traité des animaux* in *Oeuvres philosophiques*, 1: 342.

32. This is the narrative set forth in the article "Moi," *Dictionnaire des sciences philosophiques*, 6 vols. (Paris: L. Hachette, 1844–52) 4: 284–85. While this *Dictionnaire* was produced by the followers of Victor Cousin, and much that it contains is tendentious (see chaps. 4 and 5, later), the historical sequence cited here seems accurate.

33. See "Ame" in *Encyclopédie, ou dictionnaire raisonné des sciences, des arts et des métiers*, ed. Denis Diderot and Jean Le Rond d'Alembert, 17 vols. (Paris, 1751–65), 1: 327–43, quotation on 327; and "Moi" in ibid., 10: 614–15, quotation on 614. On the debate over the *âme des bêtes*, see Palmer, *Catholics and Unbelievers*, p. 147.

34. The chapter in which Condillac introduced the *moi* as a corollary of the mental operation of reminiscence is included in a section of the book called "The Analysis and Generation of the Operations of the *Ame*," an or-

ganizational device that appears to designate the *moi* as a subset of the *âme;* see Condillac, *Essai,* title of pt. 1, section 2.

35. See Locke, *Essai philosophique concernant l'entendement humain,* trans. Pierre Coste, 4th ed. (Amsterdam: Pierre Mortier, 1742), p. 264, n. 1. The first edition of the translation appeared in 1700.

36. For the well-known passages about the *moi* in the *Pensées,* see Pascal, *Oeuvres complètes,* ed. Jacques Chevalier (Paris: Gallimard/Pléiade, 1954), para. 130, p. 1123; para. 136, pp. 1126–27; para. 443, p. 1211. The rhetorical rule attributed to Pascal is found in Victor Cousin, *Des pensées de Pascal, rapport à l'Académie française sur la nécessité d'une nouvelle édition de cette ouvrage* (Paris: Ladrange, 1843), p. 45, which also quotes Pascal as saying "Christian piety annihilates the human *moi*" and "human civility hides and suppresses it." For a discussion of the annihilation of the *moi* in Pascal's theology, see Henri Gouhier, *Blaise Pascal: conversion et apologétique* (Paris: Vrin, 1986), pp. 49–53.

37. See *Oxford English Dictionary,* which gives as the chronologically first usages of "self" as a freestanding noun having the philosophical meaning of ego, works by Traherne (1674, "a secret self enclosed within") and T. Browne (1682, "in the Theater of our selves"). Locke's *Essay on Human Understanding* comes third, with the citations from pt. 2, chap. 27, para. 9, given earlier and a second citation from para. 17 of that chapter.

38. This is the contention of the article "Moi," *Dictionnaire des sciences philosophiques,* pp. 284–85. "When [Descartes] set forth the famous proposition, 'I think, therefore I am,' he truly put the *moi* in the place of the *âme* . . . [and] made it pass into language. . . . Descartes said, unmistakably and deliberately, *moi,* instead of saying *mon âme.* . . ."

39. *Discours de la méthode,* in *Oeuvres de Descartes,* ed. Charles Adam and Paul Tannery, 11 vols. (Paris: J. Vrin, 1996), 6: 33. This edition reproduces the text of the original edition of the *Discours de la méthode* published in Leyden in 1637.

40. Ibid., p. 34.

41. *Oeuvres philosophiques,* 3. By contrast, the *Dictionnaire* does contain an entry for *âme.*

42. AN: F17 1344/3, Germain Baradère, "Cours de grammaire générale: 1ère année," included with his reply to the ministerial circular of the Year VII; quotation from MS para. 48.

43. Antoine-Louis Claude Destutt de Tracy, *Elémens d'idéologie,* 3d. ed., 2 vols. (Paris: Courcier, 1817; reprint, Paris: Vrin, 1970), 1: Extrait raisonné of chaps. 1–5, pp. 391–94.

44. Ibid., p. 68.

45. Ibid., 1: 248, 397 (for the Extrait raisonné).

46. Ibid., 1: 136, 139, 143.

47. Ibid., 1: 153–55. This interpretation is borne out in a later work, *Traité de la volonté et de ses effets* (1st ed. 1815), where Tracy ascribes the idea of the existence of the *moi* to sensitivity and the idea of property to volition. I discuss this text in chap. 4, later.

48. P.-J.-G. Cabanis, *Rapports du physique et du morale de l'homme,* in *Oeuvres philosophiques,* ed. Claude Lehec and Jean Cazeneuve, 2 vols. (Paris: Presses universitaires de France, 1956), 1: 535–36.

49. Ibid., pp. 553–54; on p. 546 he implies that the fetus already possesses a *moi.*

50. Ibid., p. 538.

51. P. Laromiguière, *Leçons de philosophie, ou essai sur les facultés de l'âme,* 2d ed., 2 vols. (Paris: Brunot-Labbe, 1820), 1: 123 ("[L]a moralité et l'egoïsme sont deux contraires. L'homme moral se souvient qu'il a des frères; l'égoïste . . . ne connaît que son vil moi."), 185 ("Deux conditions sont nécessaires pour que la volonté devienne liberté morale; une délibération antérieure, pour qu'elle devienne liberté; et un but autre que l'intérêt exclusif du *moi,* pour qu'elle devienne morale.")

52. Ibid., 1: 206–7.

53. Ibid., 1: 219, where the *moi* is implicitly equated with the *sentiment de l'existence* (called the *sentiment de soi* on p. 221), and pp. 246–47, where much the same equation is implicitly made, and Laromiguière analyzes the term "consciousness" into two distinct aspects: the soul's "sentiment" of its existence and the soul's "idea" of its existence.

54. Ibid., 1: 249–50.

55. These marginal notes, available at the Bibliothèque Nationale de France, have been published in J. J. Rousseau, *Oeuvres complètes,* ed. Bernard Gagnebin and Marcel Raymond, 4 vols. (Paris: Gallimard/Pléiade, 1969), 4: 1122–30, quotation on 1129.

56. See Palmer, *Catholics and Unbelievers,* pp. 134–35: "when he sold his library in London, [Rousseau stipulated] that this volume should not be made public before his death."

57. *Notice sur la vie de Sieyès* (1794) in *Oeuvres de Sieyès,* 3 vols. (Paris: EDHIS, 1989), 3: 6–8.

58. I encountered the little loose pieces of paper that I have here called note cards during my own cursory examination of Sieyès' reading notes on Condillac; see AN: 284 AP 2, Dossiers 1–2. Since that time, some of those reading notes, though not these particular "feuilles volantes," have been edited and published; see Jacques Guilhaumou, "Le *Grand Cahier Métaphysique,* Présentation," in *Des manuscrits de Sieyès, 1773–1799,* ed. Christine Fauré (Paris: Honoré Champion, 1999), p. 56.

59. "Le *Grand cahier métaphysique,* Manuscrit et notes," in *Manuscrits de Sieyès,* ed. Fauré (henceforth, *GCM*), p. 77.

60. *GCM,* p. 85. According to Guilhaumou, the trope of the *spectateur philosophe* organized Sieyès' conception of subjectivity during the 1770s; see *Sieyès et l'ordre de la langue,* pp. 15, 22.

61. *GCM,* p. 91.

62. See AN: 284 AP2/1, "Analogie entre l'action et la reaction" and "Foyer des sensations," complementary notes to the reading notes on Bonnet in the *GCM.* My thanks to Jacques Guilhaumou for generously supplying his redactions of these texts to me; he dates the notes as 1768–70. The same passage is quoted in English translation in Murray Forsyth, *Reason and Revolution: The Political Thought of the Abbé Sieyes* (Leicester: Leicester University Press, 1987), pp. 43–44.

63. Ibid., p. 89.

64. This is one of the findings of Guilhaumou's editing of the *GCM;* see his "Présentation" in *Manuscrits de Sieyès,* pp. 51, 53–55.

65. Guilhaumou argues that, already under the Old Regime, the category of activity was the key to Sieyès's critical reading of Condillac and that Sieyès always conceptualized the *moi* in terms of a "principle of activity." See *Sieyès et l'ordre de la langue,* pp. 45–46.

66. *GCM,* p. 142 and p. 142 n. 120.

67. The political usage was his typology of citizens as active or passive in the debates over the 1791 Constitution; see William H. Sewell, Jr., *"Le citoyen/ la citoyenne:* Activity, Passivity, and the Revolutionary Concept of Citizenship," in *The Political Culture of the French Revolution,* ed. Colin Lucas, (Oxford: Pergamon, 1988), pp. 105–23, esp. 106–13.

68. See Carla Hesse, "Kant, Foucault, and *Three Women,*" in *Foucault and the Writing of History,* ed. Jan Goldstein (Oxford: Blackwell, 1994), pp. 81–98, esp. 86–89.

69. François Azouvi and Dominique Bourel, eds., *De Königsberg à Paris: La réception de Kant en France (1788–1804)* (Paris: J. Vrin, 1991), Avant-Propos, p. 11.

70. Ibid., p. 105.

71. Wilhelm von Humboldt, Journal entry of 27 May 1798, in *De Königsberg à Paris,* pp. 106–9.

72. Von Humboldt to Schiller, 23 June 1798, in ibid., pp. 109–12, quotation on p. 110.

73. Von Humboldt, Journal entry of 27 May 1798, p. 109.

74. Von Humboldt to Schiller, 23 June 1798, p. 111.

75. According to von Humboldt, Sieyès had been in contact with an earlier emissary of Kantianism to France, the Swiss diplomat Philippe-Albert

Stapfer. The result was not happy: "Sieyès drew [from Stapfer's lecture] the splendid conclusion that German metaphysics was to true metaphysics as astrology was to astronomy." Wilhelm von Humboldt, *Journal parisien (1797–1799),* trans. Elisabeth Boyer (Arles: Actes Sud, 2001), p. 123.

76. See Jacques Guilhaumou, "Sieyès et la métaphysique allemande," *Annales historiques de la révolution francaise,* no. 317 (1999): 513–35, esp. 513–14.

77. Von Humboldt, Journal entry of 27 May 1798, p. 107.

78. Von Humboldt to Schiller, 23 June 1798, p. 111.

79. Von Humboldt, *Journal parisien,* pp. 130–31.

80. Henri Gouhier dates Maine de Biran's "conversion" to "Biranism" to 1804, when he realized that an unacknowledged "revolution" had in taken place in his own thought; see *Les conversions de Maine de Biran* (Paris: J. Vrin, 1947), p. 169.

81. George Boas, *French Philosophies of the Romantic Period* (Baltimore: Johns Hopkins University Press, 1925), p. 63.

82. For these biographical details, see A. de la Valette Monbrun, *Maine de Biran (1766–1824): Essai de biographie historique et psychologique* (Paris: Fontemoing, 1914), chap. 1.

83. For the full list of his political posts, see Elisabeth G. Sledziewski, "Maine de Biran devant la Révolution," in her *Révolutions du sujet* (Paris: Méridiens Klincksieck, 1988), pp. 163–81, esp. 164–65.

84. Maine de Biran, *Journal,* ed. Henri Gouhier, 3 vols. (Neuchatel: La Baconnière, 1954–57), 3: 17–18 (25 December 1794).

85. Quoted in François Azouvi, *Maine de Biran: La science de l'homme* (Paris: J. Vrin, 1995), p. 14.

86. See Maine de Biran, *Journal* 1: 68 (24 April 1815); 128 (12 May 1816); and 3: 9 (27 May 1794).

87. See, for a similar treatment of the journal, Agnès Antoine, *Maine de Biran: Sujet et politique* (Paris: Presses universitaires de France, 1999). I learned of this work only after I had completed writing my own account of Biran.

88. Maine de Biran, *Journal,* 1: 20–23, 26.

89. Ibid., 1: 19 (22 September 1814).

90. Ibid., 1: 129 (16 May 1816).

91. Ibid., 1: 19 (20 September 1814), 24 (17 October 1814).

92. Ibid., 3: 3 (27 May 1794).

93. Ibid., 3: 13–14 (25 December 1794).

94. Ibid., 3: 8, 17.

95. Ibid., 3: 17 (25 December 1794).

96. Ibid., 1: 234 (19 November 1816), italics in the original.

97. Ibid., 3: 6 (27 May 1794).

98. Ibid., 3: 15–17 (25 December 1794).

99. Ibid., 1: 53–54 (4 April 1815).
100. Ibid., 1: 49 (26 March 1815), my italics.
101. Ibid., 1: 61 (12 April 1815).
102. Ibid., 3: 18–19 (25 December 1794).
103. Ibid., 1: 36 (1 January 1815), italics in the original.
104. Ibid., 1: 91–92 (21 June 1815, 22 June 1815).
105. Ibid., 1: 176 (23 July 1816), italics in the original.
106. Ibid., 2: 95 (25 November 1817).
107. On Maine de Biran's criteria for a science of psychology, see Azouvi, *Maine de Biran*, pp. 207–15.
108. On the weight of the manuscripts shipped by Maine de Biran's son in 1843 and 1844 to Ernest Naville, his father's biographer, see Gouhier, "Introduction" to Maine de Biran, *Journal*, 1: x.

4. An A Priori Self for the Bourgeois Male

The epigraph is from Maine de Biran, *Journal*, ed. Henri Gouhier, 3 vols. (Neuchatel: La Baconnière, 1954–57), 1: 126–27 (8 May 1816).

1. Maine de Biran, *Journal*, ed. Henri Gouhier, 3 vols. (Neuchatel: La Baconnière, 1954–57), 2: 303 (January 1821). The text cites Cousin's adherence to Schelling as the source of a disagreement with Maine de Biran.
2. This theme was already developed in a work by one of Cousin's own disciples, Jules Simon, *Victor Cousin* (Paris: Hachette, 1887). For more recent scholarship, see R. R. Bolgar, "Victor Cousin and Nineteenth-Century Education," *Cambridge Journal* 2 (1949): 357–68; Doris Goldstein, "'Official Philosophies' in Modern France: The Example of Victor Cousin," *Journal of Social History* (Spring 1968): 259–79; John I. Brooks, *The Eclectic Legacy: Academic Philosophy and the Human Sciences in Nineteenth-Century France* (Newark: University of Delaware Press, 1998); and, for the most thorough examination of the issue, Patrice Vermeren, *Victor Cousin: Le jeu de la philosophie et de l'état* (Paris: L'Harmattan, 1995). See also Jacques Derrida, *Du droit à la philosophie* (Paris: Galilée, 1990), esp. pp. 185–94, for a discussion of Cousin's founding role in modern French philosophy instruction, his relationship to Hegel, and his mystification of philosophy by attempting to naturalize it.
3. For the quotation, see V. C., "Sciences philosophiques: Programme des leçons données à l'Ecole normale pendant le premier semestre de l'année 1818 . . . ," *Archives philosophiques* 4 (1818): 86.
4. Renan, *Cahiers de jeunesse*, in *Oeuvres complètes de Ernest Renan*, 10 vols. (Paris: Calmann-Lévy, 1947–61), 9: 74.

5. Victor Cousin, "Préface à la première édition" (1826), in *Fragmens philosophiques,* 2d ed. (Paris: Ladrange, 1833), pp. 1–50, pp. 3, 5, for the quotations.

6. Duchesse de Dino (Dorothée de Courlande), *Souvenirs . . . publiés par sa petite fille* (Paris: Calmann-Lévy, 1908), pp. 132, 139.

7. Stendhal to Pauline Beyle, messidor Year X (July 1802), in Stendhal, *Correspondance générale,* ed. V. Del Litto, 6 vols. (Paris: Honoré Champion, 1997–99), 1: 56–57.

8. Martin S. Staum, *Cabanis: Enlightenment and Medical Philosophy in the French Revolution* (Princeton: Princeton University Press, 1980), p. 292.

9. R. R. Palmer, *The Improvement of Humanity: Education and the French Revolution* (Princeton: Princeton University Press, 1985), pp. 293–306, esp. 302.

10. *Moniteur universel,* 21 December 1812, as quoted in Prosper Alfaric, *Laromiguière et son école: Etude biographique* (Paris: Belles Lettres, 1929), p. 78.

11. Alfaric, *Laromiguière,* pp. 11, 14, 19–20, 25–26.

12. Ibid., pp. 29–31.

13. See Laromiguière's handwritten curriculum vitae in the Cousin manuscripts, Bibiliothèque de la Sorbonne (henceforth, Cousin MSS), vol. 236, f. 2964. The document has been bound after three brief notes from Laromiguière to Cousin; since its last entry is Laromiguière's designation as Officer of the Legion of Honor in 1837, the year of his death, it seems likely that Cousin received the c.v. as an aid in the preparation of an obituary or funeral oration for his fellow philosopher. See also Alfaric, *Laromiguière,* pp. 35–37.

14. Alfaric, *Laromiguière,* pp. 66–70.

15. See Jan Goldstein, *Console and Classify: The French Psychiatric Profession in the Nineteenth Century* (Cambridge: Cambridge University Press, 1987), pp. 246–47.

16. Laromiguière, *Leçons de philosophie,* 2d ed., 2 vols (Paris: Brunot-Labbe, 1820), 1: 67, italics in the original.

17. Laromiguière, "Discours sur la langue du raisonnement, prononcé au cours de philosophie de la faculté des lettres de Paris, le 26 avril 1811," reprinted in *Leçons de philosophie,* 1: 3–48, 34 for the quotation.

18. The adjective is that of R. R. Palmer, *Improvement of Humanity,* p. 322.

19. Alfaric, *Laromiguière,* pp. 97–98.

20. I develop this theme further in chap. 6, later.

21. "Projet d'un Collège des Pairs," in Stendhal, *Correspondance,* 2: 550–62, esp. 550 and 552–53.

22. Paris: H. Verdière, Aimé André, 1821. The books give no indication of who was behind this republication.

23. See Achille Tardif, *L'Abeille encyclopédique, ou aperçu raisonné de toutes les connaissances humaines . . .* (Paris: Rousseau, 1830), pp. 362–71; the title

page indicates the official approval of the work and its dedication to Charles X.

24. Sylvain Auroux, "La vague condillacienne," *Histoire épistémologie langage* 3 (1981), fasc. 2: 107–10, 107 for the quotations.

25. See Jean Saphary, *Essai analytique d'une métaphysique . . . dans le plan de M. Laromiguière, dont on résume d'abord les Leçons* (Paris: Brunot-Labbe, 1827).

26. A. J. H. Valette, *Cours de philosophie à la Faculté des Lettres de Paris. Discours d'ouverture. Première année* (Paris: Hachette, 1829), pp. 12–14.

27. Ibid., p. 15, 21–24.

28. Roederer to Guizot, 24 October 1832, in AN: 42 AP 289, as cited by Dudley C. Barksdale, "Liberal Politics and Nascent Social Science: The Academy of Moral and Political Sciences, 1803–1852" (Ph.D. dissertation, University of North Carolina at Chapel Hill, 1986), pp. 241–42. The term "German school" is Roederer's. As if to vindicate Daunou's opinion, a recent historical study of the Academy attributes its ultimately disappointing intellectual output in part to "the personality of Victor Cousin and his hegemony" over the institution. See Sophie-Anne Leterrier, *L'Institution des sciences morales: L'Académie des sciences morales et politiques, 1795–1850* (Paris: L'Harmattan, 1995), p. 333.

29. I owe this concept to conversations with Daniel Segal, who refers to its rough equivalent as "folk secular knowledge."

30. Francisque Bouillier, *Théorie de la raison impersonnelle* (Paris: Joubert, 1844), p. 331.

31. Louis Peisse, "Preface" to William Hamilton, *Fragments de philosophie* (Paris: Ladrange, 1840), p. v. An atypical disciple of Cousin who renounced an academic career, Peisse was proud of "mak[ing] war on medical materialism" as a freelance intellectual. See his twenty-seven letters to Cousin in the Cousin MSS, vol. 243, esp. #3971 of 14 May 1834 for the phrase just quoted.

32. Angebert to Cousin, 8 August 1829, Cousin MSS, vol. 214, #81. This letter appears in Jules Barthélemy-Saint-Hilaire, *M. Victor Cousin: Sa vie et sa correspondance,* 3 vols. (Paris: Hachette, 1895), 3: 174–85, quotation on 182.

33. "Guru" is Alan Spitzer's felicitous term for the young Cousin; see his *The French Generation of 1820* (Princeton: Princeton University Press, 1987), chap. 3.

34. The testimony is that of Cousin's student, friend, and biographer, Jules Barthélemy-Saint-Hilaire, *Cousin,* 1: 25.

35. Jules Simon, *Victor Cousin,* 3d ed. (Paris: Hachette, 1891), p. 9.

36. I have taken this information from an appendix called "Vie de Victor Cousin" in Vermeren, *Victor Cousin,* p. 353. The same information can be found

in many other sources, e.g., Barthélemy-Saint-Hilaire, *Cousin,* 1: 25; Simon, *Victor Cousin,* chap. 1; and Theodore Zeldin, *France 1848–1945,* 2 vols. (Oxford, 1973–77), 2: 411. Vermeren's version of the schoolyard story has Cousin enrolled in school; Simon's version has Cousin in the gutter, an urchin who comes to the aid of a schoolboy he does not know.

37. Adolphe Franck, "Victor Cousin," in *Moralistes et philosophes* (Paris: Didier, 1872), pp. 291–321, esp. 304 for the quotation.

38. Cousin to Royer-Collard, 20 October 1833, in Bibliothèque de l'Institut de France, MS. 3990.

39. Palmer, *Improvement of Humanity,* pp. 310, 313.

40. Ibid., p. 309.

41. Spitzer, *Generation of 1820,* p. 16.

42. Ibid., pp. 16–17.

43. Ibid., chap. 2; on Cousin's involvement in the Carbonari, see ibid., p. 63, and Vermeren, *Victor Cousin,* pp. 67–68.

44. Spitzer, *Generation of 1820,* chap. 6. On the independence of the Ecole polytechnique from the Université and the school's consequent self-regulation, see A. Bobin, *Aux pères de la famille et aux chefs d'institution. Questions importantes concernant les jeunes gens que l'on destine à l'Ecole polytechnique* (Paris: Bachelier, 1842).

45. The correspondence, covering a period from the early 1820s to the early 1840s, is in the Royer-Collard papers at the Bibliothèque de l'Institut de France; see MS 3990 for the letters from Cousin and MS 2607 for Royer-Collard's copies of his letters to Cousin.

46. For Royer-Collard's successive posts, see André Schimberg, ed., *Fragments philosophiques de Royer-Collard* (Paris: F. Alcan, 1913), p. 319; for the date of his resignation of the presidency of the Council, see Adrian Philippe, *Royer-Collard: sa vie publique, sa vie privée, sa famille* (Paris: Michel Lévy, 1857), p. 122.

47. On the inappropriateness of the name "Doctrinaire," see Dominique Bagge, *Les idées politiques en France sous la Restauration* (Paris: Presses universitaires de France, 1952), p. 99.

48. Pierre Rosanvallon, *Le moment Guizot* (Paris: Gallimard, 1986), p. 37.

49. Ibid., pp. 38–39, 41, quoting from Guizot's writings of the 1820s.

50. Perhaps because his aim is to resuscitate Guizot's political thought as an indigenous form of French liberalism, Rosanvallon does not stress the bureaucratic component of the Doctrinaire political vision. I stressed it in my discussion of the passage of the Law of 30 June 1838 and the subsequent creation of a national asylum system—a clear example of Doctrinaire institution-building by bureaucratic means; see Goldstein, *Console and Classify,* pp. 277–78.

51. Quoted in Rosanvallon, *Moment Guizot,* p. 223, from texts spanning the 1820s through the 1860s.

52. Jules Simon, "Etat de la philosophie en France: Les radicaux, le clergé, les éclectiques," *Revue des deux mondes,* 1 February 1843, pp. 365–95, quotations on p. 366.

53. V. Cousin, *Fragments philosophiques,* 3d ed., 4 vols. (Paris: Ladrange, 1838–40), 1: 371, "Appendice" (to Cousin's Ecole normale lesson plans for the years 1817 and 1818).

54. Cousin to Hegel, 1 August 1826, in *Hegel: The Letters,* trans. Clark Butler and Christiane Seiler (Bloomington: Indiana University Press, 1984), p. 639.

55. Cousin, *Introduction à l'histoire de la philosophie* (Paris: Pichon et Didier, 1828), Lesson 13, pp. 42–43. Each lesson is separately paginated in this edition.

56. Victor Cousin, "Préface de la deuxième édition," *Fragmens philosophiques,* 2d ed. (Paris: Ladrange, 1833), p. lx.

57. The use of the term *juste-milieu* to describe the signature political mission of the July Monarchy goes back at least as far as a public speech made by King Louis-Philippe in January 1831; see Paul Robert, *Dictionnaire alphabétique et analogique de la langue française.*

58. Hippolyte Taine, *Les philosophes du XIXe siècle en France* (1857), 9th ed. (Paris: Hachette, 1905) p. 311; also quoted in Spitzer, *Generation of 1820,* p. 75. See ibid., p. 73, for the age of Cousin's audience.

59. "Discours prononcé à l'ouverture du cours, le 4 décembre 1817," in Victor Cousin, *Du vrai, du beau, et du bien,* 16th ed. (Paris: Didier, 1872), p. 9.

60. Stendhal, *Racine et Shakespeare,* ed. Henri Martineau (Paris: Le Divan, 1928), pt. 2, Letter 6, pp. 137–39, my italics; also quoted in Spitzer, *Generation of 1820,* p. 81.

61. Sorbonne MS 1907, a bound notebook of notes on Cousin's course of 11 December 1819 to 18 March 1820, MS p. 9.

62. Armand Marrast, *Examen critique du cours de philosophie de M. Cousin (leçon par leçon)* (Paris: Corréard Jeune, 1828–29), p. 7.

63. Comte to Valat, 3 November 1824, in Auguste Comte, *Correspondance générale et confessions,* ed. P. E. de Berrêdo and P. Arnaud, 8 vols. (Paris: Ecole des Hautes Etudes, 1973–90), 1: 132.

64. Taine, *Les philosophes classiques,* p. 102.

65. Spitzer, *Generation of 1820,* p. 72.

66. Anne Martin-Fugier, *La vie élégante, ou la formation du Tout-Paris, 1815–1848* (Paris: Fayard, 1990), p. 244.

67. Anonymous review of V. Cousin, *Cours de philosophie,* in *Edinburgh Review* 50 (October 1829): 194–221, quotation on 198.

68. Sorbonne MS 1907, MS p. 5, my emphasis. The printed catalogue of Sorbonne manuscripts identifies the notetaker as Louis de Raynal, "then a student, later attorney general at the Cour de Cassation."

69. See Cousin, *Premiers essais de philosophie*, 3d ed. (Paris: Librairie nouvelle, 1855), p. 24. This volume provides a version of the text of Cousin's Sorbonne lectures of 1815–16 as well as a course outline for those of 1816–17.

70. Cousin, *Introduction à l'histoire de la philosophie*, Lesson 13, p. 25.

71. See, e.g., "Les fragments théoriques, 1812–1813," in *Fragments de Royer-Collard*, esp. pp. 20–40.

72. Cousin, *Premiers essais*, pp. 128–29, 132, 134, 138.

73. Ibid., pp. 134–36.

74. Cousin, "Préface à la première èdition," *Fragmens philosophiques*, 2d ed., pp. 11–12.

75. See Condillac, *Traité des animaux* (1755) in *Oeuvres philosophiques de Condillac*, ed. Georges Le Roy, 3 vols. (Paris: Presses universitaires de France, 1947–51), 1: 342.

76. Cousin, "Préface à la premiere édition," *Fragmens philosophiques*, 2d ed., pp. 13–14.

77. Cousin, *Introduction à l'histoire de la philosophie*, Lesson 5, p. 15. He said much the same thing two years earlier; see "Préface à la première édition," *Fragmens philosophiques*, 2d ed., p. 38.

78. Cousin, "Préface de la deuxième édition," *Fragmens philosophiques*, 2d ed., p. xiv.

79. For the vestibule metaphor, see Cousin, *Introduction à l'histoire de la philosophie*, Lesson 13, p. 14. For a slightly different version of the metaphor, see "Préface à la première édition," *Fragmens philosophiques*, 2d ed., p. 12.

80. Cousin to Hegel, 1 August 1826, in *Hegel: The Letters*, p. 639.

81. "Discours de M. Cousin," *Institut royal de France. Académie des sciences morales et politiques. Funérailles de M. Jouffroy . . . le 3 mars 1842* (Paris: Impr. de F. Didot, n.d.), pp. 6–7.

82. Cousin, "Préface à la première édition," *Fragmens philosophiques*, 2d ed., p. 39.

83. Victor Cousin, *Du vrai, du beau et du bien*, 16th ed. (Paris: Hachette, 1872), opening sentence of Lesson 2, p. 36.

84. While the 1818 lectures appeared in print earlier, Cousin's textbook version of them, called *Du vrai, du beau et du bien*, was first published in 1853. A second, slightly augmented edition of 1854 went through at least seventeen printings during the nineteenth century, according to the catalog of the BN.

85. See "Du Fait de conscience," a brief excerpt from Cousin's 1817 Sorbonne course, in his *Premiers essais*, pp. 242–49, reprinted in his *Fragmens*

philosophiques, 2d ed., pp. 242–52. This text discusses the three components of consciousness but does not explicitly locate the term *moi* with respect to them.

86. "Préface à la première édition," *Fragmens philosophiques,* 2d ed., pp. 17, 25.

87. "Reason is impersonal by its nature," Cousin declared; see ibid., p. 18. One of Cousin's students wrote an entire book on impersonal reason, regarding it as among Cousin's "glories" as well as the "link uniting the whole eclectic school," see Bouillier, Preface, *Théorie de la raison impersonnelle,* pp. ii–iv.

88. Cousin, *Introduction à l'histoire de la philosophie,* Lesson 5, pp. 9–10, my italics.

89. Maine de Biran, *Journal,* 2: 24–26 (17–26 March 1817). The manuscript in question was written by the aging Enlightenment philosophe, the abbé André Morellet (1727–1819).

90. Ibid., 2: 138 (29 July 1817).

91. Cousin, *Cours d'histoire de la philosophie morale au 18e siècle, professé à la Faculté des Lettres en 1819 et 1820,* ed. E. Vacherot (Paris: Ladrange, 1841), pp. 11–13.

92. John Locke, *The Second Treatise of Government,* ed. T. P. Peardon (Indianapolis: Bobbs-Merrill, 1952), chap. 5, para. 25–27, 44, pp. 16–17, 27.

93. Antoine-Louis-Claude Destutt de Tracy, *Traité de la volonté et de ses effets* (1st ed. 1815), 2d ed. (Paris: Courcier, 1818; reprint, Geneva: Slatkine, 1984), pp. 49, 60–63, 66–67.

94. Michel Foucault, *Résumé des cours, 1970–1982* (Paris: Julliard, 1989), pp. 133–34. I discuss this issue at length in "Foucault and the Post-Revolutionary Self: The Uses of Cousinian Pedagogy in Nineteenth-Century France," in Jan Goldstein, ed., *Foucault and the Writing of History* (Oxford: Blackwell, 1994), pp. 99–115, 276–80, and "Foucault's Technologies of the Self and the Cultural History of Identity," *Arcadia* 33 (1998): 46–63.

95. The more succinct "introspection" was a late seventeenth-century English coinage that enjoyed currency in both ordinary and technical language on the other side of the Channel but did not enter French until the early twentieth century; see "Introspection" in André Lalande, *Vocabulaire technique et critique de philosophie,* 16th ed. (Paris: Presses universitaires de France, 1988).

96. Victor Cousin, "Préface à la première édition," *Fragmens philosophiques,* 2d ed. (Paris: Ladrange, 1833), pp. 11–13, 49–50.

97. Victor Cousin, "Appendice," in *Fragments philosophiques,* 3d ed., 4 vols. (Paris: Ladrange, 1838–40), 1: 370–71.

98. Auguste Comte, *Cours de philosophie positive, Leçons 1 à 45,* ed. Michel Serres, François Dagognet, and Allal Sinaceur (Paris: Hermann, 1975), Lesson 45, esp. pp. 853–54.

99. Stendhal, "Sketch of Parisian Society," in Stéphane Douailler et al., eds. *La philosophie saisie par l'état: Petits écrits sur l'enseignement philosophique en France, 1789–1900* (Paris: Aubier, 1988), pp. 177–85, 183 for the quotation. This text originally appeared in 1828 in the *New Monthly Magazine.*

100. Ibid., p. 185.

101. Locke, *Essai philosophique concernant l'entendement humain,* trans. Pierre Coste, 4th ed. (Amsterdam: Pierre Mortier, 1742), p. 264 n. 2.

102. See Emile Saisset, "Sens," *Dictionnaire des sciences philosophiques* 6: 578–87, esp. 578.

103. Cousin, *Introduction à l'histoire de la philosophie,* Lesson 2, pp. 5–6.

104. Ibid., Lesson 5, p. 35.

105. Cousin, "Préface de la deuxième édition," *Fragmens philosophiques,* 2d ed., p. viii.

106. *Introduction à l'histoire de la philosophie,* Lesson 1, p. 4.

107. Cousin, "Préface de la deuxième édition," *Fragmens philosophiques,* 2d ed., p. xxxv.

108. Ibid., p. xv.

109. "When I push one billiard ball into another, it is not the billiard ball that truly causes the movement that it imparts, for that movement has been imparted to it by the hand, by the muscles that, in the mystery of our physiological organization, are at the service of the will." Cousin, "Préface à la première édition," *Fragmens philosophiques,* 2d ed., p. 26.

110. Alain Girard, *Le journal intime,* 2d ed. (Paris: Presses universitaires de France, 1986), Introduction.

111. Gouhier, Introduction to Maine de Biran, *Journal,* 1: x–xi.

112. Ernest Bersot, "La philosophie de Rousseau," *Liberté de penser* 2 (June–December 1848): 118–46, quotations on 130–31.

113. A. Charma, *Du sommeil* (Paris: Hachette, 1851), esp. pp. 4, 12–14.

114. Vacherot to Cousin, 4 April 1836, Cousin MSS, vol. 251, #5041.

115. Cousin, *Introduction à l'histoire de la philosophie,* Lesson 5, pp. 39–40. For a similar statement, see "Préface à la première édition," *Fragmens philosophiques,* 2d ed., p. 45.

116. See Roger-Pol Droit, "'Cette déplorable idée de l'anéantissement': note sur Cousin, l'Inde et le bouddhisme," *Corpus, revue de philosophie,* no. 18–19 (1991): 85–103.

117. Jouffroy, *De la politique de la France en Afrique* (Paris: Impr. de A. Henry, 1840; reprint, with a new introduction, of his 1838 *Revue des deux mondes* article of the same title). See, e.g., pp. 1, 9–13.

118. See Pauline Franck to Adolphe Franck, 31 January 1844, which quotes the newspaper *La Quotidienne* as saying of Adolphe's election to the Institut, "'Monsieur Cousin looked for his Jew to bring to the Institut. This Jew has no other qualification for being chosen than that he is a Jew.'" Pauline Franck, *Une vie de femme: Lettres intimes* (Tours: Impr. Paul Bousrez, 1898), p. 497.

119. The following material is developed at greater length in my article, "Saying 'I': Victor Cousin, Caroline Angebert, and the Politics of Selfhood in Nineteenth-Century France," in *Rediscovering History: Culture, Politics, and the Psyche,* ed. Michael S. Roth (Stanford: Stanford University Press, 1994), pp. 321–35.

120. Cousin, *Introduction à l'histoire de la philosophie,* Lesson 8, p. 19; Lesson 9, p. 15.

121. Stendhal to Pauline Beyle, 1 February 1811, in Stendahl, *Correspondance générale,* 2: 134; see also Stendhal to Pauline Beyle, July 1802, ibid., 1: 57.

122. Angebert to Cousin, 30 September 1828, Cousin MSS, vol. 214, # 77.

123. Cabanis, *Rapports du physique et du moral de l'homme* (1802), Memoir 5, "De l'influence des sexes sur le caractère des idées et des affections morales," in *Oeuvres philosophiques de Cabanis,* ed. Claude Lehec and Jean Cazeneuve, 2 vols. (Paris: Presses universitaires de France, 1956), 1: 272–315.

124. See Erica Harth, *Cartesian Women: Versions and Subversions of Rational Discourse in the Old Regime* (Ithaca: Cornell University Press, 1992), chap. 2.

125. Cousin to Angebert, n.d., in Léon Séché, *Les amitiés de Lamartine,* 1st ser., 2d ed. (Paris: Mercure de France, 1911), pp. 187–88.

126. Angebert to Cousin, 12 October 1828, Cousin MSS, vol. 214, #78.

127. "Circulaire de M. le Ministre de l'instruction publique, du 17 juillet 1840, relative au nouveau règlement du baccalauréat ès lettres," in Victor Cousin, *Défense de l'Université et de la philosophie,* 3d ed. (Paris: Joubert, 1844), pp. 363–64.

128. Victor Cousin, "Les femmes illustres du dix-septième siècle," *Revue des deux mondes,* 15 January 1844, pp. 193–203, esp. pp. 194–95. The article was reprinted as the preface to Cousin's *Jacqueline Pascal* (Paris: Didier, 1845).

129. Francisque Bouillier to Cousin, 12 October 1839, Cousin MSS, vol. 219, #778.

130. Victor Cousin, *Du vrai, du beau et du bien* (Paris: Didier, 1853), p. 43 n. 1. This book, in which Cousin sought "to assemble into a doctrinal corpus the theories scattered through our different works," was based on his ear-

liest teaching; see "Avant-propos," p. i. Hence the retrospective quality of the remark quoted.

131. BN MSS, Renan papers, n.a.f. 11481, "Notes et remarques sur cours de M. Cousin sur les idées absolues du vrai, du beau et du bien," fols. 554v–555.

132. Cousin's most sustained discussion of this topic is the undated text, "Du premier et du dernier fait du conscience, ou de la spontanéité et de la réflexion," in his *Fragmens philosophiques,* 2d ed., pp. 351–61, esp. 351.

133. Cousin, "Préface à la première édition," *Fragmens philosophiques,* 2d ed., p. 45, my italics.

134. *Introduction à l'histoire de la philosophie,* Lesson 8, p. 15.

135. Cousin, *Du vrai, du beau et du bien* (1853), pp. 42–43, my italics.

136. Renan, "Notes et remarques," fols. 555.

137. See Cousin, *Philosophie populaire, suivie de la première partie de la profession de foi du vicaire savoyard . . .* (Paris: Pagnerre, 1848), pp. 1–14, quotations on pp. 4, 13. On the "petits traités," see Leterrier, *Institution des sciences morales,* pp. 315–22.

138. Cousin, *Philosophie populaire,* pp. 14–16.

139. Jerrold Seigel, *Bohemian Paris: Culture, Politics, and the Boundaries of Bourgeois Life, 1830–1930* (New York: Viking, 1986), pp. 5, 10–11.

140. C.-A. Sainte-Beuve, "Maine de Biran," in *Causeries de lundi,* 15 vols. (Paris: Garnier, n.d.), 13: 305.

141. The key texts here are, with respect to power, *Discipline and Punish: The Birth of Prison,* trans. Alan Sheridan (New York: Pantheon, 1977), p. 194, and *The History of Sexuality,* vol. 1: *An Introduction,* trans. Robert Hurley (New York: Vintage, 1980), p. 60. See also my discussion of subjectivity in "Foucault and the Post-Revolutionary Self," pp. 108–11.

142. Foucault, *Discipline and Punish,* p. 177.

5. Cousinian Hegemony

The epigraph is from Cousin to Francisque Bouillier, 14 January 1843, in C. 'Latreille, *Francisque Bouillier: Le dernier des cartésiens, avec des lettres inédites de Victor Cousin* (Paris: Hachette, 1907), p. 188.

1. A.-Jacques Matter, "Moi," in *Dictionnaire de la conversation et de la lecture,* 52 vols. (Paris: Belin-Mondar, 1832–39), 38: 259–61, esp. 259.

2. Matter appears in the "Liste générale des rédacteurs," *Dictionnaire des sciences philosophiques,* 6 vols. (Paris: Hachette, 1844–52), 6: 1046, a sure mark of membership in the Cousinian school, as discussed later. He also corresponded periodically with Cousin, calling him his "natural protec-

tor" in a letter of 1828; see Cousin manuscripts, Bibliothèque de la Sorbonne (henceforth, Cousin MSS), vol. 239, #3425.

3. For this editorial self-representation, see the untitled preface to the *Dictionnaire de la conversation et la lecture,* 1: 3. The list of contributors on the page facing the title page confirms their claim of ecumenism: it includes Victor Cousin and François Guizot as well as their arch-enemies François Broussais and Armand Marrast.

4. The term was coined in the 1780s by Jacques Tenon, a surgeon and formulator of enlightened health policy. See Michel Foucault et al., *Les machines à guérir (aux origines de l'hôpital moderne)* (Paris: Institut de l'environnement, 1976), first page of preface (n.p.) and p. 55 n. 1.

5. Caroline Angebert to Cousin, 15 November 1830, Cousin MSS, vol. 214, #87.

6. Charles-H. Pouthas, *Guizot pendant la restauration: Préparation de l'homme d'état (1814–1830)* (Paris: Plon, 1923), p. 21.

7. Ibid., p. 326; see also Anne Martin-Fugier, *La vie élégante, ou la formation du Tout-Paris, 1815–1848* (Paris: Fayard, 1990), p. 242. Cousin was suspended in November 1820, Guizot in October 1822.

8. The letter is quoted in Pouthas, *Guizot,* p. 355.

9. Ibid., p. 445.

10. See "M. Cousin, conseiller de l'Université," *Gazette des écoles,* 12 August 1830, p. 265 and, for the quotation, "De l'ordre légal dans l'Université," ibid., 19 August 1830, p. 273.

11. For the assertion of Cousin's "never publicly claimed paternity" of this law, see Jules Barthélemy-Saint-Hilaire, *M. Victor Cousin: sa vie et sa correspondance,* 3 vols. (Paris: Hachette, 1895), 1: 378–79, 3: 228. For the contrary assertion that Cousin's claim of paternity was "an exaggeration," see Douglas Johnson, *Guizot: Aspects of French History, 1787–1874* (London: Routledge and Kegan Paul, 1963), p. 127. On the government funding of Cousin's trip to Prussia, see AN: 42 AP 21, Guizot papers, "Note pour répondre à des calomnies contre M. Cousin."

12. Cousin to a certain Monsieur Müller of Weimar, 24 June 1833, in Barthélemy-Saint-Hilaire, *Cousin,* 3: 228.

13. See Johnson, *Guizot,* pp. 128–29, which ascribes these views to Guizot. According to Charles Pouthas, however, only Cousin wanted a severe limitation of the upward social mobility of the popular classes, while Guizot intended to use the *écoles primaires supérieures* to modernize the French economy and actively encourage selective ascension into the bourgeoisie. See his unpublished typescript, "L'oeuvre de Guizot au ministère de l'Instruction publique (1832–1837)," AN: AB XIX 3760, pp. 78, 258.

14. Johnson, *Guizot,* pp. 131–33, 133 for the quotation. The state authority over the primary schools was jointly exercised by the Ministry of Public Instruction, the Université, and the prefects.

15. Maine de Biran, *Journal,* ed. Henri Gouhier, 3 vols. (Neuchatel: La Baconnière, 1954–57), 1: 24 (17 October 1814); and "Réponse à M. Guizot" (1814) in *Oeuvres de Maine de Biran,* ed. Pierre Tisserand, 14 vols. (Paris: F. Alcan, 1920–49), 10: 259–77, esp. 261.

16. Maine de Biran, *Journal,* 2: 33 (13 April 1817), 39 (4 May 1817), 39 n. 1, 54 (10–18 July 1817).

17. Guizot, "Encyclopédie," in *Encyclopédie progressive, ou collection de traités sur l'histoire, l'état actuel et les progrès des connaissances humaines,* 2 vols. (Paris: Au bureau de l'Encyclopédie progressive, 1826) 1: 1–48, p. 7 for the quotation.

18. On Guizot's central role in the development of the civilization concept, see Lucien Febvre, "*Civilisation:* evolution of a word and a group of ideas," in *A New Kind of History,* ed. Peter Burke, trans. K. Folca (New York: Harper and Row, 1973), pp. 219–57, esp. 240–48.

19. Guizot, "Abrégé: Des abrégés ou du véritable but et du meilleur mode de composition des ouvrages élémentaires," *Encyclopédie progressive,* 1: 305–20, esp. 305–7, 309 for the quotations.

20. Ibid., pp. 311–13.

21. See the letters from Jouffroy among Guizot's personal papers, AN: 42AP 145, including one dated 4 January 1836 from Pisa, where Jouffroy has gone for health reasons, in which he regales Guizot with information about his physical condition: "I will not beg pardon for entering into these details; you have too often given proof of the interest that you take in my health for me to hesitate in supplying them to you."

22. Théodore Jouffroy, "Préface du traducteur," in Dugald Stewart, *Esquisses de philosophie morale* (1st ed., 1826), 3rd ed. (Paris: Johanneau, 1841), pp. iii, v.

23. Guizot, "Abrégé," p. 312.

24. AN: 42 AP 21,"Programme de la seconde partie du cours de psycologie [sic] élémentaire," undated, MS p. 1r and separate sheet pinned to MS p. 2v. An archivist's note identifies the handwriting as Jouffroy's. The "Programme" is inside an envelope labeled "Documens philosophiques et littéraires sur l'instruction publique en France," which also contains a "Programme abrégé du cours de philosophie fait au Collège royal de Henri IV pendant l'annéee 1817–1818, et au Collège r[oy]al de Bourbon pendant l'année 1816–1817" written in a different, apparently secretarial hand. Unidentified by the archivist, the latter is almost certainly the work of Georges-Gabriel Mauger, who taught philosophy at those institutions during those

years; see Mauger, *Vues sur l'enseignement de la philosophie*, 2d ed. (Paris: Deterville, 1818), Avant-Propos, p. 1. A disciple of Royer-Collard and Scottish common-sense philosophy who was apparently unconnected to Cousin, Mauger was eager to overhaul and expand philosophy instruction in the French secondary schools. Hence the logic behind Guizot's possession of both these *programmes*.

25. Robert Gildea, *Education in Provincial France, 1800–1914: A Study of Three Departments* (Oxford: Clarendon Press, 1983), pp. 35, 42.

26. AN: F17* 1795, "Procès-verbaux des délibérations du Conseil royal de l'instruction publique" (July–September 1832), session of 28 September 1832, fol. 434–36. The quotations come from the psychology program, items 4, 10, 11.

27. "Circulaire du 8 avril 1833, relative aux questions de philosophie sur lesquels doivent être interrogés les aspirants au grade de bachelier ès lettres," in Cousin, *Défense de l'Université et de la philosophie*, 3d ed. (Paris: Joubert, 1844), pp. 362–63.

28. This point is emphasized in Pouthas, "L'oeuvre de Guizot," pp. 9–14, 257.

29. On these points, see Jean-Louis Fabiani, *Les philosophes de la république* (Paris: Minuit, 1988), pp. 9–10, and the debate over philosophy instruction in the secondary schools in the Chamber of Peers in 1844. The Duc de Broglie asserted, "In France, the last year of [secondary school] classes has always been called the philosophy class." *Moniteur universel*, 13 April 1844, p. 926.

30. See Paul Janet, "L'enseignement de la philosophie dans les lycées," *Revue bleue*, 4th ser. 1 (January–June 1894): 241–46, 246 for the quotation.

31. This is a rough formulation of Guizot's position on *capacité* and suffrage, a position that shifted in subtle ways over the course of his career while always retaining its basic advocacy of the bourgeoisie; see Pierre Rosanvallon, *Le moment Guizot* (Paris: Gallimard, 1985), pp. 121–32, and Lucien Jaume, *L'individu effacé, ou le paradoxe du libéralisme français* (Paris: Fayard, 1997), pp. 130–37. For Guizot's classic statement of the universality of the bourgeoisie, see *The History of Civilization in Europe*, Lecture 7, in François Guizot, *Historical Essays and Lectures*, ed. Stanley Mellon (Chicago: University of Chicago Press, 1972), p. 207.

32. See, e.g., some of the statistics in Gildea, *Education in Provincial France*, pp. 71, 128, 146–47, 165.

33. A.-Jacques Matter, *L'instituteur primaire, ou conseils et directions pour préparer les instituteurs primaires à leur carrière et les diriger dans l'exercice de leurs fonctions*, 2d ed. (Paris: Hachette, 1843), pp. 106–7, 117 (for the definition of "psychologie"). That the first edition of this book, called simply *L'instituteur primaire* (Paris: Hachette, 1832), contains none of the material

quoted underscores the role of Cousin's curricular changes in popularizing the term "psychology."

34. Ibid., p. 120.
35. Ibid., p. 106.
36. See "Arrêté du 28 septembre 1832," in Cousin, Defense de l'Université, pp. 359–62, esp. article 1, p. 359.
37. On the 1902 reform, see John E. Talbott, The Politics of Educational Reform in France, 1918–1940 (Princeton: Princeton University Press, 1969), pp. 16–17. On the cultural place of Latinity generally, see Françoise Waquet, Latin, or the Empire of a Sign: From the Sixteenth to the Twentieth Centuries, trans. John Howe (London: Verso, 2001).
38. Gildea, Education in Provincial France, pp. 187–88.
39. "D'une discussion entamée dans la Chambre des deputés, le 29 mai," Le Semeur: Journal religieux, politique, philosophique, et littéraire 4 (1835): 217–24, 242–44, esp. 217. In fact, Guizot was both a defender of traditional classical education and an advocate of the expansion of scientific education to meet modern needs; see Pouthas, "L'oeuvre de Guizot," pp. 165–66.
40. See "Règlement du baccalauréat ès lettres, du 14 juillet 1840" and "Circulaire de M. le Ministre de l'instruction publique, du 17 juillet 1840, relative au nouveau règlement du baccalauéat ès lettres" in Cousin, Défense de l'Université, pp. 363–64. On the nineteenth-century philosophy programmes, see John I. Brooks III, The Eclectic Legacy: Academic Philosophy and the Human Sciences in Nineteenth-Century France (Newark: University of Delaware Press, 1998), chap. 1, and Fabiani, Philosophes de la république. The long persistence of the Cousinian programme is discussed in the Epilogue, later.
41. AN: 42 AP 21, "Note pour répondre à des calomnies contre M. Cousin."
42. On Cousin's initiative in creating the philosophy agrégation, see "Facultés des lettres. Institution des agrégés. Rapport au roi et ordonnance royale," dated 24 March 1840, in Victor Cousin, Oeuvres, new ed., 16 vols. (Paris: Ladrange, 1846–51), ser. 5, vol. 1, pp. 269–82. For the quotation from the letter, see Cousin to Bouillier, 5 August 1845, in C. Latreille, Francisque Bouillier: le dernier des cartésiens, avec des lettres inédites de Victor Cousin (Paris: Hachette, 1907), p. 196.
43. Dictionnaire des sciences philosophiques, 6 vols. (Paris: Hachette, 1844–52). The brief article, "Moi," 4: 284–86, is unsigned, the indication of Franck's authorship according to the "Liste génerale des rédacteurs," 6: 1045.
44. On this point, see Lawrence Rothfield, Vital Signs: Medical Realism in Nineteenth-Century Fiction (Princeton: Princeton University Press, 1992), p. 17. The quotation is from Madame Bovary, trans. Paul de Man, Norton Critical Editions (New York: W. W. Norton, 1965), pp. 22–23.

45. As indicated on the page facing the title page of vol. 1, that firm is Panckoucke, connected not only with the two *Dictionnaires* but also with the smaller format editions of the *Encyclopédie* of Diderot and d'Alembert.

46. See Adolphe Franck to Victor Cousin, 17 October 1843, Cousin MSS, vol. 229, #2058. "Everything [concerning the first installment of the *Dictionary*] is ready, except the Foreword, whose terms must be decided in common, under your direction. I would be extremely grateful if you would convene without delay the meeting that you were kind enough to mention to me."

47. "Préface des auteurs," *Dictionnaire des sciences philosophiques*, 1: v–vi.

48. I discuss the beleaguered situation of early nineteenth-century French philosophy in *Console and Classify: The French Psychiatric Profession in the Nineteenth Century* (Cambridge: Cambridge University Press, 1987), chap. 7.

49. Max Weber, *The Protestant Ethic and the Spirit of Capitalism*, trans. Talcott Parsons (New York: Scribner's, 1958), pp. 104, 109–12.

50. Cousin's *Du vrai, du beau et du bien* (Paris: Didier, 1853), was widely adopted as a textbook and became ubiquitous in France from its first publication until the 1880s. It was, in his words, a "severely corrected" version of the foundational courses he had offered at the Paris Faculty of Letters between 1815 and 1821 and represented an effort to respond to the requests he had repeatedly received to "assemble into a corpus of doctrine the theories scattered throughout our different works." See the Avant-Propos, pp. i–ii.

51. Maine de Biran, *Journal* 2: 92 (18 November 1817).

52. See *Elemens d'idéologie*, 3d ed., 2 vols. (Paris: Courcier, 1817; reprint, Paris: Vrin, 1970), 1: 148 n. 152.

53. P. Laromiguière, *Leçons de philosophie, ou Essai sur les facultés de l'âme*, 2d ed, 2 vols. (Brunot-Labbe, 1820), 1: 195.

54. On the style of twentieth-century U.S. textbooks—their use of a single voice and avoidance of any scrutiny of the signifying practices of language—see Daniel Segal, Introduction, *Staging History: Western Civ and Its Aftermaths in American Higher Education* (in preparation).

55. See, e.g., the prefatory comments by a minor Cousinian, Antoine Charma, *Réponses aux questions de philosophie contenues dans le programme adopté pour l'examen du baccalauréat ès lettres* (Paris: L. Hachette, 1835), pp. 3–4.

56. The textbooks considered here are: A. F. Gatien-Arnoult, *Programme d'un cours de philosophie* (1st ed. 1830), 4th ed. (Toulouse: Bon et Privat, 1841) and its companion volume of readings, *Cours de lectures philosophiques, ou dissertations et fragmens sur les principales questions de philosophie élémentaire* (Paris: J. B. Paya, 1838); Charma, *Réponses*; Charles-Auguste Mallet, *Manuel de philosophie à l'usage des élèves qui suivent les cours de l'Université*

(Paris: Maire-Nyon, 1835); Amédée Jacques, Jules Simon, and Emile Saisset, *Manuel de philosophie à l'usage des collèges* (Paris: Joubert, 1846).

57. Gatien-Arnoult, *Programme,* p. 22, italics in the original.
58. Gatien-Arnoult, *Cours de lectures,* p. 81 n. 1, quoting from a journal entry made in Nancy on 21 November 1828.
59. Gatien-Arnoult, *Programme,* 4th ed., pp. 23–24.
60. Charma to Cousin, 17 April 1832, Cousin MSS, vol. 222, #1223: "J'ai traversé la psychologie sans encombre." He admitted, with more humility, that he later foundered on the "almost inevitable" shoals of ontology.
61. Charma, *Réponses.*
62. Mallet, *Manuel,* pp. 7, 23–24.
63. Jacques et al., *Manuel,* pp. 180–81.
64. Ibid., p. 181.
65. Ibid., pp. 207–8, my italics.
66. Ibid., p. v.
67. See Epilogue, later.
68. Jacques et al., *Manuel,* describes the "utility" of psychology as providing the student with the "exact meaning of that multitude of words that designate the movements and affections of the soul and that form a considerable part of the vocabularies of all languages." See "Introduction," pp. 15–16.
69. Bouillier, "Discours d'ouverture prononcé à la faculté des lettres de Lyon, le 28 novembre 1844," *Revue des Lyonnais* 20 (1844): 420–32, esp. 424.
70. Jacques et al., *Manuel,* p. 15.
71. Some of Cousin's letters to his students are accessible elsewhere, usually in published biographical accounts of the individual students. For example, Latreille, *Francisque Bouillier,* includes fifty-one of them.
72. In fact, the only personal reference to sexual matters that I found in these letters occurs in Vacherot to Cousin, April 4, 1836, vol. 251, #5041. While discussing the issues of "duty" surrounding his broken and then resumed engagement (see later), Vacherot abruptly changes register and mentions his carnal feelings for his considerably younger fiancée. "At my age, besides, after having led a strictly single life, one can fear the storms of passion; I experience no difficulty in confessing this to you. But I take myself to be a young man who has struggled [presumably with lust] and conquered, but who is not sure that he will always conquer. . . ."
73. Foucault, *The History of Sexuality,* vol. 1: *An Introduction,* trans. Robert Hurley (New York: Vintage, 1980), pp. 60, 62, 64, 68–70.
74. AN: 87 AP 9, Simon papers, Dossier 4: Les premiers travaux de Jules Simon (1836–65), "La philosophie et l'enseignement officiel de la philosophie," MS p. 5, my italics.

75. Bersot to his father, 5 July 1844, in Ernest Bersot, *Fragments de ses lettres à sa famille de 1836 à 1871* (Paris: Impr. Ch. Noblet, 1913), p. 76.

76. Paul Janet to Cousin, 28 June 1846, Cousin MSS, vol. 234, #2674.

77. Jules Barni to Cousin, 29 July 1843, Cousin MSS, vol. 215, #237.

78. Debs to Cousin, 2 December 1839, Cousin MSS, vol. 224, #1495.

79. Mallet to Cousin, 19 March 1838, Cousin MSS, vol. 238, #3248.

80. Debs to Cousin, n.d., Cousin MSS, vol. 224, #1493.

81. Mallet to Cousin, 26 June 1839, Cousin MSS, vol. 238, #3252.

82. Gatien-Arnoult to Cousin, n.d., Cousin MSS, vol. 214, #123; Charma to Cousin, 31 December (no year), Cousin MSS, vol. 222, #1225; Bouillier to Cousin, 12 October 1839, and 28 June 1840, Cousin MSS, vol. 219, #778, #782.

83. "Nouvelles diverses," *Gazette des écoles,* 19 September 1830, p. 312.

84. Jules Simon used it as the title of chap. 3 of his *Victor Cousin* (Paris: Hachette, 1887).

85. Bersot to his family, 19 August 1837, in *Lettres à sa famille,* p. 30.

86. Cousin to Royer-Collard, 20 October 1833, in Bibliothèque de l'Institut de France, MS 3990, my italics.

87. Bersot to Cousin, 9 March 1842, vol. 217, #470: "surtout quand on tient des épaulettes de vous."

88. Riaux to Cousin, 5 November 1843 and 23 January 1846, Cousin MSS, vol. 245, #4295, #4302. See also Simon to Cousin, n.d., Cousin MSS, vol. 249, #4766; and Cousin to Bouillier, 27 June 1843, in Latreille, *Francisque Bouillier,* p. 192.

89. Riaux to Cousin, 21 April 1843, Cousin MSS, vol. 245, #4294.

90. Bersot to Cousin, 18 June 1842, Cousin MSS, vol. 217, #474.

91. Delcasso to Cousin, 26 June 1842, Cousin MSS, vol. 224, #1565.

92. Ernest Renan, *Souvenirs d'enfance et de jeunesse,* ed. Laudice Rétat (Paris: Garnier-Flammarion, 1973), p. 212.

93. Barni to Cousin, 3 July 1846 and 4 July [1846], Cousin MSS, vol. 215, #238, #239. Barni's angry letter was addressed "Monsieur"; his grateful one returned to the more affectionate "Monsieur et mon cher maître."

94. Charma to Cousin, 26 August 1837, Cousin MSS, vol. 222, #1226.

95. Charma to Cousin, n.d., Cousin MSS, #1224.

96. See Charma, *Du sommeil* (Paris: Hachette, 1851), p. 10, where Charma quotes an entry in his personal journal dated 18 Avril 1836: "I cannot explain to myself how philosophy came to abandon that subject matter [madness] to physiology without at least demanding a part of it. When in 1836 Pierre Rivière of Aunay was brought before the criminal court of Calvados, six or seven physicians were consulted about his mental

state. I wondered then why some of our psychologists would not also be consulted."

97. Michel Foucault, ed., *I, Pierre Rivière, having slaughtered my mother, my sister, and my brother . . . : A Case of Parricide in the Nineteenth Century* (French ed., 1973), trans. Frank Jellinek (New York: Pantheon, 1975).

98. Charma to Cousin, 26 August 1837, Cousin MSS, vol. 222, #1226.

99. Charma to Cousin, 17 April 1832, Cousin MSS, vol. 222, #1223.

100. Charma to Cousin, n.d., #1224.

101. Charma to Cousin, 26 August 1837.

102. Charma to Cousin, 16 June 1843, Cousin MSS, vol. 222, #1227.

103. Charma to Cousin, n.d. and 7 June 1851, Cousin MSS, vol. 222, #1230, #1231.

104. Janet to Cousin, Cousin MSS, vol. 234, #2672, #2673; both letters are undated. For more on Paul Janet's subsequent career, see Epilogue, later.

105. Accounts of Cousin's involvement with Louise Colet, whose daughter Henriette he may have fathered, and of the *affaire* Colet-Karr of 1840, which resulted from Alphonse Karr's allegation of Cousin's paternity in the satirical journal *Les Guêpes,* can be found in Micheline Bood and Serge Grand, *L'indomptable Louise Colet* (Paris: Pierre Horay, 1986), Jean-Paul Clébert, *Louise Colet: la muse* (Paris: Presses de la Renaissance, 1986), and Francine du Plessix Gray, *Rage and Fire: A Life of Louise Colet* (New York: Simon and Schuster, 1994).

106. Simon, *Victor Cousin,* p. 184.

107. Barthélemy-Saint-Hilaire, *Cousin,* 2: 524.

108. Cousin to Bouillier, 7 March 1849, in Latreille, *Francisque Bouillier,* p. 204.

109. Bouillier to Cousin, 10 January [1848], Cousin MSS, vol. 219, #817.

110. Bouillier to Cousin, 4 March [1848], Cousin MSS, vol. 219, #818.

111. Bouillier to Cousin, 6 August [1848], Cousin MSS, vol. 219, #821. He repeated this phrase in #825, 28 November [1848].

112. He also believed that Bouillier possessed the requisite "firmness of heart" that would ensure that a domestic life would not interfere with his philosophical and civic life; see Cousin to Bouillier, 7 March 1849.

113. Vacherot to Cousin, 2 November 1835, Cousin MSS, vol. 251, #5039.

114. Vacherot to Cousin, 4 April 1836, Cousin MSS, vol. 251, #5041.

115. Vacherot to Cousin, 9 May 1836, Cousin MSS, vol. 251, #5042.

116. Vacherot to Cousin, 24 October 1836, Cousin MSS, vol. 251, #5043.

117. Vacherot to Cousin, 9 May 1836, my italics.

118. Vapereau to Cousin, 2 May 1843, Cousin MSS, vol. 251, #5094.

119. Vacherot to Cousin, 9 May 1836.

120. Mallet to Cousin, 21 December 1837, Cousin MSS, vol. 238, #3247.

121. See Emile Saisset, "De la philosophie du clergé," *Revue des mondes,* 1 May 1844, a criticism of the renewed clerical attack on philosophy by such

figures as Bautain and Lacordaire; and "Renaissance du Voltairianisme," ibid., 1 February 1845, a parallel criticism of Michelet's harsh attack on the clergy in the *Du prêtre, de la femme et de la famille.* The term *spiritualisme conciliateur* appears in the first article.

122. Vacherot to Cousin, 16 January 1836, Cousin MSS, vol. 251, #5040.

123. My account comes almost entirely from the letters of Bersot to Cousin, Cousin MSS. A more detailed account can be found in Vermeren, *Victor Cousin,* chap. 10.

124. Bersot to Cousin, 10 October 1840, 13 November 1840, and 2 December 1840, Cousin MSS, vol. 217, #467, 468, 469.

125. Ernest Bersot, *Réflexions sur M. Lacordaire* (Bordeaux: Impr. de P. Coudert, 1842), a reprint from the periodical *L'Indicateur.* See p. 4, for Bersot's response to Lacordaire's characterization of philosophy as a cold science bereft of the energizing power of love.

126. Bersot to Cousin, 9 March 1842, Cousin MSS, vol. 217, #470.

127. Bersot to Cousin, 11 March 1842, Cousin MSS, vol. 217, #471.

128. Bersot to Cousin, 1 May 1842, Cousin MSS, vol. 217, #473, my italics; the letter contains the phrase *maître de moi.*

129. Ibid., my italics.

130. Vermeren, *Victor Cousin,* pp. 256–57, quoting Cousin to Bersot, 10 March 1842.

131. Simon to Cousin, n.d., Cousin MSS, vol. 249, #4762.

132. See letters of Bouillier to Cousin, Cousin MSS, vol. 219: 12 October 1839 (#778); 14 December 1839 (#779); 28 June 1840 (#782). Jouffroy's loss of his Catholic faith, which occurred while he was a student at the Ecole normale and studying philosophy with Cousin, had been described by Jouffroy in his personal journal and was well known during this period; see Camille Aymonier, *Théodore Jouffroy de Pontets* (Pontarlier: Faivre-Vernay, 1919), p. 15.

133. AN: F17 4163, "Concours de sortie 1820, Résultats du concours qui a eu lieu entre les élèves qui ont terminé leur cours normal et qui se destinent à l'enseignement des lettres, Dissertation philosophique." The dossier contains twelve philosophy examinations. On the Ecole normale under the Restoration, see Pierre Jeannin, *Deux siècles à Normale Sup': Petite histoire d'une grande ecole* (Paris: Larousse, 1994), pp. 31–39.

134. Examination of Henri-Jean Pottier, in "Concours de sortie 1820," my italics.

135. Examination of Jules Thibault, in ibid.

136. Examination of Alex-Emile Lefranc in ibid., my italics.

137. Examination of Gillette, in ibid.

138. "17ème question. Du moi. De son unité et de son identité," an unnumbered document bound after letter #4563 in Cousin MSS, vol. 247. A note

in the upper left-hand corner reads "redaction en philosophie de Monsieur Emile Saisset, élève à l'école normale en 1833." Cousin, we can surmise, kept the composition because it seemed to him an exemplary response to the seventeenth question of the 1832 *programme*.

139. Angebert to Cousin, 12 November 1829, Cousin MSS, vol. 214, #82.

140. Angebert to Cousin, 21 January 1830, Cousin MSS, vol. 214, #83.

141. Angebert to Cousin, 26 April 1830, Cousin MSS, vol. 214, #84.

142. Angebert to Cousin, 22 August 1830, Cousin MSS, vol. 214, #85.

143. Franck's election took place in 1844. On his academic career and his involvement in Jewish community affairs, see *A la mémoire d'Adolphe Franck: Discours et articles* (Paris: Impr. J. Montorier, 1893), and Perrine Simon-Nahum, *La cité investie: La science du judaïsme français et la République* (Paris: Cerf, 1991), pp. 73–78.

144. See Pauline Franck, *Une vie de femme: Lettres intimes* (Tours: Impr. Paul Bousrez, 1898). The collection was edited by Pauline's daughter, Marguerite, who decided not to include her father's letters because he was already well known through his public writings; see Preface, pp. 7–8. My thanks to Aron Rodrigue for alerting me to this source.

145. On this point, see Danièle Poublan, "Les lettres font-elles les sentiments? S'écrire avant le mariage au milieu du XIXe siècle," in *Séduction et sociétés: Approches historiques,* ed. Cécile Dauphin and Arlette Farge, (Paris: Seuil, 2001), pp. 141–82.

146. P. Franck to A. Franck, 23 April 1833, in *Vie de femme*, p. 41.

147. P. Franck to A. Franck, letter of 15 April 1836, in ibid., p. 223.

148. P. Franck to A. Franck, 30 May 1836, in ibid., 249–50.

149. See ibid., p. 32 n. 1. Franck prepared for the philosophy aggregation at Toulouse under Gatien-Arnoult's supervision, receiving the highest grade on that examination in 1832 and thus coming to Cousin's attention. For another reference to Gatien-Arnoult as Franck's teacher, see P. Franck to A. Franck, 5 June 1834, in ibid., p. 103.

150. P. Franck to A. Franck, 30 May 1836, in ibid., pp. 249–50.

151. P. Franck to A. Franck, 12 June 1833, in ibid., p. 53.

152. P. Franck to A. Franck, 14 January 1834, in ibid., pp. 83–85.

153. P. Franck to A. Franck, 4 June 1834, in ibid., p. 98.

154. P. Franck to A. Franck, 5 June 1834, in ibid., p. 105.

155. P. Franck to A. Franck, 18 December 1834, in ibid., p. 123.

156. P. Franck to A. Franck, 28 December 1835, in ibid., pp. 195–96.

157. P. Franck to A. Franck, 21 March 1837, in ibid., esp. pp. 322–23.

158. Cousin, *Introduction à l'histoire de la philosophie* (Paris: Pichon et Didier, 1828), Lesson 1, pp. 11–12.

159. Damiron, *Cours de philosophie,* 1: xxvii.

160. Jacques et al. *Manuel,* pp. 6–7, 11–12.

161. See Jan Goldstein, "Eclectic Subjectivity and the Impossibility of Female Beauty," in *Picturing Science, Producing Art,* ed. Caroline A. Jones and Peter Galison (London: Routledge, 1998), pp. 360–78.

162. Guizot, *Histoire de la civilisation en Europe depuis la chute de l'empire romain jusqu'à la révolution française,* new ed. (Paris: Didier, 1846), Lesson 1, pp. 3, 5.

163. Ibid., Lesson 4, pp. 91–92.

164. Ibid., Lesson 7, p. 188.

165. See, e.g., ibid., Lesson 4, p. 99.

166. Ibid., Lesson 2, p. 57. On the linkage of barbarism and civilization in Guizot, see Jacques Billard, *De l'ecole à la république: Guizot et Victor Cousin* (Paris: Presses universitaires de France, 1998), pp. 36–60, esp. p. 51.

167. Guizot, *Histoire de la civilisation en Europe,* pp. 99–101, 119, 195–96, my italics.

168. Guizot synoptically sketches this long development in ibid., pp. 206–7.

169. Jürgen Habermas, *The Structural Transformation of the Public Sphere: An Inquiry into a Category of Bourgeois Society,* trans. Thomas Burger (Cambridge, MA: MIT Press, 1989), pp. 46–48 for bourgeois "psychological emancipation" and p. 88. Note that Guizot includes in this definition the Doctrinaire proviso about *capacité* that tempers universalism with practical restrictions on political participation.

6. Religious and Secular Access to the *Vie Intérieure*

1. For recent treatments of Renan, see Maurice Olender, *The Languages of Paradise: Race, Religion and Philology in the Nineteenth Century,* trans. Arthur Goldhammer (French ed., 1989) (Cambridge, MA: Harvard University Press, 1992), esp. chap. 4; and Tzvetan Todorov, *On Human Diversity: Nationalism, Racism, and Exoticism in French Thought,* trans. Catherine Porter (French ed. 1989) (Cambridge, MA: Harvard University Press, 1993), esp. pp. 140–52, 219–29.

2. Ernest Renan to Henriette Renan, 17 January 1843, in Ernest and Henriette Renan, *Lettres intimes, 1842–1845* (Paris: Calmann-Lévy, 1896), quotations on pp. 117–18, 120.

3. Ernest Renan to Henriette Renan, 11 July 1844, in ibid., p. 184.

4. Issy was not a separate seminary but rather the country annex of Saint-Sulpice where the seminarians spent two years before moving on to Paris. See Ernest Renan, *Souvenirs d'enfance et de jeunesse,* ed. Laudice Rétat (Paris: Garnier-Flammarion, 1973), p. 135.

5. Renan to his mother, 12 January 1842, in Ernest Renan, *Lettres du séminaire, 1838–1846* (Paris: Calmann-Lévy, [1902]), pp. 164–65.

6. On the source of Renan's earliest knowledge of Cousin, see Jean Pommier's introduction to Renan's notes on Cousin's course of 1818, *Cahiers renaniens,* no. 3 (Paris: Nizan 1972): pp. 110–11. For Renan's familiarity with the anti-Cousinian polemics of the clergy, see his *Souvenirs,* p. 157, which also indicates another source of Renan's initially secondhand information about Cousin: a classmate who had studied at the Sorbonne before entering the seminary.

7. "Notes et remarques sur cours de M. Cousin sur les idées absolues du vrai, du beau et du bien," BN MSS, Renan papers, n.a.f. 11481. On this manuscript and the problem of dating it, see note 91, later.

8. Jean Pommier, ed., "Travaux et jours d'un séminariste en vacances (Bretagne 1845)," *Cahiers renaniens,* no. 2 (Paris: Nizan, 1972): p. 197 for the quotation, my italics.

9. See "Index des noms propres" in *Oeuvres complètes de Ernest Renan,* ed. Henriette Psichari, 9 vols. (Paris: Calmann-Lévy, 1947), 9: 1595.

10. The "Liste génerale de rédacteurs" in the sixth and final volume includes "Renan, orientaliste [E.R.]." See *Dictionnaire des sciences philosophiques,* 6 vols. (Paris: L. Hachette, 1844–52).

11. Ernest Renan, "De l'influence spiritualiste de M. Cousin" (1858), as reprinted in *Oeuvres complètes,* 2: 55–85, 79 for the quotation.

12. Renan, review of Paul Janet, *Victor Cousin et son oeuvre* in *Journal des débats,* 13 June 1885, as reprinted in *Oeuvres complètes,* 2: 1109–12, quotation on p. 1111.

13. Ernest Renan to Henriette Renan, 17 January 1843, in *Lettres intimes,* p. 119. Renan is referring to Cousin, *Des Pensées de Pascal: Rapport à l'Académie française sur la nécessité d'une nouvelle édition de cette ouvrage* (Paris: Ladrange, 1843); see that work's Avant-Propos, pp. xxxiii–xxxiv, xxxviii.

14. Ernest Renan to Henriette Renan, 22 September 1845, in *Lettres intimes,* p. 300.

15. Ernest Renan, *Cahiers de jeunesse,* in *Oeuvres complètes,* 9: 64, para. 35.

16. *Souvenirs,* p. 137.

17. See, e.g., *Souvenirs,* p. 156, where he notes the logically inconsistent position of one of his teachers at Issy by saying, "He never dreamt that if, to find the true and the good, man had only to plumb the depths of his heart, then the *Catechism* of Monsieur Olier would crumble at its base."

18. The catalog of the Bibliothèque nationale de France lists copies of twenty-four editions of the *Catéchisme,* of which five were published in the seventeenth century, one in the eighteenth century and, strikingly, twelve between 1800 and 1851. I have consulted the earliest of these nineteenth-century editions.

19. Ernest Renan to François Liart, 6 November 1841, in Renan, *Correspondance générale,* 2 vols. (Paris: Honoré Champion, 1995), 1: 253–54. At

about the same date, another seminarian observed, "No more than on the pyramids does the scythe of Time encroach on Saint-Sulpice"; see M. Theron, "Le séminaire Saint-Sulpice au XIXe siècle d'après deux ouvrages récents," *Compagnie de Saint-Sulpice. Bulletin du comité des études,* no. 25 (April–June 1959): 586–93, quotation on p. 591. See also Renan's comment in the *Souvenirs* (p. 141) that in Saint-Sulpice after the Revolution, "the seventeenth century had a location in Paris where it continued without the slightest modification."

20. See Theron, "Saint-Sulpice au XIXe siècle," pp. 591–92; and Irénée Noye, "L'héritage bérullien dans la compagnie de Saint-Sulpice," *Bulletin de Saint-Sulpice,* n.s. no. 22 (1996): 164–83, esp. 174ff.

21. Renan, *Souvenirs,* p. 137.

22. On the late nineteenth-century origins of the rubric "French school," its subsequent popularization by the third volume of Henri Bremond's influential *Histoire littéraire du sentiment religieux en France,* 11 vols. (Paris: Bloud et Gay, 1916–36), and the still lively debate over its suitability and defining characteristics, see Yves Krumenacher, *L'école francaise de spiritualité: Des mystiques, des fondateurs, des courants et leurs interprètes* (Paris: Cerf, 1998), chap. 1. I am grateful to Dale van Kley for introducing me to Bérulle.

23. See Bremond, *Histoire du sentiment religieux* 3, esp. pp. 461–62.

24. See Paul Cochois, "Etre sulpicien aujourd'hui dans un séminaire," *Bulletin de Saint-Sulpice,* n.s. 9 (1983): 16–33, esp. p. 24.

25. This point is made by Bremond, *Histoire du sentiment religieux* 3: 64ff. See also "Etats de Jésus," *Dictionnaire de spiritualité ascétique et mystique,* 17 vols. (Paris: G. Beauchesne, 1932–95), 4: col. 1403–1406 and "Intérieur de Jésus," ibid., 7, pt. 2, cols. 1870–1877.

26. Bremond, *Histoire du sentiment religieux* 3: 65, 74.

27. Renan, *Souvenirs,* p. 109.

28. See Bernaud Pitaud and Gilles Chaillot, *Jean-Jacques Olier, directeur spirituel* (Paris: Cerf, 1998), p. 21; this work also includes a modern edition of the 1831 text, *L'Esprit d'un directeur des âmes, ou maximes et pratique de M. Olier touchant la direction.*

29. Ernest Renan to François Liart, 6 November 1841, p. 253.

30. Renan, *Souvenirs,* pp. 151–52.

31. Renan's earliest known writings are the manuscripts edited by Jean Pommier and published as Ernest Renan, *Travaux de jeunesse 1843–1844* (Paris: Belles Lettres, 1931). Those with exclusively religious content are drafts of sermons or comments on the Old Testament psalms; they thus provide no evidence that Renan was engaging in any kind of explicitly religious introspection.

But negative evidence is always inconclusive, and we have, furthermore, no textual evidence at all from Renan's two years at Issy.

32. Olier, *Catéchisme chrétien pour la vie intérieure*, new ed. (Lyon: Rusand, 1822), pp. 1–2. For a discussion of the English translation of Olier's key term, *anéantissement*, see Lawrence B. Terrien, "Translating Father Olier: Some Reflections on the Project of Publishing our Founder's Writings," *Bulletin de Saint-Sulpice*, n.s., no. 22 (1996): 203–206.

33. The theme of self-annihilation runs through Sulpician piety. A biography of Olier by one of Renan's Sulpician contemporaries even lists suspension of self-hatred as a spiritual lapse that Olier admonished members of his order to guard against through self-examination. [Etienne-Michel Faillon], *Vie de M. Olier, fondateur du séminaire de S. Sulpice*, 2 vols (Paris: Poussielgue-Rusand, 1841), 2: 316.

34. Olier, *Catéchisme*, pp. 17–18, 81, my italics. See also p. 137: "Jesus Christ is within us to sanctify us . . . and to fill all of our faculties with himself."

35. Ibid., pp. 96–97, 99 for *"déiforme,"* italics in the original.

36. Ibid., pp. 101–2.

37. [Faillon], *Vie de M. Olier*, 2: 306–7. On Renan's familiarity with this text, see Jean Pommier, *Exposition Ernest Renan, "Souvenirs d'enfance et de jeunesse"* (Paris: Institut pédagogique national, 1959).

38. Renan to his mother, 28 April 1843, in Ernest Renan, *Lettres du séminaire, 1838–46* (Paris: Calmann-Lévy, 1902), p. 184.

39. Renan to Henriette Renan, 16 June 1843, in *Lettres intimes*, p. 138.

40. Olier, *Catéchisme*, p. 104, title of pt. II.

41. Ibid., p. 106.

42. Ibid., p. 147.

43. [Faillon], *Vie de M. Olier*, pp. 315–16.

44. Renan, *Souvenirs*, p. 144. The nineteenth-century Sulpician works cited in this chapter (those of Faillon and Manier) bear out Renan's assertion: the author's name, given in the catalog of the Bibliothèque nationale de France, is absent from their title pages. The anonymity rule apparently applies during the author's lifetime only. Thus, all the seventeen-century editions of Olier's *Catéchisme* in the B.N. were published after his death in 1657, and their title pages include his name; those of his works published before 1657 omit his name.

45. See Michel Foucault, "What Is an Author?" in *Language, Counter-Memory, Practice: Selected Essays and Interviews*, ed. Donald F. Bouchard (Ithaca: Cornell University Press, 1977), pp. 113–38, and Mark Rose, *Authors and Owners: The Invention of Copyright* (Cambridge, MA: Harvard University Press, 1993).

46. On the relationship of Olier and Le Brun, see Henry Jouin, *Charles Le Brun et les arts sous Louis XIV: Le premier peintre, sa vie, son oeuvre, ses écrits, ses contemporains, son influence* (Paris: Impr. Nationale, 1889), pp. 86–95.

47. [Etienne-Michel Faillon, ed.] *Vie intérieure de la Très-Sainte Vierge: Ouvrage recueilli des écrits de M. Olier,* 2 vols. (Rome: Impr. de Salviucci, 1866), 2: 419–23, my italics. The stained glass window dates from 1674 and bears a different caption than the engraving: "Regina cleri" (queen of the clergy); see Marguerite Huré and Valentine Cordier, "Les Vitraux de Saint-Sulpice," in Gaston Lemesle, ed., *L'église Saint-Sulpice* (Paris: Bloud and Gay, 1931), pp. 115–23, esp. 117–18. The title of Le Brun's original drawing is given in Jouin, *Le Brun,* p. 568, which also indicates the wide contemporary popularity of this image.

48. For the classic program in intellectual history that identifies authorial intention as the goal of the historian's investigation, see Quentin Skinner, "Meaning and Understanding in the History of Ideas," *History and Theory* 8 (1969): 3–53.

49. Jules Barthélemy-Saint-Hilaire, *M. Victor Cousin: Sa vie et sa correspondance,* 3 vols. (Paris: Hachette, 1895), 2: 2; see, e.g., ibid., Cousin to Lamennais, 4 August 1825, p. 7.

50. Cousin to Lamennais, 4 August 1825 and 12 September 1825, in ibid., pp. 7–8, 14.

51. Maine de Biran, *Journal,* ed. Henri Gouhier, 3 vols. (Neuchatel: La Baconnière, 1954–57), 2: 303 (January 1821).

52. Abbé G. Bazin, *Vie de Mgr Maret,* 3 vols. (Paris: Berche et Tralin, 1891), 1: 73–74; and Louis Foucher, *La philosophie catholique en France au XIXe siècle* (Paris: J. Vrin, 1955), p. 156.

53. H. Maret, *Essai sur le panthéisme dans les sociétés modernes* (Paris: Sapia, 1840), pp. v–vii.

54. Ibid., pp. viii–ix.

55. Ibid., p. 4. Maret did not pioneer this usage but built upon the work of the abbé Louis Bautain, a former student of Cousin's turned cleric; see Foucher, *Philosophie catholique,* pp. 149–50, 153.

56. Le comte de Saint-Priest, *Moniteur universel,* 24 April 1844, p. 1056. For an account of the 1844 legislative debate, see my "Foucault and the Post-Revolutionary Self: The Uses of Pedagogy in Nineteenth-Century France," in Jan Goldstein, ed., *Foucault and the Writing of History* (Oxford: Blackwell, 1994), pp. 99–115, esp. 105–7.

57. See Alasdair MacIntyre, "Pantheism," in *The Encyclopedia of Philosophy,* ed. Paul Edwards, 8 vols. (New York: Macmillan, 1967) 6: 31–35.

58. Maret, *Essai,* pp. 5–8.

59. See Maret, *Essai*, pp. 11–13, and his *La religion et la philosophie, les philosophes et le clergé* (Paris: W.-A. Vaille, 1845). This pamphlet is discussed in Claude Bressolette, *L'Abbé Maret: le combat d'un théologien pour une démocratie chrétienne, 1830–1851* (Paris: Beauchesne, 1977), pp. 266–67.

60. Maret, *La religion et la philosophie*, pp. 11–14.

61. Ibid., pp. 14–15, 18.

62. Renan to François Liart, 6 November 1841, *Correspondence générale*, 1: 254.

63. Renan, *Souvenirs*, pp. 142, 166.

64. For the quotation, see *Travaux de jeunesse*, p. 44; the bibliography in ibid., p. 262, indicates that Renan consulted the 43-volume edition of Bossuet's *Oeuvres* (Versailles: J. A. Leibel, 1815–19).

65. Dugald Stewart, *Esquisses de philosophie morale*, new translation preceded by an introduction by the abbé [Pierre-Hippolyte] Mabire (Paris: Librairie catholique de Périsse frères, 1841), esp. pp. ii–iii. On Renan's use of this edition while a seminary student, see the bibliography of Renan, *Travaux de jeunesse*, p. 264, as well as the published version of Renan's annotations, Ernest Renan, "Notes marginales aux *Esquisses de philosophie morale de D. Stewart*," ed. Jean Pommier, *Cahiers renaniens*, no. 3 (Paris: Nizet, 1972).

66. Anonymous review of Mabire's translation of Dugald Stewart, *Esquisses de la philosophie morale*, *L'Ami de la religion. Journal écclésiastique, politique et littéraire* 113 (1842): 481–86, esp. 484–85.

67. Victor Cousin, *Cours de philosophie*, 2 vols. (Paris: Pichon et Didier, 1828–29), 2: 556.

68. Victor Cousin, *Pensées de Pascal*, Avant-propos, pp. l–li.

69. *Souvenirs*, p. 156. For the identification of the Old Testament phrase that Renan quotes in Latin and for biographical information about Jacques-Alexis-Augustin Manier, see Jean Pommier, ed., Renan, *Souvenirs d'enfance et de jeunesse* (Paris: A Colin), p. 300, nn. 170 and 173.

70. Mabire, "Avertissement du traducteur," in Dugald Stewart, *Esquisses*, p. iii.

71. "Notes et remarques sur cours de M. Cousin," f. 555v.

72. "Observations et faits psychologiques," XL, in *Travaux de jeunesse*, pp. 41–42. Renan is referring to the clerical use of "freedom of instruction" as its battle cry against the Université. For other examples of Renan's characteristic formula, see, for example, XI, XIV, XVI XXVII XL, LXXIV.

73. Ibid., XX, p. 35. For Renan's Baconianism, see his "Notes sur *D. Stewart*," in his *Travaux de jeunesse*, pp. 81–86.

74. Ernest Renan, "Notes marginales aux *Esquisses de philosophie morale de D. Stewart*," p. 20: "It would be desirable for some observant psychologist (*psychologiste observateur*) to keep a journal of his main associations of ideas as well as of his dreams and of everything that he regards as having

given rise to them; that would be a means to infer something about that subject."

75. In his letters to Liart, Renan initially calls the course simply "psychology" but later expands the name to "rational and experimental psychology." See Renan to Liart, 3 May 1842, *Correspondance générale*, 1: 301. Manier published both parts of the course, the former in Latin as "Psychologia Rationalis," in [J.-J. Manier], *Compendium philosophiae*, 2 vols. (Paris: Firmin-Didot, 1847), 2: 257–368, the latter in French in [J.-J. Manier], *Traité élémentaire de psychologie expérimentale* (Paris: Firmin-Didot, 1849). The definition of the two parts of the course is given in the *Traité*, p. 2.

76. Renan, "Observations et faits psychologiques," XVII, p. 34.

77. Ibid., XLIII, p. 42.

78. Ibid., LXXXVII, pp. 55–56; LXXXVIII, p. 56; XLI, p. 42.

79. Renan made marginal notes on passages on habit in Dugald Stewart's *Esquisses;* see Pommier, ed., "Notes marginaux," pp. 34–35. On habit in Idéologie, see George Boas, *French Philosophies of the Romantic Period* (Baltimore: John Hopkins, 1925), pp. 44–45.

80. Renan, "Observations et faits psychologiques," II, p. 28; LXXXIX, p. 56.

81. On Renan's belief in the validity of what he calls "psychological induction from oneself to others," see ibid., LXXV, p. 52.

82. Ibid., XI, p. 32.

83. Ibid., LVII, LVIII, LIX, p. 47.

84. Pierre Janet, *Manuel du baccalauréat. Seconde Partie: Philosophie*, 6th ed. (Paris: Vuibert, n.d.), pp. 12–14.

85. Ernest Renan, "Essai psychologique sur Jésus-Christ," *Revue de Paris* 27 (15 September 1920): 225–61, quotation on p. 234. For a discussion of this text, see Jean Pommier, "Un opuscule inédit de Renan," ibid., 27 (1 September 1920): 52–62.

86. Renan, "Cahiers de jeunesse," in *Oeuvres complètes*, 9: 69–70.

87. Garnier's *Précis d'un cours de psychologie* (Paris: Hachette, 1831) and *La psychologie et la phrénologie comparées* (Paris: Hachette, 1839) more than justify this label, even though Renan recorded Garnier's private criticisms of aspects of Cousin's philosophy in the mid-1840s; see *Cahiers de jeunesse* in *Oeuvres complètes*, 9: 74–75, 145.

88. Renan, "Observations et faits psychologiques," XC, p. 57.

89. Ibid., XIX, p. 35; for other instances of religious explanation of psychological phenomena, see IV, p. 28, and LI, p. 45.

90. Ibid., XXXVII, pp. 40–41.

91. Renan, "Notes et remarques sur cours de M. Cousin," fols. 555v, 556v. The notes are undated, and their BN cataloguer has suggested the 1840s or 1850s as the probable date of composition. Textual evidence I gleaned

from the notes, especially the numbering of the individual lessons, indicates that Renan was working from the 1836 edition of the lectures prepared by Adophe Garnier, who used the redactions made in 1818 by students from the Ecole normale, which they had at the time duly deposited with the *maître*. See *Cours de philosophie professé à la faculté des lettres pendant l'année 1818 par M. V. Cousin sur le fondement des idées absolues du vrai, du beau et du bien* (Paris: Hachette, 1836), Préface de l'éditeur, pp. vi–vii. That Renan did not use Cousin's own published version of 1853 strongly suggests that he read the lectures before 1853. I am here accepting the dating of the manuscript by the Renan scholar Jean Pommier, who opts for late 1844 to early 1845 on the grounds that the letters "S.S." appear atop the first page; Pommier takes this to mean that Renan produced the notes while still a seminarian at Saint Sulpice. See his editor's introduction to the published version of the manuscript in *Cahiers renaniens* no. 3, pp. 110–11.

92. Ibid., fols. 554–554v.

93. Ibid., fol. 555.

94. Ibid., fol. 560v.

95. Ibid., fol. 553v.

96. See, e.g., Marie-Stanislas Rattier, *Cours complet de philosophie, mis en rapport avec le programme universitaire et ramené aux principes du catholicisme,* 6 vols. (Paris: Gaume, 1843–44), 1: 16–18.

97. Renan, "Notes et remarques sur cours de M. Cousin," fol. 556, Summary of Cousin's Lesson 4: "Thus are derived three faculties: activity, sensibility, reason. Activity is the basis of the *moi;* but on that basis are drawn sensation, which perceives the world, and reason, which perceives the truth." See also fol. 559v, Summary of Cousin's Lesson 6: "Unlike liberty, reason is not an individual faculty."

98. Ibid., fol. 560.

99. H. Renan to E. Renan, 30 October 1842, in *Lettres intimes,* p. 106.

100. H. Renan to E. Renan, 5 August 1845, in ibid., pp. 257–58.

101. See Ernest Renan, "Ma soeur Henriette" (1862), in *Oeuvres complètes,* 9: 445–80, p. 447 for the quotation.

102. The correspondence between Henriette and Ernest is an extremely moving document, revealing two people intimately bound together in a single project: the self-realization of Ernest Renan. When Ernest leaves the seminary, the hardly affluent Henriette seeks to cushion his material insecurity by sending from Poland 1,500 francs payable to him at the Rothschild bank in Paris. See H. Renan to E. Renan, 16 September 1845, in *Lettres intimes.* This sibling soul-union was, of course, predicated on the nineteenth-century gender conventions that, denying self-realization as

a legitimate goal for Henriette, freed her considerable energies for her brother.

103. Renan, "Observations et faits psychologiques," LXXXIX, p. 56.
104. Renan, "Séminariste en vacances," pp. 143, 145.
105. Renan, *Cahiers de jeunesse* V, 39.
106. Renan, "Observations et faits psychologiques," XXXV, p. 39.
107. See Jean Pommier, "Les idées de Michelet et de Renan sur la confession en 1845," *Journal de psychologie normale et pathologique* 33 (1936): 514–44. My account of this essay follows Pommier's.
108. Ibid., pp. 539–42.
109. Ibid., p. 543.
110. Relying on the Renan manuscripts, Pommier cites this passage in ibid., p. 544. It has since been published in Renan, *Cahiers de jeunesse*, in *Oeuvres complètes*, 9: 18.
111. *Cahiers de jeunesse*, in ibid., 9: 64, para. 35.
112. *Souvenirs*, p. 144.

7. A Palpable Self for the Socially Marginal

For the source of the epigraph, see note 143.

1. *Gazette des tribunaux*, 29 November, 4 December, 5 December 1839.
2. AN: F17 6649, Dossier: Allier, Director of General Police to Minister of the Interior, 27 April 1843; University of France to Minister of the Interior, May 1843; Minister of Public Instruction to Rector of the Academy of Clermont, 8 May 1843. The two most important secondary works on phrenology in France are Georges Lantéri-Laura, *Histoire de la phrénologie* (Paris: Presses universitaires de France, 1970, 2d ed., 1993), which focuses on the brain anatomy and physiology underlying the theory, and Marc Renneville, *Le langage des crânes: Une histoire de la phrénologie* (Paris: Institut d'édition Sanofi-Santhélabo, 2000), which focuses on the milieux in which phrenology was propagated. Virtually all of my research for this chapter was done well before the appearance of Renneville's book.
3. See the excerpts from a variety of provincial newspaper accounts of these demonstrations, reprinted by Béraud in his book, *De la phrénologie humaine appliquée à la philosophie, aux moeurs et au socialisme* (Paris: Durand, 1848), pp. 367–80. See also the copy of his printed handbill, "Prospectus: Phrénologie expérimentative et démonstrations particulières" (Grenoble: Prudhomme, Impr., n.d.), in AN: F17 6649, Dossier: Allier, esp. pp. 3–4. Béraud charged a fee for each cranial inspection, but the amount, left blank on the handbill, was presumably written in by hand and subject to change.

4. Béraud, *De la phrénologie humaine.* (See note 3, earlier.)

5. For his father's occupation, see his birth certificate, dated 18 September 1818, Etat Civil, Mairie de Lyon. Béraud's passport deceptively gave Paris as his birthplace; see Archives de la Loire, 10M25, sub-prefect to prefect, 25 February 1843.

6. See Félix Herbet, "Auguste Luchet (1805–1872): etude bio-bibliographique," *Abeille de Fontainebleau,* supplement of 3 January 1913, n.p.

7. "Procès de l'Almanach populaire de la France," *La Phrénologie,* 20 December 1837, p. 1.

8. On Dumoutier's early enrollment at the Paris Faculty of Medicine, see AN: AJ16 6425, AJ16 6426. His later records are located at the Paris Medical Faculty itself because the Archives Nationales took over from the Faculty only the files of those students who actually completed the medical degree.

9. On the choice of Dumoutier for this post, see Renneville, *Langage des crânes,* pp. 206–8. A fellow phrenological adept criticized Dumoutier for political timidity; see Théophile Thoré, *Dictionnaire de phrénologie et de physiognomie, à l'usage des artistes, des gens du monde, des instituteurs, des pères de famille, des jurés, etc.* (Paris: Librairie usuelle, 1836), "Dumoutier," p. 135.

10. See Bibliothèque du Musée de l'Homme, Paris, MSS 72 and 227. Renneville, who consulted the Dumoutier papers held by the phrenologist's family, specifies that in the late 1830s Dumoutier was almost 10,000 francs in arrears in his rent payments; see *Langage des crânes,* p. 206.

11. On Guépin's first exposure to Gall, see his undated letter to Emile Souvestre, Archives de la Loire-Atlantique, 19 J 12. My thanks to the chief archivist, X. du Boisrouvray, for sending me a photocopy. For a recent treatment of Guépin's political career, see Pamela Pilbeam, "A Forgotten Socialist and Feminist: Ange Guépin," in *Problems in French History,* ed. Martyn Comick and Ceri Crossley (Hampshire, UK: Palgrave, 2000), pp. 64–80.

12. A. Guépin, *Lettre à Ribes, de Montpellier, sur divers sujets de chirurgie, de médecine et d'hygiène* (Nantes: Prosper Sebire, 1835), pp. 60–62.

13. See, e.g., A. Guépin, "Lettres phrénologiques à Monsieur Dejort," *La morale indépendante,* 17 July 1870.

14. This portrait derives from the letters to his mother of 20 July 1833, 31 December 1834, 4 January 1836, and 29 March 1836, in *Thoré-Bürger peint par lui-même: Lettres et notes intimes,* ed. Paul Cottin (Paris: Nouvelle revue rétrospective, 1900), pp. 16, 21, 25, 27–35. See also the biographical sketch in ibid.

15. Thoré, *Dictionnaire de phrénologie,* "Art," p. 48, and "Propriété," pp. 359–60.

16. Angebert to Cousin, 8 August 1829, Cousin manuscripts, Bibliothèque de la Sorbonne, (henceforth, Cousin MSS), vol. 214, #81. This letter also appears in Jules Barthélemy-Saint-Hilaire, *M. Victor Cousin: sa vie et sa correspondance*, 3 vols. (Paris: Hachette, 1895), 3: 174–85, quotation on 182.

17. Adolphe Garnier, *La psychologie et la phrénologie comparées* (Paris: Hachette, 1839), "Avertissement," pp. i–ii.

18. Amédée Jacques, Jules Simon, and Emile Saisset, *Manuel de philosophie à l'usage des collèges* (Paris: Joubert, 1846), p. 40.

19. Gall expressed annoyance at this confusion very early in his career; see "Lettre du docteur F. J. Gall en 1798 à M. Joseph Fr. de Retzer," in G.A.L. Fossati, *Questions philosophiques, sociales et politiques traités d'après les principes du physiologie du cerveau* (Paris: Amyot, 1869), pp. 287–302, esp. 300.

20. "Note de l'éditeur allemand," in ibid., p. 287.

21. Gall supplies this autobiographical anecdote in *Sur les fonctions du cerveau et sur celles de chacune de ses parties*, 3 vols. (Paris: J.-B. Baillière, 1825), 1: 3–4.

22. On Gall's dissection method, see, e.g., J. B. Mège, *Manifeste des principes de la Société phrénologique de Paris adopté dans sa séance du 9 décembre 1834* (Paris: Impr. de Pihan Delaforest, 1835), p. 12.

23. For this expression, see, e.g., ibid., p. 14.

24. M. Delabosse (pseud. for Jean-Baptiste Dubois), *M. Têtu, ou la cranomanie* (Paris: Barba, 1808).

25. For an overview of some of these parodies, see Renneville, *Langage des crânes,* pp. 83–86.

26. See MM. Tenon, Portal, Sabatier, Pinel, and Cuvier, *Rapport sur un mémoire du MM. Gall et Spurzheim relatif à l'anatomie du cerveau* (Paris: Baudouin, n.d.), pp. 1–3, 52; Renneville, *Langage des crânes,* pp. 78–83; Lantéri-Laura, *Histoire de phrénologie,* p. 130.

27. See Barbara Haines, "The Athénée de Paris and the Bourbon Restoration," *History and Technology* 5 (1988): 249–71, esp. pp. 253, 267, for the adjectives quoted; and Martin Staum, "Physiognomy and Phrenology at the Paris Athénée," *Journal of the History of Ideas* 56 (1995): 443–62, esp. p. 452.

28. Maine de Biran, *Journal,* ed. Henri Gouhier, 3 vols. (Neuchatel: La Baconnière, 1954–57), 2: 9. The lecturer was the physician Etienne Pariset.

29. Renneville, *Langage des crânes,* pp. 88 and, for the quotation, 91.

30. On Gall's dislike of the word "phrenology," see Fossati's note to "Lettre à Retzer," p. 300 n. 1. For Spurzheim's views, see his letter to George Combe of 22 October 1819, in National Library of Scotland (henceforth NLS), Combe Manuscripts 7204, fols. 158–59. Like all the Spurzheim letters in

this collection, this one is in English: "Phrenology is the true name of our inquiries, let it be explained by the doctrine of the relation between mind and brain since the root indicates both mind and brain."

31. Gall, "Lettre à Retzer," p. 300.

32. Spurzheim to Combe, June 1825, NLS, Combe MSS 7216, fols. 78–79.

33. Spurzheim to Combe, 8 June 1826, NLS, Combe MSS 7218, fols. 97–98.

34. AN: F17 3038, Dossier: Sociéte phrénologique, Ministry of Commerce and Public Works to Consul-general of France in London, 19 September 1832.

35. See, e.g., the letter of George Combe to his French translator, Prosper Dumont: "The French consul here . . . has been desired by the French consul in London to report the state of Phrenology in Edinburgh for the information of the Minister of the Home Department in Paris. I have given him every information. . . ." Combe to Dumont, 19 October 1832, Combe MSS 7385, fols. 399–400.

36. Spurzheim to Combe, 12 October 1830, NLS, Combe MSS 7226, fols. 108–9.

37. AN: F17 3038, Ministry of Commerce to Prefect of Paris, April 1831; Paris Phrenological Society to Ministry of Public Instruction, 20 February 1833; and Ministry of Public Instruction to Bouillaud, President of the Phrenological Society, 26 February 1833.

38. Ibid., Casimir Broussais to Minister of Public Instruction, 26 March 1834.

39. See Eugène Bareste, "Le Phrénologiste" in *Les Français peints par eux-mêmes,* 8 vols. (Paris: Curmer, 1840–42), 3: 97–104, esp. 99. For the actual regulations, see the manuscript "Règlement," dated 14 January 1831, in AN: F17 3038, and the revised *Statuts de la Société phrénologique de Paris* (Paris: Impr. de E. B. Delanchy, 1843).

40. See the 1831 "Règlement," Art. 1, and "Conseil d'Etat, Comité de l'Intérieur et du Commerce, Extrait du registre des délibérations du Comité," 25 April 1834, AN: F17 3038.

41. The *Journal de la Société phrénologique de Paris* was published from 1832 to 1835.

42. See the postscript to David Richard's report on a meeting of the Paris Phrenological Society, *Revue encyclopédique* 55 (1832): 718–27, esp. 726–27.

43. AN: F17 6649.

44. R. Verneau, "Documents inédits sur Gall et sa collection," *Anthropologie* 7 (1896): 195–98.

45. Louis Rousseau and Céran Lemonnier, *Promenades au Jardin des Plantes* (Paris: J.-B. Baillière, 1837), pp. 100–136. The authors were, respectively, an assistant naturalist at the Muséum and a professor of natural history at a Paris lycée. The collection also had iconic status among phrenologists. After Gall's death, Spurzheim commented on the succession struggle in Paris: "Fossati will wish to make a figure. If he marry Madame Gall and get

the collection and Gall's skull, he will produce some effect." Spurzheim to Combe, 11 September 1828, NLS, Combe MSS 7222, fols. 120–21.

46. *La Phrénologie,* 30 November 1837, p. 4.

47. "Procès-verbal de l'examen phrénologique de la veuve Landon, suicidée," reprinted in A. Penot, *Phrénologie des gens du monde: Leçons publiques données à Mulhouse* (Mulhouse: P. Baret, 1838), pp. 247–51.

48. See "Procès en diffamation et injures publics intenté par les héritiers de Mme veuve Chéron," *Le Droit,* 9 November 1836, p. 1276.

49. *Gazette des tribunaux,* 21 October 1836.

50. *Le Droit,* 9 November 1836.

51. Quoted from the *Le Messager des Chambres* in *Gazette des tribunaux,* 21 October 1836.

52. The three persons named in the suit were the secretary of the Paris Phrenological Society, who broadcast the affair at the Society's annual meeting; a physician who, having known the widow Chéron personally, wrote a confidential letter confirming the findings of the phrenological reading of her head; and the managing editor of *Le Messager des Chambres*. See *Gazette des tribunaux,* 9 November 1836.

53. The adjective is employed in the *Gazette des tribunaux,* 21 October 1835.

54. The *Gazette des tribunaux* of 9 November 1836, p. 29, offered that inventory of the various dimensions of the case. It was also explicit about the reason for its inadequate coverage: "Article 10 of the law of 9 September 1835, which prevents newspapers from detailing the proceedings of defamation trials, forces us to confine our report to the complaint and the verdict."

55. Raymond Villey, *Histoire du secret médical* (Paris: Seghers, 1986), pp. 59–63.

56. Quotations from *Gazette des tribunaux,* 21 October 1836. Technically, a charge of *diffamation* did not at this date require that the insult be true. The law of 17 May 1819 had revised the Napoleonic penal code, omitting the misdemeanor of calumny, which was defined as a false statement, and replacing it with defamation, a slander that could be true or false. Yet early nineteenth-century defamation law in France was very undeveloped; the terms of the 1819 law had hardly been glossed. See Etienne-André-Théodore Grellet-Dumazeau, *Traité de la diffamation, de l'injure et de l'outrage,* 2 vols. (Riom: E. Leboyer, 1847), 1: 1, 58. Hence the accusation of the widow Chéron's heirs easily slid into an attack on the validity of phrenology.

57. *Gazette des tribunaux,* 9 November 1836, p. 29.

58. [Louis Peisse], "Procès phrénologique," *Gazette médicale de Paris,* 2d ser. 4 (1836), 12 November 1836, p. 721. This is one of a series of wickedly funny feuilletons on phrenology that Peisse published anonymously in the *Gazette;* for his revelation of his authorship, see his letters to Cousin, Cousin MSS, vol. 243, #3987, n.d., and #3988, 7 August [no year].

59. *Gazette des tribunaux,* 9 November 1836, p. 30; A.-A. Ledru-Rollin, *Mémoire sur les événements de la rue Transnonain dans les journées des 13 et 14 avril 1834,* 2d ed. (Paris: Guillaumin, 1834), which concludes (p. 59) with a prediction that "le peuple" will rise up to avenge the massacre.

60. *Gazette des tribunaux,* 9 November 1836, p. 30.

61. Ibid.

62. See the speech by Fossati, president of the Paris Phrenological Society, in *Compte rendu de l'inauguration de la statue de F. J. V. Broussais au Val-de-Grâce à Paris le 21 aout 1841* (Paris: Impr. de Mocquet, 1841), esp. p. 78.

63. Garnier, "Avertissement," *Psychologie et phrénologie comparées,* p. ii.

64. AN: F17 6686, Minister of the Interior to Minister of Public Instruction, 24 April 1836, quoting a report from the Prefect of Police.

65. Broussais to Montègre in Horace de Montègre, *Notice historique sur la vie, les travaux, les opinions médicales et philosophiques de F. J. V. Broussais* (Paris: J.-B. Baillière, 1839), pp. 65–66. See also Jean-François Braunstein, *Broussais et le matérialisme: Médecine et philosophie au XIXe siècle* (Paris: Klincksieck, 1986), pp. 154–55.

66. F. J. V. Broussais, Préface, *Cours de phrénologie* (Paris: Baillière, 1836).

67. Hippolyte Bruyères, *La phrénologie: Le geste et la physionomie mis en scène* (Paris: Aubert, 1846), pp. 444–45 and Plate 85.

68. Ibid., p. 486.

69. See Roger Cooter, *The Cultural Meaning of Popular Science: Phrenology and the Organization of Consent in Nineteenth-Century Britain* (Cambridge: Cambridge University Press, 1984).

70. Spurzheim to Combe, 14 April 1823, NLS, Combe MSS 7211, fols. 85–86, in English (or Franglais) in the original; Fossati to Combe, Paris, 26 January 1838, MS 7238, fol. 221.

71. *Discours prononcé par M. le docteur Gall à la première séance de son cours public, le 15 janvier 1808. Introduction au cours du physiologie du cerveau* (Paris: Didot, 1808), pp. 3–4.

72. Béraud, *Phrénologie humaine,* p. ii.

73. Spurzheim to Combe, Paris, 18 November 1817, NLS, Combe MSS 7202, fol. 111.

74. Spurzheim to Combe, Paris, 20 December 1820, NLS, Combe MSS 7205, fols. 156–57.

75. Spurzheim to Combe, London, 20 May 1817, NLS Combe MSS 7202, fol. 115, my italics.

76. Spurzheim to Combe, March 1830, NLS, Combe MSS 7226, fol. 101.

77. Félix Pyat and Auguste Luchet, *Le brigand et le philosophe, représenté pour la première fois à Paris sur le théâtre de la Porte-St-Martin, le 22 février 1834* (Paris: Impr. de Mme Lacombe, n.d.), p. 10. See also p. 26: "Education

corrects nature. The good penchants combat the bad and even reduce them to impotence."

78. Mary Pickering, *Auguste Comte: An Intellectual Biography*, vol. 1 (Cambridge: Cambridge University Press, 1993), pp. 303–5, 349, 420, 600–604.

79. Bernadette Bensaude-Vincent, "Auguste Comte, la science populaire d'un philosophe," *Corpus, revue de philosophie* 4 (1987): 143–67, esp. pp. 151–53.

80. Ibid., pp. 143–47; and Annie Petit, "La diffusion des savoirs comme devoir positiviste," *Romantisme* 19 (1989): 7–25, esp. 10–11. Comte published the substance of the course in 1844 as the *Traité philosophique d'astronomie populaire*.

81. Bruno Latour, "Visualization and Cognition: Thinking with Eyes and Hands," *Knowledge and Society* 6 (1986): 1–40, esp. 6–7.

82. Charles Villers, *Lettre à Georges Cuvier . . . sur une nouvelle théorie du cerveau, par le docteur Gall* (Metz: Collignon, Year X–1802), pp. 4–5.

83. Guépin to Souvestre, n.d., Archives de la Loire-Atlantique, 19 J 12.

84. F. Imbert, *Avis aux artistes lyonnais* (Lyon: Impr. de Brunet, 1829), p. 2, my italics.

85. Spurzheim to Combe, 20 May 1831, NLS, Combe MSS 7227, fols. 197–98.

86. Combe to C. Broussais, 26 September 1831, NLS, Combe MSS 7385, fols. 127–28, my italics. On "development," see the checklist prepared for use at the Musée Phrénologique, where the "degrees of development" are given as "very great, great, medium, little"; AN: AJ15 562, Dumoutier papers, Dossier: Ouverture du Musée phrénologique.

87. AN: F17 6649, Dossier: Allier, Director of General Police to Minister of Public Instruction, 27 April 1843.

88. See Imbert's reference to this incident in *Avis aux artistes lyonnais*, nonpaginated introductory material and its note 1.

89. See AN: F17 6667, Dossier: Rhône. The other petitioner was a Dr. Duchêne of Givors. Imbert's proposed course was the "exposition of a new medical doctrine," left unspecified, but almost certainly having phrenological content.

90. AN: F17 6701–2, letters of 5 December 1846, 4 January 1847, 3 February 1847.

91. "Almanach," *Encyclopédie nouvelle*, ed. P. Leroux and J. Reynaud, 8 vols. (Paris: Gosselin, 1835–41), 1: col. 352–55.

92. See "Affaire de l'*Almanach populaire*," *Gazette des tribunaux*, 25–26 March 1839, p. 527; and André Fortin, *Frédéric Degeorge* (Lille: Collection du Centre régional d'études historiques, 1964), esp. pp. 92–98, 118–26.

93. AN: BB18 1242, doss. 4359, letter of 21 January 1837.

94. Procureur général, Cour royale de Lyon, to Minister of Justice, 9 February 1837, AN: BB18 1366, doss. 4753.

95. The passage from the newspaper is quoted in a letter of 29 September 1837 from the director of general police in the Ministry of the Interior to the Minister of Justice; AN: BB18 1257, doss. 7271.

96. *Le Semeur* 8 (25 December 1839): 410–12.

97. The advertisement, in Degeorge's newspaper, *Le Progrès du Pas-de-Calais*, 25 January 1838, also noted that the 1838 edition was already in its sixth printing of 10,000 copies. The endorsement described Luchet's "article on the phenomena of intellectual organization" as "written with as much profundity as verve."

98. "Un mot sur la direction à donner à l'enseignement de la phrénologie," *Almanach populaire de la France*, 1838, pp. 43–47; author identified in table of contents (p. 141) as "A. Luchet."

99. Eugène Bareste, "Curiosités: Le Musée phrenologique," *Almanach prophétique*, 1842, pp. 74–80, esp. 75, 80.

100. See, e.g. "La prophétie de Gall," ibid., 1841, pp. 154–56, where Gall correctly unmasks as a murderer a suave aristocrat at a party who is mocking phrenology; and "Mademoiselle Lenormand," ibid., 1843, pp. 81–99, esp. 93, the story of a young woman possessing powers of divination, who consults Dr. Gall; he tells her she can become the greatest sorceress in Europe and takes her under his wing "to teach her phrenology and the techniques of palmistry and necromancy."

101. See Joseph-Pierre Chasson, *Traité des délits et contraventions de la parole et de l'écriture de la presse*, 2d ed., 2 vols. (Paris: Videcoq, 1845), 1: 314.

102. See his membership certificate signed by, among others, Auguste Luchet, in the Dumoutier papers, AN: AJ15 562, Dossier: Phrénologie: Documents divers.

103. In both the *Almanach de la communauté* and the *Almanach de l'organisation sociale*, the article appears on pp. 94–130. Barthel refers to it as an *abrégé* on p. 110n.

104. C. Pellarin, "Les physiologistes et M. Fourier," *La réforme industrielle, ou le phalanstère* 2 (1833): 100–104, 138–41, esp. 100–101.

105. Ch. Fourier, "Les alliés dangereux," *La réforme industrielle* 2 (1833): 149–52, esp. 149, italics in the original.

106. Renneville, *Langage des crânes*, p. 154.

107. Dr. Ombros (pseud. for Fleury Imbert), *A M. Victor Considérant: Lettre d'un disciple de Gall à un disciple de Fourier* (Lyon, Impr. G. Rossary, 1836), esp. pp. 18–19, 23.

108. Guy Frambourg, *Le Docteur Guépin, 1805–1873: un philanthrope et démocrate nantais* (Nantes: Impr. de l'Atlantique, 1964), p. 109; and Jean Maitron, *Dictionnaire biographique du mouvement ouvrier français* (Paris: Editions ouvrières, 1964–), pt. 1, vol. 2, pp. 309–11. Guépin seems to

have been more influenced by Saint-Simonianism than by Fourierism, turning to the latter after the demise of the former.

109. A. Guépin, *Philosophie du socialisme, ou étude sur les transformations dans le monde et l'humanité* (Paris: G. Sandré, 1850), p. 627.

110. Charles Pellarin, *Souvenirs anecdotiques: médecine navale, saint-simonisme, chouannerie* (Paris: Librairie des sciences sociales, 1868), pp. 40–41. Like his fellow physician Guépin, Pellarin had allegiances to both Fourierism and Saint-Simonianism, as well as to phrenology.

111. Dumont to Combe, 3 November 1832, NLS, Combe MSS 7228, fols. 86–87.

112. See the history given in Raucourt's newspaper, *L'Educateur: Journal de l'Institut de la morale universelle* 1 (1836): 1–2. On Raucourt's relation to Saint-Simonianism; see Broussais, *Communication faite à la Société [phrénologique de Paris] dans sa seance du 25 janvier 1837 sur la méthode d'enseignement qui suit M. le colonel Raucourt* (Paris: Impr. de Dezauche, n.d.), p. 4. For the 1832 petition of the manufacturer A.-J. Beauvisage for authorization to instruct his workers in Raucourt's method with Raucourt's assistance, see AN: F17 6685.

113. Luchet, "Un mot," p. 43.

114. Broussais, *Communication sur Raucourt*, pp. 3, 5–6, 12, 14–16, my italics.

115. For Raucourt's comments, see *L'Educateur* 1 (January–February 1836): 2; and 2 (May–June 1837): 65 and 69 n. 13.

116. See Jacques Rancière, *Le Maître ignorant: Cinq leçons sur l'émancipation intellectuelle* (Paris: Fayard, 1987); and Jean-François Garcia, *Jacotot* (Paris: Presses universitaires de France, 1997).

117. "Philosophie panécastique: éducation des abonnés," *Journal de l'émancipation intellectuelle* 2 (1830): 441–48, esp. 448.

118. Ibid., p. 441. Jacotot seems not to know that Cousin, a bachelor, had raised no children.

119. "Variétés," *Journal de l'émancipation intellectuelle* 2 (1830), p. 477.

120. See H. V. Jacotot, "3e lettre au dr. Broussais," *Journal de l'émancipation intellectuelle* 3 (1835): 17–32, esp. 20–21, 31. The first two letters are absent from the Bibliothèque Nationale's incomplete collection of this journal.

121. A. Guépin, *Résumé de la méthode de Jacotot, par M. [Emile] Souvestre*, 2d ed. (Nantes: Mellinet-Malassis, n.d.), p. 10.

122. Spurzheim to Combe, Paris, 14 April 1823, NLS, Combe MSS 7211, fols. 85–86.

123. See "Athénée de Paris . . . Extrait du Programme pour l'année 1823," *Revue encyclopédique* 16 (1822): 420–21.

124. Renneville, *Langage des crânes*, pp. 91–92.

125. Scoutetten, "Avertissement," *Leçons de phrénologie* (Metz: S. Lamort, 1834), n.p.

126. See AN: AJ15 562, Dossier: Musée phrénologique, both for the mission statement in the manuscript "Discours d'inauguration" and for the invitation.

127. Pyat and Luchet, *Brigand et philosophe,* p. 26.

128. Mme A. Dupin, "La Leçon de phrénologie," *Journal des femmes* 1 (1832): 169–76, quotations on 169. On the aims of the journal, see "Aux abonnés," ibid., 313–15.

129. For the canonical text, see Comte, *Cours de philosophie positive,* 2d ed., 5 vols. (Paris: Baillière, 1864), 1: 32–33. Comte articulated the argument much earlier; see Comte to Valat, 24 September 1819, in Auguste Comte, *Correspondance générale et confessions,* ed. P. E. de Berrêdo Carneiro and P. Arnaud, 8 vols. (Paris: Mouton, 1973–1990), 1: 58–59.

130. Auguste Comte, *Cours de philosophie positive, Leçons 1 à 45,* ed. Michel Serres, François Dagognet, and Allal Sinaceur (Paris: Hermann, 1975), Lesson 45, pp. 842–82, esp. 857. On this theme, see also Jean-François Braunstein, "Antipsychologisme et philosophie du cerveau chez Auguste Comte," *Revue internationale de philosophie* 52 (1998): 7–28.

131. Comte, *Cours de philosophie positive,* ed. Michel Serres et al., Lesson 45, esp. p. 858.

132. Auguste Comte, "Discours préliminaire sur l'esprit positif," *Traité philosophique d'astronomie populaire* (Paris: Carilian-Goeury, 1844), pp. 72–74.

133. Fossati, "Phrénologie," *Dictionnaire de la conversation et de la lecture,* 52 vols. (Paris: Belin-Mondar, 1832–39), 43: 449–61, quotations on 450, 455.

134. F. J. V. Broussais, "Du sentiment d'individualité, du sentiment personnel et du *moi,* considerés chez l'homme et chez les animaux," *Mémoires de l'Académie des sciences morales et politiques* 3 (1841): 91–146, esp. 92, 95–96.

135. Ibid., pp. 101, 105, 110, 135–37, 144. For commentary on this and other relevant texts by Broussais, see Braunstein, *Broussais et le matérialisme,* pp. 136–38.

136. Thoré, *Dictionnaire de phrénologie,* "Professions," p. 357; see also "Spécialités," p. 389, and "Père," p. 330.

137. Béraud, "Prospectus."

138. Garnier, *Psychologie et phrenologie comparées,* p. 16.

139. Spurzheim to Combe, 10 June 1819, NLS, Combe MSS 7204, fols. 106–7.

140. Spurzheim to Combe, August 1818, NLS, Combe MSS 7203, fols. 111–12. On the claim to fame of the individual Spurzheim identifies only as "the shoemaker Spence," see Arthur W. J. G. Ord-Hume, *Perpetual Motion: The History of an Obsession* (London: Allen and Unwin, 1977), pp. 85–86; Spence's invention was written up in the *Annales de chimie* in 1818.

141. Spurzheim to Combe, 7 November 1818, NLS, Combe MSS 7203, fols. 115–16.

142. Spurzheim to Combe, 12 August 1820, NLS, Combe MSS 7205, fols. 160–61.

143. Spurzheim to Combe, February 1824, NLS, Combe MSS 7214, fols. 50–52.
144. Spurzheim to Combe, London, March 1825, Combe MSS 7216, fols. 74–75.
145. Spurzheim to Combe, 21 August 1822, NLS, Combe MSS 7209, fols. 107–8.
146. David seems to have adopted a dualist version of phrenology. As he wrote in 1839 about listening to the music of Cherubini at a funeral mass and then catching sight of the heads of the singers: "One is pained to see such sublime sounds come out of such a ridiculous machine. That's what proves that mind (âme) is independent of matter. . . ." *Les Carnets de David d'Angers*, 2 vols. (Paris: Plon, 1958), 2: 40.
147. Ibid., 1: 172.
148. Ibid., 2: 93.
149. Ibid., 1: 225.
150. Thoré to his mother, 27 December 1835, in *Thoré-Bürger peint par lui-même*, p. 25.
151. Dumont to Marion Cox, 23 April 1833, NLS, Combe MSS 7230.
152. Hippolyte Tampucci, "Remerciement aux souscripteurs aux oeuvres de Magu," in Magu, *Poésies nouvelles* (Paris: Delloye, 1842), p. v. The worker-poet Magu was well-known for his connections with the Paris Phrenological Society; see, e.g., A. Carro, "Biographie littéraire de Magu," in ibid., pp. vii–viii.

Epilogue

The epigraph is from Jean-Paul Sartre, "An Interview," *New York Review of Books*, 26 May 1970, p 23.

1. See AN: F17 4180, unpaginated brochure entitled "Etat des candidats présentés par les recteurs pour le concours de l'Ecole normale en 1832."
2. *Rapport de M. Cousin suivi des dissertations de MM. Emile Saisset et Amédée Jacques* (Paris: Paul Dupont, 1843), pp. 5–6.
3. See AN: F17 7647, Dossier: Lycée Louis-le-Grand, "Observations générales sur l'enseignement de la philosophie," 24 March 1850. The comments on Jacques were elicited by the complaints of his fellow philosophy professor, the aging Idéologue Valette, that Jacques was stealing his students.
4. See Amédée Jacques, "La liberté de penser," *La Liberté de penser* 1 (December 1847–May 1848): 1–6.
5. A. Jacques, "De l'enseignement de la philosophie dans les lycées nationaux," ibid. 1: 493–96.
6. See the notice in ibid. 5 (December 1849–May 1850): 633.
7. Amédée Jacques, "Essais de philosophie populaire, I: Exposé des motifs," ibid. 7 (December 1850–March 1851): 1–21, esp. 8, and "Suite de l'exposé des motifs," ibid., pp. 171–87.

8. AN F17*1864, Conseil supérieur de l'instruction publique. Assemblée générale, Registre unique, 13 August 1850–14 August 1851, meetings of 24 February 1851 and 14 March 1851. For an account of the proceedings by a supporter of Jacques, see H. Bellouard, "Avant-Propos," in Amédée Jacques, *Le christianisme et la démocratie* (Paris: Au bureau de la Liberté de penser, 1851), pp. 5–18.

9. A. Jacques, "Essais de philosophie populaire: Suite et fin de l'exposé des motifs," *Liberté de penser* 7: 171–87, esp. 183.

10. Ibid., 181–82.

11. A. Jacques, "Essais de philosophie populaire. De l'Homme 3: Le libre-arbitre, l'âme," ibid. 8 (June–November 1851): 340–53, quotations on 347, 352.

12. For these biographical details, see article "Jacques (Amédée Florent)" in Pierre Larousse, *Grand dictionnaire universelle du XIXe siècle* (Paris, 1866–79, reprint, Paris: Slatkine, 1982).

13. Minutes of the Commission relative à l'enseignement secondaire des jeunes filles, AN C3279, dossier 1379 (a small unpaginated notebook), meeting of 19 February [1879]. I learned of this source in Françoise Mayeur, *L'enseignement secondaire des jeunes filles sous la Troisième République* (Paris: Presses de la Fondation nationale des sciences politiques, 1977).

14. See Steven C. Hause with Anne R. Kenney, *Women's Suffrage and Social Politics in the French Third Republic* (Princeton: Princeton University Press, 1984), pp. 13–14, 16, 60.

15. For the text of this 1882 *programme,* see Camille Sée, ed., *Lycées et collèges de jeunes filles: Documents, rapports et discours* (Paris: L. Cerf, 1884), pp. 488–89. On the justification for applied psychology, see Henri Marion, *L'education des jeunes filles* (Paris: A. Colin, 1902), p. 358.

16. Henri Marion, *Psychologie de la femme* (Paris: Armand Colin, 1900), pp. 14–15.

17. "Nouveau plan d'études pour les lycées et les Facultés," 10 April 1852, *Bulletin administratif d'instruction publique,* no. 28 (April 1852), pp. 53–63, quotation on 53; and "Classe de logique," ibid., no. 32 (August 1852), p. 139.

18. For the quotations, see Victor Duruy, *Notes et souvenirs (1811–1894),* 2 vols. (Paris: Hachette, 1901), 1: 198–99, 279. On the general point, see Stéphane Douailler, Christiane Mauve, Georges Navet, Jean-Claude Pompougnac, and Patrice Vermeren, eds., *La philosophie saisie par l'Etat: Petits écrits sur l'enseignement philosophique en France, 1789–1900* (Paris: Aubier, 1988), introduction to Chapter 4, p. 444.

19. See *Bulletin administratif du Ministère de l'Instruction publique,* n.s. 17 (1874): 490–91; n.s. 23 (1880) 960–61; n.s. 71 (1902): 760–61.

20. Pierre Janet, *Manuel du baccalauréat (Seconde Partie) (Série Mathématiques) Philosophie,* 8th ed. (Paris: Vuibert, 1929), p. vii.

21. A. Cuvillier, *La dissertation de philosophie au baccalauréat* (Paris: Armand Colin, 1933), pp. 9–10. This text, a study guide for students preparing for the all-important examination, contains sample questions from previous years and, in some cases, answers as well.

22. Henri Marion, "Le nouveau programme de philosophie," *Revue philosophique* 10 (1880); 414–28, esp. 422–23, 423 for the quotation.

23. Emile Beaussire, "L'enseignement de la philosophie avant les nouveaux programmes," *Revue internationale de l'enseignement* 3 (January–June 1882): 59–65, quotation on 65.

24. See Jean-Louis Fabiani, *Les philosophes de la république* (Paris: Minuit, 1988), pp. 32–33, 60.

25. Henri Joly, *Cours de philosophie, répondant au nouveau programme officiel des lycées et du baccalauréat,* 6th ed. (Paris: Delalain, 1881), pp. 15, 30, 35–36.

26. John I. Brooks III, *The Eclectic Legacy: Academic Philosophy and the Human Sciences in Nineteenth-Century France* (Newark: University of Delaware Press, 1998), p. 55. For an account of a dispute over the philosophy *programme* in the 1890s, see Daniela S. Barberis, "Moral Education for the Elite of Democracy: the *Classe de Philosophie* Between Sociology and Philosophy," *Journal of the History of the Behavioral Sciences* 38 (2002): 355–69.

27. See J. E. S. Hayward, "The Official Social Philosophy of the French Third Republic: Léon Bourgeois and Solidarism," *International Review of Social History* 6 (1961): 19–48, and Janet R. Horne, *A Social Laboratory for Modern France: The Musée Social and the Rise of the Welfare State* (Durham, NC: Duke University Press, 2002), pp. 118–20.

28. For a fully developed version of this argument, see Jan Goldstein, "The Advent of Psychological Modernism in France: An Alternate Narrative," in *Modernist Impulses in the Human Sciences, 1870–1930,* ed. Dorothy Ross (Baltimore: Johns Hopkins University Press, 1994), pp. 190–209.

29. My examination of the relevant editions of Janet's *Manuel*—the textbook that Sartre probably used—suggests that Sartre did not encounter even cursory references to Freud in his philosophy class. Freud seems to have entered the philosophy curriculum of the French lycée only with Armand Cuvillier's textbook, *Manuel de philosophie,* 2 vols. (Paris: A. Colin, 1931), whose first volume, "Psychology," contained a brief discussion of the Freudian theory of repression (pp. 158–59). My thanks to Emmanuelle Saada for bringing Cuvillier to my attention.

30. For an example of this pedagogical discourse, rooted in Pierre Janet's 1889 philosophy dissertation, *L'Automatisme psychologique,* see Pierre Janet, *Manuel du baccalauréat de l'enseignement secondaire (Classes de Philosophie A & B), Philosophie,* 3d ed. (Paris: Vuibert et Nony, 1905), pp. 173–74, 178–79, 181. Janet had revised this edition of his textbook "in such a way as to put it in complete conformity with the new *programme* of the philosophy class"; "Avertissment," n.p., dated September 1904.

31. Pierre Janet, *Manuel du baccalaureat (Seconde Partie) (Série Mathémathiques) Philosophie,* p. 111.

Note on Sources

While the individual endnotes to this book furnish a nearly exhaustive, if piecemeal, account of the sources consulted, this note provides a concise overview of the principal manuscript and archival sources.

My discussion of the place of disordered imagination in the discourse of the late eighteenth-century guilds (Chapter 1) was immeasurably aided by the collection of memoranda protesting Turgot's 1776 abolition of the guilds that forms part of the extensive Joly de Fleury papers housed in the Manuscript Department of the Bibliothèque Nationale de France in Paris. In treating the curricula of the central schools of the Directory and especially the professors' lesson plans for presenting the philosophy and psychology of Condillac to their charges (Chapter 2), I have made use of the Ministry of Public Education archives in the Archives Nationales in Paris, F17 1339–1344.

Also at the Archives Nationales, the private papers of Emmanuel-Joseph Sieyès (284 AP)—rendered difficult both by the author's handwriting and by his often compressed and cryptic mode of expression—enabled me to sketch out the adherence of that great Revolutionary theorist and politician to Condillac's psychology as well as his criticism of Condillac's conception of the self (Chapter 3). Since I began research on this book, some but not all of the relevant portions of those papers have been published in Christine Fauré, Jacques Guilhaumou, and Jacques Valier, eds., *Des Manuscrits de Sieyès, 1773–1799* (Paris: Honoré Champion, 1999). Again, at the Archives Nationales, the private papers of François Guizot (42 AP), especially those pertaining to his tenure as minister of public instruction, provided confirmation of his deep commitment to the post-Revolutionary renovation of psychology (Chapter 5).

Since this book has placed the institutionalization of Cousinian psychology at its heart, I have relied heavily on the voluminous correspondence of Victor Cousin, housed at the Bibliothèque de la Sorbonne in Paris, to investigate the operations and informal culture of Cousin's network of disciples, strategically implanted by him in teaching posts throughout France (Chapter 5). This carefully bound, alphabetically organized manuscript correspondence of forty volumes includes only the letters to the *maître*, not, unfortunately, the drafts of Cousin's part in the dialogue. Some of the relevant letters have been published by Cousin's personal secretary Jules Barthélemy-Saint-Hilaire in his *M. Victor Cousin: Sa vie et sa correspondance*, 3 vols. (Paris: Hachette, 1895); but most often Barthelémy gravitated to Cousin's famous correspondents rather than to the more workaday material that interested me.

Another valuable source on the intimate impact of Cousin's teaching is a full set of philosophy exams written at the Ecole normale supérieure in 1820 and conserved in the Archives Nationales (F17 4163). Cousin's pivotal relationship with his mentor Pierre-Paul Royer-Collard is illuminated by the letters conserved among the Royer-Collard papers at the Bibliothèque de l'Institut de France (MSS 2607 and 3990).

The reading notes taken by the young Ernest Renan on a basic philosophy text by Cousin can be found in the Bibliothèque Nationale de France, Manuscript Department, n.a.f. 11481. Apparently dating from the period of Renan's abandonment of his religious vocation, they provide precious information about Renan's intellectual relationship to the Sorbonne *maître* at that critical juncture; information about the difference between the religious and the secular-psychological models of the inner life can also be inferred from them (Chapter 6).

Because the nineteenth-century French phrenological movement (Chapter 7) was institutionalized only in a relatively ephemeral fashion, its manuscript and archival traces tend to be more dispersed than those of its victorious Cousinian rival. One of the best manuscript sources for understanding the movement is located outside of France: the papers of the leading British phrenologist George Combe, housed in the National Library of Scotland in Edinburgh. These papers include Combe's correspondence with a number of French phrenologists, most importantly Johann-Caspar Spurzheim, the originally German collaborator of Gall who settled in Paris in 1807. Spurzheim's running commentary to Combe over a period of many years seems remarkably free of self-censorship and offers a perspective on the comparative success of phrenology in Britain and France. Some of the papers of Pierre

Dumoutier, a prominent if underachieving figure in French phrenology during the July Monarchy, can be found at the Archives Nationales (AJ15 562); these papers focus on his activities in the Société phrénologique de Paris and its associated Musée phrénologique. (The AJ15 series comprises a portion of the archives of the Muséum d'histoire naturelle that were deposited at the Archives Nationales.) Dumoutier's papers from his voyage to the South Seas as the phrenological member of a scientific mission can be found at the Bibliothèque du Musée de l'Homme in Paris. The points of contact between early nineteenth-century phrenology and the French state are detailed in two types of documents at the Archives Nationales, both part of the F17 (Public Instruction) series: requests to the government for the authorization of scientific associations (see especially F17 3038) and requests for authorization to teach public courses outside the state educational system (F17 6649–6705).

Index

abrégé, 93, 95, 187–88, 290
absolutism, 7, 43, 126
Académie française, 193
academies (educational administrative units), 149, 189, 216
Academy of Besançon, 43
Academy of Moral and Political Sciences, 146, 178, 193, 308, 319
Academy of Painting and Sculpture, 44
Academy of Sciences, 276–77
activity (mental): Cousin on, 158–59, 161–62, 169, 180, 262; definition of, 169; and good government, 137, 157, 169; Humboldt on, 127; Jouffroy on, 189; Laromiguière on, 127, 143; Maine de Biran on, 130, 133–36; in philosophy curriculum, 189, 220, 326; and private property, 162–63; as recognized through introspection, 169, 179, 202; Rousseau on, 122; Royer-Collard on, 158; Sieyès on, 124–26. See also will
Addison, Joseph, 46
agrégation, 193, 317
Alembert, Jean le Rond d', 30–31, 116
Algeria, Jouffroy on, 173
Almanach de la communauté, 297–98
Almanach de l'organisation sociale, 297
Almanach populaire de la France, 270, 294–95, 300
Almanach prophétique, 297
almanacs, 292, 294–98
âme: in Buffon, 114; in Condillac, 116, 119, 121; in Descartes, 116; in Encyclopédie, 116; in Laromoguière, 121–22; in Lignac, 111; in Malebranche, 35; meaning of term, 115; in philosophy programme, 325;

relation to term moi of, 116–18; in Sulpician discourse, 241, 256; as used by Pauline Franck, 227–28
Ampère, André-Marie, 132
analysis (method of Condillac), 68–69, 146, 165
Angebert, Caroline: compared to Pauline Franck, 226–27; correspondence of, with Cousin of, 174–76, 222–24; on Cousin's career path, 183–84, 195; deconstruction of Cousin's philosophy by, 201, 321–22; on intellectual tastes of the masses, 147, 273; sense of exclusion of, 222–23, 303
animal magnetism. See mesmerism
anonymous publication as self-annihilation, 243, 379n44
antibourgeois satire, 12, 180
anticlericalism, 319, 323
Aquinas, Thomas, 32
Archives philosophiques, politiques et littéraires, 186
Aristotelianism, 142
Aristotle, 32
artisans: Condillac on, 67, 70; as an état, 29, 38, 40–41; Quesnay on, 63–65; training of, 44–46, 88; unincorporated, 21, 39, 46, 49, 53, 57, 66, 70; as worthy of confidence, 41–42, 72. See also working class
association of ideas, 105, 257, 265, 381n74
Athénée de Paris, 277, 303
attention, mental faculty of, 23, 134, 199, 256
Augustine, 16
authorship as self-assertion, 243
autobiography, 92, 123, 170, 235, 237, 239
automatism, psychological, 325

403